The War Against the Greens

The "Wise-Use" Movement, the New Right,

and Anti-Environmental Violence

DAVID HELVARG

SIERRA CLUB BOOKS

SAN FRANCISCO

The Sierra Club, founded in 1892 by John Muir, has devoted itself to the study and protection of the earth's scenic and ecological resources—mountains, wetlands, woodlands, wild shores and rivers, deserts and plains. The publishing program of the Sierra Club offers books to the public as a nonprofit educational service in the hope that they may enlarge the public's understanding of the Club's basic concerns. The point of view expressed in each book, however, does not necessarily represent that of the Club. The Sierra Club has some sixty chapters coast to coast, in Canada, Hawaii, and Alaska. For information about how you may participate in its programs to preserve wilderness and the quality of life, please address inquiries to Sierra Club, 730 Polk Street, San Francisco, CA 94109.

Lyrics from the following songs have been used by permission:
Dirty Laundry
(Danny Kortchmar, Don Henley)
© 1982 WB MUSIC CORP. & CASS COUNTY MUSIC.
All rights administered by WB MUSIC CORP.
All Rights Reserved.
(Nothing But) Flowers by David Byrne (ASCAP)
© 1988 Index Music, Inc.

Library of Congress Cataloging in Publication Data
Helvarg, David, 1951–
    The war against the greens : the "Wise-Use" movement, the new right, and anti-environmental violence / David Helvarg.
        p.   cm.
    Includes bibliographical references and index.
    ISBN 0-87156-459-9
    1. Wise Use Movement—United States—Citizen participation.
    2. Environmentalists—United States—Political activity.   3. Right of property—United States.   I. Title.
GE197.H45   1994
363.7'00973—dc20   94-1493
                                                          CIP

Production by Janet Vail
Jacket design by Big Fish Books, San Francisco
Book design by Amy Evans
Composition by Wilsted & Taylor

Printed in the United States of America on acid-free paper
containing a minimum of 50% recovered waste paper,
of which at least 10% of the fiber content is post-consumer waste

10 9 8 7 6 5 4 3 2 1

IN MEMORY OF MY PARENTS,

MAX HELVARG & EVA LEE

Contents

Acknowledgments

Many people helped make this book possible. I'm hoping that a significant number of them won't regret it. Although some may not agree with my analysis or conclusions, I appreciate the cooperation I received from the approximately five hundred people I interviewed over the course of a year. Less than a dozen people whom I asked refused to be interviewed—several for political reasons and about an equal number out of fear. A number of others would only speak off the record, although I generally tried to discourage this practice. I found that most people—including many anti-enviro activists—who were suspicious of the "liberal" and "preservationist" media were nonetheless anxious to tell their sides of the various conflicts reported in this book. I have attempted not only to convey their statements and positions accurately but also to describe fairly the settings and contexts in which their stories unfolded.

In late 1992 Tom Athanasiou—a friend whose writings on the deep issues of environment and world systems will no doubt create much intellectual ferment in coming years—put me in touch with literary agent Joe Spieler, who in turn got me involved in this project. Joe, a bold figure in the publishing jungles of New York, represents a slew of green adventure writers, whose impressive work proves that testosterone can serve humanity as well as provoke wars and cause baldness. Sierra Club Books publisher Jon Beckmann provided me with early and essential assurance that I would not face any political strictures or constraints in my pursuit of the backlash story. He was as good as his word and as comforting as a smooth gin martini. David Spinner, my editor for the more than eighteen months it took for the manuscript to see print, served as a helpful sounding board and provided friendly, insightful feedback.

Once I began the book, I quickly discovered I wasn't the only person trying to make sense of this latest wave of environmental backlash. Among those who provided thoughtful and generous help in my understanding of this political counterrevolution were Tarso Ramos, at the Western States Center in Portland, Oregon; Chip Berlet, at Political Research Associates in Cambridge, Massachusetts; and Don Judge and his research staff at Montana State AFL-CIO headquarters in Helena, Montana. Antipesticide activist Carol Van Strum and Attorney Paul Merrell were also generous, letting me look through their files and records. My membership in the Society of Environmental Journalists (SEJ), a four-year-old professional association with some one thousand members in print and broadcast journalism, proved invaluable both in supplying contacts and providing help in framing some of the questions I've tried to answer in this work.

Many journalists were willing to share with me tapes, articles, and information they had developed over long periods of time, disproving much of what is said about the cynical and cutthroat nature of our profession (at least the cutthroat part). Among the reporters who deserve my thanks are Peter Dykstra, of CNN; Katherine Bouma, of the *Montgomery Advertiser;* Glenn Pontier, of the *River Reporter;* Will Nixon, of *E* magazine; Jon Christiensen, of *High Country News;* Ginny Graybiel, of the *Pensacola News Journal;* Don Behm, of the *Milwaukee Journal;* Wendy Miller, of the *L.A. Times;* Jane Kay, of the *San Francisco Examiner;* Jean Hayes, of the *Wichita Eagle;* Neil Modie, of the *Seattle Post-Intelligencer;* and Connie Matthiessen and Jonathan Franklin, of the Center for Investigative Reporting. Franklin is the first reporter to have broken the story of the rising wave of anti-environmentalist violence—in the Fall 1992 issue of *Muckraker,* the CIR journal. He later provided me with valuable assistance in recontacting a number of these victims and in confirming several of the numerous incidents that have occurred since his report came out.

Dan Junos, author of the forthcoming *Moon Rising*, was generous in sharing his insights, collected from years of research he had gathered on the Reverend Sun Myung Moon and his business empire, as was Eric Nadler, the reporter for a PBS "Frontline" documentary on the same subject. The Edmund S. Muskie Archives and archives director Christopher Beam, at Bates College in Lewiston, Maine, provided essential documentation on FBI spying on Earth Day 1970. Authors Pat Choate, Osha Gray Davidson, Carl Deal, Susan Zakin, and Lynn Jacobs were friendly and patient in responding to my queries. A good friend, Professor George Katsiaficas, put me through a one-day tutorial and provided a helpful reading list on social movements theory. Steve Talbot, another good friend and an award-winning documentary producer, was key to my understanding of the Earth First! bombing case. In 1990 he hired me in my capacity as a private investigator to work on *Who Bombed Judi Bari?*, a one-hour documentary on the attempted murder of Ms. Bari that aired on the San Francisco and Los Angeles PBS stations. The adventures we had in tracking that story from the streets of Oakland and San Francisco's federal building to the backwoods of northern California helped convince me that environmental reporting did not have to be boring.

Several congressional staffers and government agency research officials in Washington proved both intelligent and instructive in helping me secure documents and figure out the byzantine pathways and the political bludgeons and barters by which various bills become the laws of our land. Given their disparate feelings about public recognition, I will keep my thanks to them generic. Anne Harrington provided some valuable research assistance during a period of intense deadline pressure. An international fisheries trade negotiator in the making, she is also tall proof that environmental ethics have taken root among a new generation of post-territorial Alaskans.

While the FBI passed on several interview requests, other law enforcement professionals proved more than willing to take time out from their pursuits to share their knowledge, experience, and opinions with me. Among this group were Steve Robinson, who oversees fire and law enforcement for the Bureau of Land Management; BLM Agent Felicia Probert; Pete Person and Rich Cybeck, of the New York State Police Bureau of Criminal Investigation; Agent Carla Jones, of the Forest Service; and Scott Curley, a senior instructor at the Federal Law Enforcement Training Center. My old roommate and body-surfing partner, Manny Ramos, now a professor at the Stetson College of Law in St. Petersburg, Florida, took time out from his work schedule to review and provide useful comments on the chapter titled "Up Against the Law." Smart advice on other authorlike problems and complications was never more than a phone call away to my old bud, river codger, and Billings-born kayaker Steve Chapple, of Montana. For additional advice, computer assistance, toleration, travel company, photo documentation, good over-the-shoulder editing, and general love and support, I couldn't ask for better than what I've got with my own life's love, Nancy Ledansky.

If I've failed to acknowledge about 480 other people who were essential to the writing of this book, I hope their contributions are well reflected in the following pages. I salute the courage of some and remind others that it is a crime to use the U.S. postal system or telephonic communications for purposes of making a terrorist threat.

David Helvarg
December 8, 1993

First Encounters

"Are you an environmentalist or do you work for a living?" reads the bumper sticker on the jacked-up four-by-four flatbed crawling down Main Street. A plastic yellow ribbon flying from its radio antenna, it's one of a dozen pickups in a block-long procession going nowhere fast before making three-point turns at the end of town and heading back up Main Street towards the lumbermill. A couple of hometown patriots waving Old Glory and a portly family of five done up in yellow tee shirts, bill caps, and hair ribbons cheer from the sidewalk. A spirited young woman in a tank top and teased hair streaked an unnatural shade of yellow holds up a hand-printed sign reading "God Bless America."

You'd think Terry Anderson and the other American hostages still being held in Beirut had been freed or that U.S. troops were homebound from some CNN simulcast war. While the yellow ribbon, a symbol appropriated from a Tony Orlando and Dawn song about a felon returning home from prison, has come to be identified with people trapped in places they don't want to be, this is an entirely different use of the yellow cloth (or polypropylene, as the case may be). These ribbon wavers want to be right where they are, doing what they and theirs do best, which is cutting down trees and turning them into lumber for the Georgia-Pacific mill that blocks their view of the ocean right here in the small coastal town of Fort Bragg, California.

"Fuck you, faggots," shouts a high school kid with a buzz top as a van full of counterculture longhairs pulls into the empty dirt lot just north of the timbermill. Ben and Jerry's people are passing out free samples of their new Rainforest Crunch ice cream to some fifteen hundred demonstrators gathered here for an Earth First! "Redwood Summer" logging protest.

Across town, at Green Memorial Field, between a thousand and fifteen hundred people, many decked out in tee shirts reading "Timber Families . . . An Endangered Species," are attending a community-solidarity rally organized by the anti-environmentalist Yellow Ribbon Coalition. Here they can buy beer, soda pop, hamburgers, or "fried spotted owl" (southern-fried chicken, actually) at a dollar a body part. On nearby Harold Street, the airhorns of mammoth logging trucks bellow like cattle in the slaughter shoot.

Between the two opposing rallies, 425 riot-clad police, sheriff's deputies, and highway patrolmen from throughout northern California keep a wary eye out for any trouble not of their own making.[1]

At the environmentalists' rally, speakers talk about preserving the state's last 5 percent of old-growth redwood, attack the timber corporations for cut-and-run logging (Louisiana Pacific has opened mills in Mexico and Venezuela while closing mills in California), play fair to middling acoustic music, and read some bad poetry.

At the Yellow Ribbon rally, the talk is of jobs and how those who work in the woods are best able to manage them sensibly. Congressman Doug Bosco, a Democrat who thinks he has a keen sense of the political winddrift, plays the crowd like a pro, smirking that the young enviros should go back where they came from, to New York or New Jersey, to clean up their own messes. "We need wood products, not another Woodstock," he thunders to enthusiastic applause (Bosco will go down to defeat at the next election, in large measure because he's alienated local environmental supporters, who see him as too close to the timber industry).

It's July 21, 1990, and I've driven north from San Francisco for four hours to cover these protests and any possible confrontation that might develop. Tension has been running high in Mendocino, Humboldt, and other northern counties for some time now as environmentalists move to protect California's ancient forest remnants and timber companies—such as Georgia-Pacific, Louisiana Pacific, and Pacific Lumber—which has recently fallen into the hands of corporate raider Charles Hurwitz—respond by accelerating their timber cuts on public and private reserves well beyond what state foresters consider sustainable yield levels. There are competing initiatives on the upcoming November ballot (both will go down to defeat). The environmentalists' "Forests Forever" proposal would limit clear-cutting while allocating millions of dollars of state funds to buying up privately held redwood forests for parkland. The industry-backed "Californians for New Forestry—Global Warming Initiative" would leave the timber companies free to operate as they have been. Supporters of this initiative justify its enviro-sounding title by arguing that since young trees absorb more carbon dioxide than "decadent" old trees, clear-cutting ancient redwood forests and replacing them with new tree farms will reduce global warming.

But the timber wars are not limited to ballot fights and protest marches. On May 24, 1990, organizer Judi Bari, the main force behind the Redwood Summer campaign, had been maimed when a pipe bomb exploded below the driver's seat of her Subaru station wagon as she drove down a busy street in Oakland, California, with fellow Earth First! activist Daryl Cherney. They were driving through the Bay Area to recruit college students for these protests. Firefighters arriving on the scene had to use the Jaws of Life to cut the badly mutilated but still conscious Bari from her crumpled car, where it had crashed into a guardrail in front of an elementary school. (Cherney, who had been riding in the passenger seat, suffered injuries to one eye and his face.) Within minutes, the FBI's domestic terrorism squad was on the scene, waving off the Alcohol, Tobacco and Firearms (ATF) agents normally responsible for investigating criminal bombings. Two months later, Bari, still in the hospital and recovering from her near-fatal injuries, faced FBI-inspired charges accusing her of knowingly transporting the pipe bomb.

Many of the Yellow Ribbon supporters in Fort Bragg, including some loggers who had been holding secret negotiations with Bari to try and prevent violence, believe the bomb was in fact hers, part of a terrorist plot aimed at their worksites, families, and communities. This belief is strongly reinforced when Hill and Knowlton, the PR firm hired by Pacific Lumber to counter the environmentalists, passes out photocopies of faked Earth First! fliers calling for violence during Redwood Summer, "to fuck up the workings of the Megamachine." (An internal memo later released as part of a lawsuit reveals that the timber company was aware that the fliers were probably fakes at the time that they were distributed to the media.[2])

At 2 P.M., Redwood Summer protestors begin marching down Main Street toward the front gate of the century-old lumbermill. By now several hundred angry men and teenage boys, spillovers from the solidarity rally, have gathered at the corner of Main and Redwood directly across from the gate. Some are slamming six-packs. Others have been drinking throughout the afternoon. One run-down fellow wears a tee shirt reading, "Save a Logger, Eat an Owl."

"A lot of these guys are the same troublemakers we pick up every Saturday night," a local cop confides.

As they head toward the gate, the marchers, accompanied by motorcycle and riot police, are heckled by a couple of leather-vested bikers. ("The only good tree is stumps" is an example of the bikers' poster prose.) As the first line of marchers, twelve across and filling the width of the street, approaches the corner of Main and Redwood, a throaty chorus of boos goes up from the sidewalk followed by a booming chant of "Go Home! Go Home!"

"We Are Home! We Are Home!" the protest crowd counter-chants. As the marchers' soundtruck comes to a halt in the middle of the intersection, people start milling, unsure of what to do next. A line of the protesters carrying a fifty-foot-long banner reading "We support the timber workers, not the timber industry" try to attach their politically correct logo to GP's padlocked security gate. Private guards hired by Georgia-Pacific videotape them from inside the yard. (Fort Bragg police chief Tom Bickle later confides that he had to talk GP out of bringing in "goons from Georgia" to help out with crowd control.)

"Trees grow back, trees grow back," the yellow-shirted crowd starts to chant. A number of young men at the front of the crowd think this is a wussy chant. "Fuck You! Fuck You!" they shout, getting red in the face, flashing the bird at the enviros, and trying to psyche each other up to move out onto the street despite a riot cop's repeated warning for them to keep back. A second cop comes up beside the first. They give each other worried looks. A few more cops move in. A California Highway Patrol motorcycle officer drives slowly into position along the sidewalk. There's some name calling directed at the police. The officers push the Yellow Shirts back, holding their long riot batons in two-handed grips and thrusting them out at chest level. Before there's time for any of the local toughs to recover or regain their balance, a line of motorcycle cops, sirens wailing, rolls up the street cavalry fashion. They're followed by dozens of quick-stepping cops in blue jumpsuits and helmets who form a defensive line facing the Yellow Shirt crowd, riot sticks ready. Four men in the still rowdy crowd are arrested, including one guy waving a billyclub at the enviros. After that, nobody seriously challenges the cops' authority. A few moments later a second line of CHP officers marches into position, turns to face the larger but more peaceable enviro crowd, and gradually opens up a corridor between the two opposing factions.

A woman gets up on the soundtruck and tries to address both crowds. "Lesbian, lesbian," come cries from the sidewalk as she begins to talk about the biosphere, one of those eco-buzzwords that seems to set off the protimber crowd.

The protimber crowd begins another chorus of "trees grow back." Someone on the soundtruck starts singing "America the Beautiful." As the environmentalists join in the chorus, the Yellow Shirt chant falters and fades into confused silence.

An Earth Firster gets on the mike and offers it to anyone who wants to speak from the other side. Despite some razzing from his friends, a young man of about nineteen with longish light-brown hair peeking out from under his bill cap steps through the police lines. He climbs up onto the soundtruck and looks around for a moment.

"We want to work. We don't want to go on welfare. And we don't need you people coming up here and telling us what to do. Why don't you just go home?" he asks the enviros.

"We *are* home," several voices shout back.

"How many of you are from Fort Bragg?" he asks skeptically. Only a few hands go up. "How many of you are from Mendocino County?" he asks more confidently. About two-thirds of the crowd raise their hands. He looks dismayed, confused. "This is just bizarre!" he says after a moment's hesitation. The crowd responds with a heartfelt round of applause.

Only two years earlier, Fort Bragg had been the scene of a larger unified protest of some two thousand Mendocino residents, including fishermen, loggers, shopkeepers, homeowners, and local politicians, along with old-time hippies, rednecks, and hipnecks (the product of two generations of cross-breeding), all united in their opposition to a federal plan to lease the area's salmon-rich offshore waters for oil and gas drilling. Now this same community is split into warring factions. The Yellow Ribbon loggers and millworkers and their white-collar bosses are part of a new campaign, a self-styled "movement" whose members call themselves either Wise Use or property rights activists and support not only unrestricted timber cutting on public lands but also offshore "energy development"; mining and drilling in national parks and wilderness areas; abolition of the Endangered Species Act; a rollback of clean-air, water-quality, and pesticide legislation; and cost-plus compensation from the taxpayer whenever a property owner or corporation is prevented from filling in a wetland, mining a river bottom, or grazing cattle on public rangeland. With deep roots in the political Right, the anti-environmentalists aim to undermine and destroy the "radical preservationists" and "pagans" of Earth First!, the Sierra Club, The Nature Conservancy, the National Wildlife Federation, and Greenpeace as well as small, community-based protest groups and their perceived cohorts in the National Park Service, Bureau of Land Management, Environmental Protection Agency, Army Corps of Engineers, Hollywood, the liberal media, universities, Congress, and the Democratic party.

This is my first encounter with the anti-environmentalists, and although ignorant of their history, aims, and ambitions, I am impressed by their ability to mobilize grassroots power on the side of industry. The polarization of the community, open hostility, riot troopers on the streets, and general atmosphere of violence remind me of "Marching Days" in Northern Ireland, when I'd covered Protestant "Orangemen" and "green" Catholic nationalists clashing on the streets of Belfast over conflicts almost as ancient as the California redwoods while the British Army, with their Saracan tanks, rubber bullets, and CS gas, got to play peacekeeper for a week.

Of course, that was during wartime, and even with the violence around Redwood Summer (a Labor Day protest greeted with a hail of eggs and rocks, the beating of several activists on local backroads, and the head shaving in jail of four longhairs who had sat down to block a logging truck), it is hard for me to imagine that environmental conflict in the United States might ever begin to resemble some of the haunting scenes of violence and hatred I had come to know as a war correspondent in Northern Ireland and Central America. But today, four years later, having seen the bomb and arson damage firsthand, and having met and talked to people who have been beaten, shot at and terrified, had their dogs mutilated, their cars run off the road, and their homes burned to the ground, I'm not so certain.

"When I say we have to pick up a sword and shield and kill the bastards, I mean politically, not physically," explains Ron Arnold, a founder and leader of the anti-environmentalist movement. "I'll tell you one thing, though. There are people out there today who are ready to pick up guns and form their own armies. I've told them, look, we already fought one civil war and lost. This isn't the way to go," he is trying to reassure me minutes into our initial phone conversation.[3] It's the winter of 1993 and Ron, who prides himself on his understanding of social movements (he's a big fan of Lenin's, having read the old Communist's forty-five-volume collected works) is aware that his movement has taken some serious hits in the media because of the parallel development of vigilante violence directed against environmental activists. His rhetorical style—"We're out to kill the fuckers. We're simply trying to eliminate them. Our goal is to destroy environmentalism once and for all"[4]—hasn't helped his cause much lately. So he's reinventing himself, trying to create a new, slightly more centrist image. He's excited about an "intermovement antiviolence treaty" he's planning to sign with Scott Trimingham, a dropout from the Sea Shepherd Society, a small, radical, direct-action environmental group known for ramming pirate whaling ships and Japanese driftnetters on the high seas.

"Philosophically, Scott and I are both followers of Gandhi," claims Ron.

Chuck Cushman, another Wise Use leader and close ally of Arnold's whose organizing style has earned him the nickname Rent-a-Riot, agrees. "The violence issue is just something the preservationists use to try and get at us by implying we want to advocate or promote violence. I've never advocated or called for violence," he insists. "Personally, we've always advocated nonviolence like Martin Luther King or that guy from India, what's his name?"[5]

Most Americans have probably never encountered the Wise Use/Property Rights philosophy except in the rhetorical prose of a Rush Limbaugh or Pat Buchanan. Nevertheless, the movement has developed its own social base, idiomatic language, ideological alliances on the Right, and support network, which reaches from unemployed loggers, off-road motorcyclists, and rural county commissioners to the top levels of industry and government. On the political spectrum, the Wise Use/Property Rights movement appears larger than white separatist or militant tax-resistance forces but far smaller than the Christian Right or progun campaigns of the NRA and the Citizens Committee to Keep and Bear Arms (whose founder, Alan Gottlieb, is also Ron Arnold's boss).

While many Wise Use/Property Rights leaders claim the participation of millions of people (by adding up constituent memberships from antigreen groups such as the American Farm Bureau Federation, the NRA, and timber, mining, and other resource associations), people who pay individual dues or actively participate in ongoing Wise Use efforts number far fewer than a hundred thousand. To date, the strength of anti-environmentalism has been not in its membership rolls but in its ability to mobilize a network of core activists to intervene in and politicize local conflicts, creating a perception of power that they hope can be used as a springboard for further expansion. Whenever a local election is turned in favor of a prodevelopment Republican, or a fax campaign skews a Sunday newspaper poll to suggest that a majority of readers think environmentalism has gone too far, or public land-use hearings are disrupted by hundreds of angry protestors, or the *New York Times* seeks out policy responses from "leaders of environmental, industrial, and property rights groups,"[6] anti-enviro leaders such as Arnold and Cushman score it as a victory for their "guerrilla warfare tactics."

At the same time, they and other key members of the cadre find themselves fighting a constant battle against narrow-focus activists who "can't get beyond their own issues." They also view themselves as under the threat of localized agreements between labor and environmentalists or farmers and government resource agencies that might undermine the fever of indignation and outrage needed to fuel a national movement's growth.

At its core Wise Use/Property Rights is a counterrevolutionary movement, defining itself in response to the environmental revolution of the past thirty years. It aims to create and mold disaffection over environmental regulations, big government, and the media into a cohesive social force that can win respectability for centrist arguments seeking to "protect jobs, private property and the economy by finding a balance between human and environmental needs." Simultaneously the movement pushes a more radical core agenda of "free-market environmentalism," "privatization," and the deregulation of industry. Despite their insistence that they are not fronting for industry, many anti-enviro groups with green-sounding names—such as the Alliance for Environment and Resources (AER), Environmental Conservation Organization (ECO), and National Wetlands Coalition— have the same relationship to timber, oil companies, and developers that the smokers rights movement has to the tobacco industry. In fact the logging industry's Wise Use rallies in the

Northwest were recently used as a template by the tobacco industry when it shut down its North Carolina mills and warehouses, paying some 15,000 of its workers to march on Washington, providing them with free buses, box lunches, and banners for a protest against a proposed health tax on cigarettes.

Other anti-environmentalist organizations—such as the Alliance for America, which Ron Arnold defines as "a bizarre hybrid of industry groups and grassroots"—like Nicaragua's Contras during the 1980s, have grown beyond their corporate sponsorship to take on a fragile life of their own, complete with an internally self-validating protest culture. This culture includes Wise Use scientists, who argue that there are no real environmental threats facing the world today, conspiracy theorists who see "environmental hysteria" as part of an "antihuman" agenda to reduce world population through mass starvation, and Wise Use political prisoners who have done short jail terms for filling in wetlands and dumping garbage. With direct-mail contact lists, fax campaigns, meetings, demonstrations, "battle books," lawsuits, and legislation aimed at the destruction of "the environmental establishment," they hope to win acceptance from the media and the public as a mainstream citizens movement. "Property rights will be the civil rights movement of the nineties," argues Michael Greve of the Washington-based Center for Individual Rights, one of a network of conservative think tanks that have historically opposed civil rights legislation for minorities and women.

While there is much overlap in both leadership and membership among the hundreds of anti-environmentalist groups scattered around the United States, some broad generalities can be made. In the West, Wise Use has been primarily about protecting industrial and agricultural access to public lands and waters at below-market costs, with the primary emphasis on timber, mining, and grazing. Although hoping to broaden their appeal to recreationists (off-track motorcyclists, snowmobilers, and hunters out of touch with the conservation ethic of their sport), the core constituency in the West consists of workers and middle management in limited-resource industries such as timber and mining whose livelihoods are threatened by industry cutbacks and who are open to the argument that environmental protection means lost jobs (an argument reinforced by the disinterest conservation organizations have historically shown in the social consequences of wilderness protection).

Wise Use also appeals to western ranchers, corporate farmers, and businesspeople whose margin of profit is directly threatened by any fee increases on grazing, water reclamation, and other uses of public lands. As a general rule, however, people in these categories are more likely to express themselves through established antigreen organizations such as the Farm Bureau and the Cattlemen's Association.

East of the Mississippi (and in some western suburbs), the movement is more oriented toward property rights, appealing to a constituency of landowners, developers, and developer wannabes whose opportunities for subdividing land and building commercial equity is limited or restricted by regulations governing wetlands, endangered species, wild and scenic rivers, and other environmental protections broadly favored by the American public. While the key players in the property rights movement are upscale conservatives, more likely to own a second home than a second mortgage, they try to portray their interests as compatible with those of rural, low-income property owners. On several occasions in Connecticut, Nebraska, and elsewhere, they have won broad community support, only to see it erode when the scenic river designations they were opposing were shown to enhance rather than undermine property values. This reflects another key truism about the anti-enviro movement. At its core it is not about differing conservation philosophies or ecological world views, religion, or politics, but about basic economic interests.

"People are losing their jobs, rural communities are becoming ghost towns, education for our children is suffering, social services are being starved of income. There's a lot of real pain out there," says Bill Grannell of the anti-enviro group People for the West. It's a refrain that has resonance in a time of massive layoffs by industry giants such as GM, IBM, Bank of America, and Boeing; of wrenching structural dislocations as defense industries try to retool for the post–Cold War world market; of massive government debt slowing economic recovery following a decade of leveraged buyouts, hostile takeovers, and other nonproductive economic activity.

The Wise Use/Property Rights response to the crisis has been to argue that environmental protection is costing jobs and undermining the economy. This appealingly simple argument doesn't always hold up in the face of complex economic realities, but for out-of-work loggers in dying timber towns, workers in polluting factories being challenged by vocal community activists, or struggling farmers unable to fill or sell off wetland acreage, it answers the question of why the American dream seems to be slipping from their grasp. For people in desperate circumstances whose needs are not being met by the system, Wise Use has provided an identifiable enemy, "the preservationist," on which to focus their anger and vent their rage.

If, as Ron Arnold has put it, Wise Use is engaged in a "holy war against the new pagans who worship trees and sacrifice people," it's the pagans who have suffered most of the casualties.

"We were told if we killed any of them there was $40,000 that was there to defend us in court or to help us get away," says Ed Knight, an ex-logger and Hell's Angel describing how he was hired to lie in ambush with an Uzi, waiting to shoot Earth Firsters in the California woods.[7]

"I was driving home from a concert and saw a glow in the mist. By the time I got to my house a mile and a half in from the highway it was burned to the ground," recalls Greenpeace USA's toxics coordinator Pat Costner of the arson fire that destroyed her Arkansas home of almost twenty years.[8]

Maine antilogging activist Michael Vernon recalls another arson fire, which destroyed his house and almost cost him his life.[9] "I'm not sure if it was the smoke alarm that woke me up or if it was just light in the house," says Vernon, "but I jumped in my boots and threw my coveralls on and I opened the door and the flames were starting to come up the stairs. There was a porch right outside the door, so I ran out and jumped off the porch into the snow."

Antitoxics activist Paula Siemers remembers the night two men attacked and knifed her on a Cincinnati street near her home, following earlier incidents of harassment in which she'd been stoned and knocked unconscious, her dog had been poisoned, and her house too had been set on fire. "They ran up behind me and they punched me and hit me. They just came out of nowhere and I didn't even know I was stabbed. I just thought they'd beat me and they ran off, and someone screamed and said you're bleeding and I don't remember much after that."[10]

"After they cut my throat they poured water in it from the river and said, 'Now you'll have something to sue about,'" says Stephanie McGuire, a local activist who was raped and tortured by three men in camouflage utilities after she protested water pollution on the Fenholloway River in Taylor County, Florida.[11]

"We think it was murder," says a friend of Leroy Jackson, a Native American environmentalist whose body was found by the side of a New Mexico highway several days before he was scheduled to fly to Washington to testify against clear-cut logging on the Navajo reservation.[12] A coroner's report found that Jackson had died of a methadone overdose although those who knew him described him as a healthy man who never drank alcohol or took drugs.

Along with the growth of Wise Use/Property Rights, the last six years have seen a startling increase in intimidation, vandalism, and violence directed against grassroots environmental activists. Observers of this trend have documented hundreds of acts of violence, ranging from vandalism, assaults, arsons, and shootings to torture, rape, and possibly murder, much of it occurring in rural and low-income communities. Simple acts of intimidation—phone harassment, anonymous letters, and verbal threats of violence—may number in the thousands. "Death threats come with the territory these days," admits Andy Kerr, Conservation Director of the Oregon Natural Resources Council, who was told he'd be killed at a public meeting.[13] Lois Gibbs, Executive Director of the Citizens' Clearinghouse for Hazardous Wastes, a coalition of eight thousand local groups, adds, "People have been followed in their cars, investigated by private detectives, had their homes broken into. I'd say 40 percent of people protesting toxic waste sites and incinerators around the country have been intimidated."[14] And while only a small part of this violence can be directly linked to organized anti-enviro groups (Yellow Ribbon, the Sahara Club, People for the West, Adirondack Solidarity Alliance), much of the rhetoric and anger springs from a common fount of explosive rage that blames greens for everything from the contracting of resource industries to the closure of the American frontier.

The anti-environmental backlash represents both a danger and a challenge—not only to conservationists and antipollution activists but to all citizens concerned about their right to speak out and protest without fear and intimidation. In the last six years, the anti-enviro ranks have grown from resource users protecting their federal subsidies and property owners unhappy with land-use regulations to the fringes of America's expanding underbelly of violence, where social causes become excuses for sociopaths motivated by fear, greed, and hatred, or private security agents working on behalf of outlaw industries. As issues of sustainability and survival become more critical in the closing years of the twentieth century, affecting the things people hold most dear, such as families, health, and property, the urges to heap blame and deny reality will inevitably increase. And if people don't begin finding ways to live well on an increasingly crowded planet without destroying the carrying capacity of their natural resource base—if they let short-term special interests define their long-term strategies for maintaining clean air, clean water, and biological diversity—they may end up deceiving themselves and denying their children's future. Unfortunately, killing the messenger has already become a favorite sport for far too many Americans, who have begun to act like disoriented coal miners, crawling around at the bottom of a poisoned mine shaft in their "Save a Miner, Eat a Canary" tee shirts.

Inside the Beltway

If you can't shoot it, hook it, or screw it, it's not worth conserving.
FORMER INTERIOR DEPARTMENT OFFICIAL AND
NRA EXECUTIVE VICE PRESIDENT G. RAY ARNETT

If you want a friend in Washington, get a dog.
PRESIDENT HARRY TRUMAN

Flying in a commuter prop plane into Washington, D.C., it's hard not to be impressed by the grandeur of our nation's capital, with its broad boulevards designed on the European model, wide enough to be swept of rabble by cannon fusillade. Washington is a low-rise city, with no office building higher than the Washington Monument. It's a city of parks and fountains, white government buildings and Black neighborhoods, war monuments and Salvadoran war refugees. The federal triangle and the Mall appear above the wing as the plane banks along the Potomac. The Mall is alive with tourists, pixels of color on a greenbelt of summer grass. There's the Kennedy Center and the Lincoln Memorial, the FBI's J. Edgar Hoover Building looming over the Justice Department, the palatine Capitol Building, grown huge with the country, a stunning white confection in the summer haze. The top of its 180-foot dome is covered in scaffolding where the cast iron and bronze statue of Freedom has been removed for her 130-year makeover. Beyond Capitol Hill is southeast Washington, a domestic war zone. Twenty-five people will be murdered here and in other poverty-wracked sectors of the city during the ten days

I'm in town, and a group of six kids will be shot and wounded for no apparent reason at a municipal swimming pool. None of the lobbyists, environmental staffers, or politicians I interview will mention these shootings, not even the folks at the NRA. Gunfire has become the background noise that separates the city of Washington from the business of government.

We pass by the aging Pentagon Building on our final approach into National. It's a smooth landing. A wall of warm, muggy air, thick as damp cotton, greets us as we climb out of the plane and pick our bags off the tarmac. Washington, founded on a swamp in 1791, still has the feel of a semitropical bog, a place where longhorn cattle lie down in cattail wallows to keep the mosquitoes off their hides. It is a place out of touch with social change, more insular and culturally conservative than the rest of the country. With its beltway hierarchies of strategic think tanks, industrial foundations, trade associations, PAC-addicted politicians, corporate attorneys meeting with agency officials whose jobs they used to have—not to mention eighty thousand lobbyists, more paid persuaders than there are employees of the departments of Energy, Education, and environmental protection combined—Washington is closer in feel to Paraguay than Peoria. The Clinton team, six months into office, is still feeling its way along. An early attempt to write public land reforms into the budget has been derailed. Many environmental policy positions in the departments of Interior, Commerce, and Agriculture and the EPA remain unfilled or unconfirmed. The environment, never a front-burner issue in Washington, seems unlikely to become one during this summer of budget battles, base closures, Bosnia, and Baghdad.

It doesn't take long, however, to begin identifying the beltway power base of the anti-environmental backlash. As I leave the airport, I pick up a copy of the *Washington Times*, the ultraconservative daily newspaper published by self-styled Korean Messiah and convicted tax felon Reverend Sun Myung Moon. Its Sunday edition has extensive front-page coverage and special reports on grazing, mining, and Wise Use.[1] Under the top headline "Main Street's Verdict: Budget Is a 'disaster'" is a second one: "Western Showdown—Fight Looms on Fees for Use of U.S. Land." The story, illustrated with a color photo of a rancher feeding his cows off the tailgate of a pickup, tells of widespread rural opposition to change on the range.

"The seriousness of this grassroots movement," reads the article, "was evident last month at a series of hearings on grazing fees held by Interior Secretary Bruce Babbitt. Thousands of ranchers packed auditoriums from Bozeman, Montana, to Grand Junction, Colorado, turning the meetings into rallies and outnumbering their environmentalist opposition as much as 100 to 1." According to newspaper clips from Bozeman, Reno, Grand Junction, and Albuquerque, the four towns where the hearings took place, turnouts ranged between five hundred and a thousand, with ranchers outnumbering environmentalists by four to one.

Washington Times special reports in the same issue, headed "Miners Say Royalty Bill Would Cripple Industry," " 'Wise Use' Drive Fights Environmentalists," and " 'Extreme' Views Create Opposition to Interior Pick" portray an American West rising up in revolt against the Clinton administration and its emerald-green backers. The last story focuses on George Frampton, the former president of the Wilderness Society, whom Clinton has nominated to be Assistant Secretary of Interior for Fish, Wildlife, and Parks. It quotes Republican Senator Frank Murkowski of Alaska as saying that Frampton "has opposed without exception our timber, oil, gas and mining industries. . . . He comes from an extreme point of view." The article fails to quote any Senate supporters of the nominee.

The Moon paper (daily circulation 92,000) appears to be acting as a media stalking horse for the anti-enviros. Having failed to sidetrack the confirmation of mining-reform advocate Jim Baca for director of the Bureau of Land Management (BLM), Wise Use/Property Rights activists are now cranking up their fax networks to oppose the Frampton nomination. Chuck Cushman has established a get-Frampton committee chaired by Alaska's Lieutenant Governor Jack Coghill and blasted out fourteen thousand fax messages from his farmhouse headquarters in Battle Ground, Washington. The D.C. end of the campaign is being coordinated by Myron Ebell, Cushman's Washington lobbyist. Despite their best efforts, Frampton's confirmation, like Baca's before it, will be unanimously approved by the full Senate after a 13–5 vote in committee.

The next morning—Monday, June 21—the *Washington Post* runs an $11,000 quarter-page ad from the Oregon Lands Coalition (OLC), the main anti-enviro umbrella group in the Pacific Northwest. During the April 1993 Forest Summit in Portland, Oregon, the OLC ran a number of expensive TV ads extolling the timber industry's good forestry practices. Headlined "An Open Letter to Our President," the *Washington Post* ad is a plea for Clinton to follow up on the Forest Summit with a plan that favors continued high-yield logging on public lands. "Lately, we have been greatly troubled," reads the ad, "by a steady leak of reports in our daily papers that the plan you may offer will not provide enough timber to support our jobs and way of life we've worked so hard to preserve. If these reports are true, tens of thousands of people will lose their jobs. That would be a calamity, Mr. President, and we don't believe the American people want this to happen or that you would let it happen. . . . The national environmental groups are calling you names. We're calling you our President. Please don't let us down."

Nine days later, having kept a panel of scientists, sociologists, and economists working full-time for three months, Clinton releases his Option Nine Forest Plan, which would allow 1.2 billion board feet of lumber to be cut in the Pacific Northwest while reducing the overall amount of logging on federal land; preserving watersheds and habitat to protect salmon, owls, and rivers; and offering a $1.2 billion aid package to help timber communities diversify their economies. Predictably, neither the timber industry nor environmentalists are happy with the compromise plan. "We have to play the hand we were dealt," the president says, looking back on a decade of overcutting, court injunctions, and federal inaction.

"Funeral Services, dead trees & abandoned communities. It's all part of what Bill Clinton calls a 'fair' solution," reads the Oregon Lands Coalition flyer that soon goes out in the mail. "Option

9 is the work of young, inexperienced staffers. . . . We can help the president see that his wet-behind-the-ears process people have deceived him by sending him pacifiers & Pampers. Mail within 10 days to: President Clinton, 1600 Penn. Ave. NW, Washington, D.C. 20500."

One of my early interviews in Washington is at the Heritage Foundation, the $20 million-a-year think tank that set much of the policy agenda for the Reagan administration and serves as the model for dozens of conservative "baby think tanks" that have since sprung up around the nation. Heritage is housed in a nondescript slab of an office building a few blocks up from the Capitol on Massachusetts Avenue. Amidst the antique furnishings of the lobby hang oil paintings of favored conservative icons: Ronald Reagan, William F. Buckley, Milton Friedman, and Clare Boothe Luce.

"By denying ourselves material wealth today, by slowing the accumulation of wealth, we are denying our children. You deny the future by not using resources now." I am talking with Heritage's John Shanahan. Thirty-something, with forest green eyes, dark hair, and the unconscious mannerisms of a Bill Buckley, John is the foundation's policy analyst for environmental affairs. He works out of the "Coors Research Offices" on the building's sixth floor, four floors up from ALEC, the American Legislative Exchange Council, which is sponsoring anti-environmental "takings" legislation in a dozen states. Before coming to Heritage, John was a labor-management specialist in the Bush administration. "I'd wanted a position in the Department of Interior, but they didn't like my free-market environmental theories. You have to wonder if they were real Republicans," he smiles, one eyebrow arched ironically.

John lays out some of the precepts of free-market environmentalism, which in economic terms translates into the total deregulation of industry. "The free market by its very nature is a conservation mechanism," he claims. "All our energy and mineral resources are increasing in terms of our ability to get at them. And we'll be able to do that for quite a while. But eventually we'll start to run out and begin to use what's cheapest and most efficient, which will be renewable resources like wood. You have to ask why would people in the future want to burn oil when they'll have better battery power and renewable solar technologies? So you can see if we don't use the oil now it'll just be left lying there in the ground. Conservation just for the sake of conservation is not a legitimate goal.

"The best thing to reduce air pollution is to make energy cheap," he continues. "There would be some short-term pollution increases as countries moved from agricultural to industrial societies, but once you reach an individual income of $5,000 per capita, air pollution goes down. As people get wealthier, society pollutes more, but once you hit that income level, people begin to demand pollution reduction as a quality-of-life issue. That's why in the U.S. it would be ridiculous for us to pour out pollution the way they do in the Third World." His $5,000-income-trigger theory is based on a 1991 Princeton study funded by the Mexican government as part of its push for free trade.

How would the Heritage Foundation feel about more pragmatic mixes of regulation and incentives to achieve environmental goals—for example, Bruce Babbitt's proposal that grazing fees on public lands be adjusted or permits extended according to how well ranchers manage range ecology?

"We favor variable pricing, although the best option would be privatization, of course," Shanahan says, returning to a free-market theme popular in the early days of the Reagan administration, the selling off of public lands to private industry. "Privatization is the highest priority for the environment," he insists.

The Heritage Foundation, wedded to a robber baron's vision of unrestrained free enterprise, has taken a leading role in attacks on public resource agencies and "leftist" (legislated) environmentalism. In 1990 it issued a report on "Ecoterrorism" timed for the twentieth anniversary of Earth Day, and more recently, in its *Policy Review* magazine, it singled out the environmental movement as "the greatest single threat to the American economy."

Despite some philosophical differences with Wise Use over government subsidies for motorcycle trails and timber sales, Heritage is one of a network of well-funded think tanks and legal foundations that provide important technical support and political access for anti-enviro activists around the U.S. Reports David Howard, a leader of the Alliance for America in the June 1993 Alliance newsletter, "I was asked to be a featured speaker at the Heritage Foundation Resource Bank annual meeting. The keynote speaker was former attorney general Edwin Meese. The contacts we established at that meeting will serve the Alliance in many ways."

Other major anti-enviro think tanks operating inside the Washington beltway include the $4-million-a-year CATO Institute, a right-wing libertarian tank that also promotes free-market environmentalism while publishing books downplaying environmental dangers such as ozone depletion. Ben Bolch and Harold Lyons, authors of a recent CATO book, *Apocalypse Not*, argue that "much of the modern environmental movement is a broad-based assault on reason and, not surprisingly, a concomitant assault on freedom."[2]

The Science and Environmental Policy Project (SEPP) was founded in 1990 as an affiliate of the Washington Institute for Values in Public Policy, a Moon-funded think tank that provided SEPP with free office space.[3] Since severing its ties with the Moonies and strengthening its links with the conservative Virginia-based George Mason University, SEPP has gone on to hold a number of conferences and seminars attempting to discredit ozone depletion, global warming, acid rain, pesticide exposures, and toxic waste as real or potential threats to human health. Its executive director, Fred Singer, has become the most popular science speaker on the anti-enviro rubber-chicken circuit since the death of ex–Washington Governor Dixy Lee Ray.

Defenders of Property Rights, which was founded in 1991 by former Reagan Justice Department officials Roger and Nancy Marzulla, plays a key role in promoting anti-environmental lawsuits through the U.S. Court of Federal Claims, the conservative third tier of the federal judiciary whose sixteen judges were all appointed by presidents Reagan and Bush.

The Defenders group works closely with the Federalist Society, the Competitive Enterprise Institute, and the Washington Legal Foundation, three members of a nationwide network of twenty-two probusiness "public interest" law firms that do anti-environmental lawsuits and litigation on a pro bono basis, providing the antigreen movement with tens of millions of dollars in free legal services. The firm's directors coordinate strategy through an annual meeting sponsored by the Heritage Foundation.[4]

Walking from the metro to the NRA's headquarters, I pass a video crew shooting a thick-set bald man in a wheelchair being loaded into a van. It takes me a moment to realize that it's James Brady, Ronald Reagan's former press secretary, shot in the head during John Hinckley's 1981 assassination attempt on the president. Still paralyzed but politically active, the ex-White House official has given his name to the Brady bill (that will later become law), the federal gun-control measure that requires a seven-day waiting period before purchase of a handgun.

I enter the boxy office headquarters of the National Rifle Association. A lobby model of its new Virginia office complex suggests that even the armed defenders of the Second Amendment have given up and joined the district's "white flight" to the suburbs. I'm escorted upstairs to a spacious corner office to meet one of the most powerful lobbyists in Washington. NRA Executive Director Jim Baker, tanned and relaxed, reaches for the small automatic pistol on his desk, points it towards his handsomely planed face, and pulls the trigger, lighting his cigarette off the flame that pops up from the silver-plated look-alike lighter. Richard DeChambaugh, director of hunter services for the three-million-member gun organization, joins us for the interview session, lighting up his own coffin nail as he takes a seat. "Our position on wilderness is, we're against it unless it provides for hunting, access, and active management," Baker explains. DeChambaugh quietly nods his agreement.

Does the NRA see environmental groups as part of the opposition?

"In many cases, yes," Baker admits after brief reflection. "The environmental groups, many of them are opposed to hunting.

Many groups are. But we try to work with those we consider conservation groups versus preservation groups. . . . We like to take our environmental cues from state fish and game departments [whose revenues come from the sale of hunting tags and fishing licenses]. They're the people who know what the real science and game management requires."

Although familiar with hunting issues, competitive shooting, and other support functions of his organization, Baker's personal rise to prominence as head of NRA's Institute of Legislative Action has been based primarily on his effectiveness as a Capitol Hill lobbyist battling to prevent passage of any type of gun-control laws. Since the mid-seventies the NRA has evolved from a hunting and sportsman's group into an uncompromising gun-rights lobby whose board of directors includes a number of "God, Guns and Guts" hardliners including *Soldier of Fortune* magazine publisher Robert K. Brown.[5]

DeChambaugh, sleek haired, heavyset, and dressed in a getup that includes a blue paisley tie, gold cowboy belt buckle, and hand-tooled leather boots, is the point of contact between this most feared and powerful of national lobbies and the anti-environmentalist movement. He ran a hunting club in Amador, California, for twenty years before the Sierra foothills got overdeveloped, and led the NRA board at its 1987 Reno meeting in declaring its opposition to the expansion of federal wilderness and national parks. The following year he attended a seminal anti-enviro conference in Las Vegas, and in 1989 he was named by Baker to represent the NRA on land-use issues. He has since led an NRA campaign to overturn the century-old ban on hunting in national parks and monument areas.

"We develop coalitions with other organizations," he explains, putting down one cigarette and lighting another. "We work with the Wildlife Legislative Fund of America, with the Safari Club International. We recently scored a victory in Arizona, defeating Prop 200 [which would have banned the state's wildlife-trapping program]. We lost on Prop 117 in California [a ban on mountain lion hunting]. The Alaska wolf hunt is still up in the air—we haven't seen the end of that one yet. We've targeted legislators over hunting issues as well as gun rights. We've worked with the American Farm Bureau Federation. We toured with an NRA/Farm Bureau show in Oregon in 1992 to talk about gun ownership. Timber people have called on us to talk about impacts on elk herds from restricted logging. If you don't harvest enough trees you don't have as large elk herds. Logging road closures in wilderness areas also impact availability of game. Hunters feel, 'If we can't get there, who cares what you do with it.' We want to make sure the reauthorization of the Endangered Species Act takes hunting into consideration. . . . It's a balance we're looking for. We've communicated with [anti-enviro leader] Clark Collins. Clark and I are good friends. We've talked about getting together with his ATV [all-terrain vehicle] volunteers for handicapped hunting trips. You also have these wildlife refuges and proposed refuges, like this one in Sacramento I was told about that I put Chuck Cushman onto. They were just going to lock it up. Our position is, let's negotiate this, let's get the local landowners involved so that hunting, fishing, boating, and these other uses are preserved."

DeChambaugh also helped raise funds for sports video producer Dick Davis, who did a series of tapes for anti-enviro leader and fellow Safari Club trophy hunter Grant Gerber that aired on cable TV. One, on the *Exxon Valdez* oil spill, argued that the spill's impact was distorted by the media and that the oil had no significant or lasting effect on Prince William Sound or its wildlife.

While the NRA's DeChambaugh numbers antigreen activists Gerber, Collins, and Cushman among his organization's friends, NRA officials will have nothing to do with Alan Gottlieb, Ron Arnold's sponsor, who along with the Center for Defense of Free Enterprise, runs two progun outfits, the Citizens Committee to Keep and Bear Arms and the Second Amendment Foundation. Between them, these two groups generate some $4 million a year.

"See what is spent versus what is raised," suggests Jim Baker when asked his opinion of Gottlieb's work. "Obviously, we compete for the same dollar, but I think we do a much better job. NRA is the only group that has a staff of seventy-five dedicated to the political and legislative arena."

I mention the niche market Gottlieb has created with his *Women and Guns* magazine that he's put his wife, Julianne, in charge of.

"Sonny Jones started *Women and Guns* magazine. She now works here," Baker says dismissively.

What about the anti-environmental backlash in general? How does the NRA relate to Wise Use and Property Rights?

"We have had similar interests with many of these people, but we don't buy into a lot of baggage that goes along with those titles. . . ." He glances across the table at Richard DeChambaugh. "Sometimes we support consumptive users of resources but we've been on both sides. Guns and hunting are our primary issues." DeChambaugh nods his agreement. DeChambaugh's assistant, Gary Kania, promises to put together a sampling of cases in which the NRA has opposed logging, mining, and other resource industries. The package never arrives.

"No one's ever shown that anyone died from long-term exposure to pesticides. There is no threat to consumers from pesticide residues," claims Mark Maslyn, the long-faced, red-bearded director of government relations for the American Farm Bureau Federation (AFBF). "We've grown up in a chemical era in agriculture. If there was a problem with long-term exposures to pesticides, it would be showing up with us, the third generation of farmers, and it hasn't."

Like many other interested parties across the capital, Maslyn, director of the bureau's ten full-time Washington lobbyists, is somewhat skittishly awaiting the release of a five-year study on pesticides conducted for Congress by the National Academy of Sciences. The report, released a week later, indicates that there is "potential for concern" that some children may be ingesting unsafe amounts of pesticides and that "there should be a presumption of greater toxicity to infants and children," with exposure standards ten times higher than presently applied.[6] The EPA responds to the report by announcing new standards for pesticide residues on food that will no longer attempt to balance economic benefits with health risks based on figures for adult consumption.

"Farmers are using a lot less of everything," Maslyn explains, "because, health and environmental concerns aside, agricultural chemicals are expensive."

I ask what advantage agrochemicals have provided if crop losses to pests have pretty much remained the same or actually increased slightly, from 35 to 37 percent, over the last fifty years.

"Chemicals are a substitute for other inputs," he responds.

"Labor?"

"Yes, labor. You can't get people to work on the farms pulling weeds anymore. Housewives, students, they'd rather work at McDonalds. I know an apple grower who couldn't get people to pick his apples for $8.50 an hour."

Among its labor recommendations to its farmer members, the AFBF suggests that they demand a search warrant before allowing INS agents onto their fields to search for illegal immigrants. Following the death of United Farm Workers leader Cesar Chavez in April 1993, *Ag Alert*, the newspaper of the California Farm Bureau, quoted state president Bob Vice's backhanded eulogy: "He was no saint but he certainly changed the face of California agriculture. . . . His strength was his ability to publicize his cause, but he lacked the administrative ability to carry it through."[7]

With almost four million members, some 25 percent of them farmers, the American Farm Bureau Federation functions as a multifaceted political force, a powerful and influential farm organization, a $2 billion nationwide insurance company with some of the best rates in the industry (all policy holders automatically become bureau members), and a not-for-profit business league with huge investments in agricultural chemical and biotech companies.[8]

"My view is we've gone through three or four revolutions in U.S. agriculture from the horse to mechanical power to chemical technology and now are transcending to biotechnology if the critics let it survive," Maslyn explains.

In the 1950s and sixties, the Farm Bureau was a leading influence encouraging American farmers to make the transition from organic inputs to nitrogen fertilizers, pesticides, and other agrochemicals, part of what was then called the Green Revolution. During the farm crisis of the 1980s, the bureau favored large-scale, export-oriented agriculture over debt-strapped family farms. At its 1985 convention in Hawaii, the Farm Bureau passed a resolution (over heated objections from Iowa and other mid-western state delegations) calling for the government to sell off farmlands acquired through foreclosure.[9]

"Out of some 2.4 million farmers remaining today, most have to supplement their incomes driving a school bus or whatever. There are really less than half a million full-time farmers. The farmer you want to keep employed is that full-time farmer, that 25 percent," says Maslyn, explaining the AFBF national leadership's position.

The Farm Bureau has also been a leader in the fight against wetlands protections and other environmental reforms it considers damaging to competitive farming and to U.S. dominance of the world agro-export economy. "Legislation we're lobbying on includes water quality, wetlands, the Clean Water Act, nonpoint pollution, the Endangered Species Act, and property rights," Maslyn says, counting off the list. "Our overriding issue is private property rights. We take the view that we have an obligation to society but that society also has an obligation to us. When the benefits [of environmental regulations] are derived by society as a whole, we should have some public support in turn, some compensation . . ."

He's interrupted by an aide carrying a folder. "Excuse me. Do you have that finished language to take to Condit?"

Gary Condit is a freshman congressman and rural Democrat from California who's cosponsoring property rights legislation with Senate Republican leader Bob Dole.

"Yeah. Make sure to photocopy this. Give me back the original," Mark says, collecting a stack of papers off his desk and passing them to his aide.

I ask Mark about AFBF's differences with the National Farmers Union, Family Farm Coalition, Farm-Aid, and other advocacy groups. "We have always been more conservative than other groups in agriculture," he says. "I guess you could say we're Jeffersonian, believing the government that governs least governs best. . . . We were more successful during the Reagan administration. The farm vote split in 1992. Forty-one percent voted for Clinton, 40 percent for Bush, and the rest for Perot."

How does the Farm Bureau feel about Clinton's personnel choices?

"We're very positive on Espy and Rominger [Secretary of Agriculture Mike Espy and Assistant Secretary Richard Rominger]."

What about Vice President Al Gore and Secretary of Interior Bruce Babbitt?

"We're very positive on Espy and Rominger," he grins.

How does the AFBF function in alliances and coalitions?

"Philosophically we're closer to the Cattlemen's Association than anyone else. Their members are our members, there's more crossover. Out West it's them and us on grazing fees, public lands, predator control, wilderness. Wise Use, people like Chuck Cushman and Ron Arnold, also play a constructive role in the process, and we wish them well. If nothing else they make us look moderate."

A visit to the well-leathered Cattlemen's Association offices at 1301 Pennsylvania Avenue, three blocks up from the White House, brings a similar response. "We're closest to the Farm Bureau. We also work with Pork, Corn and Wheat [commodity groups], the Realtors Association, and Chamber of Commerce," says Greg Ruehle, their manager on environmental issues and one of seven staff lobbyists. "We're part of the Public Lands Council, which is an umbrella of the National Cattlemen's Association [with 230,000 members including the 27,000 public land grazing–permit holders], the American Sheep Industry Association, and the Association of National Grasslands. The council's executive director is also the director of federal lands for National Cattlemen."

"We're leading the [anti] Endangered Species Coalition along with the Forest Products Association," adds Alisa Harrison, the Cattlemen's director of public affairs. "Ranching is land-intensive. If government land acquisitions or regulations like Endangered Species restrict our access, that land becomes useless. . . . The whole concept of Wise Use is something we support in these battles. Sometimes Chuck [Cushman] can say things our people would like to say but can't because we have to focus on those people who can help us on the Hill as well as people who can turn out the grassroots."

"The Cattlemen's Association is a very grassroots organization." Greg Ruehle interrupts to clarify her statement. "The environmental groups are the top-down organizations. They're really special interests just like us but the press makes them out to be some sort of public interest activity."

The idea that Washington's "Big 10" environmental groups are similar in style and structure to what Ron Arnold calls the "Gang of 18" resource-industry associations—the American Petroleum Institute, National Homebuilders, Forest Products Association, Coal Association, American Mining Congress, Cattlemen's Association, and so on—is not without some merit, at least enough to gain wide credence in Washington power circles.

The D.C.-based environmental groups, with millions of dues-paying members and hundreds of professional staffers, including lawyers, lobbyists, and public relations people, use many of the same techniques as the private-sector lobbies. These include computerized mailing lists, direct-mail funding pitches, multimedia advertising, political action committees, and political endorsements. The National Wildlife Federation, with its 4.5 million members and supporters, maintains a large office complex off Dupont Circle decorated with granite frescoes of elk, bear, buffalo, mountain lions, wolves, salmon, and other wild creatures. A number of major corporations are represented on its board of directors. Audubon and Sierra have top-end media arms producing slick mass-circulation magazines, books, films, and video documentaries. Greenpeace has a national door-to-door canvassing network of a thousand volunteers knocking on forty thousand doors a night, making it the largest operation of its kind outside the Girl Scouts' annual cookie sale.

Still, these professional advocacy structures pale in comparison to the political weight and pressure industry can bring to bear.

"It's not just the number of lobbyists you have, but also *who* you have," says the director of a successful D.C. lobbying group, who asked not to be identified. "One of the surest ways to guarantee a return call from a congressman or senator is to have a former congressman or senator make the first call."

A not untypical Washington law firm based on this principle is that of McClure, Gerard and Neuenschwander, whose senior partner is former Republican senator from Idaho James A. McClure (1973–1991). While in Congress, Jim McClure won his spurs as an outspoken foe of environmentalist "tree huggers."

"I remember being at a meeting with Senator McClure and he was talking about the spotted owl and someone said, 'Well, you don't have any spotted owls here in Idaho,' and his response was, 'Well, if I thought those bastards would try and cross the border, me and my buddies would stand on the state line and shoot them down,'" recalls George Rieger, conservation editor for *Field & Stream* magazine.[10]

After leaving office, McClure continued to represent many of his old constituents, including Weyerhauser lumber and the American Mining Congress.

In 1989, in response to President Bush's pledge of "no net loss of wetlands," the law firm of Van Ness, Feldman and Curtis was hired by the Mining Congress, oil and gas industry and land developers, to lobby Congress and the White House to reopen wetlands to development. The firm established the misleadingly titled National Wetlands Coalition, which continues to lobby and write legislation that would allow the filling and drilling of estuaries, bogs, marshes, mangrove swamps, tundra, and bayous.

The nation's top public relations firms, Burson-Marsteller and Hill and Knowlton, along with the Washington-based "environmental communications" specialists at E. Bruce Harrison, have also acted as Washington spokespeople for Exxon, Union Carbide, Monsanto, and other corporate giants during environmental fiascoes such as the *Exxon Valdez* oil spill and Bhopal chemical

disaster. In *O'Dwyer's PR Services Report*, an industry publication, environmentalism has been identified as "the life and death
PR battle of the 1990s."[11]

In 1980 the nuclear industry set up its own $20 million-a-year
PR firm, the U.S. Council for Energy Awareness (USCEA), to
promote commercial nuclear power. Established in the wake of
the Three Mile Island nuclear accident, its most recent ad campaign promotes the idea that nuclear energy is the safe, environmentally friendly answer to the threat of global warming. "When
I was in college I was against nuclear energy," says the actress
playing a young mother in one of USCEA's TV spots. "But now
I've reached a different conclusion. It means cleaner air for the
planet."

Unfortunately, this conclusion puts USCEA in direct conflict
with another industry front group, the Global Climate Coalition,
founded in 1989 by forty-six corporations and trade associations
related to, among other industries, mining, oil, and utilities. The
mission of the Global Climate Coalition is to convince Congress
and the media that the concept of human-caused global climate
change such as the greenhouse effect is a myth or, where scientific
evidence is irrefutable (for example, the rise in atmospheric CO_2
since the Industrial Revolution), that the effects of such changes
are beneficial. The coalition has successfully lobbied to weaken
the U.N. Earth Summit Treaty on Climate Change, which would
reduce greenhouse emissions on a global basis, and a 1992 House
energy bill that would have required industry cutbacks of CO_2
emissions and placed a ten-year moratorium on offshore oil and
gas drilling. In 1993 the coalition distributed a $250,000 video
documentary to more than a thousand journalists across the country purporting to show that increased atmospheric CO_2 will boost
crop production, providing a solution to the world's hunger problem.[12] Congressman George Miller, the Democratic chair of the
House Committee on Natural Resources, says the coalition's real
goal is "unimpeded production of oil, gas, and coal."[13]

Not surprisingly, the argument that nonprofit environmental
groups such as Greenpeace and the League of Conservation Voters are driven by the same self-interests as major industrial lob-

bies is readily accepted by Washington politicians and the capital press corps. This follows in the wake of a decade-long crusade by Beltway conservatives—including the Heritage Foundation, the American Enterprise Institute, and the U.S. Chamber of Commerce—to redefine the term *special interest* to include public interest consumer groups, civil rights organizations, advocates for the disabled, and even "minorities and women" (a "special interest" constituting a majority of the population). Identifying environmentalists and resource lobbyists as competing special interests without considering whose interests they're representing also provides good cover for industry-dependent western Democrats opposed to the reform policies of their own administration.

"Both sides have engaged in scare tactics that are hurtful," says Mark Smith, legislative director for Democratic Senator Max Baucus of Montana. "There are groups like People for the West and Earth First! being vocal on both sides. There's a lot of anger out there on both sides." Senator Baucus led the successful resistance of western Democratic senators to President Clinton's budget plan to increase fees for mining, timber cutting, and grazing on public lands, a plan that would have generated a billion dollars in new revenues. Baucus called the proposal "unfair to the West."[14]

"First of all, not one of these senators was consulted on these changes. And second, the changes recommended were Draconian," Smith insists. "If you pursue policies insensitive to people, if you don't do it right and consider the economic effects, what's going on now will just explode. . . . There's a story about Babbitt," he continues. "A conversation he had with Clinton before he was named secretary of Interior. Babbitt is said to have told Clinton, 'Hire me and there's good news and bad news. The bad news is that you'll lose the Rockies in the next election. The good news is you'll carry California.' If the Democrats lose senate seats in the West because of these [environmental] policies, they're going to regret having taken that approach."

Western Democrats working the other side of environmental and public lands issues often find themselves under attack by both resource users at home and their own colleagues on the Hill. In this type of an ambush situation, diplomacy doesn't lessen your chance of getting killed. Ask Congressman Mike Synar of Oklahoma what he thinks of the NRA, Farm Bureau, or Cattlemen's Association, and he won't hesitate to tell you. "Thieves run in gangs. It's always been the tradition in crime," he snaps in a western twang that sounds like a gust of wind on barbwire.

"Don't hold back, Mike. Just say what you think," an aide laughs.

"It's true," he insists. "These are the people who called me uninformed until they realized I'd been a two-time national 4-H winner. Then they called me a vegetarian. I'm a fourth-generation rancher. I had steak today for lunch. Then they called me an eco-terrorist on the House floor. When all that failed, now we're socialists and preservationists. They have no facts so they're into name calling." Synar, a long-time grazing reform advocate and one of only five members of Congress who refuse to accept PAC money, has the rugged good looks of a young Charles Bronson and an attitude to match. "These are a bunch of whining welfare cowboys and the next sound you hear is the nipple coming out of their lips," he quips. "These are the same people who come into their congressman's office and say, 'I want the government to run like a business.' So I say, 'Okay, we're going to give you a dose of free enterprise. We're going to make you pay the fair market value of the assets you're using up on our federal lands, whether it's timber or grazing or minerals.'"

In the past, whenever Synar tried to push grazing reform through the House, he found his bills turned into hardtack for legislative barter by the cattle industry's many friends on the Hill. Four years ago his grazing reform bill was traded on the House floor for a moratorium on offshore oil drilling. The following year it got traded for a $100 claim fee, a symbolic wave in the direction of 1872 mining law reform. Then in 1992 there was the vote on Jesse Helms's amendment to censor the National Endowment for the Arts for sponsoring a homoerotic gallery exhibit by photographer Robert Mapplethorpe. The trade-off for keeping the NEA independent, suggested by former Democrat Les AuCoin of Oregon, was elimination of Synar's grazing bill. The trade became known as "Corn for Porn" (although beef for beefcake would have been more accurate). "Amazing, all those conservatives who suddenly discovered they could live with pornography in order to keep subsidized grazing," Synar's aide smiles wickedly, figuring if you can't restrain your boss you might as well join him.

"Corn for Porn was not a situation of trading, it was just the ugly system of democracy that actually works pretty effectively," insists cattlemen lobbyist Greg Ruehle.

The crowds of tourists in Bermuda shorts, cut-offs, tee shirts, flip-flops, sneakers, tank tops, tube tops, sun visors, and sunscreen wandering up the wide white steps and crowding the narrow arcaded corridors of the Capitol provide a refreshingly democratic counterpoint to the building's imperial Palladian architecture. Tightly packed shoals of sunblock-scented citizens, numbering some ten thousand a day, follow their tour guides through the eighteen-story-high main rotunda, learning the history and meaning of its frescoes and paintings of muscular Greek gods. Walking to the center of the white marble floor and looking up, one experiences a moment of awe, a sense of standing in the center of the world's largest Fabergé egg.

The public galleries of the House and Senate chambers are packed with tourists. More wait in line, holding the paper passes that are laid out like party favors in the office foyers of their local representatives and senators. Over the course of the evening on the final day of debate on President Clinton's first budget, Senate seating will gradually open up. Except for the C-Span posturing, the final vote is thought to be a done deal, but the Republicans and oil-and-gas Democrats led by Boren of Oklahoma manage to drag the conflict out late into the night. It will take Vice President Al Gore's tie-breaking vote at two in the morning to finally put it away.

Upstairs on the second floor of the Capitol, it's quieter. A guard points me down a polished marble corridor filled with statues of former Senate pols to the large wooden door of the Howard Baker room bearing the words "Bob Dole—Senate Republican Leader" in gold. While Democrats have divided over western resources and other environmental issues, the Republicans have unified under the hectoring leadership of Senator Dole of Kansas.

Inside, just beyond the secretary's desk, is Bob Dole, appearing as dour in real life as on TV, sitting below the office parlor's crystal chandelier. He is talking to a large, wide-girthed man in a yarmulke who's threatening to collapse a curly legged antique divan. Behind the tall, gray-suited senator, on the mantle of a marble fireplace, sits a bronze bust of himself by sculptor Friedrich M. Sogojan, a gift of thanks for the relief aid Dole and his wife Elizabeth took to Armenia following the massive earthquake of 1988.

The room, which marks the northwest corner of the original Capitol, housed the first Library of Congress until British soldiers dumped its three thousand volumes on the floor, using them as kindling to set fire to the building in 1814. Later it became the robing room for the Supreme Court and then, in the middle of this century, the Republican leader's room. It has one of the few functioning fireplaces in the Capitol. For the first few weeks of every winter, a roaring blaze warms and brightens the parlor. Then the GSA warehouse that provides the wood runs out of last year's well-aged supply and orders new green logs that smoke like greasepots. For the remainder of the winter, Dole's staff burns Duralogs from local supermarkets while writing position papers on government waste and inefficiency.

Dole, having taken up the anti-environmentalist mantle of property rights from former Republican Senator Steve Symms of Idaho, is sponsoring Senate bill 177. Based on a 1988 Reagan executive order, the bill would require government agencies to review Fifth Amendment implications for all environmental and other regulations they enforce. The bill is based on a conservative legal interpretation of the Fifth Amendment that asserts that any time the government reduces the value of private property through the regulatory process it must pay financial compensation to the property owner. Politically the bill is backed by the

Farm Bureau, the Homebuilders Association, a few other power-ful lobbies, and some fifty smaller groups from the Wise Use/Property Rights movement.

"When I introduced S. 177, I mentioned that its intention might seem curious, requiring federal employees to uphold the Constitution—an activity in which they swore to engage before they were hired," Dole declared on the Senate floor. "Maybe we should get everyone in government to take an oath every year so they would not forget."[15]

"Like the senator said, you would think those who've sworn to uphold the Constitution would have no problem with a simple declaration on behalf of a constitutional right like this," says James "Witt" Wittinghill, Dole's deputy chief of staff, who is act-ing as the bill's minder. He smiles, his eyes twinkling just a bit. Witt is a tall, straight-backed westerner with dark salt-and-pepper hair and a full mustache. He wears a black chalk-stripe suit and black cowboy boots. His corner office down the hall from Dole's is decorated with a flintlock rifle, an NRA cap, a large rattlesnake embedded in Plexiglas, various photos, newsclips, and other Dole memorabilia, and a handful of hardcover books including *With Reagan* by Ed Meese and *At the Eye of the Storm: James Watt and the Environmentalists*, by Wise Use leader Ron Arnold.

"We became aware of the property rights movement during the 1987–88 campaign when the senator was running for presi-dent," Witt tells me. "We were hearing from property rights ac-tivists everywhere. This is not just about Superfund or wetlands or hunters, but the environmentalist issues and rules are the ones trying to inject government into the middle of this deeply held belief that private property should not be regulated."

Not at all?

"I think it's a widely shared acceptance with respect to public health and safety, you cannot cause harm to others," he admits. "Local government zoning is also fairly widely accepted. But there's no scientific certainty on many of these [environmental] issues. Republicans are as committed to the environment as

Democrats. We have no intention of saying we love the environment any less than the Democrats. But before forcing an action on people, we want to show there's a tangible benefit. We won't buy a pig in a poke.

"The more sunlight put on risk assessment, for example [an EPA method of estimating health risks from pollutants such as soot smoke, sulfur dioxide, and various chemicals], the more absurd that stuff becomes. What's a one-in-ten-thousand chance of contracting cancer? If we knew that we could cure cancer. What's the impact of losing ten thousand jobs? Let's look at this as well. I don't buy that more regulation can mean more jobs. The theory Al Gore is putting forward of this green-industry stuff is if we force industry to develop environmental cleanup equipment, we'll sell this all over the world. Industry tells us we can't afford this equipment and retrofitting without job loss. Overseas they won't buy it because they can't afford it."

I ask him if there's much awareness of the Wise Use/Property Rights movement among senators on the Hill.

"Western senators have regular and constant conversations about what this new crowd's agenda is," he tells me. "They're very politically active. It's not yet to the level of the Sagebrush Rebellion [an attempt to transfer federal lands to the states launched by western resource users in the late seventies], but it will be at least as bad as that four years from now the way this administration is going. If they piss off all the grazers in the West . . . I know these people, I'm from Montana. If you get these people pissed off they could rise up again."

"Violently?"

"You know, these union methods sometimes come into play . . . I mean the labor unions, they made a contribution to the country but . . ." He leaves his antilabor thought unfinished.

Despite its claims of nonpartisanship and the active participation of a number of fringe groups, including the Birchers, the LaRouchites, and the Moonies—the anti-enviro movement, particularly in its tweedy property rights cloak, has found its strongest support in the post-Reagan Republican party. In turn Wise

Use/Property Rights can take some credit for helping to shift the political balance of at least two state houses, Oregon's and Montana's, from a Democratic to a Republican majority.

"Election of people like me is an indication of frustration on the part of people, workers and others in natural resources," grins Oregon State Senator Gordon Smith, a tall freshman Republican with the bland good looks of a game-show host. "In the ninety-two elections the [state] Senate changed from 20 to 10, Democrats, to 16 to 14, which is really a tie, because Mae Yih [a conservative Democrat] always votes with us. Our control of the House also expanded. One of the strategies of the Republican party is to work with natural-resources folks and kind of pick fights with the pure preservationists. We've found these groups are extremely effective in local returns. People like Oregonians for Food and Shelter, the Farm Bureau, these elements that are part of the Oregon Lands Coalition" [the anti-enviro umbrella group].[16]

In Texas, three institutional elements of the anti-enviro movement—the Farm Bureau, Cattlemen's Association, and NRA—ganged up to help unseat Agriculture Commissioner Jim Hightower, a maverick reformer with national Democratic leadership promise. Hightower, now a radio commentator, recalls how "they spent hundreds of thousands of dollars in television ads that were as effective as they were evil. One of them started with a flag burner setting a flag on fire, and then my picture came on the screen. You get it? The only thing that wasn't in there was having me shake hands with Noriega or someone like that."[17]

However, the anti-enviros' efforts have also been thwarted in a number of western campaigns. Montana's 1992 election for the state's sole redistricted congressional seat, seen as a plebiscite on environmental issues, went to Democrat and wilderness advocate Pat Williams, who beat out long-time Wise Use supporter and conference speaker Republican Congressman Ron Marlenee (the man who called Mike Synar an "ecoterrorist" on the House floor).

At the same time, an NRA/Farm Bureau/Cattlemen coalition led by Alan Day (the millionaire-rancher brother of Supreme Court Justice Sandra Day O'Connor) failed to unseat Mike Synar in his rural Oklahoma ranching district, whose biggest city is Muskogee, where, according to a famous song, "cowboy boots are still the manly footwear."

On the national level, Dole's "property rights" legislation has twice passed the Senate before being killed in conference with the House and is likely to surface again in the future as an amendment to an appropriations bill. While its chances of final passage are considered slim to none, its perseverance is indicative of the Republican leadership's commitment to riding the anti-environmentalist bandwagon as far as it can take them. In a 1993 appearance on CNN's "Crossfire," House Republican Conference Secretary Tom Delay identified the Endangered Species Act as the second greatest "threat" facing his Texas constituents (after "illegal aliens" but presumably ahead of drugs, crime, and political corruption).[18] Also in the house, freshman Congressman Richard Pombo of California has established an anti-enviro property rights task force that he hopes to take on the road with Congressmen Bob Smith of Oregon and Michael Crapo of Idaho.

Conservative Republican strategists, going back to the Reagan administration and including such prominent players as the Heritage Foundation, James Watt, Richard Darman, John Sununu, and Dan Quayle, have seen in the anti-environmentalist movement a way to advance their own agendas by encouraging and then responding to "popular pressure" favoring deregulation, corporate subsidies, commercial nuclear power, and the opening up of public lands to energy and mining. At the same time, conservative pundits and party ideologues, including George Will and Pat Buchanan, stymied by the collapse of communism and appalled by the broad popular support shown for the twentieth anniversary of Earth Day, have found in the environmental movement a new foe that they think might help keep the party right unified.

The danger of these strategies is similar to that the party encountered in 1992, when it allowed Pat Robertson's Christian Coalition and other elements of the Christian Right to push their antiabortion, antifeminist, antigay social agenda to the forefront of party policy, with Pat Buchanan declaring "a religious war" at their national convention in Houston (in a speech that columnist Molly Ivins suggested "may have sounded better in the original German"). Among Buchanan's targets were "radical feminist" Hillary Clinton and "Albert" Gore, whom he linked to "environmental extremists who put birds and rats and insects ahead of families, workers and jobs."[19] Most voters rejected the intolerance of the Christian Right's agenda, undermining the already shaky re-election bid of President George Bush.

Embracing the anti-environmentalist movement in the 1990s could put Republicans in a similarly vulnerable position. A May 1992 Roper poll found 80 percent of the U.S. public to be at least "sympathetic" to the environment, with more than two-thirds of Americans declaring the environment more important than the economy and believing that more, not less, environmental regulation was necessary.[20] Despite a weak economy, more recent surveys, including polls in New Mexico and Montana, continue to find overwhelming public support for environmental protection of wetlands, better range management, cleanup of mine runoff, and continuation of the Endangered Species Act.

When George Bush, in the fading days of his re-election campaign, went to Washington State to tell a rally in the timber town of Colville that if Clinton and the "Ozone man" were elected America would be "up to its neck in spotted owls," he may have gained points with the anti-enviros but he lost support overall. His campaign strategy to throw a Republican "iron ring" of support around Seattle turned into what state Democrats jokingly referred to as his "ring around Colville." In the end he lost big not only in urban, environmentalist Seattle, but statewide, even in the county where the industry logging rally was staged.

Although it's unlikely that anti-enviro groups will grow large enough to play a major role in any future Republican national convention comparable to that the Christian Right played in 1992, there are still issues tied into Wise Use that could boomerang to cause harm to the Republican party. One such response might occur if the party that claims to favor budget cutting and cost saving over its "tax-and-spend" opponents is seen as having fought too hard to protect special-interest subsidies in mining, grazing, and logging, losing taxpayers' billions by refusing to take a market-based approach to public land fees. Another might occur if a Republican-identified antigreen movement is seen to be lobbying to open U.S. resources to foreign, and particularly Japanese, interests. This view might be reinforced both by the involvement of the Reverend Sun Myung Moon's Unification Church/business empire, with its strong connections to Japanese and Korean capital, and by Canadian, South African, Japanese, and other foreign ownership of mines and cattle ranches operating on public lands in the West. Two other examples of the way foreign industry might be seen as benefiting from the anti-enviro campaigns are Mitsubishi's purchases of raw logs from U.S. timber companies operating in the Pacific Northwest and Alaska, and Japanese off-road vehicle manufacturers' support for motorized trails legislation that came out of the Wise Use movement in Idaho.

The third and most immediate danger of a boomerang involves the public's identification of the militant anti-environmentalist rhetoric of the Wise Use/Property Rights movement and confrontational tactics used in many of its protests with the physical assaults and vigilante-style attacks on environmental organizers and community activists taking place around the nation. These attacks have focused particularly in areas such as the Adirondacks and the Pacific Northwest, where anti-enviro political organizing and criminal assaults seem to be running in close parallel.

A small effort to break from the anti-enviros is occurring among California Republicans, where former EPA Administrator Bill Reilly, former Congressman Tom Campbell, and State Secretary of Resources Doug Wheeler have formed what they call the Environmental Forum. The goal of the group is to encourage their party to work with business in developing "effective conservation strategies" that would move the party closer to where the public is at.[21] Still, given the New Right/Christian Right stranglehold on party policy that sees environmentalism as both an infringement on the free market and a pagan form of nature worship, the party of conservationist hero Teddy Roosevelt is unlikely to see a green turnaround any time soon.

Nor are America's militant anti-environmentalists likely to fade

from the scene. In interviews around the country, antigreen activists have declared, with a sense of genuine outrage, that because of government restrictions on wilderness and wildlife,
"trees are being left to rot in the forest," "fish are dying of old
age," and "fresh water is just flowing out to sea." This belief in an
absolute utilitarian approach to nature, the idea that any part of
an ecosystem unused for commodity production is simply wasted,
has historical roots that go far deeper than either of our nation's
two major political parties, deeper even than the United States
itself.

Masters and Possessors of Nature

We do not inherit the earth from our fathers.
We borrow it from our children.
DAVID BROWER

I do not believe that there is either a moral or any other claim
upon me to postpone the use of what nature has given me,
so that the next generation or generations yet unborn may have
an opportunity to get what I myself ought to get.
SENATOR HENRY M. KELLER, COLORADO, FEB. 26, 1909

If the Wise Use perspective—the idea that there's too much wilderness protection and environmental hysteria and not enough clear-cut logging, pesticide spraying, and mini-mall construction—seems a bit strange by today's societal standards, it might help to remember that the environmental ethic—the idea that the earth's resources are limited and must be managed in a sustainable manner—is a new and still fragile construct within our culture. In contrast, appeals to unrestricted property rights and the promise of unlimited frontiers hold a deep and abiding place in our nation's social history going back more than half a millennium. The first major conflict between environmental sustainability and advocates of property rights in America was fought along racial lines: whites versus Native Americans.

When Columbus arrived on the island of San Salvador in 1492

in search of a trade route to India, he reported of the New World that his eyes "would never tire beholding so much beauty, and the songs of the birds large and small."[1] Other early European explorers would describe the Florida countryside as "the fairest, fruitfullest and pleasantest of all the world," and the outer banks of the Carolinas as "a land full of deere, conies, hares and fowle in incredible abundance." Having recorded their first impressions of North America's natural beauty, the discoverers quickly set about in search of gold and other objects of value.

These explorers and the settlers who followed them also encountered American Indians, as Columbus misnamed the indigenous people. These folks had been occupying the continent for upwards of thirty thousand years, ever since their ancestors first crossed the Bering Strait landbridge from Asia to kill and displace the woolly mammoths. Although initially skeptical, the Indians tried to make the newcomers from Europe feel welcome by, among other gracious acts, saving the Plymouth settlement from winter starvation.

The estimated four million Indian residents of North America, despite cultural differences among their tribal groups that often led to intercommunal raids, wars, and other common human (male) activities, were as a whole qualitatively different from these new settlers. While they practiced slash-and-burn agriculture along with fishing, hunting, and the gathering of wild edibles, they hadn't experienced the surplus-generating plow-based agricultural revolution that had shaped the European landscape with its overcrowded cities, cleared forests, and indentured peasantry. As essentially nomadic peoples with low-density populations, the indigenous groups had little lasting impact on the natural terrain and wildlife that supported them.

The Italian explorer Amerigo Vespucci (for whom America is named) found the natives "barbarous" and "shameless" even if they did show themselves to be "desirous of copulating with us Christians." He was most shocked, however, by their communal habits. "They neither buy nor sell. In short, they live and are contented with what nature gives them," he wrote. "The wealth which we affect in this our Europe and elsewhere, such as gold, jewels, pearls and other riches, they hold of no value at all. . . ."

In both the avaricious Christianity that characterized the Age of Discovery and the scientific empiricism that marked the Enlightenment, human beings were seen as apart from and having hegemony over nature, "the masters and possessors of nature" in the words of René Descartes. North American Indian cultures and religions, in contrast, were nature based, seeing humans as integral players in a larger cosmology of the spirits and seasons of Mother Earth. Today's Wise Use advocates like to portray environmental radicals (indeed all environmentalists) as "druids and pagans" or else as "Marxist watermelons" ("green on the outside, red on the inside"), but these descriptions, when not used in a purely cynical fashion, tend to reflect their own Eurocentric bias. Those of today's environmentalists who have the time or feel the need for some new paradigm of faith are far more likely to identify with Native American spirituality than with the religions and philosophies of the Old World.

The key rationale used by the white settler culture to justify the expropriation of natives' lands and displacement of their culture was the concept of private property rights as applied to land ownership. This justification was even articulated as official policy in the report of the Interior secretary for 1851: "To tame a savage you must tie him down to the soil. You must make him understand the value of property, and the benefits of its separate ownership. You must appeal to those selfish principles implanted by Divine Providence in the nature of man for the wisest of purposes, and make them minister to civilization and refinement."[2]

By contrast, the indigenous view of the land and of the white European settler's relation to it was best summarized by Sitting Bull in 1877, the year after the Battle of Greasy Grass (Little Big Horn):

> Behold my brothers, the spring has come: the earth has received the embraces of the sun and we shall soon see the results of that love!
>
> Every seed is awakened and so has all animal life. It is through this mysterious power that we too have our being, and we therefore yield to our neighbors, even our animal neighbors, the same right as ourselves, to inhabit this land.
>
> Yet, hear me, people, we have now to deal with another race—

small and feeble when our fathers first met them but now great and overbearing. Strangely enough they have a mind to till the soil and the love of possession is a disease with them.

They claim this Mother of ours, the earth, for their own and fence their neighbors away: they deface her with their buildings and their refuse. That nation is like a spring freshet that overruns its banks and destroys all who are in its path.[3]

With such diametrically opposed views, conflict was inevitable. Between 1600 and 1890 (the year Sitting Bull was murdered by Indian Police sent to arrest him), more than two hundred major battles would be fought between indigenous groups and the settlers, some four hundred treaties signed and broken, and three-quarters of the Native American population destroyed. Along with their technological edge in metallurgy, guns, and gunpowder, the Europeans' utilitarian approach to nature provided them with a range of combat strategies inconceivable to the Native Americans. These included germ warfare (General Jeffrey Amherst handing out smallpox-infected blankets to the tribes around Fort Pitts) and resource denial ("Kill a buffalo, starve an Indian" was a motto favored by General George Crook's cavalry forces in the West). The near elimination of the buffalo as part of a strategic plan to "civilize" the western plains stands as a prime example in U.S. history of this utilitarian approach to nature.

In the wake of the American Civil War, the railroad companies, army, and Texas stockmen found common cause in the eradication of the buffalo. In 1867 the Union Pacific shipped the first twenty-box carloads of cattle from the dusty Chisholm Trail town of Abilene, Kansas, to Illinois for slaughter. By 1871 it was shipping seven hundred thousand longhorn a year. The growth of a national beef industry was limited only by the competition for wild grass forage from the great herds of migratory bison. In 1869 completion of the Union Pacific railroad divided the plains buffalo into a northern and southern herd estimated at approximately forty million and twenty million, respectively. With rail towns such as Dodge City there for the shipping of hides, and rail company employees and army garrisons willing to pay for the provisioning of meat, thousands of hunters such as Buffalo Bill Cody, Charlie Rath, and Frank Mayer spread across the plains with their .55 caliber Sharps rifles, turning what had been selective hunting into industrial slaughter. The railroads joined in the carnage, advertising special excursions where passengers could shoot buffalo from the windows of passing trains. British royalty and other wealthy Europeans traveled out West for elegant week-long trophy hunts. By 1874 the southern herd had been eliminated.

General Phil Sheridan, commander of the armies of the West whose famous quote was actually, "The only good Indians I ever saw were dead," appreciated the strategic value of the bison killing. Addressing a group of Texas legislators, he admitted that buffalo hunters were "doing more to settle the vexed Indian question than the entire regular army has done in the last thirty years. They are destroying the Indians' commissary."[4] General George Crook, newly arrived on the plains from the Apache wars in the Southwest, gave standing orders to his cavalry patrols to shoot buffalo on sight.

When the hunters went out in search of northern buffalo in the spring of 1881, they couldn't find any left alive. In place of the great thundering herds were swarms of carrion-engorged black flies. The decade of slaughter complete, a number of unemployed hunters became bonepickers, spreading out across the plains in buckboard wagons to collect the "white harvest," which, shipped back East by railcar, sold for five to eight dollars a ton as phosphorus fertilizer.

The nomadic plains Indians never recovered from the loss of the buffalo and were soon driven by hunger onto government reservations, where they could be controlled and "civilized." In order to feed them, government agencies contracted millions of dollars of beef cattle from western ranchers and then cheated the tribes out of much of the meat by never delivering it. In Washington the stockmen's "Beef Ring" became notorious for feeding at the public trough. The Cherokee Strip Livestock Association, the predecessor of today's Cattlemen's Association, fought for white rancher access to reservation grazing lands. However, not all the tribes were starved into submission by the loss of the plains buffalo.

Three tribal nations—the Sioux, Cheyenne, and Arapaho—had, in the fertile Black Hills of South Dakota, plenty of elk, deer, antelope, and other game to sustain them on what they considered their sacred lands. In 1870 the army, enforcing the two-year-old treaty that had ended the Bozeman Trail war (during which the Sioux and Northern Cheyenne managed to shut down one of the four major settlement routes west), turned back a gold-mining expedition headed into the Black Hills. This led to a riot by thousands of angry miners in Sioux City and the establishment of a "Black Hills" lobby in Washington to open up the area to "advancing civilization." Charles Collins, a colorful and bombastic Sioux City promoter, argued that the "Indian monopoly" on the Black Hills, which the U.S. government had promised to honor "as long as the grass shall grow and the rivers flow," was no different than the railroad monopoly in the rest of the nation: designed to keep honest white men from earning a productive living.

In 1872 Congress passed a mining law that would allow hard-rock miners to take title to public lands for $2.50 an acre. The following year the army began doing armed mineral surveys in the Black Hills while holding private discussions with railroad magnate Jay Cooke about opening new lines through the treaty lands. Among the military commanders who sought to provoke a conflict with the Indians was survey commander George Armstrong Custer, who took several reporters along with him on his patrols. A subsequent dispatch in the *New York World* reported, "Custer's Expedition Reaches Its Destination/A Region of Gold and Silver Mines and Lovely Valleys Discovered." The gold rush that followed led to skirmishes with the Indians and increased army activity leading to war. Custer's ill-fated decision to try to take on a vastly superior (and better led) Indian army in the summer of 1876 resulted in his death, along with that of 212 of his men, at the battle of Little Big Horn. Over the next year, General George Crook was able to overcome Indian resistance in a hard-fought campaign using thousands of army troops, rapid-fire Gatling guns, and artillery. Companies such as Homestake Mining (backers of today's anti-enviro People for the West) got their starts digging gold in the Black Hills while the Indians were pushed onto increasingly smaller and less productive reservation lands. On their return east in 1877, elements of Custer's Seventh Cavalry were mobilized for riot duty in Chicago as popular resentment and worker dissatisfaction over wage cuts led to a nationwide railroad strike, the burning of thousands of locomotives and railcars, and urban street fighting in dozens of towns and cities.

The rapid growth of cities and their smokestack industries also led to bacterial diseases and epidemic outbreaks from decaying garbage piles, inadequate sewage systems, bad water, and soot smoke. Antismoke leagues were formed in New York, Pittsburgh, and other cities. In San Diego debate over whether or not to industrialize raged between self-described "Smokestacks" and "Geraniums." Late nineteenth-century urban industrialization also meant increased demand for coal, iron, lead, and copper (used for telegraph and electrical wiring). Mineworkers suffered from black and brown lung disease as well as lead and mercury poisoning. Millworkers and goldleafers lost their breath to silicosis. Tuberculosis and pneumonia were the common diseases of the meat-packing industry. Class conflicts raged in the eastern cities, taking on the appearance of industrial warfare in the intermountain West, where thousands of armed miners clashed with state militias and federal troops. Still, most people failed to link the causes of urban squalor and occupational death with the depredations of nature being practiced as part of the culture's industrial resource expansion.

The late nineteenth century was also marked by militant agricultural movements. Expanded production and industrial depressions resulted in low farm prices and a revolt amongst the farmers against industrialism and corporate power. The populist movement demanded democratic reforms, including direct elections for the Senate, graduated income taxes, and inflationary money policies that would favor the farm producer. William Jennings Bryan, the fiery populist candidate for president in 1892 and 1896, declared, "The great cities rest upon our broad and fertile prairies. Burn down your cities and leave our farms, and your cities will spring up again as if by magic: but destroy our farms, and grass will grow in the streets of every city in the country."[5]

In 1890 the U.S. Census declared the frontier officially closed, but wealthy stockmen and timber thieves, used to having their way on both the open range and the mountain range, were having none of it. The Forest Reserve Act of 1891, which set aside the first thirteen million acres of what was to become the national forest system, was angrily denounced by stockraisers, loggers, and western land developers, collectively known as "boomers." Where it was inconvenient to systematically steal timber from these new reserves, arson was employed as a tool to protest restrictions on grazing and mining.

According to Mike Weiss, in *Mother Jones* magazine, a similar pattern of arson fires is appearing on U.S. forest lands today. Major forest fires, including the 1992 Fountain Fire in California and Warner Creek Fire in Oregon, appear to have been deliberately set in order to promote salvage logging, which allows for commercial timber sales on burned-over U.S. forest lands that would otherwise be off limits to logging.[6]

The coming of the twentieth century, celebrated with millennialist fervor from Maine to California, saw a dramatic change in the government's commitment to conservation, largely as a result of three men's work: naturalist John Muir, forester Gifford Pinchot, and President Theodore Roosevelt.

Like Henry David Thoreau before him, Scots immigrant John Muir was a romanticizer of nature. His wanderings through California's Sierra Nevada and his writings about his wilderness encounters popularized in books and magazines, led to the creation of Yosemite National Park in 1890. An advocate of wilderness preservation, he also founded the Sierra Club in order to "be able to do something for wildness and make the mountains glad."

Pinchot, an avid outdoorsman, was one of the first Americans to be trained in European forest management, which sought to create a sustainable yield in wood products. Convinced that government control of the forests was the only way to stop the destructive practices of the big logging companies, he became head of the Agriculture Department's forestry division under President McKinley.

Teddy Roosevelt, big game hunter, adventurer, and politician, helped found one of the first conservation organizations in the United States, the Boone & Crockett Club (named after Daniel Boone and Davy Crockett), to protect big-game animals and their habitat. He fought to save Yellowstone Park from development and for passage of the 1891 Forest Reserve Act. Vice president of the United States when McKinley was assassinated in 1901 and elected to a second term in 1904, Roosevelt was the first chief executive to actively work on behalf of wilderness and conservation, developing close friendships with both Muir and Pinchot. He promoted the latter to chief forester.

In expanding or creating the nation's system of parks and national forests, reclamation projects, reservoirs, and wildlife sanctuaries, Roosevelt came into direct conflict with the western boomers—the "land-grabbers and great special interests," as he called them. "The rights of the public to the [nation's] natural resources outweigh private rights and must be given its first consideration," he argued. In 1906 he imposed the first fees for cattle and sheep grazing in national forests. "Whoever takes public property for private profit should pay for what he gets," he insisted to howls of protest from western resource industries and the congressmen and senators they controlled. One western newspaper called him a dictator, editorializing that if he "continued to create reserves there would be little ground left to bury folks on." The boomers also claimed that forest reserves hurt small homesteaders.

"Our policies favored the settler as against the large stockholder," Roosevelt countered in his autobiography, "although in places their ignorance was played upon by demagogues to influence them against policy that was primarily for their own interest."[7]

In many of these resource battles, Pinchot and Muir worked as a team—Pinchot as the consummate Washington bureaucrat

fighting in the halls of power while Muir beat the band to raise
public support. But Muir and Pinchot, who introduced the term
conservationist, also had strong philosophical differences. Muir
believed in wilderness preservation for its own sake, while Pinchot advocated the "wise use" of resources, believing they should
be carefully utilized to meet people's needs. During his presidency, Roosevelt often refereed their conflicts, supporting Muir
in turning down a proposal for mining in the Grand Canyon in
1906 but reluctantly siding with Pinchot over Hetch Hetchy, the
issue that would turn the two friends against each other. The city
of San Francisco wanted to dam Hetch Hetchy, a spectacular valley inside Yosemite National Park, for water and electric power.
Pinchot backed the city's plan and branded Muir and his valley
supporters "unreasonable nature lovers." In 1913 the dam was
built. A year later Muir died, his spirit broken.

Today's "wise-use" activists like to claim that they are following
in Pinchot's conservationist footsteps, although philosophically
(and often genealogically) they are direct descendants of the western boomers Pinchot, Muir, and Roosevelt all fought to defeat.
Even Ron Arnold's use of the term *Wise Use* has more to do with
marketing psychology than any deep philosophical reflection on
Pinchot's legacy. "*Wise Use* was catchy," Arnold told a reporter for
Outside magazine in 1991, "and it took up only nine [*sic*] spaces
in a newspaper headline, just about as short as *ecology*."[8]

The first two decades of the twentieth century saw increased ur-
banization and demand for food that led to a level of farm prosperity not seen before or since. Fearing a resurgence of the
farmer-based populist movement of the 1890s, agro-oriented
companies such as John Deere, International Harvester, and the
Rock Island Railroad joined with the U.S. Chamber of Commerce to help promote the Farm Bureau Federation, a conservative outgrowth of the U.S. Department of Agriculture's farm
extension program. Initially advocating mechanization of agriculture, over time the Farm Bureau would become a major
promoter of agricultural subsidies, chemical fertilizers and
pesticides, corporate farming, and low-priced agro exports. The
bureau's indifference to the plight of the family farmer and to or-

ganic crop production and its open hostility to farm laborers, wetlands, wilderness, and wildlife would make it a major anti-
environmental player in U.S. agricultural policy over the next
three-quarters of a century.

The era of farm prosperity ended on October 24, 1929, with
the stock market crash. America quickly sank into the Great Depression: the country's gross national product declined 25 percent
in three years; Wall Street traders jumped to their deaths from
high-rise buildings, whose windows still opened; bread lines
formed outside Red Cross and Salvation Army soup kitchens
while militant "unemployed councils" broke into supermarkets to
feed the hungry. In 1931 Governor Franklin D. Roosevelt of New
York established the first state relief organization in the country
to try to feed the urban unemployed. Conditions in rural America
were even worse. One-third of farmers lost their land to foreclo-
sures and evictions even as an extended drought created a vast
dustbowl that stretched across the middle part of the country
from Kansas to Oklahoma. "Okie" dustbowl refugees who tried to
find work as migrant farm laborers in California were turned back
at the border by armed state troopers.

In 1932 Franklin Roosevelt easily defeated incumbent Herbert
Hoover in the presidential election, initiating a "New Deal" policy of government intervention to "pump-prime" the economy.
Roosevelt's basic economic theory, that unlimited growth and expansion had to be replaced with well-regulated management to
assure every American a comfortable living, soon found expression in his approach to natural resources. Like his distant cousin
Teddy Roosevelt, FDR considered himself an ardent conservationist. Of the many New Deal programs he established in the
early 1930s, his favorite was the Civilian Conservation Corps.
Employing almost three million urban youths during its lifetime,
the CCC planted trees and built trails, watchtowers, and ranger
stations in national parks and forests. It ran soil-conservation projects, dug irrigation ditches and reservoirs on the plains, and created greenbelt parks around many towns and cities.

Other New Deal efforts to help America's earth and people recover from recent abuses included establishment of the Soil Conservation Service, a program of farm-price supports and rural

electrification that included the setting up of the Tennessee Valley Authority. The TVA was the first major effort to restore an ecologically and economically devastated region through programs
of soil and water conservation. But its network of publicly owned
power dams was condemned by the major utility corporations as
socialistic. These companies, along with the U.S. Chamber of
Commerce, National Association of Manufacturers, and DuPont
Chemical Company, formed the American Liberty League, a
right-wing organization of wealthy industrialists who considered
Roosevelt "a traitor to his class." FDR also faced challenges from
the radical Left and organized labor, particularly the Congress of
Industrial Organizations, whose sit-ins, rallies, and strikes were
often met by violence from police and company guards. Isolationists and "America Firsters," who believed that the nation had
gained little from its participation in World War I, were also suspicious of Roosevelt's "internationalism." Roosevelt tried to steer
a middle course between the isolationists and America's overseas
allies. But the military expansionism of Nazi Germany in Europe
and of imperial Japan in Asia soon put the United States under
tremendous pressure to come to the aid of its battered friends.
FDR's lend-lease program to Britain and the Soviet Union in
1940–41 jump-started America's industrial capacity for war production while also eliminating the last economic downturn of the
Depression era.

With its entry into World War II following the December 7,
1941, Japanese air attack on Pearl Harbor, the United States
emerged as a major world power. The nation's remarkable war
mobilization of industrial and scientific resources expanded its
productive capacity as nothing else before or since. America
tapped its natural resource base for the production of steel, aluminum, gasoline, aviation fuel, glass, lead, magnesium, wool, fiber, and myriad other components that went into the making of
airplanes, ships, and tanks. The petrochemical industry was given
a boost by the demand for synthetic rubber in 1942, rubber trees
being one of the few natural resources not available on the North
American continent.

The war effort also spurred scientific research in a number of specialized fields, including sonar and physical oceanography, which would later help the U.S. oil and gas industry expand its offshore drilling operations. The most extensive top-secret research was directed towards the development of the atomic bomb, which scientists feared the Germans might get first. However, by the time the "Manhattan Project" had a working test bomb, Berlin had fallen and the war in Europe was over. Watching the first mushroom cloud rise over the New Mexico desert test site in July 1945, project director J. Robert Oppenheimer was reminded of a quote from Hindu scripture: "Now I am become death, the destroyer of worlds."

The end of World War II, marked by the atomic bombing of Hiroshima and Nagasaki in Japan, also heralded America's emergence as the planet's preeminent power and the beginning of a forty-five-year-long "cold war" with the Soviet Union. Ironically, the only post–World War II victims of America's nuclear arsenal would be the thousands of military troops, Native American uranium miners, "downwind" ranchers, bomb factory workers, and Pacific islanders exposed to radiation from weapons development, construction, and atmospheric testing. By the late fifties, radioactive strontium 90 from bomb testing would be detectable in human bones and mothers' milk. Other Americans would be exposed to military toxins ranging from organic solvents to heavy metals to dioxin in Agent Orange defoliant as the national security state exempted the military from the environmental safeguards gradually adopted by the rest of society.

U.S. government agencies such as the Atomic Energy Commission downplayed the risks of ionizing radiation by promoting the "friendly atom" for commercial power generation. New agricultural and petrochemical products were broadly welcomed by postwar society, which saw unregulated scientific and commercial innovation as the road to prosperity. The use of chemical farm pesticides increased thirty-three-fold between 1945 and 1985. Ironically, the percentage of crops lost to insect pests also rose slightly during this same period.[9]

An affluent culture of consumer-driven conformity emerged in the 1950s. There was the postwar baby boom, the creation of

single-family suburbs such as New York's Levittown, and broadcast television, which replaced radio as the dominant medium
of communications. The American landscape was dramatically
altered by a postwar construction boom that spread with the
interstate highway system, soon accounting for 80 percent of
everything built since the arrival of the Pilgrims. The optimistic
probusiness boosterism of the 1950s was also reflected in Washington's natural resource policies. President Eisenhower referred
to the New Deal legacy of public power projects as "creeping socialism," while his secretary of Interior, a former Chevrolet salesman named Douglas McKay, was so anxious to transfer federal
lands to states and private industry that he became known as
"Giveaway McKay." One of the major resource fights of the era
was over plans by the federal Bureau of Reclamation to build a
series of power dams and reservoirs on the upper Colorado, including one at Echo Park inside Dinosaur National Monument.
Conservationists, fearing a new Hetch Hetchy that would open
the national park system to commercial exploitation, launched a
major campaign to stop the dam. Ex-mountaineer and Sierra
Club Executive Director Dave Brower led a coalition of groups
that flooded Congress with letters and testimonials protesting the
plan on both aesthetic and practical grounds. Brower's successful
effort to stop the Echo Park Dam would be followed by similar
efforts to prevent the damming of the Grand Canyon and to designate a number of now famous wilderness reserves. Still, Brower's early victory at Echo Park would prove bittersweet. As part
of the final settlement, he agreed not to protest construction of
the Glen Canyon Dam in Arizona, only later discovering the hidden wonders of the soon-to-be-flooded canyonlands below Rainbow Bridge, the highest rock arch in the world. Floyd Dominy,
the U.S. Commissioner of Reclamation appointed under Eisenhower, considered the Lake Powell reservoir that grew up behind
the dam a great improvement on nature's hidden canyons, even
penning a poem in honor of his work:

> To have a deep blue lake
> Where no lake was before

Seems to bring man
A little closer to God.[10]

"About seven hundred feet closer," Dave Brower responded with tongue firmly in cheek. Brower, like John Muir before him, would later prove uncompromising in his wilderness campaigns, helping to found a number of environmental organizations along the way, including Friends of the Earth, the League of Conservation Voters, and the Earth Island Institute.

Ron Arnold traces present-day Wise Use rhetoric that brands environmentalists as "pagans who worship trees and sacrifice people" to *Encounters with the Archdruid*, a 1971 book by author John McPhee in which Hilton Head developer Charles Frasier is quoted as saying of Brower, "Ancient druids used to sacrifice human beings under oak trees. Modern druids worship trees and sacrifice human beings to those trees." Replies Brower at eighty-two, "Really, I've just always loved people who loved trees."[11]

The election of President John F. Kennedy in 1960 marked a dramatic change in America's cultural attitudes. The youthful president's call for a "new frontier" of freedom and social involvement found resonance in the writings of Supreme Court Justice William O. Douglas, whose rulings helped establish the legal framework for the field of environmental law. Newly named Secretary of Interior Stewart Udall was among the first in government to challenge "uncritical acceptance of conventional notions of progress," and to identify links between unchecked population growth, pollution, urban decay, and wilderness protection. "The history of America," John Kennedy agreed, "has been the story of Americans seizing, using, squandering, and, belatedly, protecting their rich heritage."[12] In 1961 Kennedy, in an address to Congress, called for a wilderness bill, surveys for new national parks, and the setting up of national seashores. Governor George D. Clyde of Utah, speaking on behalf of western economic interests—the oil and gas, mining, timber, and cattle industries—warned that the new administration was threatening to "bottle up enormous quantities of natural resources." Kennedy, the witty,

aristocratic easterner already condemned by the hard Right for
not launching a full-scale invasion of Cuba during the Bay of Pigs
fiasco, now became the subject of deep distrust among the cowboy capitalists of the West.

By the early 1960s America's burgeoning urban population was
also growing increasingly alarmed by the visible by-products of
unrestrained economic growth. Smog and air pollution were
choking cities from Pittsburgh to Los Angeles. Industrial and municipal waste was poisoning the Great Lakes, seashores, and rivers. Cleveland's Cauyahoga River, covered with oil and industrial
sludge, caught fire, burning two overhead bridges, as it seeped
its way into phosphate-choked Lake Erie.

Along with Michael Harrington's *The Other America* and
Ralph Nader's *Unsafe at Any Speed*, the 1962 publication of
Rachel Carson's book *Silent Spring* gave voice to the nation's
growing concerns over poverty, consumer fraud, and environmental degradation. In an impassioned, fact-filled attack on the
use of DDT and other synthetic chemicals, Carson demonstrated
how human-made insecticides killed tens of thousands of birds
and other nontarget species, posing grave dangers to the soil,
food chain, and human health. The impact of *Silent Spring* would
prove so seminal to the development of a new ecological awareness that even today few anti-enviro conferences take place where
the late author isn't excoriated for her "preservationist hysteria"
and "bad science."

With the assassination of John F. Kennedy in Dallas, Texas, on
November 22, 1963, America suffered a political trauma that
many would later come to identify as a historical turning point for
the nation. The promise of government-sponsored political reform to ease the burdens of racism and injustice were quickly forgotten as Lyndon Baines Johnson sacrificed his "War on Poverty"
in order to pursue the "Great Frontier's" war in Vietnam.

The devastation of Vietnam's people and landscape from massive U.S. bombing and "resource-denial" strategies—using the
air cavalry to push "hostiles" out of "Indian territory"—recalled
America's earlier white-settler wars. The clearing of jungles, helicopter attacks on elephant herds (suspected Viet Cong trans-

port), and defoliation of rainforest canopy using dioxin-based herbicides in a program called "Operation Ranchhand" led to charges of ecocide. Black humor grew among the troops spraying the poisons, who shortened the U.S. Forest Service slogan "Only you can prevent forest fires" to "Only you can prevent forests."

Disillusionment over America's role in Vietnam became widespread among civil rights activists, college students, and the working poor at home. "If we are to get on the right side of the world revolution, we as a nation must undergo a radical revolution of values. We must rapidly begin the shift from a 'thing-oriented' society to a 'person-oriented society,'" said Dr. Martin Luther King in a 1967 anti–Vietnam War speech condemned by the major media.[13] In California, Cesar Chavez and the United Farm Workers began a unionization drive among migrant laborers demanding an end to stoop labor and the spraying of field workers with toxic pesticides. Countercultural hippies sought social transformation through a back-to-the-land move to rural communes and organic living profiled in the 1970 book *The Greening of America*.

On April 22, 1970, twenty million citizens, including a strong representation of the antiwar youth culture, demonstrated across America on Earth Day, a protest/celebration that marked the beginning of the contemporary environmental movement. Organized by Senator Gaylord Nelson of Wisconsin and Denis Hayes, a Harvard student, the event included local beach cleanups, tree plantings, horseback rides down interstate highways, parades of gas-masked marchers in urban centers, open-air campus teach-ins on ecology, and a thousand other innovations on a theme. The John Birch Society denounced Earth Day as a veiled attempt to celebrate Lenin's birthday, while some leftists argued that it was an establishment plot to co-opt the youth movement. In fact it was a near-spontaneous reaction by a growing cross section of Americans worried over the health effects of pollution, an issue not being addressed by traditional wilderness-oriented conservation groups. Even Richard Nixon, who had a paranoid fear of any form of political opposition, was an astute enough politician to realize that public concern over the environment was a cause better embraced than challenged. "The 1970s absolutely must be the years when America pays its debt to the past by reclaiming the purity of its air, its waters and our living environment. It is literally now or never," he told Congress in his 1970 State of the Union message shortly before ordering the invasion of Cambodia.

The Nixon, Ford, and Carter administrations would pass almost all the landmark environmental legislation that exists today and, in the process, help clean up some of the most visible and dangerous forms of pollution, including sulfur dioxide, lead, DDT, asbestos, mercury, industrial sludge, and untreated municipal sewage. In 1970 Nixon signed the National Environmental Policy Act (NEPA), which requires the government to estimate in advance the ecological impacts of its various projects and activities. This would prove so effective a piece of legislation that today's anti-environmental "property rights" bills mimic its language. Nixon also established the Environmental Protection Agency (EPA) and White House Council on Environmental Quality. The Marine Mammal Protection Act was passed in 1972, the Endangered Species Act in 1973, and the Safe Drinking Water Act in 1974, the year Nixon, facing impeachment for his involvement in the Watergate break-in and cover-up, was forced to resign. Clean Air and Clean Water acts passed in the early seventies were strengthened and reauthorized by Congress and signed into law by President Jimmy Carter in 1977.

The 1970s also saw the emergence of a new kind of environmentalism, which mixed the militant advocacy of the sixties with grassroots community organizing efforts. Direct-action outfits such as Greenpeace, which mounted maritime blockades of whalers and nuclear test sites, and neighborhood-based groups such as the Love Canal Homeowners Association, which rebelled against the toxic poisoning of communities where young children were being raised, created a powerful demand on society to restructure its industrial processes and reduce waste production. The oil embargo of 1973 and energy crisis of 1979 generated new demands for the development of renewable energy sources such as wind, solar, and biomass. President Carter called the energy problem "the moral equivalent of war" and offered a program of energy conservation tied to deregulation of domestic oil and gas. The oil industry went along with the plan once it had effectively lobbied against a proposed windfall profits tax. But attempts by the utility industry to offer a radical expansion of commercial nuclear power as an energy alternative generated widespread opposition among the new environmentalists. Antinuclear groups such as New Hampshire's Clamshell Alliance and California's Abalone Alliance led militant nonviolent blockades of nuclear power plants under construction. Industry responded by hiring private security firms to spy on and infiltrate the groups while right-wing law firms such as the Pacific Legal Foundation, established in 1973, filed nuisance suits against the protesters.

In 1974 Karen Silkwood, a twenty-eight-year-old worker and union organizer at the Kerr-McGee plutonium plant in Crescent, Oklahoma, died in a single-car accident while on her way to meet a union official and *New York Times* reporter with documents and photos she claimed would prove unsafe handling of nuclear materials at the plant. No documents were found in the wreckage of her car but dents on the left rear fender and body panel suggested she may have been forced off the road. The possibility that Silkwood had been murdered sent a chill through the antinuclear movement.[14] Nonetheless, by the time of Pennsylvania's Three Mile Island nuclear accident in 1979, issues of safety, waste storage, and widespread public hostility had effectively blocked expansion of the nuclear industry in the U.S.

The realization that environmentalism was now in a position to cripple a major industry led to some serious reflection among the leaders of corporate America. A handful of companies, recognizing the long-term benefits of pollution prevention, began to reevaluate their management systems and develop less harmful, more efficient means of production, packaging, and distribution. A much larger number of companies saw popular environmental concerns as a public relations issue and responded with a series of "greener" ad campaigns. Still others, primarily in resource-extraction industries such as oil, coal, timber, and beef, decided it was time to fight back against the environmentalists. Thirty years earlier writer Bernard De Voto had predicted where these corporate resource giants might go to find their battle champions. "The West does not want to be liberated from the system of exploitation that it has always violently resented," he'd written back in 1955. "It only wants to buy into it."[15]

Rebels and Reaganites

You chaps who are in favor of this conservation program are all wrong. You are hindering the development of the West. In my opinion, the proper course to take with regard to this [public lands] is to divide it up among the big corporations and the people who know how to make money out of it and let the people at large get the benefits of the circulation of the money.
SECRETARY OF INTERIOR RICHARD BALLINGER, 1909

We will mine more, drill more, cut more timber.
JAMES WATT, SECRETARY OF INTERIOR, 1981

Miles and miles of nothing but miles and miles may be an apt description of Nevada's bone-dry, mineral-rich landscape. Eighty-six percent owned by the U.S. government, it is both the most federalized and (surprisingly) third most urban state in the country, with more than 80 percent of its population living in either Las Vegas or the Reno–Carson City area. Yet Nevada perhaps more than any other state retains the wide-open spirit of the Old West, with legalized gambling and prostitution, easy access to guns and liquor, and lots of cheap land for transnational mining companies and government-subsidized cowboy ranchers under a system described by *The Economist* as having "tempered rugged individualism with socialist infrastructure."[1]

Still, the ranchers and rural land barons of Nevada have never been comfortable with even minimal restrictions on "their" land and water rights, often treating U.S. range managers from the

Bureau of Land Management and the U.S. Forest Service as if they were disrespectful ranch hands in need of a whipping. So it isn't surprising that fifteen years ago Nevada was the birthplace of what came to be known as the Sagebrush Rebellion, a much ballyhooed and yippie-yi-yo-ed attempt (actually the fourth of the century) to transfer control of western lands from the federal government to state authorities. Statute 633, a bill introduced into the Nevada legislature in 1979 by State Representative (now State Senator) Deane Rhodes, claimed all BLM land in the state— some forty-eight million acres—in the name of the people of Nevada. The next day *Washington Post* reporter Lou Cannon picked up on the story, giving it its handle as the "Sagebrush Rebellion." The idea of state takeovers of federal land quickly spread to Utah, Idaho, Wyoming, Arizona, and Alaska (where it became known as the "Tundra Rebellion"), gaining the support of the Cattlemen's Association, Farm Bureau Federation, oil and gas industry, coal industry, NRA, and western sports groups. In Oregon, Bill Grannell, a Democratic state representative who would later found People for the West, teamed up with Republican Denny Jones to introduce Sagebrush legislation calling for a commission to study federal land transfers.

The Sagebrush Rebellion, with its image of tobacco-chewing cowboys versus pencil-pushing bureaucrats, was a natural for the media, getting wide regional and national play. Congressman James Santini of Nevada went on network television to complain that since passage of the mildly environmental Federal Land Policy and Management Act, it had become impossible for ranchers to work with the BLM (forgetting to mention that he had voted in favor of the act). Idaho Senator Jim McClure, a sheep rancher, sponsored an amendment to an appropriations bill to limit the BLM's power to regulate grazing for environmental purposes. Utah Senator Orrin Hatch, sponsor of a federal land-transfer bill, referred to Sagebrush as "the second American Revolution" and claimed that the United States was "waging war on the West," encouraged by "environmental extremists and toadstool worshippers," whom he also branded as "land embalmers."

Some westerners didn't buy into that argument. Arizona Governor (now Secretary of Interior) Bruce Babbitt called the rebellion "a land grab in thin disguise." But when Bernard Shanks, an associate professor at Utah State University, labeled Sagebrush "the new McCarthyism," the Woolgrowers Association, Cattlemen's Association, and Utah Farm Bureau wrote to the university president threatening to block new building funds if Shanks wasn't fired. The university assured them that Shanks was on his way out.[2]

There were also acts of vandalism and intimidation associated with the Sagebrush Rebellion, although mostly of the phone-threat and tire-slashing variety, not the dog-killing, shooting, and house-burning type of violence occurring today. Ironically, elected officials often acted as vigilante cheerleaders, encouraging a sense of militancy and rebellion among the "rebels." Utah County Commissioner Calvin Black warned BLM employees to travel in pairs or groups along back roads to avoid being shot at by local people, and Congressman James Santini asked a group of angry miners for "solutions to the Bureau of Land Management short of assassination." (At a 1992 meeting in Goshen, Washington, Chuck Cushman, responding to a suggestion that environmentalists be shot, cautioned, "The idea is to participate in the public process before you have to get that excited.")[3]

"The fact that 1980 was an election year also had a lot of impact on the Sagebrush Rebellion," recalls State Senator Rhodes. "Right after the election, President Reagan sent me a telegram saying he was a Sagebrush rebel and supporter. We had a major meeting in Salt Lake, where I read that telegram. Later he called me up and invited me to Washington. That meeting at the White House lasted about forty minutes. It included Reagan and Ed Meese and Paul Laxalt. He didn't come right out and say he supported us that time, but he did say we should keep up our efforts and that he would also direct the [federal land] agencies to be more responsive to us."[4]

Ronald Reagan's 1980 election victory was a triumph for the conservative wing of the Republican party and its supporters on the religious Right. Many of the central players in today's anti-enviro movement won their spurs in the "Reagan revolution."

Colorado brewer Joseph Coors, a close friend of the new president and member of his "kitchen cabinet," established both the Mountain States Legal Foundation, dedicated to fighting "bureaucrats and no-growth advocates," and the Heritage Foundation, the conservative think tank that would emerge from relative obscurity to set much of the policy agenda for the new administration. New Right leader Paul Weyrich, who helped Coors set up Heritage and encouraged Jerry Falwell to form the "Moral Majority," hired Ron Arnold to write a subsidized biography of James Watt after Watt left Mountain States to become Reagan's first secretary of Interior.

Direct-mail fundraisers Richard Viguerie and Alan Gottlieb raised hundreds of millions of dollars for various right-wing causes. Gottlieb alone raised tens of millions for the 1980 and 1984 Reagan campaigns. A former head of "Youth Against McGovern" and board member of Young Americans for Freedom and the American Conservative Union (which led the fight against the Panama Canal Treaty), Gottlieb would take credit for being the first Republican to identify "Reagan Democrats" through selective mailings in six states. Floyd Brown, director of Gottlieb's Center for the Defense of Free Enterprise, would go on to produce the infamous race-baiting Willie Horton TV ad in the 1988 presidential campaign along with the less successful 1-800-Gennifer Flowers anti-Clinton ad in 1992. Ron Arnold would take over Brown's responsibilities at CDFE while Gottlieb was serving jail time for tax evasion.

John McLaughery of Vermont, a Reagan national campaign staffer and speechwriter, would move to the White House as senior policy advisor, where he would help assure Chuck Cushman's appointment to the National Parks System Advisory Board. Today McLaughery is a state senator from Vermont's Northeast Kingdom and leader of New England's property rights movement. Roger Marzulla was assistant attorney general under Ed Meese in the Reagan Justice Department. Today he and his wife, also a former Justice Department official, run the Washington-based Defenders of Property Rights, part of a network of right-wing legal foundations that function as the litigating arm of anti-environmentalism.

Mark Pollot, Marzulla's special assistant on land and natural resources, has become a key player in efforts to push anti-enviro
"takings" cases through the federal court system. Steve Symms,
who would become the voice of the anti-environmental movement on Capitol Hill, was first elected Republican senator from
Idaho in the 1980 Reagan landslide. The NRA, the Farm Bureau, and oil, cattle, forestry, and other resource associations
that play important roles in today's anti-environmental campaigns, were all strong backers of Ronald Reagan, the NRA
going so far as to break a 109-year tradition of presidential nonpartisanship in order to endorse the former cowboy actor turned
politician.

   After its founding in 1982, the *Washington Times*, a daily newspaper owned and controlled by the Reverend Sun Myung Moon's
Unification Church, would act as media cheerleader for the Reagan "revolution." With more than a billion dollars in U.S. investments, the self-styled Korean "Messiah" was and is a major
financial backer of various right-wing and conservative causes.
His church-affiliated efforts have included fundraising for Ollie
North and the Contras, bailing Richard Viguerie out of a financial
tailspin in 1987, and establishment of the American Freedom Coalition, which played a key role in early Wise Use organizing
drives. Today the *Washington Times* and its weekly magazine, *Insight,* continue to provide the most comprehensive and sympathetic coverage of the anti-environmentalist cause to be found in
any "major" media.

   However, despite its seminal role in the formation of much of
today's antigreen infrastructure, the Reagan "revolution" would
prove a disappointment to many of its most faithful believers because of its failure to bring about the kind of long-term institutional changes they desired: reduction of the size of government,
creation of an unrestricted free-market economy, silencing of the
demands of women and minorities, and elimination of environmental "roadblocks" to growth and development. A prime example of this disappointment can be found among the West's
former Sagebrush rebels. With President Reagan's endorsement
of the Sagebrush Rebellion, western resource users believed a

massive federal-to-state land transfer was about to take place, but all too quickly they found themselves blindsided by the more radical New Right ideologues gathered around the Heritage Foundation.

"What happened that really lost the momentum of the rebellion is people from Heritage didn't want state control, they wanted privatization," recalls Deane Rhodes. "I remember we had a meeting in Reno where someone from the Heritage Foundation started talking about this privatization angle and things quickly went back downhill from there. The sportsmen's groups were the first to drop out, because they all imagined losing access to their favorite fishing holes and hunting areas. Our intent had been, you know, there might be some privatization, but the states would make those decisions."

"We just felt that state governments would prove even more corrupt land managers than the federal bureaucrats," recalls R. J. Smith, a consultant to Reagan's Council on Environmental Quality who now works as an independent policy consultant.

Western business interests listened to these warnings of state corruption, smiled, and nodded encouragingly, but the New Right eggheads didn't seem to get it. The last thing western miners, ranchers, and logging companies wanted was to pay full market value for the public lands they were already operating on at little or no cost.

Meanwhile, Reagan advisor Senator Paul Laxalt of Nevada had been given the nod to choose a secretary of Interior. He picked former Wyoming Senator Clifford Hansen, but Hansen was unwilling to submit financial-disclosure statements. So Laxalt turned to a little-known public interest lawyer from Denver admired by Attorney General Ed Meese. James Watt, president of the Mountain States Legal Foundation, was an outspoken advocate of the conservative cause who liked to classify people as "liberals" or "Americans."[5] A Christian fundamentalist, he favored unlimited development of natural resources. While personal faith should not be a factor in evaluating political appointees, Watt seemed to take pleasure in aggressively arguing his messianic faith as justification for his policy decisions. Asked in a congressional hearing by the House Interior Committee why he was so determined to see public lands rapidly developed, he responded that there was no point in long-term conservation because "I do not know how many future generations we can count on before the Lord returns."[6] He was an early example of what the Christian Right and Wise Use/Property Rights advocates of today refer to as "dominion theology," a literal reading of Genesis 1:28: "And God blessed them and said to them, Be fruitful and multiply, and replenish the earth and subdue it."

Lanky, bald, and funereal in appearance, Watt was not above questioning the patriotism of those with whom he disagreed. "What is the real nature of the extreme environmentalists, who appear to be determined to accomplish their objectives at whatever cost to society? Is it to delay and deny energy development? Is it to weaken America?" he asked after his first run-in with the militantly moderate conservationists at the National Wildlife Federation.

Watt brought William Perry Pendley, one of his supporters from Mountain States, into Interior as assistant secretary for energy and minerals. He also lobbied for Anne Gorsuch to head up EPA. Among Gorsuch's qualifications was the fact that she was a leader of the self-styled Republican "crazies" in the Colorado statehouse, where she had opposed hazardous-waste-control laws. Her appointment was assured after she agreed with Budget Director David Stockman that the agency could easily get along with a 50 percent cut in funding, a hoop an earlier candidate for the job had refused to jump through. Her chief counsel at EPA would be a lawyer from Exxon, her chief of enforcement a lawyer from GM. She later married Bob Burford, a millionaire Colorado rancher also heavily invested in banks, trailer parks, and oil wells who had been named to head the Bureau of Land Management.

Often identified as a Sagebrush leader, Secretary of Interior Watt was in fact quite happy to see the Sagebrush Rebellion go under in order to get on with the more radical business of selling off the public lands to the private sector or else leasing them out at what the General Accounting Office (GAO) later termed "fire-sale prices."

Privatization of public lands, a bold idea in free-market theory, proved a nonstarter in the real world, with few congressmen or senators willing to tell the folks back home that their favorite fishing lake or campground had just been sold to Donald Trump or some OPEC oil sheik. Nor were most developers spinning cartwheels at the thought of a nineteenth-century-style land rush. When Watt proposed putting an initial thirty million acres out for bid, environmental lobbyists heading to the Hill to protest found themselves trampled underfoot by real estate lobbyists fearful of the consequences of that much property suddenly being dumped on the open market.

Determined to find some way to transfer all that wealth to the private sector where it could "be put to work," Watt announced that he would open up the billion acres of the outer continental shelf, along with 100 million acres of Alaskan land, to offshore oil leasing and drilling. He leased out millions of acres of western lands for shale-oil and geothermal drilling, pushed for energy development in wilderness areas, tried to block congressional funding for the National Park Service, and held the largest public coal sale in history in the Powder River basin of Montana and Wyoming north of Teapot Dome.

According to a GAO investigation, the final $67 million coal sale was underpriced by $100 million.[7] After the Mineral Management Service in Wyoming gave its estimate of the fair market value (an estimate later determined to be too low), two of Watt's deputies in Washington decided the field estimates should be lowered further. These new minimum bids were then illegally leaked to the coal companies (the Reagan Justice Department declined to prosecute). At a meeting on March 19, 1982, three of Watt's men, including William Perry Pendley, decided that the new minimum-bid system should be replaced with an "entry-level" bid, which in practice meant cutting the lowest asking price another 40 percent. Having burned a lot of calories coming up with this formula, Pendley and a fellow bureaucrat went off to dinner that evening with a couple of coal-industry attorneys, who picked up the $494.45 meal tab. When Congress decided to investigate the coal-lease system at Interior and depositions started being taken, Pendley resigned and headed back to Colorado, where several years later he was named president of the anti-environmental Mountain States Legal Foundation.

Watt—whose confrontational style was rapidly losing him points across the political spectrum, including with Nancy Reagan, who didn't like any shadows crossing her husband's untroubled visage—made several gaffs that would prove fatal to his career. First, he tried to have the Beach Boys banned from performing on the Washington Mall on the Fourth of July, believing they lacked the moral wholesomeness of Wayne Newton, another performer scheduled to appear. That attempt at eccentric moral censorship was publicly laughed off by the southern Californians at 1600 Pennsylvania Avenue. Not so easy to laugh off was his comment following a Senate vote to stop any new coal sales until a special commission reviewed his policies. In extolling the commission, Watt bragged that "we have every kind of mix you can have. I have a black, I have a woman, two Jews and a cripple."[8] Shortly thereafter, having embarrassed the Teflon president, Watt was driven out of town on a rail (with a stake driven through his heart by Nancy Reagan). Among those saddened by his departure was Carl Bagge, president of the Coal Association, who in explaining Watt's leasing policies from industry's point of view told Congress, "We're working for coal, God, and America. All we want is to make a buck and develop coal resources and bring fuel to America."

Meanwhile, a congressional investigation would find that under Anne Gorsuch the Environmental Protection Agency was failing to protect the environment and its Superfund program was being transformed into a costly lawyer-subsidy system. Illegal private meetings with regulated companies, deals for reduced fines to polluters, suspension of safety rules on waste disposal, new appointees continuing to represent old clients in conflict with the agency, and a flurry of paperwork requirements in lieu of health and safety enforcement became the agency's new standards. With industry favors flying fast and furious, the morale of professional civil servants at EPA plummeted. One middle manager hung up a hand-lettered sign in his office reading, "No good deed goes unpunished."[9]

Typical of the deals going down was a 1981 Gorsuch meeting with the Thriftway Company, a small southwest gasoline refiner that complained about the cost of conversion to unleaded gas. She told them it didn't make sense to enforce EPA regulations on removing lead from gas, since changes were being proposed. After the meeting she talked briefly with a Senate aide who caught up with the Thriftway reps and relayed the message that, although she couldn't tell them directly to break the law, she hoped they'd gotten the point.[10]

In the fall of 1982, the House Energy Committee began requesting EPA documents on hazardous waste dumps and questionable Superfund enforcement decisions. The White House ordered Gorsuch to withhold the documents under "executive privilege," a position even a conservative Republican member of the committee called "bizarre, at best." Rita Lavelle, in charge of the hazardous waste program, took this delay as a sign to begin shredding scores of subpoenaed documents. In the middle of this oversight conflict, flooding in the Midwest spread dioxin contamination throughout the town of Times Beach, Missouri, leading to the emergency evacuation of more than two thousand residents. With the media focus this brought to the congressional hearings, and with growing tales of incompetence and industry collusion at EPA, the administration decided it was time to cut its losses. In a move engineered by White House aides James Baker and Richard Fuller, the just-married Anne Gorsuch, now Anne Burford, was forced to resign along with some twenty other appointees. Rita Lavelle would eventually serve six months in jail for perjury and obstruction of justice. While later scandals (HUD, the S&L bailout, Iran-Contra) would receive greater media play, the early goings on at Interior and EPA would set the tone for the Reagan administration's approach to environmental issues.

Vice President George Bush would also make a fair stab at gutting environmental protections through his oversight of the Task Force on Regulatory Relief. Responding to what the U.S. Chamber of Commerce called the "terrible twenty"[11] business regulations, the Bush task force tried to eliminate or weaken rules for classifying hazardous waste and potential carcinogens, protecting water quality, and licensing nuclear power plants.

As the Reagan era came to a close, George Bush, despite his faithful eight years of service, found that he had few friends among the Reagan revolution's true believers, who had never forgiven him his 1980 primary campaign description of Ron Reagan's trickle-down, supply-side tax program as "voodoo economics." Seen as a pragmatic preppy in the Nelson Rockefeller mold, Bush's planned ascension to power in 1988 stirred a deep sense of dread among the party's New Rightists, Christian fundamentalists, and radical conservatives, a brooding distrust hard to fathom for people outside the hothouse atmosphere of Republican power politics.

Certainly right-wing ideologues such as CDFE's Alan Gottlieb sensed in private meetings with the then vice president what the country as a whole would come to suspect during his presidency. "My impression of him is that he tries to make you think he supports your position no matter what it is. He's a bit phony and it comes across," Gottlieb recalls, recounting a cocktail-party meeting he and other leaders of the American Conservative Union had with Bush in the spring of 1986. "He's not a very warm person. He doesn't want you to get to know him, was how I felt. I spent most of the evening with Barbara, who I liked very much."[12]

Bush's 1988 campaign rhetoric about being the "environmental president," seen as a cynical election ploy by many political observers, was nonetheless taken as a cause for worry by resource-industry leaders. Opinion polls were showing interest in the environment crossing traditional political boundaries between Democrats, Republicans, and independents, and anti-enviros feared that George Bush would not let his personal beliefs, whatever they might be, stand in the way of what was popular or expedient.

"No question, we were not greatly enamored of Bush," says Grant Gerber of the Wilderness Impact Research Foundation (WIRF), a nonprofit outfit founded in 1986 with help from the

American Farm Bureau Federation to oppose any new federal wilderness designations. "It was pretty scary when Bush came in. Bush was definitely perceived as a danger," agrees Ron Arnold of CDFE.

Once elected to office, Bush's appointment of establishment Republican environmentalists such as Bill Reilly to head EPA and John Turner as director of the U.S. Fish and Wildlife Service gave the anti-enviros a real case of nerves. "My boss told me to spend a week getting everything I could on William K. Reilly and what I found out scared the hell out of me," recalls Trent Clarke, legislative aide to former Senator Steve Symms (Republican, Idaho). "I went back and told my boss, this guy's a hardcore preservationist. Very antiproperty. Steve talked to John Sununu. John agreed we couldn't trust him but said his boss wanted the guy, so please let him be nominated."[13]

The anti-environmentalists were reassured by the presence of trusted friends such as White House Chief of Staff John Sununu, who as governor of New Hampshire had pushed hard for the Seabrook nuclear power plant; OMB Director Richard Darman, who in a speech at Harvard proclaimed, "Americans did not fight and win the wars of the twentieth century to make the world safe for green vegetables"; and Vice President Dan Quayle, whose White House Council on Competitiveness, like Bush's Task Force on Regulatory Relief before it, blocked or weakened a number of environmental initiatives on clean air, toxic incineration, and recycling.

While resource industries and special-interest lobbies like the NRA, the Farm Bureau, the Petroleum Institute, and the American Mining Congress contributed heavily to the Bush election effort, they also hedged their bets in a small but significant way by encouraging and participating in a couple of meetings designed to coordinate anti-environmental campaigns while supporting the creation of proindustry "grass roots."

"Beginning in 1985 we'd held a series of ad hoc meetings with major players from the Farm Bureau, Mountain States Legal Foundation, and Pacific Legal Foundation, a changing group of eight to twenty people, mostly meeting in Salt Lake City, Utah," recalls Grant Gerber.[14]

In June 1988 Gerber's Wilderness Impact Research Foundation (WIRF), along with MSLF and PLF, staged a two-day "National Wilderness Conference" at the Hilton Hotel in Las Vegas, a large smoke-free casino resort that would later gain notoriety as the site of the navy's sexually predatory Tailhook convention. Announced as "a gathering of groups and individuals concerned about the impact of federal wilderness policy on wildlife, recreation, cities, and industry," it drew some two to three hundred people from sixty industrial, resource, hunting, and motorized-recreation groups to respond to the "threat" of expanded federal wilderness.

"People equate preservationists with socialism, and they're right to do that because the preservationists believe government is the answer to all their problems," explains Gerber, an attorney who runs WIRF out of his single-story graystone law office in Elko, Nevada. "People don't understand that the rancher is the best range manager there is, that when you designate wilderness and take man out of the equation you actually begin to destroy habitat.

"When the first white man came to the Ruby Mountains [outside of Elko] in the 1820s, there were virtually no deer," says the stolid blond, fourth-generation Nevadan. "Now it's a cornucopia of wildlife. The reason is the cowboys created habitat. The cattle grazed off the grasslands, and shrubs and weeds came up that provided forage for the deer population to grow. Shepherds killed off the predators, the coyotes and bobcats. In the twenties they started using poisons for predator control, and then the deer population exploded. In 1910 there were forty deer in the Rubies. By the 1970s there were forty thousand."

These and similar arguments favoring "multiple use" of public lands were heard at the conference's nine official sessions. And between the panels, people from various industry associations and state and regional groupings began to network, something relatively new for conferees used to doing their political lobbying from a single issue or industry perspective. "The meeting included all the majors," Gerber recalls, "the American Petroleum Institute, American Mining Congress, Richard DeChambaugh from NRA, the Farm Bureau. Don Rollins of the Farm Bureau chaired the meeting. Clark Collins from the Blue Ribbon Coalition was there. Ron Arnold and Chuck Cushman were also there. Later, Arnold took all the credit for the movement's founding. But at this meeting, we'd already selected a national steering committee and planned a series of follow-up meetings that took place in eighty-nine, ninety, ninety-one."

"The word *movement* never occurred at Grant's meeting. We went to his conference and thought it was not sufficiently broad enough, that it was still just about wilderness with industry talking to itself," responds Ron Arnold. "Chuck and I were knocked off the program, or only given fifteen minutes each instead of the thirty we'd been promised. We did our Ron and Chuck dog-and-pony show but really we thought it was time to try another tack."[15]

Two months later, in August 1988, the Center for Defense of Free Enterprise sponsored a three-day "Multiple-Use Strategy Conference" at John Ascuagga's Nugget Hotel in Reno. This meeting also drew some two to three hundred people. In addition to the $10,000 put up by CDFE, funding and in-kind services were provided by five other groups, including Cushman's National Inholders and the Moon-affiliated American Freedom Coalition.

"Essentially this was a militant, very grassroots base. We invited panels of lawyers and citizens groups like Consumer Alert [a proindustry outfit criticized as anticonsumer by Ralph Nader and Consumers Union]. It was a very spirited conference," Ron recalls.

Despite its activist tone and commitment to "destroy" the environmentalist enemy, the Reno conference included many of the same players who'd attended Gerber's Vegas meeting: the NRA, Farm Bureau, MSLF, Pacific Legal Foundation, mining and timber associations, some big corporations such as Exxon and DuPont, and small motorized-recreation groups such as the Sourdough Snowmobile Club and Alaska Motorcycle Racing Association.

"The difference between our meeting and Grant's was we weren't going for any of that industry self-pity, that hand-wringing stuff," Arnold claims. "We had this three-hundred-pound guy we called the Cuddler, and anytime someone would start hand-wringing in a session he'd go up to them and wrap his arms around them and pat them on the shoulder going, 'There, there.'"

What really set the Reno conference apart, however, was the follow-up publication of a paperback book titled the *Wise Use Agenda*, put out by the Free Enterprise Press, a CDFE subsidiary. By soliciting suggestions from conference participants and then assembling them into a twenty-five-point agenda for a "movement" whose name he'd invented, Ron Arnold was able to advance the process of anti-environmental consolidation he'd been promoting since 1979, when he'd first argued that "industry can't stand alone; it needs a grassroots movement to fight for its goals."

Ron claims that Wise Use, a term appropriated from Gifford Pinchot, is powerful "because it taps a psychological need for symbolic ambiguity," but a reading of "The Top Twenty-Five Goals of the 'Wise Use Agenda'" suggests a complete lack of ambiguity. The goals, drawn from the written suggestions of the American Freedom Coalition, NRA, MSLF, Blue Ribbon, and other conference participants, include the following:

· Immediate development of the petroleum resources of the Arctic National Wildlife Refuge in Alaska.
· Logging three million acres of the Tongass National Forest in Alaska.
· Conversion of "all decaying and oxygen-using forest growth on [*sic*] the National Forests into young stands of oxygen-producing carbon dioxide-absorbing trees to help ameliorate the rate of global warming" [cutting down all old-growth trees to solve a problem the anti-enviros deny exists].
· A foreign policy that "takes steps to insure raw material supplies for global commodity industries on a permanent basis."
· Exempting from the Endangered Species Act, "non-adaptive species such as the California Condor, and endemic species lacking the biological vigor to spread in range. . . ."
· The right of prodevelopment groups "to sue on behalf of industries threatened or harmed by environmentalists."

· Opening up seventy million acres of federal wilderness to commercial development and motorized recreational use.
· Opening all public lands "including wilderness and national parks"
to mining and energy development.
· Expanding national park concessions under the management of
private firms, "with expertise in people-moving such as Walt Dis-
ney."[16]

The book was given a bit of symbolic weight by the reprint of
a generic telegram of greeting from President Bush, not to the
Reno conference but to a meeting of another "member organization of the Wise Use movement," and by a back-cover photo of
Bush with Alan Gottlieb. The photo was taken at the 1986 American Conservative Union cocktail party Gottlieb attended with
then Vice President George Bush. When Ron and a small delegation traveled to Washington and tried to personally present
their Wise Use agenda to President Bush, they were directed to
"some low-ranking, low-echelon official in the back of the executive office building," Ron recalls with some bitterness.

Nonetheless, as could be predicted, a number of follow-up
newspaper and magazine articles would refer to President Bush's
telegram of support "to the Wise Use Conference" and appearance with "Wise Use leader" Alan Gottlieb. It was the kind of
subtle media ploy that Arnold and Gottlieb have become re-
nowned for.

Anti-environmental organizing efforts, in abeyance during the
Reagan administration, began to increase in the wake of the Reno
conference, gaining momentum as the economy went into reces-
sion. Rising unemployment and the threat of layoffs opened a significant segment of the public to arguments that blamed the
breakdown of the traditional family, women in the workforce, immigrants, and environmentalists for their increasingly desperate
financial straits. Within a few years of the Vegas and Reno conferences, the anti-enviros would be able to claim their first
significant victories, won with the quiet assistance and encour-
agement of key Bush administration insiders.

"There were seven hundred people there. You can't imagine
the virulence of the outcry. I was Saddam Hussein, a Communist,

a fascist, everything else you could think of. One lady got up there, jaw quivering, used her time to say the Pledge of Allegiance, then looked at me and called me a Nazi. They loaded the hall," recalls Yellowstone National Park Superintendent Robert Barbee of his January 24, 1991, encounter with anti-enviros at a public hearing on the Yellowstone vision document in Bozeman, Montana.[17]

The Yellowstone vision document was a sixty-page plan that grew out of congressional hearings in the mid-eighties. It was designed to chart a long-term course of protection for the vast natural ecosystem surrounding Yellowstone National Park, a twenty-million-acre expanse of lightly settled lands that extends through parts of Montana, Wyoming, and Idaho, including the Grand Teton National Park and six national forests. Coordinating the effort for the Park Service was Lorraine Mintzmyer, the only woman to serve as a National Park Service regional director.

The Yellowstone vision draft, released in July 1990, stated that the first consideration in land management should be its environmental impact—that while logging, grazing, mining, and drilling would continue in the national forests they should in the future be done in ways "sensitive to other resource values and uses of the land." The vision plan, although modest in its aims, would limit activities such as geothermal drilling on the northern park boundary that might impact Old Faithful and that was then being planned by the Church Universal and Triumphant, a wealthy religious cult in Park County, Montana. More significantly, it could restrict plans for a massive open-pit gold mining operation being planned by Crown Butte, a subsidiary of Canada's Noranda, near the tiny mountain settlement of Cooke City on the park's northern border.

Opposition to the vision plan soon coalesced within the mining, logging, and cattle industries. Wise Use, working with these groups, began to organize grassroots resistance, focusing on three public hearings scheduled for Montana. Thousands of letters went out to local residents from the mine-industry-financed People for the West, Chuck Cushman's National Inholders Association, and a local resource users coalition. A typical People for the West letter warned, "What is being proposed is a national park 8.5 times the size of Yellowstone."

"You will lose many of your existing rights," Cushman warned in another letter. "The plan will govern your life."

"We mailed out in the neighborhood of twenty thousand letters, and the trade associations probably did another ten thousand," Cushman recalls. "We included a little postcard saying, 'Please send us a copy of the vision document.' Can you imagine what happened to the people in the vision document headquarters when they got something like ten thousand requests for copies of this? They had no money for it. They literally couldn't pay themselves, because they had to do printing after printing after printing to keep up with it. This gave us more time to organize."

"In Bozeman, a college town that's always been pro-environment, we had 600 out of 750 people on our side," Cushman continues. "We had yellow armbands and the politicians literally looked out on a sea of yellow. . . . It wasn't just us. We were in a team play with People for the West, the Western Environmental Trade Association, the Cattlemen, the Farm Bureau from three states. We crushed them in this process."[18]

People for the West dominated the Montana meetings with prehearing rallies and bus caravans bringing in angry citizen-protestors from Wyoming and Idaho. They were given yellow armbands as they got off the buses and told they were fighting for nothing less than their lives and their land. Also helping to organize the protests were staff members from Montana Republican Congressman Ron Marlenee's office (Marlenee would go down to defeat in the next election).

After the Bozeman hearing where Park Superintendent Barbee was shouted down, the Department of Interior cancelled planned additional hearings and released a shortened ten-page vision document eliminating any reference to ecosystems management or environmental priorities. Shortly thereafter, National Park Regional Director Lorraine Mintzmyer was reassigned to Philadelphia.

Wise Use activists trumpeted their "victory at Yellowstone," and soon even environmentalists were repeating the claim. The vision document had been gutted, because Wise Use "out-organized and out-shouted both bureaucrats and environmentalists at public hearings," according to the January/February 1993 issue of *National Parks* magazine.

But a congressional report released in July 1993 showed that a plan had already been under way to destroy the vision document for political reasons and then claim it was done in response to Wise Use's negative public opinion. The 461-page report put out by the House Committee on Post Office and Civil Service and titled *Interference in Environmental Programs by Political Appointees* revealed "an improper concerted activity by powerful commodity and special interest groups and the Bush Administration to eviscerate the Draft Vision document because the commodity and special interest groups perceived it as a threat." The Department of Interior and special-interest groups first destroyed the sixty-page scientific document, turning it into a ten-page "brochure," the report said. "They then developed a story that would explain the revisions and keep their actions a secret. Finally, to protect their acts and in apparent retaliation against Ms. Mintzmyer, the Department of Interior effectuated a directed reassignment which moved Ms. Mintzmyer out of the Rocky Mountain Region and away from the Vision document process."

The fifteen-month investigation of civil service abuses directed against Lorraine Mintzmyer, who resigned after her reassignment when bureaucratic retaliations against her continued, included interviews with forty-five witnesses and reviews of six thousand documents. The report traced the initial plan to destroy the vision document to a series of letters and meetings in the summer and fall of 1990, including a letter from David Rovig, president of Crown Butte Mining, to Secretary of Interior Manuel Lujan; meetings between department of Interior and Agriculture officials, Republican Senators Simpson and Wallop of Wyoming, and representatives of commodity groups, including the Wyoming Woolgrowers Association and Wyoming Farm Bureau; and a conversation between White House Chief of Staff John Sununu and Deputy Assistant Secretary of Interior for Fish and Wildlife Scott Sewell, in which Sununu told Sewell that from a political perspective the existing draft of the vision document "was a disaster and would have to be rewritten."

In one of the congressional report's chapters titled "Keeping the Concerted Activity Secret," the report explains how in the winter of 1991

1. The individuals and groups involved in the concerted activity artificially manufactured the appearance of negative public opinion at a few, select, local public meetings.
2. Mr. Sewell closed down previously scheduled national hearings to avoid anticipated positive comment.
3. The scientific interdisciplinary (ID) team was maneuvered out of the revision process.
4. The participants used the manufactured, negative public comment to explain why the revisions were allegedly necessary.

Ironically, the congressional report on these abuses was itself subject to political pressure. The original draft report, dated December 30, 1992, refers to a "conspiracy" between the Bush administration and commodity and special-interest groups. In the final report, the word *conspiracy* has been replaced with the milder *concerted activity*. [19]

On December 18, 1991, President Bush also signed a new multibillion-dollar highway bill. The bill included a rider, the Symms National Recreational Trails Act, that allocated $30 million a year for backcountry trail construction, to be paid for out of federal gas taxes. A minimum of 30 percent and possibly as much as 70 percent of that money would go for off-road motorized vehicle trails. The act was named for retiring Republican Senator Steve Symms of Idaho and is likely to be remembered as his outstanding legislative achievement during twelve years in office. Clark Collins, an Idaho trail-bike racer and founder of the anti-enviro Blue Ribbon Coalition, coordinated much of the lobbying effort for the act, considered the prime (and to date only) example of federal Wise Use legislation to be enacted into law. "This is the first time the preservationists had to accept legislation they opposed as vigorously as they opposed this bill," says Collins, a mild-mannered former electrician who refers to environmental organizations such as the Sierra Club and the Wilderness Society as "hate groups."

"We mobilized recreational users. We drove a tiny wedge between hiking societies and the hate groups," he claims. "Mountain bikers are one of the fastest growing groups in the country. We think we can reach them. We say they're already riding on two wheels, they just haven't figured how to attach a motor yet."[20]

Millions of Americans, continuing a seventy-five-year-old love affair with the internal combustion engine, own and use recreational vehicles, ranging from two-stroke dirt bikes to snowmobiles, dune buggies, and jet skis. The off-road vehicle industry, aside from providing smelly, high-speed fun and excitement, contributes billions of dollars a year to the balance-of-trade deficit, since most of these small-engine vehicles are manufactured in Japan.

Clark Collins raised his family working as a construction electrician in Pocatello, Idaho, but like tens of thousands of other guys with rangy frames and a good sense of balance, he found religion on any Sunday there was a motocross or cross-country trail-bike race. "I was Eastern Idaho 1972 Overall Motorcycle Association champion. Rode a Hodaka, a Japanese bike," he recalls proudly. As he got into the politics of racing and motorcycle associations, his whole family got involved in ORV sports. At sixty, his mother cracked her shoulder falling off a trail bike. Today she rides a four-wheel ATV.

As a member of the International Brotherhood of Electrical Workers (IBEW) Collins fought against a right-to-work law championed by right-wing Idaho Senator Steve Symms, but when a wilderness bill threatened to close down one of his favorite dirt-bike trails, he ended up working with Symms to block the Sierra Club proposal and later mobilized "motorized recreationists" for Symms's 1986 re-election campaign.

In 1987 Collins established the Blue Ribbon Coalition with Darryl Harris, publisher of several Idaho-based specialty magazines, including *Potato Grower, The Sugar Producer,* and *Snowmobile West.* Their aim was to unite motorized recreationists and resource users from around the country under the tag line "Preserving our natural resources for the public instead of from the public." Early supporters included the American Petroleum Institute, Suzuki, Yamaha, and Kawasaki. In 1988 Collins began meeting with the D.C.-based American Recreation Coalition (ARC), the Motorcycle Industry Council (MIC), and other small-engine producers and aficionados to develop off-road trails legislation. He also received a grant from the Honda Motor Company that allowed him to work full-time as Blue Ribbon's executive director, attending anti-enviro conferences, contributing his trails proposal to the Wise Use agenda, and lobbying in Washington for adoption of the trails act.[21] Japanese manufacturers of motorcycles and snowmobiles also took out full-page ads in his *Blue Ribbon* magazine (actually a tabloid newspaper) reasoning that any new U.S. wilderness trails for ORVs would quickly translate into new sales for them.

On his first trip to Washington, Collins was told that Symms, as an "outspoken Republican multiple-use advocate," might not be the best sponsor for his bill in the Democratic-controlled Congress. Principled and pragmatic, he decided to stick with the only politician he knew: "I pledged our commitment to working with Symms on this in whatever manner would be the most beneficial to him politically," he later recalled.[22] Symms, by then planning to quit the Senate when his term expired and seeing that his anti-enviro property rights legislation was going nowhere, decided to reciprocate Collins's loyalty by making the ORV-trails bill his top priority.

In 1990 Collins got motions of support for the bill from the American Horse Council and (at Grant Gerber's third annual Wilderness Conference) the United 4×4 Association. The prohunting Wildlife Legislative Fund signed on because, according to their national affairs director, "the ORV antis are undoubtedly the same people who combat hunting, fishing and trapping." Collins solicited letters of support from several western governors but ran into problems at a national meeting of state park and recreation directors because of Blue Ribbon's participation in anti-enviro attempts to torpedo the American Heritage Trust Fund. The Farm

Bureau, usually a key supporter of anti-environmentalist efforts, also failed to endorse the trails bill at its national convention in Phoenix, when farmers raised objections to the way snowmobilers and other ORV operators cut fences, trespassed, and generally screwed up and ignored their property rights. Collins tried to put the blame for the problem onto the Rails to Trails Conservancy, a "preservationist" group that ended up in an uneasy alliance with Blue Ribbon on the ORV trails bill. In D.C., Collins got Congressman (now Senator) Ben Nighthorse Campbell of Colorado to agree to become the first Democratic sponsor of the bill and gave testimony at early committee hearings. As an act of Wise Use solidarity, the prologging Oregon Lands Coalition (OLC) campaigned for the trails bill during its 1991 "Fly-In for Freedom" lobbying trip to Washington. Despite opposition from such groups as the National Wildlife Federation, Wilderness Society, and American Hiking Society, the bill gained momentum as the American Recreation Coalition (ARC), Motorcycle Industry Council (MIC), American Motorcyclist Association (AMA), International Snowmobile Industry Association (ISIA), and other off-road vehicle lobbies set up a working task force to push for the bill's passage, with ARC's Derrick Crandall running their day-to-day lobbying operations on the Hill.

"I made a lot of trips to D.C. in ninety-one—three or four when it got real intense, when it got down to the short strokes on the final passage and they were trying to sidetrack it," Collins recalls of the last-minute maneuvering that went on around the bill.[23] The Interior committee put forward a plan to divide the funds between the federal government and the states. Crandall thought they should allow the committee to "have their fingerprints on the final bill," but Clark argued that any concessions at that point in the process would be seen as a sign of political weakness. The task force rejected the Interior committee proposal. Then members of the public works and transportation committee proposed that the fund be administered through the Department of Transportation. Steve Symms agreed, transferring the bill away from Interior. Finally, on Sunday, November 24, 1991, just before a House/Senate conference committee voted in favor of the Trails Act, Senator John Warner of Virginia suggested the bill be named in Symms's honor. Three weeks later, President Bush signed off on the highway-transportation bill including the Symms rider.

Since passage of the Symms Act, the Blue Ribbon Coalition has been fighting budget cutbacks (only $7.5 million was allocated for ORV trails in 1993) while continuing to try and promote other anti-enviro causes among ORV enthusiasts. The cover story of their winter 1993 issue of *Blue Ribbon* magazine was titled "Crown Butte Mines Assist Snowmobilers," a long paean to the mining company's efforts to help snowmobilers by rerouting them around a mine-construction road near Cooke City on the border of Yellowstone, where it plans its huge open-pit mining operation. Blue Ribbon has also argued that Forest Service construction of logging roads is not really a timber-industry subsidy, since they can later be used as motorcycle and ATV recreational trails once the trees have been removed. Clark says his preservationist opponents "want all our roadless areas to be designated 'Wilderness,'" but under the Symms Act several new trails have recently been built in the mountains outside of Pocatello, Idaho, trails that Clark takes great pleasure in riding on his Honda XR-250, which he calls "a nice quiet bike."

At the end of the September 1991 Fly-In for Freedom, the second D.C. lobbying trip organized by the Oregon Lands Coalition, participants from around the country met in a room at the Marriott Hotel in Crystal City, Virginia, where they decided to hold a follow-up meeting in St. Louis on November 8. There, "where the wagon trains formed up to head West," they formed the Alliance for America, an anti-enviro network of local activists and resource associations that modestly describes itself as "the most powerful grassroots organization this country has ever seen."

They set up a steering committee that included the Oregon Land Coalition's Tom Hirons; WIRF's Grant Gerber; June Christle, a tugboat company operator from Alaska; Joan Smith, a rancher's wife from California; and Tee John Mialjevich, a commercial shrimper from Gretna, Louisiana, who'd been leading Gulf of Mexico fishing boat blockades in protest of TEDs, turtle-excluder devices, which reduce the death rate of endangered sea turtles caught and drowned in shrimpers' trawlnets. In 1989 George Bush's Secretary of Commerce Robert Mossbacher had been widely criticized after he tried to lift TED requirements in response to the "volatile situation" Mialjevich had created in the Gulf. Among Secretary Mossbacher's critics were the writers and illustrators of the *Teenage Mutant Ninja Turtles* comics, who introduced into their strip a new anti-turtle villain, the evil "Captain Mossback."[24]

David Howard, a property rights activist and resident of New York's Adirondack Park, was named chairman of the newly formed Alliance for America. Alliance funding came from the Moon-affiliated American Freedom Coalition, American Farm Bureau Federation, Cattlemen's Association, American Mining Congress, Chemical Manufacturers Association, Petroleum Institute, and several other industry groups.

The third Fly-In for Freedom, and the first sponsored under the alliance banner, was held in September 1992 and drew some 350 people from across the country, including loggers, lobbyists, lawyers, miners, a couple of farmers from Wisconsin, property rights activists from New Hampshire and the Adirondacks, and Tee John's shrimpers from Louisiana and Texas. They lobbied against the Clean Water and Endangered Species acts, argued about the need "to put people back in the environmental equation," and picketed CBS, claiming that Dan Rather was an environmentalist. Their lobbying efforts and much of their access to various government agencies were facilitated by members of the Bush re-election campaign, which in the wake of the Rio Earth Summit that June had staked out a hardline anti-environmentalist position. But not all the Bush officials they met with proved themselves particularly loyal to their commander-in-chief.

Joan Smith recalls how she and Nadine Bailey, an unemployed logger's wife from Hayfork, California, had, during an earlier scout trip with Federated Women in Timber, met David McIntosh, the policy director for Vice President Quayle's Council on Competitiveness. "He was very nice and cut to the essence and told us we needed someone to carry our banner, and I don't remember how we were then put in touch with Pat Buchanan [who was running against Bush in the Republican primaries at the time] but we were. Pat and his wife and aides later flew into Redding Municipal Airport, and we had cars there to meet him and led a caravan to Hayfork. He mentioned that visit to Hayfork during his speech to the Republican convention."[25]

While anti-enviro groups such as People for the West, Blue Ribbon, and the Alliance for America were gaining strength during the Bush years by attacking the Washington political establishment that was quietly using and supporting them, the spotted-owl controversy exploded in the Pacific Northwest. The administration's refusal to enforce the Endangered Species Act after years of government-subsidized overcutting of the old-growth forest and a subsequent federal court order suspending all logging in spotted owl habitat on the region's public lands had set off a broad-based, well-organized environmental backlash. By the spring of 1993, the growing conflict had begun to poison the region's reputation for social tolerance. Stories in the newspapers and on TV showed spotted owls shot and nailed to Forest Service signposts, long-haired protestors being dragged off of logging trucks, and angry millworkers marching through the streets of dying timber towns. But it was still hard to get a sense of who all the players were. On the environmental side there were some familiar names like Earth First!, the Oregon Natural Resources Council, and the Sierra Club Legal Defense Fund joined by several new players including commercial salmon fishermen and Native American tribal councils worried about declining fish runs and dying rivers. But to the national media it was all "owls versus loggers," or, for the factoid-oriented press like USA Today, "4,600 Owls vs. 32,100 Jobs."[26]

If environmentalists' arguments got lost in the media coverage, the timber industry's political forces were reduced to an insulting caricature of a wide-suspendered logger wearing a "Spotted Owl tastes like Chicken" tee shirt. Perhaps, as many suspected, the urban-based media were simply unfamiliar with who was doing the ground-level organizing to turn out the industry's troops.

Who were timber's frontline political warriors and how effective a force did they really have to combat the environmental revolution's advancing agenda? The only way to find that out would be to travel to the scene of the conflict and let the counterrevolutionaries speak for themselves.

FOUR

The Forest for the Trees

The working class and the employing class have nothing in common.
PREAMBLE TO THE CONSTITUTION OF THE
INDUSTRIAL WORKERS OF THE WORLD

Hungry and out of work? Eat an environmentalist.
BUMPER STICKER SEEN AT INDUSTRY-SPONSORED LOGGING RALLY

The Oregon state capitol in Salem was built in 1938 in what might be described as a World's Fair Neo-Greco-with-turret style of architecture. Two Vermont marble frescoes, of Lewis and Clark and a covered wagon, bracket the main entrance. Atop the giant thimble-shaped turret stands a twenty-three-foot-high gold-leafed statue of a bare-chested pioneer logger holding a single-bladed ax. Just inside the building, beyond the rotunda, you come to a Georgia-Pacific display case filled with old saws, axes, and logging photos. You'd never guess that timber represents less than 5 percent of Oregon's modern workforce, although admittedly a twenty-three-foot-tall gold-leafed statue of a bare-chested software designer might create its own set of problems.

I enter a meeting room on the third floor of the four-story building where sixty people have gathered from the Oregon Lands Coalition, the state's anti-enviro umbrella group. The Oregon Lands Coalition (OLC) was established in 1989 by log company operator Tom Hirons along with Valerie Johnson, sister of State Senator Rod Johnson. Financial support has come from Weyerhauser, Boise Cascade, the Oregon Farm Bureau, and the

National Rifle Association, among others.[1] An outgrowth of the 1988 "Oregon Project" campaign run by Bill and Barbara Grannell (now of People for the West), OLC has organized anti-spotted-owl and anti-endangered-species rallies, has led a boycott of a TBS Audubon special on logging, and has helped establish the Alliance for America, which sponsors annual Fly-In for Freedom lobbying trips to Washington.[2] OLC spokeswoman Jackie Lang introduces me to Marlin Aerni and three of his union brothers who have joined eastern Oregon ranchers, their rural community supporters, and logging association employees for today's state lobbying effort.

Marlin is a bluff, gregarious guy with a quick, wide smile who looks like he might be hiding a medicine ball under his black-striped engineer's shirt. His thinning blond bangs frame a squared-off, sun-weathered face. His penetrating blue-gray eyes have an edge of hardness that doesn't always match his ready smile. Marlin is president of Local 1189, the Halsey, Oregon, pulp mill chapter of the 250,000-member United Paperworkers International. Over the last five years, he has helped mobilize his 130 workers for yellow-ribbon and OLC rallies against Forest Service restrictions on logging and against endangered species protection of the spotted owl, an indicator species for the forest's health.

"Last year our local spent $9,000 on timber issues. Just this month, with the timber summit coming up and all, we're spending $6,000 on newspaper ads," he tells me. "I lobby here in Salem and also fight environmental overregulation. And the company doesn't put any restrictions on me. When they foot the bill to send me to D.C. to lobby on resource issues, they know I also lobby on the striker bill [which bars employers from hiring permanent replacements for workers on strike]. They don't mind. They know we're not going to strike, because we've got the best contract in the industry."

Beginning in 1988, companies such as Pope & Talbot, Simpson Timber, James River, Boise Cascade, and Georgia-Pacific began working closely with a number of their employees to provide paid days off and free transportation and meals for those attending anti-environmentalist yellow-ribbon rallies.[3] Some companies even paid their workers' membership dues in anti-enviro organizations. The companies also provided their unions with industry-funded research on the impact of the Endangered Species Act, log exports, and other forest issues the unions couldn't afford to research on their own (having recently been forced to accept pay cuts by many of these same companies).

Marlin Aerni was raised in Albany, Oregon, close to the Pope & Talbot mill, where he now works. His father and uncle also worked the mills. His grandfather, a dairy farmer in the Trout Lake area, used to float his cheese downriver by raft to Portland. "There were twenty-five mills in the area when I was growing up. Now there are maybe six left. The first time the company approached our local about helping them, in eighty-eight, we said we couldn't work with them. They were jerks back then," Marlin laughs. "But then the expansion they'd been planning didn't come, and we saw 100 to 150 new union jobs down the tube because of this dioxin talk. So I got a week off from the company and they gave me some names, some retired university people, and I began to research this dioxin thing. I went to the environmentalists and even the Centers for Disease Control and all them other agencies. I asked this environmentalist lady, 'What is it you want?' She said, 'We don't want you on our river.' After I almost strangled the bitch, I realized very few of these people are credible or interested in the facts. It's more like a religion for them."

So Marlin got active in the Oregon Lands Coalition. "The first time I met Charlie Janz [the outgoing president of OLC], well, he's an anti-union gyppo [independent] logger, and we just glared at each other. Finally I got in his face and said, 'Are your guys unionized?' and he said, 'Hell, no.' And I said, 'Well, you must treat your workers well, 'cause none of them have called me up.'"

I ask Marlin and the other union men how they feel about working in coalition with gyppo loggers, industry lobbyists, and Republicans. Paul Sullivan, a bald, mustachioed official with the Association of Western Pulp and Paper Workers, shakes his head morosely. "You have to understand. When I'm down here lobbying and feel depressed, I go visit a Republican, because they're the ones with us on these resource issues."

Marlin cuts off his friend. "The thing is, see, we have to get the Democrats off this liberal green, save-the-world kick and back to doing what's right for the workers here," he explains. "We had this Jim Jontz of Indiana who was going after our jobs out here, who wanted to lock away the resource, and so we took fifteen union people out to his district to canvass door to door. The way I was going to do it was to hit up local industries here for the money, but it turned out that was illegal. So Mike Drapper [head of the Western Council of Industrial Workers] said, 'Let me set up a PAC,' and we went back there and our brothers in the United Auto Workers didn't like us at all and were fairly hostile because Jontz was their man. So we agreed not to come around their factories or union halls, but we were out there in the malls and on the local talk radio and stuff and we beat him. He lost the election."

Jim Jontz, a four-term Democratic congressman from Indiana, was defeated in the 1992 elections by a combination of factors, including large oil, timber, and mining donations to his Republican opponent, Gulf War veteran Steve Buyer, who campaigned in his chocolate chip camouflage utilities. Jontz was also targeted by the Farm Bureau, because of his support for wetlands protection of the Indiana dunes area along Lake Michigan.

"Those fifteen union guys had a very marginal impact. They were a sideshow at best," says the ex-congressman, who, when interviewed in late 1993, was back in Washington lobbying against NAFTA. "They set up a $30,000 PAC, a P.O. box in Indiana, to fly themselves in and put themselves up for two weeks at the nicest motel in Kokomo, but labor wouldn't let them do anything once they got there. What had a greater impact, I think, was the $50,000 in direct donations the timber industry provided my opponent."

Jack Williams, of UAW Local 685 in Kokomo, is less sanguine in his assessment. "I hope to hell those guys come back to visit us now," he says, following with an anatomically improbable suggestion involving his union brothers and a spotted owl. "They call themselves labor but they weren't brave enough to come see us, to sit down and talk things over. Instead they were off with the Republicans, doing their dirty work. We have over 10,000 UAW members in the Fifth District, and any time we had a problem with plant closings or anything like that we could count on Jim for help and support. He had something like a 100 percent voting record for labor. Now we have a quite anti-union congressman, partly because of those guys. And the funny thing to me is they're fighting to kill their own jobs, which is what will happen in a few years if they cut down all the forests. What they should be fighting is that cheap labor overseas with those log exports and runaway shops."

I go along with Marlin and six others from the OLC lobbying group to a 3 P.M. meeting with State Representative Greg Walden, the Republican majority leader in the Oregon House. Our group is left waiting in a small conference room for fifteen minutes while Walden finishes off talks with lobbying seniors, health care providers, and sheriffs. He finally enters the room wearing the small yellow flower and lapel ribbon the OLC passed out earlier. Walden's a tall, bland-looking man with a high forehead and the flat brown eyes of a predator fish. He tells us how he remembers the first big yellow-ribbon demonstrations outside the statehouse back in eighty-eight and how he'd told the organizers they should do a similar march on Washington. He then turns to Marlin. "I heard how you guys helped get rid of Jim Jontz. You really made the difference. That was a great job you did."

Marlin flashes his wide smile. "We understand you're thinking of running for governor," says Marlin, "and we're not happy with Barbara [Roberts, the Democratic governor]. We know where you're at and we'd like to support you if certain union things could be resolved. We should talk about union issues some time."

"Absolutely," Walden agrees.

Marlin leans back, crossing his hands across his gut, a satisfied man.

"We need to do something about this salmon business," complains a rancher from eastern Oregon. "You know, most of those fish are disappearing at sea or behind the dams. There's no reason to be blaming the cattleman."

"That's federal," Walden commiserates. "I don't think there's a lot we can do about that, but I think what we can do at the state level is move back to minimal federal standards on things like the Clean Air Act. We don't need to punish ourselves by being more stringent than we have to be."[4] Although solidly Republican/ Wise Use, the eastern Oregon ranch vote has about as much real impact as the Portland grunge rocker vote. To put it another way, if elk could vote, most politicians east of the Cascades would have antlers and wet noses.

At the end of the day, Marlin invites me to visit his pulp mill any time I want. A week later I take him up on his offer.

On my way to the Halsey, Oregon, mill I stop in Centralia, Washington, a one-time railroad and logging center. On the walls of the old brick-fronted downtown along Tower Avenue are historic murals of an 1860s farmyard, the railroad station, even Buffalo Bill's Wild West show, commemorating its visit to town in 1910. Only the gunfight and lynching of 1919 are missing. I stop by the *Centralia Daily Chronicle*, where I'm guided to a framed copy of the newspaper dated Tuesday, November 11, 1919. I'm surprised at the main headline: "Coal Miner Strike Ends, Indianapolis, U.M.W." Only below that is the local banner: "McElfresh, Grimm and Casagranda killed by IWW. Five more Centrailians wounded by Wobblies, murderers are nearly lynched. Soldiers who defended our country shot down on streets by IWWs as they marched down Tower Avenue. Boys had no chance to defend themselves. Town scoured for skunks." As I'm copying this down, two young reporters are teasing a third who doesn't want to go hunting with them. "I just don't like guns," he smiles, shaking his head no.

I drive down to the Skookumchuck, a brown, slow-moving river that runs past the freeway. Where the old trestle bridge once stood is a green steel-frame span rebuilt in 1959 near a Seventh Day Adventist church. It was here on the night of November 11, 1919, that they lynched Wesley Everest, himself a World War I veteran. This was just one more incident in the ongoing labor wars then convulsing the Northwest timber industry, as lumberjacks and millworkers attempted to organize for an eight-hour day, wages they could live on, and clean camps. In Seattle a hundred thousand workers staged a five-day general strike followed by police raids and hundreds of arrests. In Spokane the Industrial Workers of the World—the "Wobblies" mentioned in the *Chronicle* article—led a free-speech fight, filling the jails in protest after their street meetings were banned. Beaten and starved, several men died in their cells before the ban was finally lifted. In Everett, Washington, vigilantes and police opened fire on two steamboats carrying three hundred IWW members to a picnic and rally. Five Wobs were killed along with two vigilantes, more than fifty people were injured, and seven were reported missing. And in lumber camps all across the north woods there were strikes, bedroll burnings, double bunks axed down to singles, and tree spikings where the industry tried to break the strikes using the Loyal Legion of Loggers and Lumbermen. In Centralia the Lumber Trust worked with the American Legion to destroy the local IWW. Legionnaires raided the union hall and beat up Wobblies with gas pipes and rubber hoses. When the Legionnaires returned a few weeks later, marching past the union hall on Armistice Day, firing broke out. It was never established who fired first, but as Legionnaires charged the hall, Wesley Everest, wearing his army uniform, was heard to tell a union brother, "I fought for democracy in France and I'll fight for it here. The first man through that door is gonna get it." He was as good as his word and shot a man, but then his rifle jammed, and he headed for the river, a pistol in his hand, chased by an angry mob. Halfway across the river he turned and, firing from the hip, killed a second man, Dale Hubbard, the nephew of the timber boss who had organized the anti-IWW raids. As he was beaten, Everest taunted the mob, "You haven't the guts to hang a man in the daytime." He was right. That night he was taken from the town jail, castrated, and hung from the Skookumchuck River bridge, his body riddled with rifle fire. "Tell the boys I died for my class," he'd told his cellmates just before he had been taken away.

No one was ever arrested for Wesley Everest's lynching, but according to a later state inquiry, six Wobblies were wrongfully convicted for the Tower Avenue shootings and served fifteen years in prison before being pardoned in the 1930s.[5]

Unlike the coal trusts in Appalachia, whose industrial wars with the United Mine Workers ended in an armed truce that has more or less held for the last eighty years, the timber industry succeeded in destroying the Wobblies and those who followed them in attempting to organize the region's widely dispersed loggers and millhands. The resulting weakness of organized labor in the Northwest has been reflected as recently as the 1980s, when, under the antilabor policies of the Reagan administration, a number of unions were forced to downsize and take $2-an-hour wage cuts at a time when the timber industry was posting record profits.[6]

Ninety minutes after crossing into Oregon, I leave Interstate 5 on my way to the Halsey mill and drive past flat green fields of grazing sheep toward white plumes of smoke rising in the distance. Several chimneys come into view, the largest, at more than three hundred feet, a red and white vapor stack. I turn in at a fenced drive with a large wooden sign reading Pope & Talbot, Inc., to admire a thick log segment in front of the company's administration building. A plaque tells me that the log is 87.5 inches in diameter and was taken from a 434-year-old Douglas fir cut down on BLM land back in 1970. The plaque doesn't say how tall the tree was, only that it produced sixty thousand board feet of lumber.

The guard at the main gate directs me through a complex of giant industrial cookers, silos, and overhanging pipes to a four-story concrete-block building. Opposite the concrete building are 150-foot-high cinnamon-brown mounds of woodchips and sawdust. Clanking around on top of these dunes are a pair of big yellow bulldozers, pushing the stuff into drifts and piles—the kind of work every child in America wants to grow up to do. Marlin, wearing a purple union jacket, comes out to meet me and lead me upstairs to a cafeteria area where the snack machines are located. We're joined there by Robert Sherwood, the company's environmental manager. Through the fourth-floor windows, I watch a dozer climb past us on its way to the top of a chip mound. Marlin and Bob begin to talk about their problems with the nearby city of Corvallis, population 4,300.

"Our discharge pipe is upriver from the city water treatment," Bob Sherwood tells me. "We have to purify 90 to 95 percent of our waste, just like they do, but our wastes are stronger."

"The city of Corvallis doesn't want to spend money on sewage treatment. They want to ratchet down on our permits, and they think if they can squeeze us down they won't have to spend the money," Marlin claims. "The people I've met are raising hysteria. It's all bullshit lies. Tannin releases are more visible is all. We used to bleach out the tannin with chlorine so our effluent wasn't visible and nobody complained, but since 1987 we stopped doing that and the color went visible."

When you stand on the bank of the Willamette downstream from the plant's outfall pipe, you can see what Marlin's talking about. There's a line in the river where the water turns from green-blue to a brown-tea color. The brown color comes from lignin (or tannin), the glue that holds wood fibers together. It looks weird, froths the surface, and stains boat hulls but is considered relatively harmless by the state Department of Environmental Quality, at least compared to the chlorine compounds the company used to use to bleach its effluent. In fact, it's the chlorine bleaching of white paper and the dioxin that process creates that has raised concern about human health and environmental impacts in recent years. The Halsey mill is now in the process of building an oxygen delignification cooker to reduce its dependence on chlorine.

"We'll meet our requirements to be chlorine-free, or almost totally chlorine-free, by 1997," Bob promises. "The technology's coming online. We can solve the dioxin problem, but wood supply and this vocal public comment is another problem. One of Corvallis's big concerns is they don't want us expanding, no matter what."

"They have this 'I got mine and I don't care' attitude," Marlin says of the plant's numerous critics in town. "A good share of them are retired and have nothing to do but keep track of us." His brow furrows as he prepares to make the most onerous charge one can hurl in Oregon. "A lot of them are from California," he claims. "The first thing I ask is where they're from, and it's either California or back East somewhere."

Marlin takes me through the shop area to his Oldsmobile Royale parked outside. We climb in and drive around to the back side of the chip pile, where we watch a big semitrailer detach from its cab, rise up on a hydraulic lift like a Patriot missile launcher box ready to fire, and spill a load of chips from its bottom doors. With some five hundred tons of pulp processed here every day, the mound receives about a hundred truckloads of Douglas fir chips and sawdust daily. Marlin takes a pinch of wintermint-flavored Kodiak Smokeless Tobacco and puts it inside his mouth up against his cheek. Soon he opens the door and spits the first of a series of brown wads onto the ground.

We pass under a pipe bridge connecting the pulp silos and the James River paper mill across the road. There's a white lime build-up on the ground and a blistery refrigerant odor in the air. As we climb a ladder above the water intake tanks, Marlin explains the pulping process to me. "We take the chips and run 'em through the digester that cooks out the lignin, the glue that holds the tree together. Then we take the fiber—the cellulose—and wash out the chemicals from the digester using lye and other caustics. We bleach the fiber with chlorine and take it to the papermaking machines across the road."

From the roof of the recycling plant, we have a sweeping vista. Sixty acres of scummy brown settling ponds are being aerated by giant blue fiberglass eggbeaters. Frank Perry, who was also in Salem for the OLC lobby day, joins us here. He's a jolly-seeming guy with full white hair, a sandy mustache, and a respectable beer belly, although nothing to compare with Marlin's. He's brought along a yellow hard hat and safety glasses for me. Frank is IBEW political director for the mill as well as the union's environmental lobbyist. Marlin and Frank explain that in the days when the plant's effluent was chlorine bleached, the clarified wastewater would be run through a fish tank to test it for toxicity.

"Those fish grew pretty big," Frank says. "Wonder what happened to them?"

"They were some good-looking fish. I wouldn't be surprised if someone didn't take them home for a barbecue dinner," Marlin smiles.

We go inside and up to the ninth floor of the roaring recovery unit, past small glass ports that look into the flaming heart of the furnace where the green and white chemical "liquors" used to process the cellulose are recycled. "The caustic cooks the chips . . . lime and calcium carbonate are used in the cellulose-washing system . . . ," Frank shouts to me over the thundering din of machinery. We enter a control room where three men are watching banks of switches. Frank points to a pair of black and white monitors showing the burning heart of the pressure vessel. "We put the green liquor through the evaporators and run it off," he continues, still shouting. "It's extremely volatile at this stage, the controlled green liquor." I nod like I understand what the hell he's talking about.

Back outside we walk past some railroad boxcars used for taking out pulp and some black chemical tanker cars that bring in the chlorine, caustic soda, and limestone used in processing the chips. We stop at the union trailer where Marlin has his office.

"Last strike we had was in eighty-eight," he recalls. "Over contract language. It lasted fifteen days. We were out there on the line and they had to operate with their own management people, so we knew that couldn't go on too long."

"Jesse Jackson was here," Frank volunteers. "Yeah, Jesse Jackson came out and spoke on the picket line, got everyone fired up. It was a great scene. Don't know who's gone off with his picture though," Marlin says, pivoting around on his chair as if to search it out. He points to a plaque hanging over his desk. "I'm kind of proud of that one."

It's a bronze and wood plaque reading "1991 APA Activist of the Year," given by the American Pulpwood Association, the industry lobby. "It's the first time they ever gave one to a union person," he grins. "We're all learning we've got to work together, because if this industry goes down our jobs go down with it."

Frank Perry motions for me to follow him out of the trailer and over to the washing unit. On the ground floor is a continuous vertical belt about eighteen inches wide, made of hard rubber segments connected with metal teeth. Small pop-up metal platforms with handholds are part of the belt coming out of the floor. I watch Frank step onto one and rise towards a hole in the ceiling above us. I follow. The belt pulls us up through concrete holes a little wider than shoulder width through the floors of the building. Looking up, I can see Frank step off the moving belt on the fourth-floor ledge above me. I step off after him. We're standing near a wide corridor flanked by big metal cookers that look like brew pub tanks lying on their sides. The first one has open side panels, and we can see yellow pulp cooking away in a goopy corn-colored mix. Down the central aisle on the other side we can see blackish pulp churning away. From the last cooker on the left, we pull out some bleached white pulp that looks and smells like wet paper towels. When this pulp crosses the pipe bridge over the road to the James River Company, the wire paper machines will turn it into "rough product" such as paper towels and toilet paper. We wave to the men and women in the computerized control room before climbing back onto the belt loop.

Outside I pause to talk with Frank. I've noticed that when Marlin's around Frank tends to keep his peace, the volume of available air in any given space being what it is. It turns out that Frank is an ex-Green Beret and seventh Dan blackbelt, but very laid back about it.

"I was in Vietnam in the early sixties doing preparation work for what was to follow. You know JFK was preparing to withdraw [from Vietnam] within eighteen months of his re-election. I think JFK was killed by the military-industrial complex. I know *they* had no intention of getting out of there." I ask him if he's seen the Oliver Stone movie based on the same premise, but he hasn't. He begins talking about the oxygenation system they're installing at the mill and mentions that they've just avoided a nine-month shutdown.

"Because of the logging restrictions?" I ask.

"No. Because Sweden devalued the kroner. That's allowed the

Scandinavians to flood the European market, which means that Pope & Talbot has lost its niche there. Pope & Talbot sells pulp at $330 a ton, versus the $243 a ton the Swedes can now offer. So instead of a $3 million loss this year from increased chip costs, they began looking at a $15 million loss. They thought that with a nine-month shutdown here they could save $10 million, but then after considering the loss of continuity and what their absence from the market might do they decided against it. It was strictly an economic decision on their part."

"So what do you make of that?"

"I take my karate students to Japan every year and so maybe that gives me a different perspective from outside the area, but I can see that it's all a part of a world economy now. These adjustments will take place, there'll be a new standard established for a sustainable yield, and some of the smaller companies probably won't make it. But that's what happens. I just hope Oregon stays affordable so that the people who were born here will be able to keep on living here. Right now, the way it's going, I think the state will be unaffordable in my kids' lifetime."

I ask him about the anti-enviro rally the unions are organizing with the Oregon Lands Coalition and Wise Use for the upcoming Forest Summit in Portland. The summit, promised by Bill Clinton during his election campaign, will bring together all the players in the Northwest timber wars to try to resolve their conflicts.

"It will be kind of a last hurrah for the timber issue," he says, surprising me. "Things are never going back to the way they were. And the thing is, I don't really blame it on the spotted owl or marbled murrelet [another endangered bird]. We let the government get away with fifty years of mismanagement and that makes me angrier than spotted owls or any of that stuff. They just did the bidding of the special interests and let things go until they reached the state they're in now."

Good forestry is a matter of perspective. For two days before the April 1993 Forest Summit in Portland, Oregon, local television was inundated with thirty- and sixty-second spots from OLC, Weyerhauser, and other industry reps showing lush ridgelines full of luxuriant second-growth Douglas firs. Shot from about five hundred feet above the ground, the ads carried the message that the region's trees were a bountiful and renewable resource for to-day and tomorrow, a message visually confirmed by the vast-seeming forest passing majestically in the foreground and the second green ridgeline visible in the middle distance. What the ads failed to show was the third ridgeline or the valley in between.

On the day after I arrive in Portland to cover the Forest Summit, I find myself flying at twenty-five hundred feet above Gifford Pinchot National Forest in a yellow and white Cessna Cardinal. From here the mountain range resembles an old retriever dog suffering from a terminal case of mange. In any direction you look you see a patchwork landscape of broken wood lots and tan-colored earth. We pass a four-thousand-foot mountain that's been stripped bare and cut up from summit to base by logging roads making cross-hatchings in the late spring snow. Banking, we fly along a ravine too steep for easy logging, passing a ragged fragment of mixed 200–300-year-old Douglas fir, cedar, and hemlock that looms above and protects a narrow blue-line stream looking like it might harbor some good-sized fish. Over the next ridgeline we spot a red front-loader and some yellow trucks parked by a raw exposed bog in the middle of yet another clearcut, a cut that goes downslope to a river without the required protective buffer of trees. I click on my headset mike and ask Jay Noyes, our pilot, "Isn't that illegal?" "Probably," Jay answers, sounding as if he's seen worse.

Jay thinks the yellow trucks might be there for replanting. The companies like to replant 80 percent Doug fir to 20 percent hemlock. Alder will also sneak in to colonize cutover areas. Alder are good trees for replacing nitrogen in the soil but lousy for lumber. The companies don't like them and, where they can, spray them with herbicide.

We fly over a serpentine hillside where forty- to sixty-year-old second-growth fir is coming back as evenly and luxuriantly as the fur on a ranch-bred pelt. As we approach its southern boundary, I wonder what forester Gifford Pinchot would think of this half-cleared national tree farm. Looking down we can see a razor-straight line of trees that marks the end of the patchy U.S. forest and the beginning of Weyerhauser's private lands, a vast denuded moonscape running down to the Swift Reservoir. The bad/worse dividing line stretches in either direction as far as the eye can see. It's a depressing example of free-enterprise environmentalism—or at least the export tax incentive program that inspired the lumber companies to ship one out of four logs to Asia during the record cuts of the 1980s.[7] Heading back towards Portland, we fly along the Columbia River, passing over rafts of logs floating below the huge Weyerhauser pulp plant at Kelso/Longview. We cross over the Cowlitz River where it feeds into the Columbia, its waters still gray-colored from ash more than a decade after the eruption of Mount St. Helen's, which rises, cloud shrouded, in the distance.

Thirty thousand feet up is another perspective worth having. If the weather cooperates, any commercial airline flight between San Francisco and Seattle will provide the opportunity. Looking down at Mount St. Helens from that height, seeing the gray landscape, the debris-filled lake, the altered rivers, and the ravages from the 1980 volcanic eruption gives one momentary pause, restoring a sense of wonder and awe at the overwhelming power of nature to mark the land. At six hundred miles an hour, you've left the volcano behind in a few moments. What you haven't left behind, what is so subtly imprinted on your mind that it takes a conscious act of will to realize, is the much greater imprint on the landscape produced by years of clear-cut logging and development. Although we still speak of the great northwestern forests, what we really see during hours of overflight is not a forest at all, but a strained ecosystem patchwork no wilder than grandma's quilt.

"Twenty Niner One, you're cleared for landing," the control tower tells us as our Cessna bumps down through the turbulence over suburban Portland. We land on a secondary runway and taxi to the commercial airport's civil aviation area. Jay, at the controls of the small single-engine plane, is also an aerial photographer who works out of Hood River, Oregon. He's tall and slim with gray-blond hair. "When I moved out here from Colorado," he tells me as his other passengers climb out from under the wing, "I fig-ured I'd rather have a plane and a small house than a large house and no plane." He admits that he bought his Cardinal "half think-ing of what would be the best plane for Lighthawk."

Lighthawk labels itself the environmental air force. It's made up of volunteer pilots from around the country who provide over-flights of threatened habitats for activists, politicians, and the me-dia from Canada to Costa Rica. On the day before the Forest Summit, they've assembled five prop planes and a helicopter for media overflights of some of the disputed logging areas. As we enter the Flightcraft terminal, a CNN crew is gearing up, hoping to beat out the storm front now gathering over the mountains. They'll be flying with George Atiyeh of Mill City, Oregon, in his blue-and-white twin Comanche.

A youthful looking forty-five, with dark brown hair pulled back in a ponytail, a cavalry man's mustache, and lively gray eyes be-hind thin gold glasses, George is an eminent member of a long-established local clan. But even his deep familial roots in Oregon's timber and mining culture—his family filed its first claims in 1859, one of his grandfathers ran Pacific Lumber, his uncle was the state's governor in the 1980s—hasn't kept George from being targeted in the ongoing timber wars.

"In the late seventies and early eighties, I was flying back and forth to our sawmill in eastern Oregon, and from the air I could see how overcut the forests were," he explains. "After a few years of this, I was having trouble reconciling my own rhetoric about sustainable yields with what my eyes were seeing."

In 1981 George sold his logging interests and began speaking out for better forestry practices. In 1983 he testified at the state-house in favor of a wilderness bill and scenic-river protections his uncle, the governor, opposed. George also spent much of the 1980s battling the U.S. Forest Service. He had an underground silver mine in the Opal Creek area, forty miles east of Salem, and a three-thousand-acre stand of old-growth forest, including eight-hundred-year-old Douglas firs. Early in the decade, he decided he was going to protect Opal Creek. Since it was inside the Wil-lamette National Forest, he expanded his "Shiny Rock" mining claims, using the 1872 mining law to block the Forest Service from logging the area. "We had to go to court and spend hundreds of thousands of dollars fighting them, because they knew that what we really intended to do was save those trees," George explains, an involuntary grin creeping across his face. In 1989 he got a bill introduced in the statehouse to try and turn Opal Creek into a state park.

"This was around the time the spotted owl was designated an endangered species. Mills closed throughout the southern part of the state and the millworkers were paid that day to go to the state capital to demonstrate. They surrounded the capitol with logging trucks, and some of the people I saw outside demonstrating had been sending out flyers for Friends of Opal Creek, this nonprofit we'd set up the day before. I went out to the rally to ask them what was going on and they said, 'When we got to work this morning they told us this was our work today.'"

"Right after that I became the focus of a lot of this anti-environmentalist anger and started getting two or three death threats a day. They slashed the tires on my wife's car. A log truck tried to run my seventeen-year-old son off the road when he was out driving my car, and they held my twelve-year-old daughter down in the schoolyard and tied her up with yellow ribbons. I heard that some guys joked about shooting my plane out of the sky."

I ask him about the phone threats. "The phone threats were like, 'You're a dead son of a bitch' and 'Get out of the canyon.' I said, 'Listen, my family's been in the state from before the turn of the century, a lot longer than you, asshole, so we're not going anywhere.' Finally it got so I just left a tape on my machine. It said, 'Please leave a message or, if this is a death threat, just calm down and take a deep breath, because you're probably nervous, and then leave your name and address and I absolutely will get back to you.' Well, there were still a few threats, but none of them had the balls to leave their names. Finally I called up the mill owner, who I figured was behind most of it. This is a guy who was born with a silver log in his mouth. I said, 'You better stop this or

be damn sure the first shot counts, because if it doesn't I'm coming after you and I know where you live.' Right after that the
threats stopped."

George was particularly angry that his family was being targeted. "After they tied my daughter up with the yellow ribbons,
I called the school authorities and said, 'Cut it out, it's like putting
a swastika on a Jewish kid.' And they did stop it after that. But it
went so far that they killed a music program in the high school and
instituted a forestry program instead, to teach the kids how to be
loggers. A bunch of kids wanted to come to Opal Creek to visit
the preserve and the school board wouldn't let them go. They
came anyway, and that became a big story. Of course, I was still
a social pariah in my town. No one would sit next to me at the high
school football games. Friends were afraid to visit my house. Mer-
chants who tried to stay neutral, who didn't go along with the
yellow-ribbon stuff, were threatened with boycotts, so they'd
hang up 'We support the timber industry' banners and tie yellow
ribbons around their stores. They'd also give money to Friends of
Opal Creek on condition we didn't publicize their names. Eventually things calmed down. I think my standing up made a difference. Plus, most of the people in my town are good people. It's
just that a few have too much power. It's still a kind of feudal economy in many of these lumber towns."

In 1992 George arranged to donate the three-thousand-acre
Opal Creek forest area to Friends of Opal Creek for eventual
transfer to The Nature Conservancy as a permanent preserve.[8]
He sees this original old-growth forest he's helped to save as compensation for some of the vigilante harassment he and his family
suffered through.

"My middle son got the most shit," he says. "Other families
wouldn't let their kids associate with him. He got flak from the
other guys at school. He decided he was going to move to Portland
to stay with my sister and finish high school up there. I agreed
that was okay if that's what he wanted. Then a few nights before
he was going to leave he was watching MTV and saw the Grateful
Dead video "You Can Run but You Can't Hide—and there were

two pictures of him, clips from this Audubon documentary, "Rage Over Trees."[9] And that's when he decided to stay. He turned to me grinning and said, 'To hell with them. None of *them* have been on MTV.'"

"Stumps Don't Lie," reads the stage banner at the Ancient Forest Concert held on Portland's Willamette River the night before President Clinton's Forest Summit Conference gets under way. Fifty thousand people have turned out in the rain to hear the music and support the cause. "What right do we have to tell other countries to stop cutting their forests when we haven't stopped cutting ours?" asks Kenny Loggins before his set. "My daddy grew up in Butte, Montana, the hole that wouldn't stop. It's a ghost town today, 'cause no one would say stop."

Black rap group U-Krew plays as a white signer for the deaf tries to keep his hand movements flipping and rolling as fast as the song. It becomes a game between them, ending with bear hugs and a big round of applause. David Crosby, still alive despite his sybaritic ways, sings "Long Time Gone." Carole King, down from her home in Idaho, does "Smackwater Jack" and a new song she calls "No More Welfare Timber." Ninety-five-year-old Pacific Northwest activist Hazel Wolfe totters to the microphone. "I couldn't believe as a young girl that the limitless forests I knew would be almost gone some day, but I'm confident now that in my life they'll be saved." Ann and Nancy Wilson of Heart sing "Dreamboat Annie." Nat Bingham, a salmon fisherman out of Fort Bragg, California, talks about how salmon are disappearing because the clearcuts are stripping away shade and putting silt in the rivers.

"Clinton and Gore, cut no more!" chants the crowd. By now the sun has set and the rain is coming down in sheets. Neil Young squints out over the rain-slickered crowd as stagehands set up his pipe organ. "Nice weather . . . for trees," he deadpans, before reeling into a final set that includes, "Comes a Time" and "After the Gold Rush." The last speaker is Native American activist Winona LaDuke, who comes up on stage with her two children. "Our lands, our forests are our sacred places. Our forests are about our survival. We all have to reduce our levels of consumption. We need to get back in order with the natural law," she tells the crowd, which responds with sustained applause before dispersing into the night.

"Enviro-elitists rock'n'roll while timber families starve," reads the sign carried the next morning at OLC's Wise Use rally by Christy Britt, the wife of an Oregon contract logger. Their "Family Forest Summit" is taking place as the official conference is getting under way across the river. "There's a lot of timber workers' suicides, a lot of broken families, there are people losing their homes," Christy tells a reporter from the *Oregonian,* Portland's daily paper.[10] "I read about that concert last night. I was struck by the difference between the people there and the people struggling to survive. From what I could see, the people who were doing the singing and playing sounded very smug and self-righteous."

Several boats cruise the river with banners. One reads, "Mr. Babbitt, where did your hardwood floors come from?" The rain is pouring down even harder than it did the night before. Up to half of the sodden crowd of ten thousand industry supporters and their families manage to squeeze under the large white tent that OLC has erected for the event. Inside they listen to a country western band and various speakers from Montana, Oregon, and Washington but seem most interested in what's being said on the television monitors carrying a live feed from the convention center. A number of the men wear their safety helmets or company bill caps. One humorist carries a placard that reads, "Hug a logger, you'll never go back to a tree." There's also a story hour for the kids featuring an original narrative about "the old-growth tree that wanted to be cut down rather than left to die in the forest so it could help supply forest products for people."

But most of the people here, like their fellow blue-collar workers facing shutdowns at military bases across the country, seem to realize that things are not going to go back to the way they were before. They're desperately concerned about their jobs and their futures. "I'm too old to retrain. I've had back surgery. If I went somewhere else, they wouldn't even look at me," says fifty-eight-year-old Dave Field, a Boise Cascade millworker. "They talk about training you on computers." He holds up his hand to show the stub of a finger lost in the mill. "I can't type. It ain't gonna work."

The rally ends with the adoption of a "vision statement" for resource management that would open up more public lands to logging. This document was written by a "grassroots" committee that includes OLC's Tom Hirons, Valerie Johnson, and Charlie Janz.

The official day-long Forest Summit takes place across the Steel Bridge at the spacious, green-glass-spired Portland convention center. Participants include President Clinton, Vice President Gore, half the Cabinet, invited guests and panelists, and just about every cop within a five-hundred-mile radius. The summit is to consist of three panels to examine the human, environmental, and economic aspects of the timber crisis. I'm expecting a lot of talk of conciliation and compromise, along with competing claims over who loves the forest most and who's been hurt the worst.

I join the six hundred other journalists covering the event as we're searched and shuttled into a large, dry basement hall wired with phone lines, minicams, radio feeds, and television monitors. Only a handful of pool reporters and photographers are allowed upstairs in the conference hall. The rest of us, like the demonstrators down by the river, follow the event on TV, exchanging gossip and snacks with old friends and young competitors.

Four or five hours into the summit, Clinton and Gore are still fully engaged in the discussions, questioning panelists about the relative merits of various fiberboard-compression techniques, value-added tax credit structures, and other minutiae that are, to policy wonks like themselves, what good poker hands are to normal men. I can't help thinking that Ronald Reagan would be three hours into his nap by now, while George Bush might be halfway to Tokyo on an urgent foreign policy matter.

After summit participants have their say, they come downstairs to talk to the press. There's Nadine Bailey, the dynamic six-foot-three unemployed logger's wife from Hayfork, California, who's been traveling the Wise Use talk circuit for the last two years. She's walking down the hall doing establishment shots with her husband and daughter for a camera crew from ABC's "American Agenda," praising Bill Clinton to Barry Serafin.

Western Industrial Workers Council union boss Mike Draper, balding, bearded, and built like the proverbial brick outhouse, makes an appearance downstairs. Testifying before the president, he expresses the hope that "together we can find a solution that protects the forests of God and the families of man." To the press he claims he's always been a strong union Democrat (Jim Jontz might disagree) and resents the way Rush Limbaugh is attacking Clinton on the radio. Local reporters more interested in bear-baiting than PR statements try to draw Draper and his equally swarthy enviro nemesis, Andy Kerr of the Oregon Natural Resources Council, into pawing range of each other, but the two manage to avoid taking notice of each other.

A reporter suggests to Kerr that he looks like a spotted owl. "That really ruffles my feathers," Kerr responds. He tells a group of reporters that he thinks it's okay if the summit results in increased lumber prices owing to old growth–logging restrictions. "Right now the number one product in landfills is paper. Number two is wood. If you get rid of the Forest Service subsidy for logging, the market price is going to go up. The free market is fine, allowing for greed with some social restraints. The problem is that the old guard of the forest industry are dinosaurs who just don't want any change or innovation."

Draper is talking to another group of reporters. "I think, for the most part, we're hearing a change in the rhetoric here today because this administration has brought a sense of optimism. This is the first time the *human* element has been brought into the debate. I'm ecstatic with the outcome. You could see he [Clinton] was captivated by the process."

President Clinton finishes the eight-hour conference with a plea to the participants. "I ask you to stay at the table and keep talking and keep trying to find common ground," he says. "I don't want this situation to go back to the posturing, to positioning, to the politics of division that have characterized this difficult issue in the past."

Bill Clinton, with his hands-on approach, seems to have established a de facto cease-fire in the timber wars that will hold for three months, until release of his Option Nine Forest Plan on July 1, 1993. The plan dramatically reduces logging on U.S. federal forest lands but does not protect all old growth, results in some job loss but also provides relief aid, protects salmon and rivers but allows some cutting in owl and murrelet habitat. In all these ways it succeeds in creating the common ground Clinton has spoken of. Both the timber industry and environmentalists condemn it for not giving them what they want.

Before leaving Portland, I arrange to meet ex-millworker Gene Lawhorn at a Chinese restaurant on the east side of town. Gene is about five foot seven, thin and wiry, with light gray eyes, silvery blond hair, and jutting beard. He has a tattoo of a flaming skull on his right forearm and the remnants of an Appalachian accent. He's wearing jeans, a jean jacket, and, incongruously, a green Earth First! tee shirt.

Gene is a relative newcomer to the Northwest and relatively poor. Looking for work, he moved to Oregon from Ohio in 1985 with his wife and two young daughters. He'd seen his town of Mansfield, Ohio, shut down after Westinghouse closed its plant and moved overseas. The Empire Steel Works, where his father and grandfather worked, had laid off most of its employees. "We were just hillbillies, just working people from the little Tennessee section of town," he smiles, stroking his beard. "There wasn't much we could do but leave." He got his first mill work in Westbrook, Oregon, working cleanup crew as a log head spotter and tail spotter for $5.80 an hour. "We had logs blow up on us when they didn't feed right. I was pinned against the wall by a board that would have killed me if my friend hadn't hit the stop button they'd just put on the line. As it was, I was knocked unconscious."

It was at the Westbrook mill that Gene first heard about the spotted owl. "They'd call a shift meeting and give us all coffee and donuts and bring in speakers, foresters from the lumber companies, and other outside speakers and tell us about the spotted owl and the preservationists. They'd have these postcards for us to sign with a collection box to drop them in—these spotted owl protests to Congress. I signed them along with everyone else. They'd scare you into thinking you'd lose your job if you didn't."

He got laid off anyway but found new work at the International Paper sawmill in Gardner, a union shop. "I was impressed with the better conditions I found there, plus I was making $8.90 an hour now, so I decided to get involved with Local 3127 of the International Woodworkers of America. I became a shop steward, but when people asked me, 'What's the union done for me?' I was bothered that I couldn't answer, so I went to the library and got out a book, *Labor's Untold Story*. And that book was like an awakening for me. I began reading labor history and understanding how history can help you find out the truth about what's going on today."

In early eighty-seven, Gene had a tee shirt printed up with "Just Wait till '88," which was when their union contract was set to expire. His whole crew began wearing the shirt, and it spread throughout the mill. "There were some guys, they'd wear that shirt all week long, and management started getting nervous. Two weeks before Christmas the company announced it had sold the mill and laid us all off."

He heard that Roseburg Forest Products was hiring and was able to get another union job at their Dixonville veneer mill. He became shop steward again and began writing history articles for the Western Council of Industrial Workers newspaper. "But they stopped running them because I wrote that the way labor had been treated in the past was like what was being done to the human rights of people in El Salvador and South Africa, and Mike Draper said you can't write that. That's un-American.

"But that didn't bother me too much, because by then we were on strike. We were out from January through May of eighty-nine, out for five months." He smiles strangely. "What I saw on the picket line, it was like that science fiction movie *They Live*, where you could see who were the aliens when you put on these sunglasses. It was like putting on those glasses. A lot of people in the

union were wearing yellow ribbons at the time to protest the environmentalists, only I began to notice this thing and I said to the
other people on line, 'What does every vehicle crossing our line
have in common? The cars and pickups of the scabs, the log
trucks, the managers' cars?' They all flew yellow ribbons. So on
the picket line the yellow ribbons started disappearing.'"

Visiting another mill on strike, Gene was surprised to find
Earth First! activists picketing with the workers. "I began to see
that they were human, not the ogres we'd been told about. They
were reaching out and talking to me and actually blocking the cars
of scabs. I went to Portland and debated them on the radio and
started seeing that they had a point of view too. But I didn't become that vocal until shortly after the strike ended, when the
timber/labor coalition was formed to protest against the spotted
owl and they announced this big September rally in Salem, where
they would shut down the mills and go protest. So me and a couple of other guys had a press conference to denounce the rally,
not liking this whole yellow ribbon business any more. Only
about four of us showed up, but because the press likes controversy we still got a lot of play on TV and in the papers, and the
union president threatened to kick my ass. Anyway, that rally was
a flop. The company rented five buses for the day and bought a
bunch of box lunches, but only about forty people went on the
buses of the four or five hundred who took the day off. Most of
the others went fishing, I guess.

"Some time after that, Roseburg Forest Products held one of
these meetings after lunch where we got an extra paid hour to listen to these OLC people. They had this Wise Use group called
TREES, Timber Resources Equals Economic Stability, and another called WOOD, Workers of Oregon Development, but nobody was joining them. So they came and talked and all you had
to do was sign up and the company would pay your $12 member-
ship fee so they could then go to lobby and say, 'Look, we have
three thousand dues-paying members or whatever.' It was a
scam."

By this time Gene was beginning to identify himself openly as
an environmentalist. The only thing he couldn't tolerate about

the Earth Firsters he was meeting was their advocacy and use of tree spiking, with its potential to injure or kill forest industry workers.

"In March of 1990 I'd talked a bunch on the phone with Judi Bari, trying to get her to renounce tree spiking. And then I got a tape of her folk music singing 'Spike a Tree for Jesus' and got real pissed off. So at this University of Oregon conference I attended, I challenged her face to face, and she immediately agreed to renounce it, which caused a big stir with some of the other Earth Firsters. But most of the environmentalists who were there thought tree spiking was wrong anyway and gave her a big round of applause.

"I thought this was a big thing, that an Earth First! leader would promise never to tree spike again, but Mike Draper called it 'just another preservationist tactic,' and the timber industry denounced it as some kind of plot. It was like they didn't want tree spiking to end, 'cause it made it easier for them to talk about eco-terrorists."

Soon, like hundreds of other grassroots environmentalists across America, Gene and his family began to encounter their own form of terrorism. "I was put back in the Dixonville plant, which was in a real rural area. There were about 125 people working there. And there was this real proindustry millwright guy who drove up to me on a forklift my first day there and said, 'Are you that environmentalist, Lawhorn?' And I said, 'Yeah, I'm that environmentalist, Lawhorn.' And he said, 'If you don't quit this plant we're going to cut your nuts off.' Well, I knew you have to come back at a threat like that, hopefully in some creative but direct way, so shortly thereafter I walked up to the guy and I handed him a small knife. I had a larger knife in my back pocket just in case. And I said, 'Here, you want to cut my balls off,' and he kind of backed down. He said he didn't mean he was going to do it, he meant someone else might. Not long after that Judi Bari was bombed and things got kind of scary. Then this guy started bad-mouthing me when I wasn't around, and someone put my name and number on the bulletin boards at different mills saying, 'This is a spotted-owl-loving son of a bitch. Call him up and tell him what you think.' So then we started getting all the calls, hang-up calls, death threats, calls telling my wife she was an owl-loving bitch. We changed our number half a dozen times, but that didn't help. Somebody broke the windshield of my Nissan pickup. People would drive up to the house in the middle of the night, break beer bottles in the driveway, and then peel out. Then they started driving by the house firing off guns. Angel and Terra, our two little girls, were five and eight at the time. I started sleeping with a loaded thirty-thirty rifle by the bed to defend my wife and family. The local cops came out a few times but didn't do much. Lisa, my wife, was at a yard sale when one cop told her, 'You people should get out of here, move somewhere else.' She came home really mad, feeling like the cops were on the side of whoever was doing this. She had this big Dodge truck with a bumper sticker reading, 'Justice for Judi Bari,' and she was twice driven off the road, off of route 42, by log trucks. The kids were with her at the time and they were shaken up, pretty scared, you know.

"Lisa was also harassed at the Pentecostal church she attended because of these environmental letters I was writing to the editor of the town paper there in Sutherlin and she couldn't get work. The manager at the Kentucky Fried Chicken where she applied for a job told her, 'We don't want you troublemakers here.'"

Gene was laid off at the mill in late 1990 and soon realized he wasn't going to be rehired. He moved his family to Portland in ninety-one, where he now works as a warehouse supervisor.

"One of the things that really changed my way of thinking," he reflects, "was going deer hunting, going after blacktail, in the Siuslaw National Forest back in eighty-six. I came to this bog with a family of beaver working in the water and I just sat down and watched those beavers for about three hours. It was just fascinating watching the way they worked together. And at some point I stretched my legs and popped my knee or something and one of those beavers heard it, slapped his tail on the water, and, boom, they were all gone, just like that. I came back to that place two years later and it was gone, nothing but clear-cut, bulldozed, scarred-over land. So you wonder about where the beaver are going, and the salmon that are threatened now, and you realize this country was once the promised land, once had everything, but now it's all polluted, its working people are living on the edge, and cutting the last ancient forests just won't get us back on our feet."

Grassroots for Sale

Alarmed by the success of the environmental movement, industries such as mining, logging and ranching are trying to duplicate it: they are forming grass-roots groups in a loose-knit coalition dedicated to the "wise use" of natural resources.
WASHINGTON POST

Because they were new organizations and active and well-funded, I think they really had an impact on the western senators and congressional delegations.
JIM BACA, FORMER DIRECTOR, BUREAU OF LAND MANAGEMENT

With the timber companies clear-cutting the ancient forests of the Pacific Northwest, the coal companies strip-mining southern Appalachia, and the plastic and petrochemical processors cracking hydrocarbons along the Gulf Coast, traditional resource-based industries find themselves under tremendous pressure to change or die as the United States enters a new world market. Here, on the global scale, the U.S. is unable to compete in nails, ceramic tile, or wood products, but leads the way in fiber optics, wind turbines, and computer drives. Those companies that can meet the next century's requirements for more energy-efficient, environmentally clean means of production will survive to play on a vastly expanded field. Those that are unable to make the transition are fated for economic obsolescence. Simultaneous to and paralleling this change is a demographic shift that is dramatically altering the American West. The expanding city- and town-based populations are putting new multiple-use demands on our public lands—for recreation, scenery, and wildlife—and threatening the monopoly long held by government-subsidized users in mining, logging, and grazing. Agriculture also faces a serious choice: whether to move towards low-input, labor-intensive forms of farming or to continue chemically mining the soil and expanding agri-biz production methods to every last river, dell, wetland, and low-lying depression that hasn't already been developed for real estate.

A handful of rearview visionaries have staked out a consistent position on these and other natural resource issues, choosing to defend the conventional against the unknown, the extractive against the regenerative, and promising industry that with a little financial support they can stem the tidal changes now occurring in the New West and across America.

Ron Arnold likes to warn and cajole; Chuck Cushman entertains and alarms; Bill Grannell plays the friend of the worker; Grant Gerber drones and deals; Clark Collins is the patient negotiator; William Perry Pendley is the supercilious lecturer. What all six of these men have in common are distinct, often competing claims to leadership in the anti-environmentalist movement of the 1990s. They are driven, fiercely self-assured individuals, suspicious of each other's motives and interests, and anxious to prove themselves the largest, most brightly colored fish in their small but growing pond. They are, in Chuck Cushman's words, "the old dogs" of a young movement whose scars and bite marks are as likely to have come from each other as from their "preservationist" enemy.

"Chuck Cushman isn't a real organizer. Chuck is a forager," Bill Grannell claims. "He goes into battle where the fights are under way but doesn't leave much infrastructure behind. Arnold and [his sponsor Alan] Gottlieb are on the extreme Right. They don't represent anyone but themselves."[1]

"Grannell's just a profiteer," countercharges Chuck Cushman. "He doesn't believe in reaching out to others. Mostly his work is about money, and so I think he views us as a threat. He and his wife are skilled organizers and could do a lot, but they're not willing to make economic sacrifices for the cause, and that turns off the grassroots."[2]

"Please don't try to tar the property rights movement with Mr. Arnold. Ron's not everything he makes out to be," Grant Gerber warns. "Most of the major players in the property rights movement—the Farm Bureau, the NRA, the Cattlemen's Association—will have nothing to do with Ron or his friend Alan Gottlieb. They're profiteers and they have some very unsavory connections."[3]

"Everyone who's ever worked with Grant Gerber knows he's a backstabber," Ron Arnold responds. "We know all the bullshit and libels you spread about us and we love you, Grant. Every time you say those things you send the media to us and get a hair up your ass."[4]

"Splintering multiplies a movement's power," Ron adds a few moments later, going on to argue that movements are by nature "segmentary, polycephalous, ideological networks." He's attempting to find a sociological rationale for the personality-driven divisions that mark the small, contentious network of anti-enviro activists who are leading the fight against the greening of America.

Environmentalists and liberal politicians have accused the Wise Use/Property Rights groups of being little more than a front for greedy corporations and public lands profiteers. "These organizations are not grassroots. They are Astroturf laid down with big corporate money," says Jay Hair, president of the National Wildlife Federation.[5] Congressman George Miller, the Democratic chairman of the House Committee on Natural Resources, says, "All of these people have their hands and their noses and their snouts deep into the taxpayer's pocket."[6]

It's a charge that infuriates ranchers, loggers, small businesspeople, and frustrated developers such as Peggy Reigle of Dorchester, Maryland. In the early eighties, Reigle, a former vice president for finance at the *New York Daily News*, along with her husband, Charles Jowaiszas, purchased an eighteenth-century house in rural Dorchester County on the state's scenic eastern shore. They also bought a nearby 138-acre abandoned farm for

$400,000, hoping to subdivide it into fourteen homesites and a site for their own "dream house." When the area was classified as a wetland, Reigle and her husband watched their investment sink like a cinderblock in wet sand.[7] In July 1990, a frustrated Reigle founded the Fairness to Land Owners Committee (FLOC) to oppose President Bush's "no net loss of wetlands" pledge along with what she calls "the ecofascist movement." In the last four years, by her own count, the group has grown to twelve thousand members (only five hundred pay dues). She and other second-tier organizers around the country—cattleman's wife Joan Smith in Yreka, California; former log company operator Bruce Vincent in Libby, Montana; Maine-second-home owner Eric Veyhl in Concord, Massachusetts—working for little more than their own self-interest, feel deeply insulted when they're accused of being corporate shills. They believe they're creating a genuine broad-based grassroots movement to oppose the preservationists, a feeling reinforced by at least some of the coverage they've received. ABC's "Nightline," in a set-up piece to a debate between Al Gore and Rush Limbaugh in February 1992, described Wise Use as a movement "ranging from . . . Exxon, which would like to use the land for oil drilling, to ordinary citizens like Peggy Reigle, who simply want to use the land to build their dream house."

In an interview for a *New York Times* article titled, "When the Bad Guy Is Seen as the One in the Green Hat," published that same month, Reigle explained to reporter Keith Schneider how "landowners, and I mean moms and pops, not oil companies and miners, are being abused by restrictions that no longer make sense. Their lives have been devastated and their land is being held hostage by these [environmental] laws."[8]

"Committee leader Reigle does not pay herself a salary, answers her own phone and counts on an array of volunteers, including public interest lawyers and former regulators, for assistance," reported a May 1993 *Insight* magazine article on Reigle's efforts to pass property rights legislation in Maryland. This Moon publication piece described "a classic David and Goliath duel" between FLOC and the Chesapeake Bay Foundation, with annual assets of $6.6 million. "Land rights activists fielded no professional lobbyists, but the environmentalists pulled out all the stops . . . accustomed to being seen as the underpaid underdog, they are taking on a small movement that receives virtually no support from major industry or large foundations."[9] The article failed to report on the intense statehouse lobbying efforts of the Homebuilders Association, Maryland Farm Bureau, Maryland Association of Realtors, and other corporate supporters of the property rights legislation, however.

Still, anti-enviro activists perceive themselves as working with, not for, resource industries, which they often disdain as being too willing to compromise with the enemy. In trying to organize among unemployed loggers, resource workers, small independent businesspeople, and frustrated middle managers, they have even incorporated a thinly veiled "anticapitalist" message, using class resentment as a cudgel by portraying environmentalists as wealthy elitists, part of a "green establishment" with links to transnational corporations, the Rockefellers, and Mellon money. Bill and Barbara Grannell claim that environmentalists are "the elitists at the top, driving Mercedes and BMWs and telling average Americans what to do."

"The Nature Conservancy is a capitalist institution designed to promote socialism," insists Grant Gerber, referring to the 200-million-dollar-a-year nonprofit organization that buys up wild and undeveloped private land for preservation, often reselling it to the national park system. "Corporate executives . . . direct seven out of every ten public affairs dollars from their firms and corporate foundations to organizations that act to destroy business and industry," claim Ron Arnold and Alan Gottlieb in their latest self-published book, *Trashing the Economy,* an "exposé" of the greens based on a classic far-right thesis that capitalism is surrendering itself to an alien force (in this case environmentalism) and needs a dynamic new movement (Wise Use) to rescue it from degeneracy.

As part of their anti-elitist rhetoric, the Center for Defense of Free Enterprise (CDFE) and People for the West disseminate figures indicating that the environmental "establishment" generates an annual gross income in the neighborhood of $3 billion

(*Money* magazine places it at $2.5 billion, *Outside* magazine at half a billion). Impressive a figure as $3 billion is, what it really indicates, if accurate, is that organized environmentalism in the United States has the same economic clout as the television home-shopping industry. In other words, if all the environmental groups in the United States agreed to pool their resources, Green, Inc., would be about one-eighteenth as big as Wal-Mart and would rank 160 on the Fortune 500 listing. Of course, it *would* be the only member of the Fortune 500 trying to change the resource utilization, production methods, and long-term strategies of the other 499.

The antigreens claim to be doing their nationwide organizing work on a gross income of between $10 million and $100 million a year, a far smaller amount than the (far larger) environmental movement has available to work with.[10] Reviews of IRS filings confirm that most of the established anti-enviro groups (Blue Ribbon, CDFE, WIRF, People for the West) operate in the $50,000-to $500,000-a-year range.[11] However, these figures can also mislead by failing to take into account "in kind" services provided by major institutional players from the corporate sector and the political Right, including the multibillion dollar Farm Bureau Federation, NRA, ALEC, probusiness nonprofit law firms, and numerous resource-industry organizations such as the California Forestry Association.

CFA's Communications Manager Kathy Kvarda, along with putting out the state industry-association newsletter, is paid to coordinate the anti-enviro Alliance for Environment and Resources (AER). "It would be nice if we could get a statewide grassroots umbrella group going that was more independent in terms of industry identification. But then again, we're a poor association," the cheerful blond publicist says brightly, explaining how AER was originally established in the mid-eighties, "when people in the Forest Service told us we needed nonindustry input to balance the preservationists in the forest planning process."[12] In 1993 Kvarda's job requirements included coordinating the Alliance for America's five-day "Fly-In for Freedom" lobbying trip to Washington.

In a few places, such as Alabama and Alaska, state governments have taken on a leadership role in creating and promoting the anti-environmentalist backlash. In 1992 Alabama State Forester Bill Moody set up his own anti-enviro group, Stewards of Family Farms, Ranches and Forests, and funneled into it from the State Forestry Commission more than $7,000 in start-up funds plus secretarial support. Moody put commission staffers to work producing videos and literature for the group and, before his activities were exposed in the *Montgomery Advertiser* by reporter Katherine Bouma, held a secret commission meeting that voted to allow him to work for Stewards on state time (Alabama paid him $80,000 a year and provided him with the exclusive use of an airplane). He had also planned to send thirty commission staff members in state cars to the group's founding meeting in December 1992. Moody, the subject of an ethics investigation and a lawsuit, retired from the Forestry Commission in September 1993. Meanwhile, the Forestry Commission has provided support for a second anti-enviro group, EAGLE—Alabamians: Guardians of our Land and Environment—whose spokesman, Colin Bagwell, equates environmentalists with Communists, "infiltrating all of the nation's institutions."[13]

Scattered in hundreds of small rural towns and suburbs across America, made up of ad hoc groups in need of constant resuscitation by paid professional organizers and right-wing legal foundations, kept in communication by fax nets, fliers, and conferences whose attendance never exceeds the low three figures, and promoted by friends in industry, government, and the media, Wise Use/Property Rights may be neither "the most powerful grassroots organization this country has ever seen"—as reported in the Alliance for America newsletter, circulation 2,500—nor the "brutally destructive anti-environmental onslaught" portrayed in a Sierra Club fundraising mailer. Rather, Wise Use/Property Rights is a new and militant force on the political Right that has the power to impede and occasionally sidetrack attempts at environmental protection, intimidate politicians and local activists, and polarize or misdirect needed discussions over jobs, health, and natural resources.

"Their very heated attacks didn't significantly change the nature of the state's environmental goals, but it certainly makes it more difficult to have a large-scale debate when people come in with this strong ideology," says Jonathan Lash, former secretary of natural resources in Vermont and now co-chair of the President's Council on Sustainable Development. Chuck Clarke, the former director of Washington State's Department of Ecology who now has Lash's old job as Vermont's secretary of natural resources, takes it a step further. "These extremists have injected fear into the political process. In Washington State they had a hard core of two hundred or so who would turn out for every meeting and protest. A few hundred people with a canned speech and canned concerns can have a tremendous impact, even if 85 percent of the public disagrees with the protestors."

Mark Smith, the legislative director for Democratic Senator Max Baucus, claims that "they have their real impact on hard-pressed local communities like Libby, high unemployment areas in the northwest of Montana. They're not a statewide force. My boss, who has a good instinct for mainstream Montana, thinks these groups represent legitimate opinions but not mainstream opinion. Their strength is in packing meetings."

"Wise Use hasn't generated much sympathy or even awareness that it exists among the general population," adds Bob Langsencamp, deputy land commissioner for the state of New Mexico. "You see it mostly in rural southeast New Mexico and in the towns of Pecos and Cuba, small northern towns outside of Santa Fe. They've really tried to focus themselves on decision makers in Washington. At the state level they haven't been terribly effective, even in coalition with the cattlemen and the Farm Bureau."

What anti-enviro activists lack in numerical strength, however, they more than make up for in a moral certitude bordering on self-righteousness that finds kindred souls among the anti-abortion militants of Operation Rescue and the lab-trashing "Meat-Is-Murder" wing of the animal rights movement. Like other political true believers, they have little problem justifying intimidation tactics or rationalizing anti-environmentalist violence. Their potential and their limitations as a social force can best be eval-

uated by looking at the different organizing styles, habits, and his-
tories of three of the movement's scrappy, meat-eating "old dogs":
Ron Arnold, Chuck Cushman, and Bill Grannell.

In terms of media presence, Ron Arnold is to Wise Use/Property
Rights what Randall Terry of Operation Rescue is to the Right-to-
Life movement, Pat Buchanan is to the Republican party, and
Reverend Al Sharpton is to civil rights. He has taken a personal
bitterness against the environmental movement, the organizing
theories of Lenin, the collective-behavior analysis of a couple of
professors in the social movements field, and a broad reading of
Abraham Maslow and other social psychologists, and synthesized
them into a new force on the political Right that sees environmental change as an imminent threat to free enterprise, private
property, and industrial civilization.

In 1979 Ron began to develop a theory that industry could no
longer stand alone, that it needed a grassroots movement to fight
for its goals. When he joined up with New Right fundraiser Alan
Gottlieb in 1984, he gained the means and wherewithal to begin
mobilizing that constituency. Labeled one of the top ten "Enemies of the Earth" in a *People* magazine poll of environmental organizers, Arnold bills himself as the chief theorist and
philosopher of Wise Use.

If you leave downtown Seattle heading east across Lake Washington's floating bridge, you quickly come to Bellevue, an edge
city with a recently constructed core of ten- and twenty-story
copper-colored glass low-rises, upscale hotels, and flippy neon
shopping malls. On the edge of this edge city is a woodsy business
park containing a two-story brown cedar complex called "Liberty
Park." The owner is New Right wunderkind Alan Gottlieb, a di-
minutive, forty-five-year-old businessman with the attentive,
wet-eyed look of an intelligent mole. Liberty Park, to which Gottlieb took title following a series of creative real estate transactions
in 1982 and 1987 involving himself, his wife, and the nonprofit
foundations he runs (the foundations paid over $700,000 for Lib-
erty Park, but the Gottliebs ended up owning it), is home to the

Center for the Defense of Free Enterprise (CDFE), Citizens Committee for the Right to Keep and Bear Arms, the Second Amendment Foundation, and the Co-op Service Bureau, which operates his mainframe computers and phone banks. Other conservative groups, such as the American Freedom Coalition, Accuracy in Media, and various county secessionists, tax rebels, and anti-abortionists, used to rent space at Liberty Park but have since moved on.

Alan is one of a handful of direct-mail fundraisers columnist George Will once called "quasi-political entrepreneurs who have discovered commercial opportunities in merchandising discontent. . . ."[14] A number of his compatriots on the Right have accused him of personally profiting from his causes. One example: In 1991 his Second Amendment Foundation (SAF), which he calls the smaller, "intellectual" part of his progun operations, paid him $35,000 as part-time director at large plus another $51,000 in rent (the *Seattle Times* reported that his nonprofits were paying him twice the fair market value for commercial rental space). The foundation also paid $474,512 to Alan's for-profit Co-op Service Bureau for data processing and other services, and $327,760 to Merril Associates, his for-profit marketing and publishing company. More than half the $1.75 million raised by SAF that year went directly to Alan Gottlieb or the corporations he controls.[15] In addition to his fundraising and publishing operations, Alan Gottlieb also maintains part interest in a couple of television stations, a radio station (KBNP-AM in Portland, Oregon, which he purchased in partnership with his two gun foundations—although the foundations appear to have provided all the cash), and a radio syndication network. "We own the western air waves at one A.M. in the morning," he brags.

Alan, who was raised in a liberal New York Jewish family, traces his political conversion to his reading as a teenager Barry Goldwater's *The Conscience of a Conservative* (as an adult he chose to make a religious conversion to Catholicism). At the University of Tennessee in the late 1960s, Alan became involved in YAF, the Young Americans for Freedom, a pro–Vietnam War group with a reputation for attracting clean-cut white males who would rather attend a William Buckley speech than a Rolling Stones concert. "You didn't join YAF to meet a girl, that's for sure," Alan admits with a laugh. "Most members, a lot of them anyway, were over-weight and had acne."

Thin and smooth-skinned, Alan quickly advanced to a leader-ship position in the group, becoming national head of Youth Against McGovern and the Student Committee to Keep and Bear Arms (which evolved into his Citizens Committee). Like Dan Quayle and other Vietnam War supporters of a certain class and disposition, Gottlieb volunteered to serve his country in the Na-tional Guard. In 1970 he ran the conservative youth campaigns of Senate candidates Jim Buckley in New York and Bill Brock in Ten-nessee. Brock ran against and defeated Senator Al Gore, Senior, the vice president's father. "I did this radio spot with this ad agency. We used the voice of a good Tennessee dirt farmer," Alan recalls, faking a southern drawl. " 'Where was Al Gore when our boys were fighting in Vietnam? Was he in Tennessee fighting for us? Was he in Washington fighting for us? No. He was in New York City at an antiwar moratorium!' We played up New York, where I was from, knowing how all New Yorkers are hated in Tennessee. We played off patriotism for the war and Tennessee as the vol-unteer state. At the end the farmer says, 'I'm a lifelong Democrat but I can't vote for Albert Gore.' It was a devastating spot, real fun," Alan grins, unembarrassed by the memory.

After moving to Seattle, Alan got involved in direct-mail mar-keting. "My first campaign was for a ballot measure for farm-workers' protection here in Washington. It was a very well written measure. It protected farmworkers so they wouldn't be taken ad-vantage of by farmers, but at the same time protected them from Cesar Chavez, from organized labor."

In 1977, working through his friend Richard Viguerie's mailing house, Alan sent out half a million Citizens Committee fundrais-ing letters reading, "From Congressman ———" with local rep-resentatives' names in the blanks. The only problem was, many of these congressmen hadn't agreed to let their names be used.

"I cannot believe there is anyone in the Congress more op-posed to gun-control legislation than I am," said Republican Representative Robert Walker of Pennsylvania. "However, I cannot and will not condone this kind of irresponsible special-interest appeal for money." When Walker called Gottlieb to demand a retraction of the letter on which his name appeared, Gottlieb hung up on him. Congressman Bob Carr, a Michigan Democrat and gun-control advocate, was even more upset by the progun solicitation that went out under his name. "It is gross and wanton fraud to use my name in a way that implied that I favor something that I actually oppose," he howled. Claiming that it was all a mistake on Viguerie's part, Gottlieb's nonprofit gun committee agreed to return the funds they'd collected.[16]

Once he had his gun foundations and private business ventures under way, Alan decided to launch a new project, a probusiness bicentennial think tank called the Center for the Defense of Free Enterprise.

In a corner space on the second floor of Liberty Park, Ron Arnold has found a comfortable niche and platform as CDFE's executive vice president. He shares an outer office with Alan's secretary. On the walls behind him and to the side are several kitschy pictures of cowboys, killer whales, and Karl Marx lighting his cigar with a dollar bill. Alan's larger inner office is decorated with original art work of cowboys, neon guns, and bullets.

Since Ron Arnold came aboard in 1984, the center has distinguished itself from a plethora of other right-wing think tanks by focusing its attacks on environmentalism and producing seminars, conferences, "battle books," radio spots, and numerous direct-mail funding pitches aimed at spreading the anti-enviro Wise Use message. Alan has also led fundraising seminars for a number of other anti-enviro leaders, including Chuck Cushman, Clark Collins, and William Perry Pendley. Of the $12 million a year he brings in with his direct-mail operations, about $2 million goes to various anti-environmental clients.[17] The year Ron Arnold joined the center, 1984, was also the year Alan served eight months of a one-year federal prison sentence for tax evasion. In 1978 he'd claimed an income of just over $17,000 but forgot to report some personal expenditures, including $10,000 he spent on his fiancee's engagement ring and $8,000 that went into his stamp collection. His parents refused to confirm his story that he'd borrowed the money from them. His lawyer then called the charges politically motivated, an accusation Gene Anderson, the Reagan-appointed U.S. attorney prosecuting the case, called "infantile."[18]

Still, a man like Alan Gottlieb, both personally pleasant and able to generate cash faster than an ATM, does not lose friends over small things like felony tax convictions. "I'm well aware of his classic battle with the Internal Revenue Service. I've seen him go through meat-grinder situations and come out stronger than ever," wrote (then) Senator Steve Symms of Idaho in his introduction to Alan's self-published book, *The Gun Grabbers*.[19] CDFE's recent congressional supporters include Republican Senators Alfonse D'Amato of New York, Ted Stevens of Alaska, and Jesse Helms of North Carolina. Its 1992 list of Distinguished Advisors included former Secretary of Defense Dick Cheney, Chuck Cushman of National Inholders, and Richard Ichord of the American Freedom Coalition.

CDFE claims a membership mailing list of 125,000, 52,000 of whom, according to Gottlieb, can be counted on to pay their dues. Of this group all but 8,000 are Wise Use members, he says. Ron Arnold claims that of these 44,000, about 14,000 are "hardcore activists," although it would be difficult to image anyone as hard-core as Ron himself.

I ask Ron about his distinctive beard. "I've worn it this way since I was twenty-three," he tells me, sounding oddly defensive. "Preservationist journalists have attacked me, claiming it's a Mennonite or an Amish beard." In a December 1991 article titled "Brown Fellas," *Outside* magazine described Ron as "a dour man with a Mennonite beard."[20] For the sake of accuracy, it should be noted that the beard is a full snowy white facial adornment sans mustache, a classic full-lipped patriarch's beard of nondenominational character. The only other person I've ever met with a beard like Ron Arnold's is C. Everett Koop, the AIDS- and cancer-fighting surgeon general under Ronald Reagan. Koop is a larger man than Arnold, with a broader face and lively blue eyes.

Ron's slate-colored eyes are cool and wary behind a pair of metal-frame glasses. At fifty-six, tall, trim, and trenchant, Ron is perhaps the most competent Wise Use leader when it comes to press relations. He understands the value of a good quote. During our eight-hour interview, he will periodically toss out little prepackaged sound bites as if chumming for media sharks. "King Bruce Babbitt will generate a genuine insurrection in this country," he'll say, referring to the mild-mannered secretary of Interior. Or, "The National Park Service is an empire designed to eliminate all private property in the United States."

I'm reminded of the Guatemalan army major who told me that the North American Jew Sol Linowitz was the main agent of the Communist International in the Carter White House. Ron once told a reporter he was the Darth Vader of the capitalist revolution, but now prefers to quote Princess Leia, identifying Wise Use with the federation forces battling the evil empire of environmentalism. He has the complete Star Wars trilogy in movie-screen letterbox format at home, a dark, tree-shaded, four-bedroom ranchhouse set back from a pleasant residential street three minutes from the office. He understands the mythic power of the Skywalker cowboy archetype that George Lucas created three years before Ronald Reagan cantered into the White House, although Arnold himself seems closer in spirit to a postmodern riverboat gambler, calculating the odds as he ups the ante.

Born in Houston, Texas, in 1937 at the tail end of the Depression, Ron was abandoned by his father as a toddler. With his mother incapacitated by illness, he was adopted and raised by his grandparents, who moved to San Antonio when he was eight. His grandfather ran a hobby shop, where Ron worked after school. He played French horn in the high school band. On Saturday nights the band would play on the riverbanks of the Río San Antonio.

The river has since evolved into a major tourist mecca of outdoor cafes, shops, and malls, but San Antonio remains best known for the Alamo, a surprisingly small stone and adobe fort where Davy Crockett, Jim Bowie, and other Anglo heroes of the West fell in the battle for Texas independence. The Alamo seems an appropriate symbol for Ron Arnold's coming of age. Today Ron must

feel similarly besieged trying to build a counterforce to environmentalism. It's got to be hard arguing that the only real ecological
problem facing America is "preservationist hysteria" when the
dominant culture offers network miniseries on global warming,
NASA shuttle flights to study the ozone hole, General Norman
Schwartzkopf joining The Nature Conservancy, and green business books like *Costing the Earth* and *The E Factor* infiltrating
business schools and corporate management seminars. There's
even the national Color Marketing Group announcing that "the
colors of 1995" will include "cricket: a bright, clean, soothing,
healing, back-to-nature color"; "coastal: an environmental color
that captures the essence of clear water"; and "everglade: the
color of new growth, a fresh green devoted to regeneration."[21]

After high school, Ron attended the University of Texas for a
year before drifting west in 1956 with a couple of buddies, ending
up in Seattle. There he met a young woman, got married, and
found work assembling B-52 bombers for Boeing. Eventually, after taking a few courses at the University of Washington, he became a production illustrator and computer graphics artist for
Boeing. He worked on a range of government contracts, from the
SST supersonic transport to the B-70 bomber. "We had some
weird stuff going through there in the sixties, like the moon rover
and all sorts of top-secret gear, including giant lathes for the Sat-
urn booster O rings," he recalls. "I couldn't believe NASA found
guys dumb enough to sit on top of rockets built by the lowest bid-
der, but they did."

Ron went through a lot of turbulence in his personal life during
those years. He's been married three times and has a schizo-
phrenic adult daughter from his first marriage. He lost a son in
infancy before his second wife, Phoebe, an opera singer, died of
a brain tumor. "They misdiagnosed it as a nervous breakdown.
She spent time with a shrink and when she got worse was put into
an institution for six weeks. But when her motor functions began
going, that indicated there was an organic cause. She was operated on and they removed a tumor the size of a tennis ball. The
doctor told me she had nine months left to live. Her shrink suggested I not tell her or our daughter Andrea. He said, 'Why have

death hanging over them when you could be helping them to live life to the fullest?' In a way I regret I listened to him, and I didn't tell them. I developed an ulcer instead. But we did have a wonderful time. We got a mobile home, toured all over the country, went to Disneyland. When Phoebe went back into the hospital, I remember going to pick up my little daughter from the babysitter. I said, 'Mom is in the hospital again.' She said, 'Will she die?' I told her yes. Then she looked at me and said, 'If we're alone we'd better take good care of each other.' To hear this greatness of spirit coming from this six-year-old child is something I'll never forget."

He goes on to rhapsodize about his daughter, as many fathers will. Andrea's a Stanford graduate, plays cello with the Seattle Philharmonic, and has written a book, *Fear of Food: Environmentalist Scams, Media Mendacity, and the Law of Disparagement*, for the center's Free Enterprise Press. "She's brilliant," says Ron. "She had an IQ of 176 last time we tested her. Mine's only 163."

In 1974, a year after his second wife died, Ron married his current wife, Janet. "It was love at first sight," he says with a rare smile.

Surprisingly, it was Ron's recreational interests that would turn into an obsession and new career path. In 1960 he joined the Sierra Club, which he saw primarily as a hiking outfit. "I hiked all the trails in the Olympics, some seven hundred miles. It was great. I was young and fit and would keep running into these other backpackers, most of whom belonged to this group, so I joined." He took a Sierra Club mountain climbing course but was terrified when he got up onto the rockface. "I thought they were really crazy. It seemed like a good way to kill yourself," he recalls. "After a while the club suggested I join their conservation group, and we began doing these industrial tours on the weekends, dog and pony shows put on by the timber companies and dam builders. Brock Evans was the Northwest lobbyist for Sierra back then. I did some slide shows for the club in sixty-five with two projectors synched to music and narration. It was a big thing at the time, similar to the work I was doing at Boeing for the SST."

But the defense plant design man soon began to feel out of place among the generally liberal, antiwar heirs of John Muir. "Sierra was getting very political in the sixties. I was familiar with how they exaggerated and stretched the truth in their conservation campaigns and I didn't mind that. Still, I could see how they were changing from a nature and hiking orientation to more rabid environmentalism," he claims.

In the late sixties, Ron began working with the Alpine Lakes Protection Society, which he says was funded by a small Sierra Club grant. He recalls spending several years hiking and charting a proposed area for wilderness and multiple-use forest designation, drawing maps, and putting together a slide show of the backcountry's hidden wonders. "At the last minute the Sierra bigwigs came in and expanded the wilderness area. Our more moderate multiple-use proposal was sabotaged," he complains.

He then tells of his moment of apostasy, when the scales fell from his eyes and he saw environmentalists revealed for the power-hungry elitists they really were, a story he's repeated hundreds of times over the last two decades.

"We had this guy come into one of our meetings with some photos of a deck of logs that had fallen into a creek. I knew enough about the timber industry by that time to see that it was a mistake, that these were some valuable logs, that the couplings maybe broke on them without the yarding crew's knowledge. And I said to Brock, 'Look, I know Weyerhauser's cleanup guy. Why don't I call him?' And Brock looked at me and said, 'Our demographers tell us environmentalism only has two or three years of public popularity left. Why give that company a chance if we can smear them now?' It ended up as legislation by headline, with that picture of those downed logs running in the newspaper. That's when I realized they didn't give a damn about saving that creek or the forests or anything. They were only interested in their own political clout."

"That sounds like horseshit of the highest order," says Brock Evans, now vice president in charge of national affairs at Audubon. "Basically I remember Ron as a weird loner kind of guy. I don't think I ever spoke to him much at all. I remember he had a slide show he wanted to sell to us on Alpine Lakes, and we said, 'Look, we're a volunteer group. We don't really have the money for that.' He got disgruntled and quit a short time later. Some people thought he might have been a plant when he turned around right away and started attacking us at these forestry council meetings in 1970. You have to remember this was in the Nixon era, and that sort of thing, political spying, wasn't uncommon."

Dave Knibb, a Seattle-based attorney who was active in the Alpine Lakes Protection Society, also questions Ron's reconstruction of events. "I think it helps Ron's cause to say he was betrayed in some dramatic way, but I just remember that he was never really in step with us philosophically. And as time went on he felt less and less comfortable and just kind of faded from the scene.

"I think Ron might have gotten involved with ALPS because it was a smaller group than Sierra and he could gain more recognition. We never got any grant money from Sierra. He's wrong about that. We got more closely aligned with them years later when we were getting the Alpine Lakes legislation through Congress, but nobody felt like we'd been sold out. We thought it was a great victory.

"Ron had a special talent for putting together these slide shows with sound and narration," Knibb continues. "And when he offered his services, we thought that was wonderful. The one he did for us was great, and we used it a lot but that was pretty much the extent of his role. I don't remember his making any maps or doing any surveys. I do remember he always asked questions that were different from the kinds of questions everyone else was asking at the time. Some people in the group were very suspicious of him, but I tried to give him the benefit of the doubt. He appeared to me to be very gullible. He'd already quit Boeing and was working for timber companies for his bread and butter and would say, 'My clients in the timber industry told me this, and isn't this the truth?' He was easily led astray, was my impression."

By 1971 Ron had left Boeing and started his own graphics company. "The first business I got was the result of work I'd done in the Sierra Club," he says, going on to describe a $6,000 slide show he produced for Simpson Timber. He did thirty to forty films for

Weyerhauser and a slide-show history of floor waxing for the GAO. "I was familiar with industrial processes. I had developed this vast knowledge of industry and of resources and of how fragile the whole system of economic interdependence was, and I understood our opponents wanted to destroy industry and transfer power into their own hands," he explains. He soon began giving anti-environmentalist lectures and became a contract writer for various industry publications, including *Coal Age* and *Agrochemical Age*. In 1977 he was hired by three lumber companies— Simpson, Arcada, and Louisiana Pacific—to fight the expansion of the Redwood National Park in California. "I told them, 'Look, you can't win. Redwoods are a sacred cow, but I can help you give away only half of what they want and make them pay you top dollar for that.'" As part of his antipark campaign, he helped organize a convoy of twenty logging trucks from California to Washington, D.C., arranging for them to do three laps around the Indianapolis speedway en route.

In 1979 Ron wrote a series of articles for *Logging Management Magazine*, warning industry against attempts at compromise with the environmental movement. For his hardline advocacy, he was chosen by the Committee for a Free Congress, Paul Weyrich's New Right action group, to pen a subsidized biography of Reagan's first secretary of Interior, James Watt. Following the 1982 publication of *At the Eye of the Storm: James Watt and the Environmentalists*, Ron gained popularity as a speaker for chemical manufacturers such as Dow and Union Carbide looking to counter the growing antipesticide movement in the Northwest and Canada. In a 1981 lecture to the Washington State Weed Control Association, he declared that "antichemical activists are the world's number one crop pest. Once you recognize that, you must treat them like a noxious weed or a pernicious disease that attacks public opinion and public policy. They are just another hostile organism that must be controlled."[22]

In another industry presentation, he suggested an effective fumigant. "We can't let motives go by without mentioning the fact that marijuana cultivators do not like pesticides at all because some of them kill their cash crop. I have found that the public has come to realize and accept this motive of antipesticide activists as a fact. If you find such a motive to be credible in your local situation, I would strongly suggest that you do everything possible to associate the word *antipesticide* with the word *marijuana*. Keep hammering at that one long enough and it may do more to win your ultimate battles than all the science you can ever get someone to listen to."[23]

In 1984 Alan Gottlieb, in the middle of raising $10 million for the Reagan re-election campaign, was browsing in a D.C. bookstore, looking at the flyleaf of James Watt's biography, when he saw that the author was based in Bellvue. Returning home, he gave Ron a call and the two of them got together. "Reagan was killing us at the time," Alan recalls without irony. Like other conservative fundraising outfits, the center was losing its base of support as the Reagan administration made everything else on the Right seem redundant. Ron pitched Alan his idea for building a movement that would target "runaway environmentalism."

"At the time, we picked it up and played with it only because we really didn't have a good issue for the center to sink its teeth into," Alan admits ten years later. "It worked out far better than I would have predicted. I've never seen anything pay out as quickly as this whole Wise Use thing has done. What's really good about it is it touches the same kind of anger as the gun stuff, and not only generates a higher rate of return but also a higher average dollar donation. My gun stuff runs about $18. The Wise Use stuff breaks $40."

Once ensconced at CDFE, Ron began turning out a series of books and working with fellow anti-enviros such as former insurance salesman and national parks nemesis Chuck Cushman. "Throughout the seventies, I'd known what the problem was but didn't have a solution to offer industry in my talks and seminars," Ron recalls. "Then I read *People, Power, Change* by Luther Gurlick and Virginia Hayne, and their analysis helped me to realize that in an activist society like ours the only way to defeat a social movement is with another social movement. So now we had a nonprofit mechanism to work with and told industry, let us help you to organize our constituencies."

People, Power, Change is a minor work in social movements theory that nonetheless reflects the progressive changes that overtook the field in the late 1960s and early seventies. Going back to the late nineteenth century, Gustave Le Bon, known as the father of social psychology, had written *The Crowd*, in which democracy and popular social movements were seen as a pathological break with traditional (or "natural") hierarchies. At the beginning of the twentieth century, sociological theories tried to explain social movements through analogies with nature. Lyford Edwards, for example, thought revolutions were like elephants, slow-breeding but powerful creatures. Harvard's Talcott Parsons wrote *The Structure of Social Action*, introducing "unit acts" theory, which viewed societal goals as determined by the inputs of various social units in an almost mathematical formulation paralleling the mechanistic economic theories of Adam Smith.

In 1957 Parsons's student Neil Smeleser wrote *Theory of Collective Behavior*, a book that analyzed crowd psychology from a normative point of view. Crowds and disruptive social groups were compared to electrical "short circuits" in the smooth functioning of society. This theory of social aberrance made sense in the context of the 1950s, with its invisible underclass of Negro ghettos and rural sharecroppers. This was a time when only Beatniks and Communists were perceived as standing outside the dominant paradigm, and society's response to a perceived threat was to short-circuit Julius and Ethel Rosenberg, the so-called atom bomb spies, at Sing Sing prison.

However, with the emergence of the civil rights and antiwar movements of the 1960s, oppositional groupings were seen as having a rational basis rather than simply being an irrational response to a rational society, and sociologists turned from looking at crowds to analyzing organized, long-term social movements. John McCarthy at Catholic University and Meyer Zald at the University of Michigan developed a "resource mobilization theory," arguing that social movements were as strong as the resources— people, money, and media—they could mobilize. Anthony Oberschall wrote about "rational calculation," suggesting that social movements exist because people know they can gain more through their participation. In 1971, responding to conservative social critics such as Eric Hoffer and Bruno Bettelheim, Gurlack and Haynes wrote their book *People, Power, Change,* closely following the better-known models established by McCarthy, Zald, and Oberschall in recognizing the catalytic role social movements can play in pluralistic societies such as the United States and Canada. Exposed to collective behavior theory through this relatively obscure work, Ron adopted a utilitarian/evangelical approach to social change, preaching the need for industry to support anti-environmental groups. "Give them the money. You stop defending yourselves, let them do it, and you get the hell out of the way. Because citizens' groups have credibility and industries don't," he preached.[24]

Along with identifying the need to create proindustry grassroots, Ron was also among the first on the political Right to link environmentalism with communism. As real communism faded towards oblivion around 1990, this trend would become increasingly popular with right-wing think tankers, magazines, and conservative pundits such as George Will and Pat Buchanan.

In a 1984 talk to a pesticide trade group in Canada, Ron explained how "the Soviet Union would never allow such a thing as a wilderness area in which valuable resources of petroleum or timber or nonfuel minerals could never be extracted, yet they encourage the Free World to voluntarily lock up more and more of their natural resources from economic production. . . . Environmentalism is an already existing vehicle by which the Soviet Union can encourage the Free World to voluntarily cripple its own economy."[25]

The following year, Ron speculated that the Union Carbide disaster in Bhopal, India, which killed twenty-five hundred people, might not be his former client's fault. "Sabotage is not far-fetched," he wrote. "The Soviets were certainly the propaganda beneficiaries. What really happened? We may never know. It may be another failure of human technology. But it could also be another Soviet mass murder."[26] He also wrote that Fernando Pereira, a photographer killed in 1985 when French secret agents bombed the Greenpeace ship *Rainbow Warrior*, was "reported to be" a contact agent for terrorists and the KGB.[27]

Ron's ongoing travels in Canada, helping timber giants such as MacMillan Bloedel set up proindustry groups, did not go unnoticed by that nation's media and politicians, whose fear of foreign meddling was not limited to the Soviet Union. A 1992 report by the Canadian Library of Parliament, entitled *Share Groups in British Columbia*, states that "the forest companies have provided these 'local citizens coalitions' with much of their organizational impetus and financial backing. Their apparent objective has been to pit labour against environmentalists and environmentally-oriented persons. Their effect has been to divide communities and create animosity in the very places where honest communication and consensus should be encouraged.

"While the rank and file membership of the Share movement may not be aware of its connection with the Wise Use movement," the government report continues, "the tactics and language of the two movements indicate a common source of counseling and training, namely Ron Arnold and his associates."[28]

Today Ron is promoting a new threat: his own people's potential for violence and insurrection. In the course of one interview, he brings up this possibility eight times. "Things are so regulated and restricted that people are sensing themselves as an oppressed class, and that's how you get revolutions," he'll say. Or "Try telling a logger who's lost his job and house and whose neighbor is molesting his daughter because he has nothing else to do that he should remain nonviolent—that we'd rather see him work within the system. I've had calls in the middle of the night to talk to a guy who was armed and wanted to kill someone, an environmentalist or whoever. I've driven two hundred miles to tell him, 'Listen, you silly son of a bitch, this will just get you killed and the government will be in here with army regulars and cannons. There'll be nothing left of your town.'"

I ask Ron why he thinks President Clinton held a Forest Summit in Portland, Oregon, rather than an Auto Summit in Detroit, where GM has laid off more than a hundred thousand people, more workers than are employed in Northwest logging.

"There's not a civil war rising there," he claims unblinkingly. "There are not people there ready to march with guns." I must look somewhat skeptical, thinking that Ron might never have been to Detroit. "Ask the FBI," Ron tells me. "They're very concerned and they should be. There's a war brewing."

Wise Use organizer Chuck "Rent-a-Riot" Cushman spends much of his time on the road.

"I try and get people to let go of their anger and have some fun," says Chuck to the crowd of sixty-five timber workers, ranchers, and lobbyists gathered in a conference room of the Sacramento Raddisson Hotel for a meeting of the Alliance for Environment and Resources (AER). Chuck has turned down the offer of a dais and microphone. He's more comfortable pacing, getting close to his audience, taking off his jacket, putting it down, picking it up, moving around, laughing, letting them see what he's made of.

"How many of you have heard me talk before?" he asks. About half the people in the small audience raise their hands.

"What's your biggest problem right now? You think it's timber supply, but I think it's [Democratic Senators] Boxer and Feinstein, because there's no balance left. So either we're going to have a second Boxer rebellion or have to do something to offset these guys. . . . This desert [protection] bill is your first opportunity to fight. It's an opportunity for you to say to Dianne Feinstein, 'Your pollsters are all wet. I'm going to fight you on the desert and make this a statewide issue.' If that bill passes and they create a national park down there, you know the Sierras are next. I've always said wilderness is like aspirin. Two are good for you; one hundred will put you in the hospital."

While not as big as all outdoors, Chuck Cushman still cuts an impressive figure at 6'2" and 260 pounds, with his wattle-hugging white beard, lively blue eyes, and toothy, bad-boy grin. The most active anti-enviro field organizer in the United States, Cushman operates the National Inholders Association and other letterhead organizations out of a rambling farmhouse in Battle Ground, Washington. He figures he attends six to eight meetings a month, many with small local groups, providing them with needed resources and inspiration. Others he advises by fax and phone. His speech to the AER meeting follows the same broad outline, including many of the same anecdotes I'll hear repeated, live and on tape, at half a dozen meetings in California, Washington, Nevada, and Michigan.

"The preservationists have become like a new religion, a new paganism that worships trees and sacrifices people," he tells his listeners. "They say they want to be reasonable, they want 50 percent. So you agree and go on with your life. Five years later they're back. And what do they want? Fifty percent. Understand that these guys have a gun at your head and they want to take what you've got. So you're going to have to draw a line in the sand somewhere. The key to this is creating controversy because that opens people's minds. . . . Our side always wants to fight with facts, with truth. The other side is fighting with perception. Congress operates on perception, not reality. It doesn't matter what's true. It's what people *believe* is true and what people contacting them believe is true. So we have two jobs to do: education and building public awareness. But we also have to drive up the front steps with people so that they get the perception that all hell is going to break loose if they don't allow some of our people to survive.

"What are the three most important words in political action?" he asks rhetorically. "*Lists, lists, lists.* If you don't have a list you're not in the game. We have a list on computer of every miner in the country, every rancher who has a grazing permit, every timber purchaser on federal land. Every special use permittee in a national forest. This is not rocket science to realize we have to stay competitive with the other side. The next most important words are *network, network, network.* So, okay. Let's talk solutions."

He's got his audience paying attention now. Some are even leaning forward in their chairs.

"First of all, try and be nonpartisan, be team players," he tells them, moving around, smiling, working the room like the top-flight insurance salesman he once was. "Encourage entrepreneurship, encourage new groups to form. Bring in other multiple-use groups. Make it fun, share information. Put aside anger. . . . Let me give you some examples of how we've helped people be creative. How many of you have heard of Jim Jontz? He was a congressman in Indiana, past tense. The timber industry played a big role getting him defeated in Indiana. This is the arch enemy of the timber industry. Let me tell you a brief story— but if that tape recorder's on, could I get you to turn it off while I tell this story?" The tape recorder is turned off.

"We were going to picket Jim Jontz's office the day he announced the Ancient Forest bill. As a dig at Jim, Congressman Don Young [Republican from Alaska] had introduced a bill to declare Jontz's Indiana district an ancient forest. We asked Young to reintroduce it while we demonstrated, but he didn't have the time. We said, 'You do it. We'll cover the PR.' So we put out nationwide press faxes from our office, changing the internal ID and time code on our nine machines to make it look like it was coming from Young's office in D.C. Next, we redid the machines and put out protest fax releases that looked like they were coming out of Indiana, saying, 'Why the hell is Jontz messing with this forest stuff instead of taking care of business here at home?' I had a list of the Indiana talk-radio stations, and we flooded them with calls from people in the Northwest saying they were calling from Jontz's district and why did this other congressman want to turn Kokomo into a national forest? It was a stealth operation. We had a lot of fun with it."

With the tape running again, Cushman tells a few of his other favorite war stories.

"We heard that Congressman Ron Wyden [Democrat from Oregon] was going to have a hearing in Portland on retraining loggers. He hadn't done a thing to help loggers up to that point. I called up this friend of mine and said, 'I need to know the name of the biggest logger you know.' And he said, 'There's Nils Madson, about 6'6" and 320.' I talked to Nils and said, 'Come dressed for work and bring the biggest chainsaw you can find,' and he came down in front of Wyden's office with that chainsaw on his back and we put a sign on him saying, 'Congressman Wyden, I want to be retrained. I want to be your brain surgeon.'"

He segues into his next story. "Last year the preservationists were going to propose a bill called the High Desert Preservation Act [sic] in eastern Oregon. They said they wanted to eliminate ranching and announced that they were going to have this conference at a place called the Malheur Field Station. So we were asked to come down and show these local folks, who had a lot of anger, how to do something that was nonviolent and fun. We did a silent protest. We got the ranchers prepared with signs at this place way out in the middle of the desert, and I had them walk inside this building where the preservationists were meeting and up each side of the aisles and just turn in towards these people and for the next two hours we didn't say a word. This preservationist guy was visibly nervous and stumbled over his speech. All their speeches were screwed up; they could hardly talk. And then, when the head guy gets up to talk, I had everyone move in about two feet. It made them feel like the building got smaller. Worked great. We had lots of press, lots of fun. That's 1991. In 1992 people called me up and said, 'They're doing it again.' Now, our people had had so much fun the previous year, we had lots of new folks. So visualize a mile-and-a-half-long line of cars, coming over this dusty hill just as the sun is rising. Imagine Butch Cassidy and the Sundance Kid. Who *are* those guys? If I was a preservationist waiting there looking out for us, like I know they were, I would have run for the head real fast. Anyway, we came up and they'd moved into this metal building maybe twenty feet from the road and we brought with us two logging trucks and two cattle trucks and we pulled the cattle trucks on either side and we put the mama cows in one truck and the baby cows in the other truck and for the next three hours we had stereophonic cow." This gets a big laugh from his audience. "They couldn't hear themselves think. A national newspaper story said '. . . through the din of bawling cattle.'"

The "national newspaper" was the *Portland Oregonian*, which reported, "About seventy-five people picketed the conference at the Malheur Wildlife Refuge, thirty miles south of Burns, Saturday. Signs carried slogans such as 'Save the Desert, Plant a Preservationist,' and protestors marched to the accompanying din from bawling, stamping cattle in two, huge metal stock trucks."[29] The article went on to reprint the poem that Scott Greacen, one of 170 people attending the environmentalist conference, recited to the 75 ranchers:

> Thank you for coming and bringing the press.
> A well-informed public will help us clean up your mess.
> You'll give us some grief, but the conference is full.
> 'Cause we don't want your beef, and we don't need your bull.

The *Oregonian* also quoted "protest organizer" Chuck Cushman as accusing environmentalists of "systematic, cultural genocide of rural America."

Rural Clark County, Washington, across the river from Portland, is a reminder of why zoning has become popular over the last seventy years. Turning off the highway past the Volcano View Llama Ranch, you pass by beer delis, gas stations, and garden supply stores, drive through a quiet county park, pass a few struggling truck farms and a large cluster development of identical tract homes looking out of place in a weedy green field. In several yards stand double-width trailers, old trucks, or satellite dishes. By an unpainted barn, a small herd of cows grazes, and next to their owners' new exurban ranchettes, several horses and ponies are corralled. Beyond the clutter of dying agriculture and new real estate construction is a stunning view of snow-capped Mount St. Helens.

I pull in at the fifteen-acre "Cushbaum Farm." It's named for Chuck and his "spouselike person," Christine Bauman, who are in the process of breaking up, even though the property is still in her name. As a property rights activist, Chuck Cushman seems to have an ambiguous relationship to real property. Aside from the farm bought in his girlfriend's name, he has two park inholdings (private lots within a public park—one in his son's name) and a string of tax liens, small claims, and civil losses totaling more than $20,000 in the California counties of Tulare and Sonoma. While living in Sonoma before moving to Battle Ground in 1991, he also twice defaulted on a $50,000 home mortgage.[30]

The front yard of the farmhouse is planted in decorative wooden pinwheels. Half a dozen cars and vans are pulled into the drive. In addition to the brown three-bedroom farmhouse there's a prefab garage, a flat-topped red building, and an old dairy barn where Christine keeps her Vietnamese pot-bellied pigs. A possum recently killed the chickens, but there are still some ducks and three Pinscur beef cattle on the small spread.

At the back of the main house is an extra door leading to the office for National Inholders. Inside are a couple of copiers, two free-standing fax machines, and fax boards attached to half a dozen IBM clones. A heavy-set woman and two local teenage girls are busy at a long table doing Chuck's secretarial work. "Right now we have three ladies working here full-time. Well, one full-time, two part time. But that's because technically, according to the state, I'm only allowed one woman here. The others work very full part-time jobs," Chuck will later tell me with a conspiratorial grin. With its mismatched furniture, boxes of paper, yellowed carpet, and general sense of clutter, the office has the feel of a small-town environmental center without the wildlife posters or macrame wall hangings.

Chuck greets me dressed hobby-farm casual in jeans and a checked western-style shirt. His private office is a scene of impressive disorder, with piles of newspapers, reports, and open cardboard boxes on wall shelves labeled "mining law," "mailings," "land use," "receipts," and so forth.

"What I like is the combat, the excitement when the phones are all ringing and the faxes are going, and the office is full of people, and we're up all night, maybe contacting three or four thousand people. I just love it." He stops to take a phone call from Washington. Into the receiver he says, "I'm frustrated with [American Mining Congress attorney] Jack Gerard. Rome is burning and we're fiddling. What?" His brow furrows. "We're not going to lose on the mining law? All I can tell you is your perception and what's happening there don't jibe. We don't have team play. I can't get a call back from them unless I tell them it's an emergency. I can still get twenty to thirty thousand letters out, and I can get a few thousand comments on the record for the Senate hearings, but I don't have the resources right now. . . . I'm not taking in a dime. We can turn this around if you have the resources to help. We're down to the short hairs now. I spent three months building a relationship with them, but now either they don't know how to work with the grassroots or they don't care to. Industry is not taking advantage of all the tools available to it to save itself."

Chuck is a natural player, simultaneously making his funding pitch and making sure I'm getting down his end of the argument, shifting blame away from Wise Use in case the 1872 mining law goes down the tubes, which seems increasingly likely. He once interrupted an interview with another reporter for a call from Washington, explaining that Congress was about to take a crucial vote. "And they need your permission?" the reporter wondered.

Chuck was born and raised in the suburbs of Los Angeles, attending North Hollywood High where he wrestled and played football. His father Dwight, an L.A. teacher and former Boy Scout official, owned a cabin in Yosemite and worked there as a naturalist and interpreter during the summers (Chuck has told a number of rural audiences he was raised in Yosemite). In 1962 Dwight Cushman was forced to sell his cabin to the National Park Service or else lose his summer job. It was an injustice that would be long remembered and many times avenged by the oldest of his three sons.

Chuck's first brush with fame came in 1963, when, at the age of eighteen, he was profiled in the *Los Angeles Times* as Dodger Stadium's loudest, most successful peanut vendor. Within a few years he'd taken his sales abilities to a new level, becoming one of the top insurance salesmen in Los Angeles and Beverly Hills, for thirteen years in a row selling more than $1 million a year in coverage. He invested in property, including a private cabin inside the Yosemite park boundary (an inholding). In 1975 he divorced his first wife, with whom he'd had the first two of his four

children, and in 1977, suffering from migraine headaches, he retired on full disability and moved to South Lake Tahoe. A man of
boundless energy, Chuck bought a four-wheel-drive truck, had a
brief second marriage, and looked for other ways to keep himself
entertained. Then, on September 14, 1977, he received a letter
from the National Park Service saying cabin owners in Yosemite
were prohibited from modifying their homes or building on their
property and that new laws and regulations were under consideration to limit development inside national parks. In Chuck's
mind, this was a repeat of the abuse his father had suffered, although he claims not to have been immediately aroused to action.
"I didn't pay much attention to it until January of seventy-eight,"
he recalls, "when a group of six or eight of us met in a room at the
Holiday Inn in Sacramento and decided to form the Inholders Association. I had the time to work on it. Using Freedom of Information requests and threatening to sue one regional park
superintendent a week until I got the names, I got lists of other
inholders from the Park Service."

With those names, Chuck began a campaign of lawsuits and
protests targeting the Park Service. The Inholders Association
grew rapidly, forcing the Park Service bureaucracy to reform
some of its more arbitrary activities: to open up hearings on land
acquisitions and limit the use of condemnations against unwilling
sellers. But Chuck also developed a reputation for shooting from
the hip and the lip and for creating conflicts where none had previously existed.

In 1979, after an insurance investigator took note of his hectic
cross-country organizing schedule, Chuck's former employer,
Mutual of New York, cut off his disability payments. Chuck
briefly moved to Washington, D.C., as an antiparks lobbyist, but
didn't last long. "In Washington you dance together on Saturday
and beat each other's brains out on Monday," he tells anyone who
will listen. "I was better at the Monday part." Still, with Ronald
Reagan's election he found he had a number of new friends in
high places. John McClaughery, a senior policy analyst in the
White House, pressured James Watt to appoint Chuck to the National Parks System Advisory Board. "Chuck is a loud force, and

I figured he'd shake things up, which he did," McClaughery says.[31] Chuck recalls fondly the time he served alongside astronaut Wally Schirra, Lady Bird Johnson, and other distinguished board members. "I was the skunk at the lawn party," he says. He also met and became fast friends with Watt biographer Ron Arnold. "We're like brothers. I have absolute trust and faith in Ron," Chuck says today. When Ron hooked up with Alan Gottlieb, Chuck began taking fundraising courses from the sweet-natured New Right tax felon. He also developed contacts with the Farm Bureau and other groups that were likely to support him in his organizing against the National Park Service and any other agencies that might attempt to establish new federal parks, wildlife sanctuaries, or wilderness areas.

In the 1960s, the Army Corps of Engineers targeted the Middle Delaware River valley of New York State for a series of dams to provide power and water to New York and other big cities. Before the plans fell through, hundreds of rural residents had been forced from their homes. When the Park Service took over administrative control from the corps, it had houses bulldozed that had been occupied by squatters. By the mid-1970s, the Upper Delaware River had become a favorite recreational area for thousands of weekend canoeists from New York City. The local population was divided between those who favored the economic benefits of this new industry and those who disliked the impact of the mostly young, urban weekend partiers. In 1978, when Congress declared the Upper Delaware valley "wild and scenic" and ordered the Park Service to develop a land-use plan for it, the canoe outfitters began to fear that they would become a regulated park concession. After years of debate and discussion over land use, the outfitters hired Chuck to fly in and mobilize the local populace against the Park Service. It was here on February 6, 1984, dressed in his buckskins, that Chuck earned the moniker "Rent-a-Riot."

"They're going to come in and strangle you! You're going to lose your valley! The Park Service wants to get rid of you!" he shouted to the many valley people who had gathered that night at a local school gym. He warned that hunting and fishing would be restricted, farms and stores shut down, ancestral lands seized.[32] He still remembers the three-hour barn raiser of a presentation as something very special.

"I came to that meeting and it was a magic experience. There were nine hundred people in Eldred, New York, in this small brick schoolhouse gym. It wasn't far from where that big concert took place, Woodstock, and it had some of that electricity. People were standing there shoulder to shoulder in the middle of this snowstorm outside, and I showed a movie, *For All People for All Time*, that John McClaughery produced. And it showed the Park Service bulldozing thousands of homes, some not far from there, and these people were just stunned. That night someone slashed tires and painted a swastika on a Park Service vehicle, and that was the only thing that happened while I was there. It could have been some misguided person who was too upset to act effectively or it could have been something done to discredit us."

In the following weeks and months, a campaign of harassment against local environmental activists developed under the aegis of the Upper Delaware Alliance led by Don Rupp, a real estate agent still active with the property rights movement in New York and New England. When the *River Reporter,* the local newspaper, exposed numerous inaccuracies in Chuck's presentation, residents organized a boycott of the paper and threatened to burn down its office. By 1986 Rupp and his followers, having lost much of their local support, were disrupting public planning meetings and talking about tar and feathering town officials and burning out or shooting "traitors" who participated in the land-use process.[33] "Don Rupp wrote a letter to my paper saying he was in 'gorilla warfare' with the U.S.," recalls Glenn Pontier, editor and publisher of the *River Reporter.* "So we did an editorial cartoon of him as a gorilla jumping up and down on a conference table. A short time later my house burned down." Despite police and FBI investigations, no one was ever arrested in connection with the fire.

"I'm no apologist for the Park Service, but you cannot come in here and tell people they'll lose their homes and sow dissension and tear the fabric of a community apart and then walk away as if nothing happened," said Pontier. "That's what Cushman did, and I can never forgive him for that."

"Unfortunately," recalls Chuck, "there were some extreme conservative folks out there, and I had to sever my relationship with them. And as a result I got killed financially. They never paid me what they owed me."

Since that time Chuck has led dozens of other anti-enviro fights, helping to derail congressional funding for the National Heritage Trust and blocking a Tallgrass Prairie Reserve in Oklahoma and "Wild and Scenic River" listings in Washington and Oregon. "The only fight I ever lost was for the Columbia Gorge in Oregon," he claims.

The Niobrara River in northern Nebraska is a favorite recreation area for high-plains hunters, fishermen, and canoeists. It is known for its whooping cranes, wild turkeys, and bald eagles, its cool flowing waters, and its dramatic river bows and green mantled bluffs. In 1989 Chuck was hired by backers of a proposed 180-foot-high Bureau of Reclamation dam to organize opposition to a "Wild and Scenic River" listing for the Niobrara, protection that was passed into law by Congress in 1991.[34]

"We had a good time in Nebraska. We had a big parade and demonstration with a mile-long line of tractors and combines and angry farmers. But the problem was with the group there," Chuck explains. "They weren't all working together. We gave them the tools for the plans but they didn't follow through. Also, the *Omaha Herald* was outrageously biased against us. Still, we won," he insists, although others might count the "wild and scenic" designation as a loss for the dam builders. "We felt good that we got an improved bill from Congress that builds a high wall of protection for property owners," he explains, taking credit for agreements negotiated into the bill by local farmers opposed to the dam.

In 1991 NRA's Richard DeChambaugh put Cushman in touch with wine vintners and developers in Sacramento who were opposing the creation, on one of the last undeveloped green spaces left in California's Central Valley, of a 25,000-acre Stone Lakes National Wildlife Refuge. "If you like the IRS you'll love the Fish and Wildlife Service," Chuck warned a group of forty landowners he addressed in Walnut Grove, California, near the southern border of the proposed migratory waterfowl refuge. Shortly after Chuck's visit, opponents of the refuge formed the South Stone Lake Preservation Council.

Richard Spotts was the Sacramento representative of Defenders of Wildlife, one of the environmental groups supporting the refuge. "When Cushman came on the scene," he says, "it turned into what I'd call a borderline violent situation. I was incredibly heckled, and a couple of farmers came close to beating me up. Lots of environmentalists were so intimidated they left the hearings without testifying." A short time later, a nine-page letter went out to thousands of homes in the area signed by Marcie Spears, a "concerned mother and housewife," warning of the danger of killer mosquitoes. The letter explained that if the refuge was established, mosquito-borne encephalitis outbreaks could easily leave dead and brain-damaged children in its wake. "Don't get me wrong, I care very much about wildlife and the environment too," the letter read in part. "But this refuge just goes too far. If just one person dies or one child suffers permanent brain damage because of these extremists, I just couldn't live with myself if I didn't speak out."

The local Mosquito Control District, which favored the refuge, explained that the amount of water in the refuge during mosquito season would be smaller than what was already stagnating in the area's irrigation ditches. Contacted by reporter Glen Martin of the *San Francisco Chronicle*, Spears denied having written the letter, saying it was put together by several activists close to Cushman.[35] Chuck denies having had anything to do with the letter, but insists that killer mosquitoes are a legitimate issue of concern.

In 1992 Chuck got active in his home state and county around land-use and growth-management issues, helping to form the Washington Private Property Coalition, which paid him just under $2,000 a month as a part-time consultant (his normal rate is $500 to $1,500 a day plus expenses). He first organized his semi-rural Clark County neighbors against a proposed wetlands protection law, sending them letters warning that the county intended to take away their property and raise their taxes. The letter predicted that future regulations would "strangle and curtail farming and home ownership," and asked them for donations to help lead the resistance. Hundreds of people donated money and turned out for a series of public hearings, shouting down elected county officials and insisting on delays and revisions until, with police standing by to maintain order, the county agreed not to pursue any wetlands protection or set up any long-term land-use planning programs. In May 1992, the *Columbian*, Clark County's main newspaper, located in the Columbia River city of Vancouver, Washington, ran an in-depth profile of Chuck titled "The High Priest of Property Rights." In the article reporter Loretta Callahan quoted Robin Winkes, a Yale University history professor who had served with Chuck on the National Parks advisory board. "One of the things I always felt about his approach is, he starts with a grain of truth, then the sky is falling on your head," Winkes said. "The bottom line is, as a person, I kind of like Chuck. But I also think he's mischievous, dangerous, and often out of line."[36]

In 1993 Chuck and a Pacific Legal Foundation lawyer filed suit against Clark County for establishing a construction moratorium on cluster suburbs in rural areas. He also threatened to lead a secession movement in his semirural neighborhood. A *Columbian* editorial suggested he might want to name the new entity "Cushman County."

Chuck also continued to finance his hectic nationwide organizing efforts through fundraising. He claims he raises $300,000 a year and pays himself $35,000. Exact figures and parameters between Chuck's personal and organizational income are hard to come by, since the Inholders Association and his other groups are private, for-profit operations. "He was able to raise a great deal of money, but when it came in I didn't see him being responsible about how it got spent," Kathleen Rueve, one of his former bookkeepers, told the *Columbian*.[37]

Chuck claims that his National Inholders Association has sixteen thousand members who help finance its work. "Those names Chuck has are really more of a client list than a membership list," says Andy Neal, chief lobbyist for the California Farm Bureau. "We always get calls from Chuck and these other groups for money, and really all I see from Chuck is funding requests."

In trying to keep his accounts balanced, Chuck has borrowed large sums of money from several elderly members of the Inholders Association, failing to repay his debts until ordered to by a judge. In 1983 J. R. and Betty Tallackson, who owned land along a "Wild and Scenic River" near Oak Ridge, Tennessee, loaned NIA $6,700 on agreement that Chuck would pay it back with 10 percent interest within the year. By 1987, when only $1,450 had been paid back, the Tallacksons got a Sonoma municipal judge to order Chuck to make good the difference.

Daniel and Mary Defoe, lifelong California ranchers who have had a vacation cabin in the King's Canyon area of the Sierra since 1932, met Chuck in the late 1970s when the Park Service was trying to buy their cabin from them. He helped them to hang onto it, and Daniel later loaned Chuck more than $7,000, interest-free. "It was a verbal agreement that he'd borrow it for a certain amount of time. It was done on a handshake," Daniel Defoe recalls. "That agreed time passed, and I didn't feel he was doing everything he could do to repay his loan. We had to put a lien on his house. Eventually he paid it off when he sold the house. I still respect what he's doing, but I was discouraged that he didn't carry through on his promise. I'm not much of a sport for this Inholders stuff since that happened."[38]

On October 15, 1993, Clark County sheriff's deputies seized about $13,000 worth of antiques from Chuck's farm to settle another old debt. The widow of Bernard Vandewater of Oregon, who had loaned Chuck and National Inholders about $10,000, hadn't received the majority of payments Chuck had been ordered to make following a 1989 court case. According to the *Columbian*, Chuck said he believed Bernard Vandewater had made a contribution, not a loan, to the Inholders Association, but lawyers for Mrs. Vandewater said her deceased husband had won his case by producing a signed promissory note from Chuck.

The IRS has also filed a $22,379.87 tax lien against Chuck. In a December 1992 deposition, Chuck complained that "they're on me like stink on a pig."[39]

Chuck's personal life seems as unstable as his financial status. "Every woman I know has a bone to pick with me," he jokes. "Christine is an environmentalist, you know. She does total recycling, no chemicals in the garden, doesn't believe in that stuff. . . . She and I are just on two different pages. It makes a relationship more difficult. She doesn't share my interests; she doesn't go on political trips. I was married the first time for almost ten years," he continues. "My second marriage I wanted a mother for my kids. I had a housekeeper who was wonderful with kids but I had a hard time affording her economically, so I made a mistake, rushed into that marriage. We're still good friends, though. I'm good friends with all my wives," he laughs, going on to talk about what "a great gal" his former third wife is. "I've never had to have two lawyers in a divorce yet," he grins.

Bluff and engaging in a bearish sort of way, Chuck at fifty-one is back into the singles lifestyle. One woman recalls him hitting on her at a singles volleyball group; another recently spotted him at a dance put on by the *Columbian*'s classified ads section. And bar talk overheard after one of his Wise Use presentations reveals keen interest among the forty-something country women in acid-washed jeans.

"My problem is I don't have a committed partner. If you can do things together, if you can go on trips, it's much better," he muses. "Ron [Arnold] has that with his wife, Jan. She's a wonderful lady and real support for him, something I don't have right now."

So with little obvious control over his organizational, financial, or personal life, Chuck Cushman has been forced to go for the adrenaline rush: fighting new battles while raising funds to pay off his old ones, eating on the run, worrying about his health and weight, catching flak from the media. Almost by default, he has taken on the role of the anti-enviro movement's smoke jumper, flying from place to place across America looking for local brush-fires to break out so he can add fuel to them.

"When [Assistant Secretary of Interior] George Frampton shuts down logging communities," asserts Bill Grannell, "it's really not that different from when the militia shot down all those miners in the [1914] Ludlow massacre [in which more than two dozen striking miners and their families were killed by guardsmen in the pay of the Colorado Fuel and Iron Company]. The only difference is the militia killed them outright while Frampton is leaving them to live in poverty with their kids unhealthy and uneducated. It's like what the coal companies created in Appalachia with their strip mines. Frampton and the Sierra Club are the new set of elitists ruling our country."

Pug-faced and tenacious, bald-domed with a fringe of gray-brown hair, a jutting beard, and pointy cowboy boots, Bill Grannell, of People for the West, looks like a mid-sized John Ehrlichman, talks with the pneumatic cadence of a John Wayne, and numbers sixties organizer Saul Alinsky and radical labor leader Harry Bridges among his heroes. His vision is to apply the organizing techniques they used to mobilize dockworkers and the urban poor in building a rural, chapter-based anti-environmentalist movement.

Reeling from declining farm income, the depressed commodity prices of the eighties, and unrelieved depopulation going back more than thirty years, small-town rural America has become disenfranchised in much the same way as the inner city, with its declining tax base, deteriorating schools, and increasing dependence on social welfare programs. The members of the social elite of these rural ghettos—mine company operators, wealthy ranchers, and gyppo loggers—anxious to deflect their neighbors' anger and frustration away from themselves and their corporate sponsors, have become the local leaders and champions of Grannell's People for the West.

Like Charles Collins, the nineteenth-century Sioux City promoter who campaigned to open the Black Hills to white gold miners with arguments equating Native American "land monopolies" with the railroad trusts, Bill Grannell and his wife, Barbara, aim to convince the rural poor that their predicament is the result of an elitist power structure. This elite, they argue, is typified not by Homestake, Phelps-Dodge, Energy Fuels, and other giant mining companies that have scarred their landscape, irradiated their families, and polluted their rivers, but by the West's new "preservationist" settlers, who are gentrifying towns like Boise, Bozeman, and Santa Fe.

People for the West (PFW) is a project of the Western States Public Lands Coalition, established by the Grannells in 1988. With more than twelve thousand dues-paying members and several full-time organizers, it is the largest of the anti-enviro groups, although careful to distinguish itself from Wise Use. Says Bill, "The Western States Public Lands Coalition is not part of Wise Use. That's our official position. They're too far right, too shrill. The game of political extremism doesn't work."

But PFW's critics, such as former Bureau of Land Management Director Jim Baca (who once accused PFW of fomenting violence and compared Grannell to ex–Ku Klux Klansman David Duke), point out that the group's claimed 1992 budget of $1.7 million was almost wholly provided by mining companies looking to fight reform of the 1872 mining law. "These are the industry types who just don't want to get off the gravy train," he says.[40] It's a credible argument, given that twelve of the group's original thirteen board members were mining executives.

"Those who pay, play," shrugs Bill Grannell, drinking a cold Bud to the plinging sound of slot machines at a casino bar in Reno. Having just finished promoting his group at an anti-enviro meeting, he's more than happy to kick back and reflect on what he sees as the seamless flow of his political evolution from Democratic union organizer to defender of corporate mining. "My grandfather was an IWW organizer in Terre Haute, Indiana, where [Socialist party leader] Eugene Debs was from. My father was a labor organizer for the Carpenters Union. I organized for the National Education Association (NEA) for a couple of years.

"My father worked in construction, and we moved around the West and Midwest a good deal while I was growing up," he goes on. "I went to the University of Denver in sixty-three and one and a half years to the law school before deciding that wasn't what I wanted. I moved to Coos Bay, Oregon, in my early twenties, where I bought a boat and started fishing for salmon. I got involved with the Democratic party and joined the county central committee. That's when I became friends with Senator Wayne

Morse. Imagine. I'm twenty-two, twenty-three, sitting in a bar in Coos Bay drinking with Wayne Morse and [Longshoremen's leader] Harry Bridges. It was heady stuff."

"You were against the Vietnam War?" I ask, recalling that Morse was one of the earliest, most consistent critics of the war in the U.S. Senate.

"Pretty much," Bill admits reluctantly. Among the constituency Bill's now trying to organize, Vietnam is still considered a winnable war lost by traitors in the media and Congress. It's also the bitter core of an anecdote repeated regularly at Wise Use/Property Rights events. The story may be apocryphal, combining as it does elements of hostility towards the rich, leftists, women, the media, and the West's new settlers. As it's told, Ted Turner and his wife, Jane Fonda, try to cut in line at a popular steakhouse in Manhattan, Montana, not far from Turner's fifty-thousand-acre ranch. Told that they have to wait their turn like everyone else, they go into the bar. The bartender, either a decorated Vietnam veteran or the brother of someone who'd been killed in Vietnam, depending on who's telling the story, looks Turner in the eye as he sidles up to the bar, shakes his head, and says, "I'll serve you, but the bitch has to go." The punchline is usually followed by appreciative laughter.

After working salmon for a few years, Bill Grannell sold his boat and became a union organizer with the NEA, attending Saul Alinsky's organizer training school in Chicago, where many of the most effective sixties radicals honed their skills. "I find that what I learned there is still very useful," Bill says. "It was everything from how to organize a strike to how to shut down a shop to how to make a peace. Saul said if you make a war be sure you can win it. Also be sure you know how to negotiate the peace that comes afterwards."

In 1972 Bill was elected a Democratic state representative from Oregon's Fourth District. He would serve ten years in the Oregon statehouse before quitting in 1982. During that period he also published a weekly newspaper, the *Bay Reporter*, distributed up and down the south-central Oregon coast.

"I became chairman of the revenue committee in the Oregon

House," he recalls. "The first bill I carried in seventy-three was for public employees' right to collective bargaining. . . . Natural resource production was also vital for the state. It provided revenue for the schools and I fought hard to protect it."

"Bill was not a liberal," says Larry Campbell, the square-jawed Republican speaker of the Oregon House. "It was hard for Bill to move legislation that was favorable to the natural resources industries, because he was part of a very liberal caucus and at loggerheads with them. But Bill himself was not a liberal."[41]

Democratic Senate Majority Leader Dick Springer agrees. "He was a collective bargaining leader but was not known as an environmentalist, not coming from Coos Bay."[42]

White smoke billowing from the stack of a lumbermill marks the far end of Coos Bay, across the water from the oceanside fishing harbor and lighthouse park. The old, brown ten-story Tioga Hotel, set back from Bayshore Boulevard's railroad tracks, is the largest building in this sleepy town of fifteen thousand, but the old flophouse is dwarfed by the white superstructure of the *Neptune Jacinth* tied up at the waterfront. A massive log freighter out of Singapore, the *Jacinth*'s four yellow deck cranes are ready to pick up a new load of Douglas fir, fill her hull, and stack the surplus logs topside between the upright steel beams that picket the deck. Three of her Asian crew are leaning on a rail sharing a cigarette, looking out over the misty town and the green and brown checker-cut hills just beyond it. For these sailors from Singapore, a high-tech city-state where it's against the law to own a car more than three years old, Coos Bay, Oregon, must seem a lot like Sibu, Sarawak, or Kompong Som, Cambodia, or any of the other Third World ports where they tie up to collect raw logs. For the people of Coos Bay, however, it's a nice place to call home, even if the cutthroat trout are disappearing from the Umpqua River because of siltation and shade loss from the clearcuts.[43] Coos Bay is also a nice place to visit if you want to try to understand the politics of resource-industry Democrats like Bill Grannell.

Back at the turn of the century, the O & C Railroad was involved in real estate speculation on public lands it had been given to build a rail line. As it became clear that there would be no rail-line built, the federal government decided to reclaim the property and provide 50 percent of future timber revenues to the local counties that had been cheated out of the promise of transportation and development. Coos County was one of eighteen O & C counties in western Oregon that would use this income to run their school systems, eliminating the need for local property taxes. Residents of O & C counties—like the residents of Alaska, where the state collects 90 percent of all federal oil, gas, and mineral revenues—quickly developed a sense of entitlement, a belief that they shouldn't *have* to pay the same taxes other Americans did because their areas created "new wealth" from the ground. That sense of entitlement would spread rapidly during the Reagan years, fueled by supply-side economic theory, which argued that tax cuts, particularly for the rich, would increase federal revenues by stimulating investment, creating "new wealth" that would trickle down from above.

After retiring from the statehouse with his ten-year severance in 1982, Bill Grannell got a job as a lobbyist with the Association of County Governments. "They hired me to come up with an answer to the school-funding crisis. We put a sales-tax initiative together, but it failed. The voters weren't interested," he recalls. "This was at the time of the tax rebellion—Jarvis-Gann and Proposition 13 in California. Howard Jarvis even came up here to Oregon to campaign against our measure. I was also lobbying in Washington for the BLM and Forest Service budgets [in order to generate timber sales]. This was when the Gramm-Rudman balanced-budget deal was passed in 1984. The first mandated cuts would sequester 14 percent of shared revenues. The only amendment, the only exception, that got passed was sponsored by Senators James McClure [of Idaho] and Mark Hatfield [of Oregon]. It protected our natural resource revenues and I authored it.

"Groups like the Wilderness Society, Audubon, and Sierra were always against us," he continues. "They would argue that forest sales were below cost—saying, for example, that the roads the Forest Service constructed should be charged to the timber companies. But those aren't just logging roads, you know. They serve recreation; the Forest Service can use them to study wildlife or respond to fires. So it became obvious to me that they just wanted to stop timber harvesting in all public forests. At the local level, I was finding the same kind of groups—like the Oregon Natural Resources Council, Andy Kerr's group, which was appealing each and every timber sale. It wasn't just fiscal conservatives we were up against but this other agenda put out by the antiharvesting, anticattle groups, and it didn't take a rocket scientist to figure out that these people were out to one-up themselves. They had had some successes in the past with environmental protection, and now they were into the realm of environmental extremism, of New Age religion. . . . It was very frustrating. In the eighties, under Reagan, we had no revenue sharing, plus Gramm-Rudman, plus the environmentalists cutting out what revenue base we did have."

Given a choice of enemies to go after, the most popular president in the nation's history or owl-loving environmentalists, Bill Grannell, like a number of other rural Democrats, including House Speaker Tom Foley, chose the easy target.

Bill met his wife Barbara in 1982. She was a legislative staffer in Salem working against Oregon's tax-limitation initiative. They got married in 1984 while she was leading the school-tax-initiative campaign. For the next six months, she continued to work for the schools initiative in Oregon. Bill went back to Washington to lobby for the counties. This would set a pattern of separation and reunion that still continues in their highly politicized, on-the-run marriage.

Bill recalls, "Around that time my father died and my mother was pretty elderly, so we went back to Denver and I became the city's lobbyist." He campaigned for construction of the Two Forks Dam, an environmentally risky water project cancelled in the early days of the Bush administration. "We also began publishing a newsletter, *Public Lands Report*, out of our home that went to county offices, the BLM, Congress. The environmentalist problem kept accelerating. All the timber, oil, and gas leases were being appealed. Industry folks asked me if I thought we could create a coalition to oppose them. Barb and I spent a year talking to corporations that were looking for support to organize a grassroots response. We talked to 220 corporations, but only four bit: Chevron, Medford Timber, Energy Fuels [a uranium-mining company in Colorado], and Homestake Mining [which got its start mining gold in the Black Hills following the battle of Little Big Horn].

"We incorporated Western States Public Lands as a nonprofit that allowed us to lobby. Our first issue was the spotted owl in Oregon. We put together the Oregon Project in eighty-eight, pulling together a coalition of sixty-two groups in ninety days. Barb and I were the main organizers. Later we added Joe Sand, the ex-AP bureau chief up there. He did the press for us. Joe died of a cerebral hemorrhage, driving back from a lands meeting last year. Joe was a dear friend of ours," he pauses. "We put the project together for $120,000, half from our four companies, half from the Counties Association. By the end we had fourteen timber companies involved. We got over 170,000 names on a timber harvest petition. We had Hatfield with us and turned Bob Packwood around. We got the Hatfield-Adams amendment that said all the lumber caught up in legal appeals shall be cut. In terms of separation of powers it probably wasn't legal, but it sure sent a message. . . . The local groups we organized into the Oregon Coalition. The Oregon Coalition, along with the Yellow Ribbon, to their right, later became the Oregon Lands Coalition (OLC), which helped form the Alliance for America."

People close to the OLC claim that the Grannells left Oregon when the timber companies wouldn't pay them an $80,000 fee to continue organizing. Bill Grannell says the OLC got co-opted by the timber corporations and moved too far to the right.

"By ninety-one the timber companies had bailed on us. They put their money into the American Forest Resource Alliance (AFRA), a beltway operation where they hired a bunch of D.C.-based experts on 'grassroots' organizing. They also put money into the Oregon Lands Coalition. But Medford stayed with us and Homestake and Energy and Chevron were still with us. We decided to move from Denver to Pueblo. A lot of our supporters think big cities like Denver are the problem. We also decided to apply the lessons of Oregon to the mining industry. We got a lot of response because of the success we'd had in Oregon. When the Society of Mining Engineers joined us, which included many middle-level managers and CEOs, that brought us the mining companies and industry support."

Mining supporters included Nerco Minerals, which donated $100,000; Cyprus Minerals, which donated $100,000; Chevron, $45,000; Hecla Mining, $30,000; Bond Gold, $30,000; Pegasus Gold, $15,000; Homestake Mining, $15,000; Minerex Resources, $15,000; Energy Fuels, $15,000; and the American Mining Congress, $15,000.[44] Fifteen thousand dollars was the minimum price demanded for membership on the board of directors for Western States Public Lands, although this rule would later be amended to allow "grassroots" members from states with ten or more PFW chapters to be represented. The first grassroots member named to the board was Marvin Watts, a small-mine owner from New Mexico.

PFW spokesman Joe Sand told reporters that Western States had collected $1.7 million from the mining industry for their organizing work, although IRS records show that in 1991 they raised just over $500,000, a figure that increased to just over $625,000 in 1992.[45] Whichever figure is accurate, the investment would prove worthwhile to the mining industry, which was desperately looking for new means of defending the 1872 mining law. That law has given mining companies the right to extract "hard-rock minerals" such as gold and silver from millions of acres of public lands without paying the government any royalties. It's also allowed them to take title to land for as little as $2.50 an acre, a price originally set in 1872 to encourage development of "unsettled" Indian lands. With no modern-day provisions for cleanup and reclamation, the mining law contributed to environmental degradation associated with abandoned mines and runoff that has polluted streams and rivers throughout the West. It wasn't surprising, then, that a poll commissioned by the industry in 1991 found 82 percent of respondents thought mine companies should be forced to pay royalties and restore abandoned mining sites.[46] The pollsters cautioned the industry not to debate the mining law in public forums. However, the creation of People for the West provided the industry a way of advancing its cause in the name of populist empowerment. PFW's strategy would be to argue that any restriction on mining was a first step in a preservationist plot to limit multiple use of federal lands for logging, ranching, and recreation.

PFW's early campaigns targeted Montana and New Mexico, two states where mining proposals for test drillings and cyanide-leach gold processing were meeting stiff environmental opposition. When congressional hearings on the 1872 mining law were held in Santa Fe, New Mexico, PFW turned out five hundred protestors, many of them Phelps-Dodge and MolyCorp employees bused in by their companies. MolyCorp had earlier donated $10,000 to Western States. Ed Cordova, MolyCorp's head of security, was also chairperson of the local PFW chapter in Questa, New Mexico, a boom-and-bust company mining town in the northern part of the state.[47]

"We started out looking at the mining law, which is the mining companies' major cause," Bill Grannell admits, "but in our organizing efforts we got a range of people involved, which necessitated a more moderate broad-based approach. . . . You can't empower people and think you have a string attached to their back," he says.

Still, PFW's efforts to organize people around nonmining issues—be they cattle grazing, off-road recreation, predator control, or Spanish land-grant rights—always seem to circle back to protection of the mining industry.

Recent PFW campaigns have included efforts to organize trail-bike riders and loggers in southern Missouri's Mark Twain National Forest, where test drilling by the Doe Run Lead Mining Company was recently completed (PFW's Missouri campaign is being coordinated by the president of the state Mining Industry Council). PFW is also trying to organize the 130 or so residents of Cook City, Montana, around the issue of water rights. Two miles outside Cook City, on the northern border of Yellowstone National Park, is where Noranda wants to open its huge New World Gold Mine.

Montana rancher Paul Hawks complains: "Mining is given

preference over all other uses, but they don't tell you that at their [PFW] meetings. I have yet to see them lay out what the 1872 mining law does."[48]

Says former Bureau of Land Management Director Jim Baca, "I've never understood why a cowboy who's expected to be a steward of the land would want to go to bat for a miner who comes in, makes a mining claim, takes the land, pollutes the water, and leaves without paying anything for it."

Public lands mining in the West is "a license to steal and the biggest scam in America," adds Senator Dale Bumbers (D-Ark.), leader in the fight to reform the 1872 mining law.

The Golden Rooster

*Five men are known to be dead and 16 are already in the hospital:
the Frisco mill on Canyon Creek is in ruins: the Gem mine has
surrendered to the strikers, the arms of its employees have
been captured, and the employees themselves have been
ordered out of the country.*
SPOKANE WEEKLY REVIEW, JULY 14, 1892, reporting on
a typical labor/management dispute in U.S. mining history

The biggest gold heist since the days of Butch Cassidy.
SECRETARY OF THE INTERIOR BRUCE BABBITT on the 1872 Mining Law

There's a golden rooster in a glass display case between the registration desk and the slot machines at John Ascuaga's Nugget Ho-
tel/Casino in Reno. It's eighteen-karat gold, weighs more than
fourteen pounds, and is insured for $140,000. Aesthetically, I'd
rate it the equal of some of the nicer tin roosters I've seen for sale
on the streets of Tijuana, although it's not really my place to be
judging poultry art. It's the 206.3 troy ounces of gold in the
statue, or more specifically how that gold was mined, that has
brought me here today.[1]

"Mineral Information Network Exchange"—Mine Net to
those in the know—is listed on the hotel's meetings board along
with a wedding, the World Dreambuilders, an AA meeting, and
a drumming workshop. About sixty people are attending this one-
day conference, which was organized by Chuck Cushman. The
event has been billed as an attempt to create "grassroots support"

for the 1872 mining law, that legacy of the nineteenth-century Indian wars that allows mining companies to "patent," or take title
to, federal lands and mine the hard-rock minerals they find there
without paying fees. Today, the law results in a loss to the treasury
estimated at half a billion dollars a year. According to a 1989 GAO
report, the law has also led to widespread real estate speculation
on public lands. The report cites one example in 1986 where mine
patent holders bought 17,000 acres of public land for $42,500 and
resold it a few weeks later for $37 million.[2] Under this patenting
process, 3.2 million acres of public land, an area the size of Connecticut, have already been sold. Moreover, twelve thousand miles
of western rivers have been contaminated by acid, arsenic, and
heavy metals in mine runoff, and mine tailing piles have contaminated soil, lakes, watering holes, and drinking wells from Appalachia to the Rocky Mountains. Half a million acres of worked-over
mine sites now lie abandoned, and forty-eight such sites have been
deemed EPA Superfund cleanup sites. The Berkeley open-pit
copper mine in Butte, Montana, is the largest hazardous waste site
in the country.[3] Given its history and impact on the U.S. taxpayer
and the environment, the 1872 mining law is about as likely to win
broad popular grassroots support as pedophilia for profit.

Among those in attendance at today's Mine Net conference are
Chuck's co-chair, Steve Borell, from the Alaska Miners Association; Jim Burling, an attorney with the Pacific Legal Foundation;
an exploration geologist for Amex Gold; a representative from the
Independence Mining Company; a general manager for a
Canadian-owned mine; someone from Kennecott; an Elko, Nevada, city council member; a couple of mining engineers; a couple of drill operators; some recreational miners; and three people
from a group called "Grassroots for Multiple Use."

Chuck paces in front of the room, flashing his big grin. Today
he's wearing a western-cut sports jacket, blue shirt, grizzly bear
belt buckle, brown slacks, and cowboy boots. "My role here is to
pretend I'm Phil Donahue, to let people talk as much as possible
and keep it informal," he explains. Then, as a group-dynamics exercise, he has everyone stand up and rearrange their tables into

a U shape. Five minutes later, as if on cue, someone says, "Look, just getting us to reorganize the room is an example of the unity we have to solidify, to get things done."

Chuck points out that "since the press is here" there should be no attribution—that is, no speaker should be quoted by name, in order to keep the discussion "unrestrained and free-flowing." During the first break I get him to agree that people appearing on the panels can be quoted by name.

The key panel includes Duane Gibson, a sallow young assistant to Senator Ted Stevens of Alaska, and Jack Gerard, an amiable, round-faced lawyer in a red and white striped shirt from McClure, Gerard and Neuenschwander (McClure, as in James A., the former Idaho senator). Jack's representing the major transnational corporations of the American Mining Congress.

"Pegasus and the other majors are bailing on us," complains an unattributed (or UA) conferee.

"Can we sue the majors for negligence? Because if they don't initiate [property rights] 'takings' suits, they're not doing right by their stockholders," another UA suggests.

"It's true the judiciary now has more friendly Reagan-Bush appointees for life, but before we go the litigation route we have to fight our perception problem in Congress," Jack points out. "The perception is you're buying land for $2.50 an acre, converting it to golf courses, and selling the minerals for your South African owners, and we have to alter that perception. We have to point out that 60 percent of western mining is U.S.-shareholder owned, so it's not all foreign owned."

"We just don't want the AMC shooting us in the foot as they go around the back door," says a suspicious UA in a cowboy hat.

"Look, the AMC is not there to stick it to you," Jack Gerard tries to reassure the group. "But we're going to have to give something up. That's just realistic. So maybe we can't live with a royalty on gross, but maybe we can accept a royalty on net."

A militant from Idaho stands up to speak. "The majors in mining give us nothing. Maybe they kicked some money in for People for the West, but they haven't done anything in Idaho. But I'll tell you if my little eight-man mining company goes down the shitter, I'm going to put logging roads all through the Frank Church Wilderness Area and trash it, 'cause I have the permits for logging [as part of his mining patent] and we should just tell George Miller [chairman of the House Committee on Natural Resources] you're going to piss off a lot of people and we can trash your Endangered Species Act and anything else we choose, and maybe if you're lucky we'll let you keep something."

"That's not the perception they have in Congress," Chuck points out.

"How many people here work at actual mining operations right now?" asks Ivan Urnovitz from the Northwest Mining Association, one of the speakers on the next panel. About twenty out of sixty participants raise their hands. Discussion begins to shift to preservationist congressmen and to Al Gore's plan to destroy all industry west of the Mississippi. "We're dealing with religious zealots who want to turn the country into a national park. And when you're dealing with irrational people, you have to start acting irrationally too, so that's what I've started doing," says Dave Parkhurt, a panelist with Nevada Miners and Prospectors. Duane Gibson returns the focus of the discussion to the third planet from the sun, saying that his boss, Senator Stevens, believes that people in the mining industry should try and work to influence the Clinton administration through the Western Senate Coalition.

A month later, western Democrats led by Max Baucus of Montana will get Clinton to drop mining, grazing, and timber-sale reforms from his 1994 budget plan. The president agrees to their demand because he is hoping to gain support for his jobs bill, but since no western Republicans are asked to trade anything for his concession, he ends up losing on both deals.

"These guys must have never played poker. It's like they're getting on-the-job training up there," complains Bob Langsencamp of the New Mexico Land Commissioner's office, expressing a widely held feeling among public land-reform advocates in the early days of the Clinton administration.[4]

Chuck and Bill Grannell (reluctantly attending Chuck's meeting as a personal favor to Steve Borell) each take time from the mining meeting to make pitches for their respective groups.

"National Inholders is essentially a phone company to facilitate all you people in Mine Net," Chuck explains, rubbing his beard with his knuckles. "We're a political guerrilla fighting outfit. That's what we do best. We have nine faxes and can reach three to four thousand people overnight. Ours is a grassroots, bottom-up operation, so please don't view us as competitive with your work."

"People for the West has over one hundred chapters. We have organizers in Montana, Colorado, Arizona, New Mexico, and California," Bill explains. "We've had hearings where we've shown up from Denver to Anchorage to Salt Lake City. We fax selectively. We try and reach out to labor. We realize that we gotta be moderate and mainstream. It may be therapeutic to say, 'Let's burn down the White House,' but it ain't gonna happen. We have to live in the world as it is."

Jack Gerard points out that money, waste, and reclamation remain the main perceptual issues that supporters of the 1872 mining law have to address.

A woman consultant in a red dress with short, stylishly feathered hair offers a suggestion. "After the Summitville incident in Colorado, it's important we be perceived as opposing bad actors. Rather than always saying how awful the existing environmental regulations are, we should say, 'We're very happy with them because they do what needs to be done to protect the environment, but we don't want things to go too far over in the other direction.'"

"So you're talking window dressing? Just restating what we're already doing?" asks another UA.

"Exactly."

Her reference is to the ongoing pollution that began in 1986 at the Summitville Gold Mine in southern Colorado's San Juan Mountains, where cyanide used in heap-leaching operations has poisoned seventeen miles of the Alamosa River, a tributary of the Rio Grande. Galactic Resources, Ltd., the Canadian company that opened the mine in 1986, declared bankruptcy in early 1993, leaving the state of Colorado stuck with the $20 million cleanup bill and a 170-million-gallon tailings pond built into a dammed-up valley that continues to leak cyanide.[5]

I head down to the casino lobby for a drink thinking I'm not half as cynical a reporter as I thought I was. Over a Cuervo and orange juice, I decide that while here in Nevada I'll try and visit a working mine site.

Although best known for its gambling and irradiated sheep, Nevada really got its start with pick-ax mining. In 1859, Nevada was the empty quarter of the Utah territory also known as Zion, a vast forgotten desert basin considered, even by the Latter Day Saints of Salt Lake City, too barren to bother with. Then two Irish miners, Patrick McLaughlin and Peter O'Riley, digging on the eastern slope of the Sierra Nevada, unearthed the greatest silver strike since the Spanish conquistadores found their mountain of silver at Potosi. It was named the Comstock Lode, after Henry Comstock, the man who cheated McLaughlin and O'Riley out of their claim. Over the next five years, gold and silver strikes in the Great Basin would attract more than seventy thousand people to the area, including a number of Forty-Niners who'd failed to strike it rich in California's gold rush. Mining for gold, silver, quicksilver, gemstones, and copper would provide Nevada with the wealth and population it needed for statehood.[6] Nineteenth-century mining strikes throughout the West would help fuel America's expanding Industrial Revolution, but at a terrible price. Within twenty years of the Sutter Creek gold rush, California's Indian population would decline from a hundred thousand to thirty thousand people as peaceful tribes were decimated by the miners' guns, forced slavery, diseases, and liquor. More than any other industry, American mining has been marked by violent conflicts over territory and labor. These have left a bitter legacy still seen today in the strip-mined mountains and shotgun-shack poverty of Appalachia, the twelve thousand miles of mercury and heavy-metal poisoned rivers that criss-cross the intermountain West, and the hospital wards of Arizona's Navajo nation, where former uranium miners are dying from an epidemic of lung cancer.

The history of the mining industry is probably best summed up in *Dave Barry Slept Here.* In this humorist's history of the United States, the author explains that labor unrest was "caused by coal miners emerging from the ground and making radical demands such as: (1) they should get paid; or, at least (2) they should not have the tunnels collapse on them so often. The coal companies generally responded by bringing in skilled labor negotiators to bargain with the miners' heads using clubs. This often resulted in violence, which forced the federal government, in its role as peacekeeper, to have federal troops shoot at the miners with guns. Eventually the miners realized that they were safer down in the collapsing tunnels, and there was a considerable decline in labor unrest."[7]

This style of labor negotiation was first practiced beginning in the middle of the nineteenth century against Irish immigrant miners in the anthracite coal fields of Pennsylvania. Irish survivors of the potato famine, working for starvation wages in the mines, organized a clandestine group called the Molly Maguires, named after an Irish widow who took great pleasure in shooting British landlords and their agents back home.

In their "long strike" of 1874–75, the Mollies dynamited mineshafts, shot a number of unpopular mine superintendents, and threatened to shoot any miner who went back to work. The Mollies' organization was eventually broken up after being infiltrated by a Pinkerton detective named James McParland. In the summer of 1877, the state of Pennsylvania hung nineteen miners named as Mollie gunmen by McParland. It was no secret that the mine owners, railroad tycoons, and other leading industrialists of the time hoped these mass executions would mark an end to American labor unrest. But it was not to be.[8] Just a month later a nationwide railroad strike broke out that rapidly reached insurrection-level violence in major towns and cities with hundreds killed by state militias or, where the state militias sided with the rioters, by federal troops. It was after the railroad strike of 1877 that National Guard armories were constructed in major cities across America to guard against future uprisings.

The United Mine Workers were next. They tried to unionize

the coalfields of Pennsylvania, leading a hundred thousand miners out on strike in 1897. This was the first in a series of bitter strikes for union recognition, decent wages, and mine safety that would, over the decades, convulse the coalfields in Ohio, Indiana, Pennsylvania, Tennessee, Kentucky, and West Virginia.

But it was in the Rocky Mountain West that turn-of-the-century mining conflicts took on the appearance of industrial wars, complete with major gun battles, broken treaties, and political assassinations.

In 1892 striking miners in the Coeur d'Alene region of Idaho began a generation of deadly warfare with armed and deputized strikebreakers. By 1899, with the mineowners refusing to recognize the miners' unions, and mines and mills being dynamited by wildcat strikers, Governor Frank Steunenberg declared parts of Idaho "in a state of insurrection and rebellion." President McKinley sent in federal troops, and martial law was declared. Thousands of miners were rounded up and held in specially erected "bullpens" until the strikes were broken. Governor Steunenberg, who when elected had been a man of modest means, left office a wealthy individual. He didn't get much time to enjoy his prosperous retirement, however. In December 1905, someone tied some fishline to the front gate of his huge sheep ranch. When he opened the gate it set off a charge of dynamite that killed him instantly.[9]

In Colorado the Western Federation of Miners led the fight for the eight-hour workday. The WFM was headed up by William Dudley Haywood. A one-eyed giant of a man, "Big Bill" Haywood was a cowboy turned miner turned revolutionist with a penchant for packing a six-gun when he went out to the mining districts to organize his "boys."

In 1901 the gold and silver miners of Telluride went out on strike. After the first month, Arthur Collins, superintendent of the Smuggler-Union Mines, decided to reopen his operations using armed and deputized strikebreakers. The Telluride chapter of the WFM sent a purchase order to a Denver gun dealer for 250 Winchester rifles and fifty thousand rounds of ammunition. On July 3, with their consignment delivered, the local union miners ambushed the Smuggler "deputies" in a gun battle that lasted the better part of a day. Finally the strikebreakers raised a white flag, and the miners allowed them to take their dead and wounded and leave the area. Later the governor of Colorado sent a commission of inquiry, which reported, "Everything is quiet in Telluride: the miners are in peaceful possession of the mines," thereby sending shudders through the national business community. The following year somebody shot Arthur Collins dead as he sat reading by a lighted window in his home.

In 1902 the Colorado Mine Owners Association blocked passage of state legislation for an eight-hour workday. Bundles of cash were reportedly passed out to lawmakers on the assembly floor of the statehouse. The following year Cripple Creek miners, frustrated with the legislative process, went on strike for the eight-hour day. Governor James Peabody, a banker and close friend of the Mine Owners Association, declared Cripple Creek and Telluride to be "in a state of insurrection and rebellion" and sent the Denver militia to take control. When a newspaper editorial declared the action unconstitutional, the state judge advocate replied, "To hell with the Constitution: we are not following the Constitution."[10]

Miners were seized on the streets and taken from their homes at gunpoint. Hundreds were held without charges in barbed wire bullpens for weeks on end. The editor of the *Victor Record* was arrested after his paper questioned the actions of the militia. When a civil judge tried to hold habeas corpus hearings, the military surrounded the courthouse and put a bayonet to his chest. Stores that sold provisions to the miners were looted and burned. An ex-congressman was shot and wounded by soldiers. The Citizens Alliance, a mineowner-organized vigilante group, beat up and terrorized strike supporters with impunity. Big Bill Haywood and WFM president Charles Moyers snuck in and out of Cripple Creek armed and ready to shoot it out with militiamen if they attempted to capture them. The WFM decided to spread the strike to other mines around the state. The governor responded by putting those districts under martial law. In 1904 a train bringing strikebreakers into Cripple Creek was dynamited and derailed.

The state retaliated by forcibly deporting dozens of union officials to Kansas and New Mexico. With most of their leadership jailed, shot, or in exile, the strikes eventually faltered and the miners returned to their ten-hour shifts in the mines.[11]

In 1905 Bill Haywood and Charles Moyer journeyed to Chicago, where, along with Eugene Debs, Mother Jones, Emma Goldman, Daniel DeLeon, and two hundred other militant labor leaders of their day, they formed the IWW, the Industrial Workers of the World. The Wobblies, as they came to be known, believed in "one big union" open to all races and nationalities. In their vision, through general strikes and without great violence, the union would put the mines, mills, and factories into the hands of their workers. This was a very western, shoot-the-moon kind of idea, based more on organizers' personal strike experiences than on the ideologies of European Marxists. Still, it was the kind of class-based revolutionary proposal guaranteed to send shivers up the spines of America's industrial elite.[12]

Within months Haywood, Moyer, and an associate, George Pettibone, were kidnapped by state marshals and taken to Idaho, where they were charged with ordering the murder of former Idaho Governor Frank Steunenberg. They'd been named by sometimes union member Harry Orchard. During a three-day jailhouse interrogation by James McParland, the same Pinkerton detective who had infiltrated and condemned the Molly Maguires almost thirty years earlier, Orchard himself had admitted to the actual assassination by dynamite.

The arrest of the three raised a cry of "frame up!" from the working class movement as newspapers across America and Europe reported their arrest, trial, and possible execution. One hundred thousand marchers in New York demanded their release. Nationally famous attorney and defender of lost causes Clarence Darrow traveled to Idaho to represent them. In Terre Haute, Indiana, IWWs (including, in all likelihood, Bill Grannell's grandfather) rallied around Socialist party leader Eugene Debs. Debs, until then a lifelong advocate of nonviolence, wrote to Darrow to suggest that a worker militia be raised to march on Idaho and free the prisoners from the gallows. In the newspaper

Appeal to Reason he wrote, "If they attempt to murder Moyer, Haywood and their brothers a million revolutionists, at least, will meet them with guns. . . . If the plutocrats begin the program, we will end it."

President Teddy Roosevelt, after reading these words, sent a copy of them to his attorney general with a note: "Is it possible to proceed against Debs and the proprietor of this paper criminally?" In another letter to a politician friend, Roosevelt referred to Haywood, Pettibone, and Debs as "undesirable citizens." Soon thousands of college students began wearing buttons reading "I am an undesirable citizen."

In May 1907 the Idaho trial began. Clarence Darrow, the consummate defense attorney, called Orchard "the most monumental liar that ever existed," tearing his testimony apart as the fabrication of Pinkerton's McParland. During his testimony McParland remained impassive as Darrow called him a paid professional liar and asked him how it had felt to befriend the Molly Maguires in order to send them to their hanging deaths. (McParland replied that he had just been doing his job.)

In his eleven-hour summation, Darrow, wearing a rumpled gray suit and clutching his eyeglasses in one hand, told the jury that they had the power to kill Haywood. "If you kill him, your act will be applauded by many: if you should decree Haywood's death, in the great railroad offices of our great cities men will sing your praises. If you decree his death, amongst the spiders and vultures of Wall Street will go up paeans of praise for those twelve men who killed Bill Haywood. . . . But if you free him there are still those who will reverently bow their heads and thank you twelve men for the character you have saved. Out on the broad prairies, where men toil with their hands: out on the broad ocean, where men are sailing the ships: through our mills and factories: down deep under the earth, men who suffer, women and children weary with care and toil . . . will kneel tonight and ask their God to guide your judgments . . . to save Haywood's life."

On July 28 the jury returned a verdict of not guilty. It would prove a sweet if short-lived victory for the defendants and their mining unions.[14]

With the horrific conditions that existed in the mining industry—with thousands of miners dying from cave-ins, slate falls,
coal dust, and gas and dynamite explosions, and living conditions
in the aboveground mine camps not much better—labor unrest
continued to expand. The most dramatic confrontation of the era
grew out of a western coal strike organized by the United Mine
Workers. In 1913, eleven thousand coal miners in southern Colorado, many of them foreign-born Italian and Greek immigrants,
went out on strike against the Rockefeller-controlled Colorado
Fuel and Iron Corporation. Evicted from their shacks in isolated
company towns, the miners set up tent cities in the hills. John D.
Rockefeller hired gunmen from the Baldwin-Felts Detective
Agency to help break the strike, but after a series of unprovoked
shootings the miners began to collect arms to defend themselves.
There followed a series of gun battles, during which the miners
succeeded in driving back an armored train and disabling an armored truck known as the Death Special. The governor of Colorado responded to the shifting balance of forces by sending in
the militia to help reopen the mines (Rockefeller agreed to pay
their wages). The strikers, refusing to give in, held out in their
tent cities throughout the cold winter of 1913–14. In the spring
the militia, including many company gunmen who had simply
changed uniforms, set up machine-gun positions in the hills
above the tent colony at Ludlow, where a thousand men, women,
and children were encamped. On the morning of April 20, after
a miner and a guard got into a fight, the militia opened fire with
their machine guns. When strike leader, Lou Tikas, approached
to ask for a cease fire, he was shot dead. A number of people, unable to find shelter in the shallow trenches the miners had dug for
protection, were cut down by the guards' bullets. At dusk the militia moved down from the hills with torches and set fire to the tent
colony. The next day a telephone linesman going through the
ruins counting bodies found a shallow pit beneath a cot. Inside
were the charred bodies of two women and eleven children; they
had been burned to death. In all twenty-six people died in what
came to be known as the Ludlow Massacre.

After burying their dead in the town of Trinidad, armed miners moved out into the hills, where they began destroying mines, dynamiting mineshafts, and killing mine guards. The governor asked for federal troops to restore order. The army arrived in force and a few months later the strike was broken.[15]

The following year IWW balladeer and organizer Joe Hill was arrested in Salt Lake City and charged with killing a grocer during a robbery. Although there was no hard evidence against him, Hill's prominence in the IWW and recent union work with local copper miners assured a vigorous prosecution. The state copper trust, the newspapers, and the police were convinced of his guilt, as was a local Mormon jury. Thousands of telegrams from prominent citizens, foreign ambassadors, the government of Sweden (where Hill was born), even President Wilson, asking Governor William Spry to commute Hill's death sentence went unanswered. In his last note to Bill Haywood, Hill wrote, "Don't waste any time in mourning. Organize." On November 19 Joe Hill was executed by a five-man firing squad in the yard of the Utah State Penitentiary.[16]

Frank Little was an outspoken member of the IWW's general executive board. A one-eyed part Indian with a warrior's courage, he was widely known as the "hobo agitator." In 1916–17 he was active in leading strikes in Montana and Arizona, including one in Bisbee, Arizona, where the vigilante Loyalty League rounded up twelve hundred miners at gunpoint, put them on open rail cars, and shipped them out into the desert. In June 1917, while Little was engaged in that strike, an industrial accident at Montana's Speculator Mine took the lives of 190 men, not an untypical occurrence at a time when a mine owner could claim that it was easier to replace a lost miner than a mine mule. In late July Little traveled back to Butte, Montana, to help lead a miners' strike against Anaconda Copper. Mystery writer Dashiell Hammett, working as a young Pinkerton at the time, later recalled how an Anaconda Copper official offered him $5,000 to kill Little, an offer he declined.[17] On July 31, 1917, Frank Little got into a shouting match with a group of Anaconda company guards. In the early hours of the next morning, six armed men broke into his hotel room, beat him up, and dragged him in his pajamas to their car, where they tied a rope around him and dragged him three miles to the Milwaukee Railroad trestle. There they lynched him, pinning a note to his body that read, "First and last warning." No one was ever arrested for the murder.[18]

Through force of arms, the western mining industry was able to break the militant Western Federation of Miners and, with the help of the federal government, the IWW. Woodrow Wilson's Justice Department used the Wobblies' opposition to World War I as an excuse to raid dozens of their meeting halls throughout the country and put 101 IWW leaders on trial for conspiracy to encourage draft evasion. All 101 were convicted. Fifteen Wobblies, including Big Bill Haywood, were given twenty-year prison sentences. Haywood jumped bail and fled to Russia, where a revolution had broken out. He remained there, a son of the West in exile, till his death in 1928.

Under a determined leadership, the UMW continued to carry on its strikes, win industry concessions, and organize new membership in the eastern coal belt, where miner populations were both more settled and more numerous than in the mining boom towns of the West. Still, the conflicts were intense and deadly. In West Virginia the army was called out when armed miners and company militias fought in the mountains, and General Billy Mitchell led the first and only domestic air force bombing raid against American citizens, using his biplanes to attack the UMW's positions. With the onset of the Depression, the UMW began a new organizing drive in Appalachia under the leadership of John L. Lewis, another gruff giant of a man who helped unify labor, under the banner of the Congress of Industrial Organizations, the CIO.

With their mineral rights bought out from under them, the mountain folk, hillbillies, and immigrant mine laborers of Appalachia were forced to live in a kind of indentured servitude in and around mining towns built, owned, and operated by the coal companies. When, in 1930, union organizers from Pennsylvania, Indiana, West Virginia, and other UMW strongholds began holding secret meetings in the hill country of Kentucky, the mineowners hired "goons" and gangsters from Chicago to root them out.

In places like "Bloody Harlan" County, coal company death squads carried out a reign of terror that included the kidnapping and murder of suspected union organizers. Victims' bodies were dumped by the sides of roads and in streambeds as warnings to the miners. But with unemployment in the coalfields skyrocketing, miners, desperate to find some way to feed their families, continued joining the union. Many began carrying .38 revolvers, known as "John L. Lewis peacemakers," for self-defense.

On May 5, 1931, in Evarts, Kentucky, a fight broke out between miners and the coal companies' industrial police. The goons drew their pistols, as did many of the miners, and a shootout ensued. One miner and three company guards were killed. Evarts shattered the mining industry's grip of fear and intimidation on the region. Although the violence would continue for years to come, the miners now began to call openly for strike actions and demand collective bargaining agreements. By the end of the decade, they had won recognition of their rights as union workers.

The UMW never admitted to arming or encouraging the coal miners in their violent means of defense. Unlike the WFM or the Wobblies, the UMW was not looking for a revolution so much as a square deal for its membership, and the union had a keen strategic sense of when to pull back from a fight it couldn't win. Several times during the thirties, Governor Flem Sampson of Kentucky sent the National Guard into the coalfields, calling coal country "a hotbed of Reds and Communists." Each time, the striking miners hung out American flags in greeting and peacefully sat out the guards' occupation of their communities. As John L. Lewis noted in 1948, when President Truman sent the military into the coal mines to try and force a strike settlement, "You can't dig coal with bayonets."[19]

Unfortunately, by the end of World War II it was possible to dig coal seams with bulldozers and dynamite. Surface mining—or strip mining, as it came to be known—reduced the mining industry's need for workers while massively expanding the environmental destruction wrought on the coal-, copper-, and gold-producing regions of America. To the miner's risk of cave-ins, explosions, silicosis, and black and brown lung disease could now be added community and regional impacts from river and ground-water pollution, earthen dam breaks, erosion, flooding, soil contamination, and subsidence.

By the 1970s the UMW had joined several other unions, including the United Steel Workers and the Oil, Chemical and Atomic Workers, in rejecting management attempts to form common fronts for what union spokespeople have called "environmental blackmail," attempts to win industrywide exemptions from toxic-emission standards, mine-reclamation requirements, and the Clean Air and Clean Water acts. Even though the UMW did come out during the Bush administration in opposition to acid-rain controls on coal with high sulfur content, when it comes to occupational health and environmental protection, its spokespeople still insist on drawing a distinction between themselves and the industry's Coal Association.

"They're very strident, and had to be dragged kicking and screaming into the twentieth century," says Mike Buchner, director of research for the UMW. "Our position is, we think coal production can be done in a responsible manner, which means better standards and no harm to the community from land subsidence, stream pollution, and other environmental impacts. We view things like reclamation and mine safety as part of the costs of production, which should be internalized into the price of coal. Historically the industry has externalized them into this system of waste [pollution] that society as a whole has had to pay for somewhere later down the line."[20]

Today the hard-rock mining industry is trying to win its workers' backing for 1872 mining law "reforms" that would guarantee minimum change in the Jesse James–era law. But the number of miners involved in these massive public lands operations is relatively small, and hard-rock miners organized by the steelworkers have rejected industry's overtures. To people who have lived in places like Butte, Montana; Alamosa, Colorado; and Coeur d'Alene, Idaho, mines and mining have always represented quick wealth for a few and deadly trouble for everyone else. As new people move to the West looking for a clean and safe environment in which to raise their kids, locally based opposition to the big mining operations has increased. Even some of the old-timers who have historically benefited from these operations, seeing the growth of foreign ownership of the mines, have begun to ask why the multinational industry should continue to get a free ride from Uncle Sam.

I leave the Howard Johnson's motor lodge in Elko, Nevada, on a cold winter morning. The dry desert air freezes my hair, still damp from the motel shower, into brittle furrows. KELK radio reports that "Good Morning, America" is sending a camera crew to town next week to cover the big story. Elko has just been named the most livable small town in America by some author who must put a high premium on clean air, open vistas, fast food, easy freeway access, legalized gambling, prostitution, and gold. Lots of gold. Elko is the fifth largest gold-producing area in the world, helping Nevada turn out some 6 million troy ounces a year, enough for close to thirty thousand golden rooster statues. The second KELK news item is that a ferret has escaped from its owner and there's a $100 reward for the fugitive varmint's recovery.

"Just head up Mount City highway past the Raley's and keep going forty-four miles," I've been instructed. "Then turn right at the sign for the mine and it's seven miles to the mill site." Within a few minutes I'm past the last outlying suburban ranchettes, alone on the two-lane blacktop humping through snow-blown dells and arroyos. The slush and splatter muddy up the windshield on my red box, a rusting '83 Toyota wagon with four-wheel drive if needed. What I need now is some window-washer spray, but the plastic lines are frozen up. I pull over to clean off the glass with a handful of snow, a few black and white magpies by the side of the road my only company. I'm a little surprised I'm being allowed to visit a mine on such short notice. When I called Newmont at 7 A.M. this morning, they'd said they needed ten days notice for a press tour but the Independence Mine is working out. "We're interested in staying open to the public but we can't really trust reporters who just want to portray us as scarring the land

and exploiting the West," Bob Zurga, the company's CEO, explained on the phone from Reno before reluctantly agreeing to let me go up to the mine. "I think one of the major things that will come out over the next year, you're going to see great disappointment in the role of environmental restrictions across the earth," he went on. "You have to protect the earth, but with efficiency. Already we're seeing a 35 percent increase in lumber prices. We're the biggest taxpayer in Elko County. What will happen when we have to cut back because of increased royalties? We're all being hurt by this approach, which takes people out of nature."

I cruise along at a sedate seventy-five miles an hour through vast snowfields that run up against distant ice-dusted mountains framing barren valleys of truly Arctic proportion. A passing truck or a three-strand barbed wire fence become the connective tissue of civilization. Somewhere behind me are the Ruby Mountains and an eighty-six-car railroad train running west out of Salt Lake. There's a sterile beauty in the icy sea of sage and scattered stands of windblown aspen that dot the hills. A shaft of sunlight cuts through the low white clouds to illuminate a single jagged five-thousand-foot peak, and I have to smile at the pure grandeur of it.

"Independence Mining Co. FMC Gold. Jerritt Canyon Mine," reads the small sign on the side of the road. I turn onto the private road heading up into the cloud-obscured Independence mountain range. Ridges of rock jut towards the low white sky as the mill complex, with its three big smokestacks, comes into view. White steam rises into the white clouds, cream on porcelain. Large semis going in the other direction pass me near the tailing ponds that cover several hundred acres in front of the mill. I pull up at the guardpost and am directed to the mine office, where I sign a liability release and receive a yellow hardhat and safety glasses. Through the window I can see a flatbed truck pull up to the gate. Its chained-down load consists of a single huge tire for a 150-ton truck. I'm directed down a hallway to the office of Scott Barr, the mine manager.

We shake hands and Scott offers me a seat. He has a smooth,

friendly face with narrow gray eyes and a truly impressive gut hanging over his "Nevada" belt buckle. The buttons on his striped, coffee-stained shirt strain against the pull of the cloth.

He tells me his mill operates like a chemical plant. They have a chlorine-bleaching process for their slurry along with an oxidizing "roasting" process. "Half the mill's operations are roasting, half bleaching," he explains. "We get a little cyanide in our wastewater, but that's kept in our runoff ponds. We haven't had any wildlife mortalities or serious environmental problems since we opened in eighty-one." The big operators like Newmont (the largest gold producer in the United States, mining in the nearby Carlin Mountains) use heap leaching with cyanide, whereby a weak solution of cyanide is sprayed over exposed ore and the gold is processed out of the liquid runoff. "It takes no pretreatment but the recovery is low, about 60 to 70 percent. Our mill uses fine-grain rock, almost like face powder, and we get 90 percent recovery from our feedstock, which has about one part gold per million."

"How much rock do you have to dig for an ounce of gold?"

He does some quick calculating. "We get 0.14 ounces of gold per ton of ore. We process about eight thousand tons of rock a day and produce three to four hundred thousand ounces of gold a year out of the Jerritt Canyon mine. We employ seven hundred workers. Newmont and Barrick [a Canadian-owned mining company also operating in the Carlin range] produce about ten times that amount."

He shows me a wall map of the area. "Our claims and operations area covers some two hundred square miles, although the area of disturbance is only a few square miles."

"On public lands?"

"Our mining is all taking place on Humboldt National Forest land."

I ask if Independence is a locally owned mine.

"Independence used to belong to Freeport Gold but is now a subsidiary of Minorco, a Luxembourg-based company owned by the Oppenheimer group."

"DeBeers?"

"Right, DeBeers."

I begin to understand why the American Mining Congress is worried about a perception problem in Congress. If the general public realizes that long-time pillars of South Africa's recently defeated apartheid system are digging gold for free on U.S. public lands, the little remaining support for the 1872 mining law might erode down to bedrock. Today non-U.S. corporations control fifteen of the twenty-five largest gold mines in the United States, most of which operate on public, or "patented," land. The Jerritt Canyon mine produces about $155 million in royalty-free gold for DeBeers every year.[21]

"And the gold goes where?" I ask.

"We ship our gold offshore for the jewelry market—direct export of the dorey with some silver impurities still in it to Europe, Italy, Switzerland. The tax credit on exports favors that."

Barr, a fourth-generation miner whose grandfather worked the Comstock Lode, accepts that the mining law of 1872 will probably be reformed. "A royalty payment would mean we'd become more selective, only mine the higher grade ores. The impact would probably be felt for two or three years. We're really concerned the eastern power lobbies may not see the 14 percent of mineral production that comes from public lands as that important, even though a lot of it is gold." He pauses. "Frankly, the validity of any mining on public lands is being questioned. That part of multiple use will be difficult to sustain."

Scott Lewis, the environmental supervisor for Jerritt, drives me up to the mine site. He's a tall, youthful-looking man, six-foot-four with reddish hair and a trim mustache, dressed in a fleece-lined winter coat, boots, and jeans. He graduated from Montana State in range science in 1983 and later worked coal in Colorado and Texas, where he met his wife. We climb the looping haul road, an eighty-foot-wide strip of oily dirt and gravel that is damp from drifting ground fog. Scott points to the four-foot raised berms along the cliff sides, which OSHA requires. He tells me about the NEPA (National Environmental Policy Act) requirements the mine has to meet. He says that state concern over mining has also increased since some mining mercury showed up in

Carson City's water supply. I ask him if there are any environmentalists in the Elko area. "There's people here who like to hunt
and play. We've got people with mule deer groups who keep an
eye on the agencies and on us to make sure we mitigate for mu-
lies."

We pull up in front of a prefab metal building. Inside I'm introduced to Jim Collord, the mine operations superintendent.
Jim's also six-foot-four. They grow 'em big in Nevada, I figure, because of either the open space or the nuclear testing. Jim looks to
be in his fifties, with a solid build and a noticeable resemblance
to actor Richard Crenna, including the weathered face full of
finely etched character lines. He has warm brown eyes that are
friendly and unchallenging, which one appreciates when meeting
a miner half again as large as your standard black bear.

"To me mining is basic. It's creating new wealth out of the
ground," he muses, munching his way through a lunch of carrots
and salad. "I'm a third-generation gold miner. My grandfather
worked central Idaho mine claims, staked the Thunder Mountain
claim. I was born in Idaho in the mining town of Stibnine, a boom
town of a thousand people that's now a ghost town. My dad was
injured in a logging road accident in '49, so we moved to California, where he worked quicksilver on the Hearst ranch. He got radiation burns watching an A bomb go off while flying around in a
light plane with a Geiger searching for uranium deposits back in
the 1950s. Said he could see the blast wave move across the desert
floor. I got my master's degree in exploration from the Mackey
School of Mines. Since then I've lived in a number of towns—
Rawhide, Nevada; Wolf Fang, Idaho; and Paradox, Utah, among
other places."

He also has a sixteen-year-old son he named Jerritt, after the
mine. "I couldn't recommend Jerritt go into mining. I think the
future of mining in the U.S. is pretty bleak," he admits. "I get
very depressed sometimes. The excitement of prospecting has
been my history, but now we're coming up against a massive foe
in environmentalism."

He removes a Sierra Club fundraising letter that he's tacked up
on the bulletin board. "I'm a member of The Nature Conser-

vancy, so I get stuff like this in my mail," he says, handing me the letter.

It's an attack on the Wise Use movement, and has that non-partisan, direct-mail style of three-dot urgency and barely suppressed hysteria common to the fundraising medium. "We must confront the most dangerous challenges in our history," it reads, lest Wise Use "open up our precious wilds so energy companies can drill for oil and gas and dig for minerals . . . destroying crucial wetlands . . . clear-cutting our few remaining ancient forests . . . inviting massive construction in our most beautiful national parks and wild areas. . . ."[22]

"The media goes for this kind of garbage," Jim complains. "The general public doesn't understand that on public land you don't just rape and scrape."

Scott concurs. "They don't know the extent of the permitting process. Our original Environmental Impact Statement cost $2 million."

"I myself am a charter member of People for the West," Jim continues. "We tried to get an Elko chapter going but it's pretty inactive. The smaller splinter groups tend not to hang together. The mining companies themselves are more involved. The way I see it, Elko is a mining town, and so in a way it doesn't do much good to preach in Elko, you're pretty much preaching to the choir. I mean this is a town where Clinton came in a distant third [behind Bush and Perot]. But if you look at the media trends and stuff, I feel like we're fighting a losing battle."

I ask him if anyone else in the mine is active in People for the West or similar groups. "Not really. Most of these guys driving the trucks here aren't political, but if you tell them, 'Hey, you're going to lose your job if this mining law goes through,' they'll catch on."

We head outside, climbing into the cab of his four-wheel-drive utility vehicle. The cold air is bracing and smells of diesel, dirt, and sage. He pulls out onto the haul road, oil-blackened and as wide as the Transamazon Highway.

"Some people like to look at mountains or rivers," he tells me as I look out over the edge of the mountain. "I find ore pretty unique. Like what you have in these mountains is 34-million-year-old gold formations that came out of ancient hot springs. I hunt for big structures, follow fault lines, and look for sediments and rock outcroppings that indicate where hot spring systems once existed. We take samples. Maybe drill a thousand holes. I find a lot of beauty in ore bodies. They're a rare part of nature." He points out a jasperoid outcrop, a knobby hill to us laymen. It's an indicator of past flows. "Hot water once moved through these rocks with gold in solution, some kind of chloride solution, within it. Then the carbon in these rocks locked onto the gold, just like in the milling process."

"How's that?" I ask.

"We run cyanide and gold through activated carbon, coconut charcoal does a good job, the husks are reusable. So we'll flush the gold out onto steel wool, then melt the steel wool, then use a chlorine solution to remove it or else heat the carbon off it, roasting it in an oxygen fire."

We drive up towards a high pass as a muddy hundred-ton truck with a ninety-ton load of rock and ore in its shallow, jacked-up bed passes us, heading down the mountain. Behind it a larger yellow truck rumbles into a turnoff to one of the mine's faces. The truck is worth a million dollars and makes Bigfoot look like a standard Chevy. Each of its eight-foot-high tires costs $52,000. The road we're driving on is salted, but the salt washes away with every rain and a new application has to be laid down—for $82,000.

We pass an ore pile almost black with crushed carbonatious rock mixed with striations of orange-colored arsenic and then cross over a snow-flurried divide. On one side of the mountain, the waters draw down to the Owyhee River, a tributary of the Snake, which wanders eight hundred miles north through Hell's Canyon and beyond. On the west side of the mountain, the water percolates down to the Humboldt River, which flows west to Lovelock and beyond to the outskirts of Reno. The hillside is terraced with past mining cuts. At close to eight thousand feet above sea level, more caterpillar haul trucks roll past us.

"Mining's a damn tough job, and this mine is probably one of the toughest, with its elevation, its hilliness, its snow, and its mud," Jim reflects, "working through these freeze-and-thaw cycles, 24 hours a day, 360 days a year. You're fighting the weather and these complex little ore bodies. You have to move a lot of rock to get to the ore. This is tough work."

I ask him about the irregularity of the terrace faces. "We move more material when prices are up, less when they drop. You can track price changes in the angle of the mine faces. Here we blast three or four hundred holes per pit. Our ore is mainly gold with trace amounts of silver, arsenic, and mercury, but mostly waste rock attached."

Scott points to a future cut site across the valley, where a rare stand of aspen, like anorexic dogwoods, bend in the frosty high-country wind on the rolling face of a snowswept virgin hillside. "Aspen is important," says Scott. "You have raptors like the gos-hawk that are indicator species for the aspen. Also cavity nesters, woodpeckers."

"There's some neat country here in Nevada," Jim adds. He likes to cross-country ski as often as he can get away from his work. We pass an old waste dump, where tons of "growth medium" soils have been piled up along the roadside for future reclamation work. Jim gets on the radio. "Hey, I think we ran out of muck for Dan's dump back there. Why don't you move that loader to the 7,060 elevation." "Okay, boss, if that's what you want," a voice crackles back from the dash-mounted unit. "I just drove past the 7,750 bench. I'll move it around."

I ask about some broad lines in the exposed rockface running along the mine terraces above us. "Up this pit, you can see that bedding. That's old ocean floor, about 280 million years old," Jim grins.

We pass a big shovel with a blue cab that looks like the prow of an ocean-going tug. "That's a fifteen-yard shovel, a $2 million ma-chine made by Harvish Figer out of Milwaukee [a company Bill Grannell has approached to help fund People for the West]."

The road begins winding down a steep canyon ravine—or at least that's my initial impression. It takes me a minute to realize this isn't a ravine but an artificial pit. We pull out onto the crater floor three hundred feet below ground level. I climb out of the truck, looking up towards the rim thirty stories above us. Thirty million tons of rock and ore have been moved out of this hole since 1986. That's about three hundred nuclear aircraft carriers in weight. There are wooden stakes off to our left decorated with multicolored plastic flags where new twenty-five-foot-deep blasting holes are being prepared. "We're still chasing that block of ore body," Jim explains. "Mining twenty-foot slices using our computer models to tail it down."

I'm disappointed to find out there's no new blasting going on today. The trick with industrial blasting is to pack your holes with ammonium nitrate fertilizer and diesel oil, a formula long popular with truck-bomb terrorists in Ireland, Colombia, Lebanon, and, more recently, New York. You use your dynamite as your blast initiator.

We drive over next to a pickup truck where a safety flag man is waiting to watch a mechanized ballet of behemoths. Even from a hundred feet back, I feel like we're in Tonka Toys as the world's largest frontloader, a 1,300-horsepower 994 Caterpillar, takes thirty-five- to forty-ton bites out of an ore pile. The Cat operator sits in a cab twenty feet off the ground, moving his machine's segmented body, on eleven-foot-high tires, in tight radial turns. His machine's radiator block is the size of a garage door. In four railcar-sized scoops, he fills up a 150-ton mud-splattered yellow haul truck and is ready for the next. This is as big and rudely basic as man's industrial processes get. These miners eat mountains and shit gold.

"It moves twenty-one yards of muck in a scoop," Jim says proudly. A boxy, mechanized drill hammer sits on the far side of the pit readying another twenty-five-foot grid for blasting. "We'll blast six hundred holes at a time. About four hundred tons is loosened per hole. Once I did an eleven-hundred-hole shoot."

"That must have been spectacular," I say, thinking of the five-hundred-pound bombs I used to watch turning half-block sections of Managua into rubble and the IRA's nitrobenzine car bombs blasting downtown Belfast. "It doesn't look that spectacular if you do it right," he tells me. "The trick is to shake the rock loose but leave it in place so that afterwards the diggers can come in and muck it out."

I'm relieved to see that the snow-capped peaks around us still dwarf this human work as we climb back up onto the main haul road.

"This is a small hole," Jim says, referring to the entire Jerritt operation. "We move up to 150,000 tons a day. Barrick or Newmont probably move 500,000 tons a day. You go visit a copper pit like they've got in Butte, Montana, you'll see what really big is."

"The hole that ate a town."

"That's right."

The hole that ate a town and is now the world's largest Superfund cleanup site.

I ask him if he's really worried about his company having to pay the same royalties as a coalmine operator or oil company.

"People don't understand that this is a different operation from coal or gas. We don't set the price. The royalty will just shorten the mine's life. People will be out the gate a year earlier. Some of the low-grade ore won't be worth milling. In other words, we wouldn't be maximizing the use of the resource."

As much as I respect Jim Collord and his work, before maximizing this mine's resources for DeBeers of South Africa I'd rather see the Humboldt National Forest given over to cross-country skiers, deer hunters, and endangered goshawks.

SEVEN

Save It for What?

*These "Wise Use" extremists claim that economically you're going
to take their jobs away from them; they're all going to become
poor; their children are going to starve; and it's all because you're
a bunch of fuzzy-headed tree-huggers. . . . It's blatant lying
in many cases is how they present things.*
GENERAL NORMAN SCHWARZKOPF (RET.),
AT A NATURE CONSERVANCY PRESS CONFERENCE

*The APA [Adirondack Park Agency] will take all of our private
property. The APA will be a total dictator. Adirondackers will
be forced to live in concentration camps working as slave
laborers for the APA.*
LT. COLONEL CALVIN CARR (RET.),
LEADER OF THE ADIRONDACK SOLIDARITY ALLIANCE

A redtail hawk rides a warm thermal above the Pemigewasset
River as it bubbles past the green yards and century-old field-
stone foundations of the small Victorian town of North Woodstock, New Hampshire. The town has established a postage-
stamp-sized park where a strip of white sand and a wide granite
bar reach out to a sudden dropoff in the river bottom, a natural
swimming hole deep enough for a breathtakingly cold morning
plunge or cannonball dive to the clear rocky bottom. Right now a
couple of young boys are keeping themselves amused chucking
rocks into the hole. Beyond the pool-sized depression, the Pemi,
as it is known locally, rushes knee-high around a thickly wooded
island that divides it just above a rumbling set of rapids that could

prove fast thrills for a kayaker or skilled canoeist. The rushing sound of the crystal whitewater bridging over glacial boulders has also provided the perfect tonic for my tired bones, assuring a good night's sleep at a local inn along the river.

While loggers, ranchers, and multinational mining corporations fight for continued economic access to western public lands under the rubric of Wise Use, quietly scenic parts of America east of the Mississippi, including a forty-mile stretch of the Pemigewasset, have become the prime battlegrounds for the property rights movement. As rural life has been increasingly altered by the growth of highways, cluster developments, and shopping malls, people have begun to debate how best to preserve areas, such as northern New England, that still manage to maintain their unique mix of stable populations, pastoral landscapes, and intact ecosystems. Competing ideas have included proposals for environmentally oriented state and local land-use planning, federal protections for unique rivers and vital wetlands, maintaining the values and choices of private property owners who have protected these areas in the past, or a combination of all three that can assure sustainable rural development. For leaders of the property rights movement, only the third of these four options is acceptable, a no-compromise defense of landowners' rights to do with their property as they please without any form of restriction.

The night before arriving at the Pemi, my travel mate, Nancy, and I had driven south through the Franconia Notch from the north-country town of Lancaster. Before leaving there, Jeff Elliot and his wife had warned us to drive carefully, and not too fast. Over the last six months, there had been a number of car/moose collisions, several fatal to both parties, since three-quarter-ton moose when challenged tend to turn broadside to their attackers. This sounded like a fair warning, and more reassuring somehow than the ones running on the news back home, where a spate of armed car-jackings had San Francisco Bay Area drivers on edge.

Jeff is a bearded high school teacher and former state Fish and Game biologist. He was dressed in jeans and a "Stop Acid Rain" tee shirt the day he took us to see where his house had once stood.

Just before sunset we parked by the side of a two-lane blacktop road and walked five minutes up a trail lined with wild ferns, painted trillium, and pink moccasin flowers, accompanied by swarms of blood-hungry mosquitoes. In a clearing stood the remains of Jeff's two-story cabin, burned to the ground three years ago. Part of the floor is charred but still intact where his 250-gallon hot water tank ruptured in the flames. A rusting metal stove leans against a remnant of a wall beam and a scattering of twisted nails and hooks. The rest of the building is all blackened charcoal timbers tangled up with blackberry bushes and wild grasses and surrounded by a half-crescent of scorched trees.

"I'd gone to visit a lady friend in Worcester, Mass., turning off my propane gas before leaving Friday night," he tells us. "On Wednesday around noon a fellow teacher saw the fire from the heights and called the fire department. She described it as a fireball-type explosion. By the time the fire department got here, there wasn't much they could do. The fire inspector said it was arson."

We climb around the blackened remains. Some broken glass bottles, empty beer cans, and cigarette butts suggest that local teens have made the place their hangout. "Look at this," Jeff calls out, leaning down while slapping a mosquito off the back of his neck. I approach, thinking he's found some forgotten keepsake, but what he wants to show us is a cone-shaped morel mushroom growing out of the black ash. "I'd been living here four years and lost everything in the fire," he says, slapping at another mosquito that's alighted on his face. "I wasn't the only one who lost his home," he smiles, and points to where a weasel had lived just outside his front door.

He takes us further back into the woods, searching for a rare iris he'd spotted on his last trip out to his property. I offer to pick a Canadian mayflower for Nancy, but she'd prefer more Avon's Skin-So-Soft, which we're all using as mosquito repellent. Jeff, who's a trained entomologist and freshwater ecologist, shows us a hole in a rotting tree trunk leading to a shallow burrow below. He tells us that there are unexplored ecosystems of shallow caves and burrow networks in the forest floor. We hear a woodpecker knocking nearby. He says there are also flying squirrel, moose, coyote, beaver, and bear in the area. The Highway Department used to dump road-killed moose and deer at the front end of his property, which attracted black bears.

In 1989 Jeff Elliot led a campaign against the clear-cutting of New Hampshire's forest domain. "Philosophically I aligned myself with Earth First!" he says. "The natural world has a right to exist regardless of the human condition. It's not that I don't sympathize with women's rights or fighting poverty or whatever. That's just not my main concern. I was brought up here in New Hampshire. What I know and what I'm going to fight to defend is the wilderness—all of it that's still left, all of it, without compromise.

"A state policeman told me an angry logger burned my place down," he continues on our way back to the car, as we pass the ruins of his former home once more. "He wouldn't tell me what he based his information on." Jeff has his own theory about a local logger who had been an outspoken opponent during the clear-cutting campaign, but admits he'll probably never know for sure who torched his house.

Since that fire two other anti-logging activists he knows have been burned out by arsonists, Michael Vernon and fellow New Hampshirite Jaimie Sayen. Vernon, a town official in Solon, Maine, woke up with his house on fire and had to dive off a second-floor porch into the snow to escape the flames that eventually gutted the building.[1]

Says Jaimie Sayen, who lives on the edge of a wilderness area north of the White Mountains, "I don't think it's a coincidence that in the last three years Jeff Elliot, Michael Vernon, and myself have all experienced arson. The thing is, I'm not intimidated. I've been involved in this forest stuff for years and I'm not going away. These guys who inspire this stuff, like Don Gerdts in the Adirondacks or Ron Arnold, are not going to last, because they are only negative. They only know what they're *against*. They have no vision. They will have some limited success as demagogues for a while, but the question really is how to swat them off before they do too much damage." Swatting, I find, is a popular term in the northeast forests during mosquito and blackfly season.

Since 1988, when a French holding company put half a million acres of Diamond Match timberland in New York, Vermont, New Hampshire, and Maine on the international real estate market, the region's environmentalists, state governments, and congressional delegations have been trying to develop a land-use plan to protect the northern forests.[2] The increasingly militant property rights movement has been attacking the idea of forest protection as an attempt to steal land from its rightful owners.

Having lived in New England for five years, I'm aware that more than 90 percent of the land in this region is privately owned and well maintained by people who take pride in their seasonal enterprises and pastoral landscapes. Like everywhere else, New England has seen population shifts, particularly in southern New Hampshire and Vermont, with people migrating northward from the cities. For the most part, however, the new arrivals have adapted to the region's traditional ways of viewing the world, which include a healthy skepticism towards ostentatious wealth and all levels of government above the town meeting. Respect for private property rights is as natural to a New England Yankee as are thrift, patriotism, and the conservation ethic. So New England would seem to be fertile ground in which the property rights movement could take root. Of course, the devil, as they say, is in the details.

The New Hampshire Landowners Alliance (NHLA), with a core of about twenty activists, has been one of the most high-profile property rights groups operating in New England. In 1993 it led a successful campaign to block a "Wild and Scenic River" designation along a forty-mile stretch of the Pemigewasset River, a portion of land that included the North Woodstock/Lincoln area. This designation would have prohibited dams and federal water projects on the Pemi, keeping it protected in its present free-flowing state. However, six out of seven towns along the proposed stretch voted against that designation after NHLA convinced area residents that the 1968 Wild and Scenic Rivers Act was part of a government plan to take control of their property, even though the New Hampshire congressional delegation had tailored the Pemi agreement to exclude any land acquisitions.[3]

NHLA is headed by Cheryl Johnson, a short-haired, bright-eyed native New Hampshirite who runs a computer graphics business out of a small office above the nineteenth-century Mad River Inn in Campton. Dressed casually in jeans and a man's dress shirt, with her NRA bill cap on a nearby shelf, she takes time out from assembling the national Alliance for America newsletter to talk about how she first became politically active.[4]

"For me it started in January of ninety-one, when the Pemi was nominated for state protection," she says. "I was totally apolitical. I'd never read a newspaper. I went to this river-management meeting with about two hundred people. Friends of my husband said they needed support, so that's why we went."

One of her husband's friends (and his employer at the time) was Ed Clark, part owner of Clark's Trading Post, a local tourist attraction, and of several hydroelectric facilities. Ed Clark hoped to erect a dam across a steep gorge on the river at a point called Livermore Falls, the site of a nineteenth-century mill. State river protection would prevent any dams from being built.

Says Cheryl, "Our feeling was the rivers were protected, local zoning already protected them enough. But they wanted to establish locally based appointees named by the governor. It turned into a major battle and people got stomped on. The hydro dam didn't go in, even though historically this had been a working site. There had been a grinding mill there for logs going to the paper-mill in Lincoln. Ed Clark had planned a detailed historic restoration. He wanted to rebuild the old mill so that it would have attracted tourists. He spent fourteen years and $450,000 working on the project. Now the owner of that land has had to sell it to the state for two to three hundred thousand because if it can't be developed it's just a liability. College kids use the beach there for drinking and jump off the rocks and sometimes kill themselves.

"Anyway, in May of ninety-one, the river got state designation," she continues. "Then, in February of ninety-two, the federal study began. It was the same thing again, only a bigger deal.

We didn't want the feds involved. I never intended to be a leader. I wanted to do the group's newsletter, but this guy dropped out and I was left doing more and more of the work. Gradually I started reading the newspaper and watching the news on TV. At first I thought it was just us fighting this designation. Then I realized there was something bigger going on. I went to the Fly-In for Freedom in D.C.[5] and met all these other property owners and other types like ORV operators and got educated about what the preservationists were trying to do to us. I became real angry seeing how their magazines were all putting out the same propaganda. When I got home I mailed eleven years of environmental magazines back to *National Wildlife*. Then I went to St. Louis for the founding of the Alliance for America. It was my first flight on a commercial airliner. Now I'm secretary of the group. You have to understand this is a real grassroots movement. We have to pass the hat around to finance our work.

"In 1992 to ninety-three we built our [NHLA] membership up to 1,500 and began to educate people," she continues. "We brought in speakers like Don Rupp from the Upper Delaware Valley, Joe Wrabek from the Columbia River Gorge in Oregon, and David Howard [from the Alliance for America]. Personally, I think Don Rupp goes too far. He said if this becomes a scenic river then it's a national park, and in a park you can carry a gun. I think he did more harm than good.

"I've heard [Adirondacks leader] Don Gerdts speak in Vermont, and he can really fire people up. He's very much like Chuck Cushman, with a 'Rent-a-Riot' personality. We didn't bring Chuck in because he wanted $1,500 a day for a weekend presentation."

In its campaign to block the wild and scenic designation, the NHLA put out fliers and press statements claiming that the federal government wanted to turn the Pemi into a national park and seize people's land. They got editorial support from the *Manchester Union Leader*, the state's largest (and notoriously conservative) newspaper. They also told people that the scenic river designation would decrease their property values, although studies of the more than 150 Wild and Scenic Rivers established to date shows that the opposite is far more likely to occur.

"The real problem is not property values declining but gentrification," says Glenn Pontier, editor of the *River Reporter* in New York's Upper Delaware Valley. "Our property values have gone up with the Delaware River designation, and this hurts the old-timers around here. What Chuck Cushman, Don Rupp, and people like that do is prevent real discussion of what's going to happen, so that we now have people having to sell their homes because nobody made the right plans or asked the right questions back when the issue was first debated."

I ask Cheryl if she'd been involved back in 1979, when the EPA shut down the old Lincoln Paper Mill. The mill had polluted the Pemi, making the river unsafe for swimming, wading, or fishing and giving the town the derisive name of "Stinkin' Lincoln."

"No. It was polluted, but you were just used to it. It wasn't anything you really thought about, because it had always been that way," she says.

As we leave she gives us copies of the two most recent Alliance for America newsletters. The cover story in the April 1993 issue is headed, "Signing Away America," and begins, "As of April 2, 1992, the United States as we know it no longer exists." The article goes on to explain that by signing the U. N. Covenant on Civil and Political Rights, the U. S. government has betrayed God and the Constitution. The story is reprinted from the *New American Magazine*, a publication of the John Birch Society.[6]

Nancy and I pull off by the side of Route 3 behind a couple of cars with Plymouth State College stickers, cross a railroad track, and scuttle down a steep path on a thickly wooded hillside, sliding through brambles, loose dirt, and tangled branches, before regaining our footing just short of a rusting coil of barbed wire. The Pemi River is fifty yards across here. Opposite the boulder-strewn bank we stand on is a white sand beach where two young college women in bathing suits and tee shirts are wading in the cool water. To our left 130 feet above the river is the red, rusting remnant of the Pumpkinseed Bridge, a slender double bow extending from granite outcroppings on either side of a steep gorge where the waters narrow. To our right, along the riverbanks are rolling emerald green hills so lush they make you wish you were an ungulate.

After taking in the river view, we climb back up to the railroad tracks and walk along them a short way to the red brick pumphouse of the old grinding mill. Moss- and lichen-covered rocks lead down to a second beach by a cataract of thundering white water, where the gorge has narrowed to no more than twenty-five feet across. Four students, three guys and a girl, are sitting high up on the beach. One of the lads, ponytailed and bare chested, plays the guitar, a cigarette dangling from his lips. We walk out on a granite ledge next to the thundering falls, fast tons of white water shooting across an exposed staircase of granite rock. It sounds like Dolby white noise and is as visually hypnotic as fire.

We return to the car and move on, then make another stop at the Mill at Loon Mountain, a wood and brick complex of boutique shops and restaurants which along with the Lincoln Center Shopping Mall and the River-Green Condominium/Hotel have surrounded what's left of the abandoned papermill. We climb around inside the original mill's hollowed-out red-brick boiler building. Just behind it I find the old effluent canal out to the river, its water still a bright orange color. Inside the Loon Mountain shopping complex, between a cookie shop and a bookstore, is a display case of old photos showing the mill in operation and the spruce logging camps that fed its pulpers before the turn of the century. Pictures of steam boilers date from 1915; one shot of the mill's front parking lot dates from the 1950s.

Peter Gould, who works for Lincoln Mill Associates, the real estate agency that oversees the mall, has heard that there was some conflict over lost jobs and environmental regulations back in 1979, when the EPA shut down the mill. "Luckily, the whole town of Lincoln retrofitted from a mill town to a resort town in a pretty short time," he says. "The Loon Mountain ski area had opened in 1966, and so that gave a head start to the effort."

At its peak, the contaminated papermill employed some five

hundred workers, roughly the same number as are now employed in the shopping mall, restaurant, and condominium complex alongside the restored river.

On our way out of town we make a final stop at Clark's Trading Post. There's a billboard on the riverbank just before you get there, but the low-slung brown-shingle cabin that's been stretched a city block long would be a hard place to miss in any case. Inside, the trading post is filled with all sorts of gimcracks: chipmunk postcards, Indian tomahawks, feathered headdresses, leather bullwhips, the Last Supper on a cross section of pine wood, Davy Crockett coonskin caps, jawbreakers, maple sugar candy dolls, saltwater taffy, costume jewelry. Ed's not around, but his black bears are—nine of them in cement-walled and -floored compounds next to the trading post. Behind the pens is a small circular bear stadium used for weekend performances. You can peek through ceramic chutes in the concrete walls or pay to drop food down to the pacing animals, whose black coats appear patchy from mange. Next door to the trading post is "Clark's Station," a theme park with miniature train rides and bumper boats. Clark's Trading Post conveys a hint of what a "historically authentic" Livermore Falls dam restoration project might have looked like, including the waterslide and leaping-trout show.

About sixty-five miles south of Canada, near the Vermont border, Nancy and I realize we've crossed an undefined boundary and have entered the much debated northern forest. We're looking out across endless miles of low, forested mountains stretching to a blue-tinted horizon that is unbroken by visible clearcuts or any discernible towns of size. Occasionally a small village will outline itself against a hillside, a white New England church steeple pinning it to the landscape like some exotic proof that, given the right opportunity, humans can complement the natural terrain as easily as a herd of deer on a sunlit ridgeline.

We drive into Vermont, where much of the woodland has been cleared to make way for tidy red-barned dairy farms, following directions that take us off the tarmac and onto one of the area's many interconnecting dirt roads. "Pat Buchanan is right," grins State

Senator John McClaughery, a six-foot, blue-eyed, square-jawed, not-quite-handsome politician and conservative philosopher. "There are two cultures at war—an educated elite, who want good government, control of antisocial tendencies, and a smooth-running system, and the other culture—an independent, freedom-loving culture of low-level anarchy resistant to order and authority. We see this battle on gun control, property rights, land-use control. It's the American glory."

After a brief stint in the Reagan White House, McClaughery left Washington and returned to the green fields of Vermont.

"Many of my friends stayed on there in D.C. and got rich," he says. "I chose not to." Looking out of the picture window in his multiroom, high-roofed red pine-log cabin five miles up an unpaved country road in Vermont's Northeast Kingdom, it's easy to believe he made the right choice. Beyond his wide wooden porch on the front sixteen acres of his two-hundred-acre spread is a field of daisies, purple lilac bushes, a few poplar trees, and a ridgeline view of the green mountains. Anxious for at least one sighting, Nancy asks him if there are any moose in the area.

"I lose constituents to moose every year," he says. "They come through their windshields. They're so high off the ground that when you hit one you end up with two thousand pounds of animal in your lap." He's fought to pass a bill that would allow the shooting of nuisance animals. "It's not a sport to shoot them but the problem is they've become a sacred animal here in Vermont, a symbolic issue for the other side. The moose is our whale!" he shakes his head more perplexed than offended. He accuses the governor, Howard Dean, of being in the pocket of the environmentalists.

"You ran against him in ninety-two?" I ask.

"So they say," he smiles.

Governor Dean beat Republican state senator and property rights leader McClaughery three to one, with the latter drawing around 23 percent of the vote.

The property rights movement in Vermont has focused on repealing two state laws, Act 250 (passed in 1970 and requiring permits for development) and Act 200 (passed in 1988 and requiring each town to develop its own land-use plan). Supporters of the movement include a mixed bag of farmers from the economically depressed Northeast Kingdom, a Burlington real estate developer, backers of a planned Wal-Mart that's running into popular opposition in the town of Williston,[7] and the management of the Killington ski resort, which hopes to siphon off state-owned riverwater for snow making. Legal support has been provided by the New England Legal Foundation (NELF), one of the twenty-two right-wing public interest law firms coordinated through the Heritage Foundation. But the movement may have peaked early during McClaughery's 1992 election campaign. In June of that year, Citizens for Property Rights (CPR), the state's major activist group, held a rally at the Killington ski resort. The hotel's lobby was decorated with twenty effigies hanging from the ceiling with nooses around their necks. Each bore a placard with the name of a liberal state politician or environmental leader, including Democratic gubernatorial candidate Howard Dean. After Nadine Bailey, the unemployed logger's wife from Hayfork, California, gave one of her stump speeches, a CPR spokesman introduced his group's favorite candidate, declaring, "There is the scent of a lion in the political arena, and that lion is John McClaughery."[8]

"This movement was not useful for my campaign at all," McClaughery complains. "I mean, of the 100 to 120 people who showed up at that rally, they all voted for me but none delivered their towns. Citizens for Property Rights is now basically defunct. They had this constant mantra of 'Repeal Act 200,' but no real grasp or desire to develop plans and political strategies. Most of these folks are all heart but sadly unsophisticated. Historically we rally to meet a threat but can't sustain a drive. It's like herding rabbits. The preservationists at VNRC [the Vermont Natural Resources Council] by contrast know how to hunker down with defeats and stay the long term.

"It's really two different world views at work here between us and the environmentalists," he reiterates. "They don't want the woodchucks [native Vermonters] to be able to buy a home and raise a family. They look down on woodchucks and don't want growth. They think anything that increases comfort or convenience should be banned. It's part of what I call the Green Church, this religious compulsion to make people suffer for our sins against nature. These elitist land planners also dominate the liberal media. Seven of the state's nine daily newspapers are pro-preservationist, one is nondescript—kind of eccentric—and one is progrowth. That's the *Caledonian Express* here in the Northeast Kingdom."

John helps to balance what he considers the "liberal bias" of the media by sitting on the editorial board of the Moon-controlled *Washington Times.* He is also active in ALEC, the American Legislative Exchange Council, having proposed the first state compensatory takings legislation in 1991, and has co-written a book titled *The Vermont Papers,* a plan for decentralizing Vermont into a county shire system. Much to his annoyance, the ideas in his book have won a following among some of the state's leftists.

I ask him about some of the right-wing radicals who have attached themselves to the property rights movement. "We had a northern forest lands meeting here and the idiot John Birch Society showed up," he says, frowning like he's just found a deer tick in his coffee mug. What does he think about Bircher activity and the vigilante violence going on in the Adirondacks Park, just across Lake Champlain from Vermont?

"You have to understand the Adirondacks people. Back in 1973 I spoke to eight hundred people in the town of Saranac Lake. They've been so put upon and colonized for so long over there I can see why they'd be driven to extremism."

Two days later we cross the lake in order to investigate the property rights movement in the Adirondacks for ourselves. A handful of small sailboats bob at their moorings as we approach the nineteenth-century port hamlet of Essex on the car ferry from Charlotte, Vermont. As far as we can see along the western shore of Lake Champlain run the dense green forests of the Adirondack Mountains—what we in the West would call foothills, actually— a five-million-year-old geological dome 160 miles wide and a mile high. From satellite photos you can see water running off this dome in all directions to form the Hudson, Saranac, and a hundred other rivers. The mountains are thick with a profusion of first-, second-, and third-growth oak, maple, beech, spruce and fir, hemlock, yellow birch and white pine, sumac, black cherry, and wild apple. On reflection, these hilly mountains are as quietly breathtaking in their own arboreal way as any bare-rocked, snow-capped mountain crag the Rockies might offer up. The Adirondack uplift is contained within a century-old park boundary larger than the state of Vermont, larger than any U.S. park outside Alaska.

It seems odd, then, that one of the most militant property rights movements in the United States today, one that has escalated from protests to punches to vandalism and an organized campaign of terror involving death threats, arson, and gunfire, should be carried out by people who have chosen to call a park their home. But then there are many unusual aspects to the Adirondacks Park scene, not the least of which is its location. Normally when you think of great wildernesses, New York is not the first place that comes to mind. But in 1894 New York State amended its constitution to declare the Adirondack Mountains "forever wild." This followed decades of massive overcutting of the upstate forests. By 1850 New York was producing a fifth of the timber cut in the U.S. The Hudson River was choked with log rafts heading towards the mills at Glens Falls. Along with white pine for lumber, spruce was being milled for paper, hemlock bark used in tanning, and almost anything with roots and branches converted into charcoal for industry.

The Adirondacks timber boom had its price, however. Loggers clear-cut more than two-thirds of the mountains, stripping forest cover and leaving behind only those hardwoods that couldn't float. In addition, game hunters using hounds and fishermen blasting streams for fish decimated the area's wildlife: deer and trout, moose, beaver, cougar, bear, wolf, and bald eagle all but disappeared from the countryside. Sportspeople and hunters began complaining of this destruction of the wilds in the pages of *Forest and Stream* magazine. The logging industry dismissed these early preservationists as "Denudatics," for their opposition to the denuding of the mountains. But the Adirondacks also serve as the watershed for New York City, and by the 1870s the loss of forest cover was causing increased erosion and flooding, which in turn threatened the water quality of the Hudson River and commercial transportation on the Erie Canal. Influential members of the New York Board of Trade and Transportation, including the Vanderbilts, who owned the Erie Canal, soon joined the outdoorsmen of *Forest and Stream* in demanding protection for the Adirondacks. *Harper's Weekly* and other popular magazines ran drawings of vast fields of stumps and raging forest fires set off by the sparks thrown from charcoal-burning lumber trains. The *New York Times* editorialized in favor of making the Adirondacks "the Central Park" of the world. Governor David B. Hill, a quiet conservationist in his own right, began the legislative process that would lead to the establishment and constitutional protection of the park.

Initially, the blue-line park boundary encompassed 2.6 million acres, including private lands that the state planned to buy up. Over time, however, the blue line expanded to almost 6 million acres, of which only 42 percent is today owned by the state. Half the remaining land is owned by park residents, with the rest divided between outside ownership and the forest products industry.

The early years of the park saw the growth of small hamlets and villages sustained by a mixed economy of selective logging, tourism, and health care. The town of Saranac Lake became famous for its sanatorium, established by Dr. Edward Trudeau (great-grandfather of "Doonesbury's" Gary Trudeau), and private lodgings with open porches known as "cure porches" where people with TB came to "take the airs." Among the town's more distinguished visitors were Mark Twain, Robert Louis Stevenson, Margaret Sanger, Albert Einstein, and Somerset Maugham. The nearby town of Lake Placid would also gain fame as the site of the 1932 and 1980 Winter Olympics. Farming inside the blue line was widespread in the early part of the century, as much of the Adirondacks had been reduced to field and pasture. The forest cover didn't begin to fully reestablish itself until the 1930s. Even then it was a new kind of forest, 50 percent softwood to 50 percent hardwood contrasted to the earlier 80/20 mix. As the number of paved roads running through the park grew during the 1950s, tourism increased. Still, much of the area remained economically depressed, its local population dependent on seasonal jobs provided by resorts, logging, and wilderness guide work. With the opening of the Interstate 87 "Northway" in the mid-1960s, real estate interest in motels and second-home developments along the shorelines of the area's 2,700 lakes and ponds skyrocketed. Lake George, in the southern part of the park, became one of the first towns overrun with strip developments consisting of motels, marinas, amusement parks, and apartment complexes.

In 1968, worried that there was almost no form of land-use control or zoning inside the blue line to protect the park's wild and natural aspects, Governor Nelson Rockefeller appointed a "commission on the future of the Adirondacks." In 1971, responding to the commission's recommendations, the state legislature established the Adirondack Park Agency (APA) to develop long-range land-use plans for both public and private property in the park. Some local residents of the hamlets were outraged at the idea of having to follow zoning guidelines established by a state agency (although only 10 percent of the hamlets had set up any zoning of their own). Developer Anthony D'Elia and Saranac businessman Frank Casier were among a number of early "home rule" advocates who founded the League for Adirondack Citizens Rights, which held town meetings (including the one attended by John McClaughery) and demonstrations demanding the abolition of the APA. In 1976 local State Assemblyman Ron Stafford sponsored a bill that would have replaced the APA with a locally elected board. Days before the bill was to be voted on, an arsonist was caught trying to set fire to the newly constructed APA headquarters building in the park town of Ray Brook.

"I'd given a speech in Canton. I think I'd actually told this community group that the troubles were over," recalls the athletically built director of the APA, Bob Glennon, his green eyes sparkling. Glennon, a newly hired agency employee at the time, had gone for some beers with his friend and APA colleague Dick Beamish after the 1976 community meeting. "That's why it was two in the morning when I pulled in behind our building to fuel up my state car," he admits, smiling. "When I got out I smelled gas. I went inside and saw these two cans and noticed a guy dressed in black with a black ski mask kind of hunkered down in a corner. I remember being mad and knocking him down. The adrenalin kind of took over. I knocked him down and then kneeled on him and reached for this phone on the desk and called the state troopers. They arrived a few minutes later and arrested him and began reading him his rights off this little card. It was kind of weird. The next day there were bail fund cans in all the local bars," he laughs.

The arsonist was quickly identified as Brian Gale, a Tupper Lake resident. Gale had been paid to torch the building. Who paid him and why have never been established, although there were persistent rumors about a Saranac-based home rule leader. Gale was allowed to plead guilty to a charge of third-degree burglary and sentenced to sixty days in jail. Stafford's proposal to abolish the APA was voted down at the State House in Albany.[9]

"This was similar to what we're seeing today: contrived violence timed to influence legislation," claims former APA man Dick Beamish, who now works as the Audubon Society's representative in the Adirondacks.

Things quieted down over the next decade. The park's permanent population grew to some 130,000. Incomes, which had been among the lowest in the state, rose gradually to meet the norm for rural New Yorkers. The park, only a day's drive from seventy million people, began to attract close to ten million visitors a year. They enjoyed a multiuse range of activities from swimming and water skiing at lakeside resorts to hiking and canoeing across countless miles of isolated backcountry wilderness. Then the building boom of the late 1980s touched off a new round of conflict between those who saw the park as a natural treasure to be preserved and those who felt they had a right to profit from developing their scenic surroundings as they chose. Soon, a thousand new homes a year, including huge lakeshore condominium complexes, were under construction. Ninety thousand acres of prime forest land was put up for auction by land speculators, and by 1989 the real estate industry had replaced logging, tourism, and the state payroll as the mainstay of the Adirondacks economy.

Worried for the park's future, Governor Mario Cuomo established what he called the Commission on the Adirondacks in the Twenty-First Century. He appointed fourteen people, including six park residents, to the commission. One of the Adirondackers was Robert Flacke, a former APA chairman and owner of three motels and nine other businesses in Lake George. Flacke had a falling out with park environmentalists after they opposed his 1979 plan for a sewage-transfer system that would have shipped Lake George's wastes out of the lake basin and over the hills to the Hudson River, allowing his small city to continue growing. Even before the commission completed its 245 recommendations,[10] Flacke was leading a campaign to kill new land-use proposals, particularly one that called for a year-long construction moratorium while new environmental and lakefront protection standards were being established. In May 1990, weeks ahead of the official findings, Flacke's dissenting report was released to the media. Its release helped to mobilize several militant property rights groups, including the Citizens Council of the Adirondacks (CCA), led by retired Long Island ad man and failed real estate developer Donald Gerdts, and the Adirondack Solidarity Alliance (ASA), headed by retired army Lt. Colonel Calvin Carr.

On May 5 Gerdts and Carr held an anticommission rally, attended by some two hundred people, in the park hamlet of Elizabethtown. "This is Day One of the Adirondacks rebellion," Gerdts declared.[11] Following the rally they marched on the office of the Adirondack Council, the park's long-established eighteen-thousand-member mainstream environmental group best known for its willingness to compromise on almost anything. The protestors, in no mood to dialogue with "radical preservationists," painted the council's windows with swastikas. A dozen men led by Gerdts then went to the home of Eric Siy, a council staff person. "They threatened to burn down my house," Siy recalls. "Gerdts said things like, 'I should have dropped you the first time I saw you.' My neighbor, who's a deputy sheriff, finally came over and got them to go away."[12]

Over time other Adirondack Council members would receive similar death threats. Further, rotten vegetables and skunk oil would be dumped on the sidewalk in front of their office, bent roofing nails would be left on the street to flatten their tires, and used condoms would be sent to them in the mail. Liquid manure was also sprayed on the building shortly before a planned picket by the ASA. "Some good Adirondacker decided to give them some back," Calvin Carr sniffed, grinning, when he arrived on the scene with his picket sign a few hours after the vandals struck.[13]

"My car was vandalized at my home with the fender bashed in," says Adirondack Council Administrator Donna Beal, a third-generation park resident whose parents were local schoolteachers. "It sickens me if, because of your beliefs, you're subjected to violent tactics. It just goes against everything this country stands for."

Events quickly escalated that summer, with Gerdts and Carr vying to outdo each other in the realm of the outrageous. They organized a motorcade protest drive to Albany with several hundred cars, slowing down I-87 traffic to a fifteen-mile-an-hour crawl. Gerdts directed the rally by CB radio from an exit ramp while Carr flew overhead radioing his own directions from his personal helicopter.

Next, a group calling themselves the Minuteman Brigade, or Liberators, started sending out threats that they would burn down the state forest reserves if any of the commission's recommendations were carried out. Tee shirts appeared with the slogan, "Only Cuomo Can Prevent Forest Fires." Flaming arrows were fired at the APA and Adirondack Council offices, the home of a Department of Environmental Conservation (DEC) police officer, a state police substation, newspaper offices, and other area buildings. Daniel Sage, a Schroon Lake property rights activist and vocal defender of the brigade, compared supporters of the Twenty-First Century report to Communists who should "be burned out and executed."[14]

Gerdts faxed a warning memo to Governor Cuomo, declaring, "Only your direct and immediate intervention will prevent bloodshed and major property damage."

"This guy comes from Queens. He was probably born on a piece of asphalt. He's now up there telling everybody he's ordained to tell you how to deal with the forests?" the bemused governor commented to a group of upstate reporters.

By now intimidation was becoming a fact of life in the park. People who wrote letters to local newspapers arguing in favor of the commission report—including Elenore Webb, a Blue Mountain Lake resident in her eighties—got threatening phone calls at home. After making a threatening call to a man whose letter to the *Adirondack Daily Enterprise* he didn't like, Gerdts was charged with harassment. When George Davis, executive director of the governor's commission, tried to give a speech in the park, he was disrupted by dozens of angry hecklers. His state police escorts were so unnerved they had a police car parked outside with its motor running in case Davis was forced to flee.

Meanwhile, Bob Flacke established the Blue Line Council, which, along with other prodevelopment groups such as the Adirondacks Fairness Coalition, portrayed itself as a moderate group staking out the middle ground between the "radical preservationists" of the Adirondack Council and the "understandably angry" property rights activists, whose violent tactics they refused to condemn.

"Flacke positions himself in the middle by encouraging the crazies," claims Audubon's Dick Beamish. "It's a phony strategy but it's had some success."

The Blue Line Council and other park "moderates," together with the New York State Farm Bureau and Ron Stafford (who, since his 1976 bill to abolish the APA, had become chairman of the state senate's powerful finance committee), were able to pull together a statewide coalition to defeat a 1990 bond act that would have provided hundreds of millions of dollars worth of funding for new state land acquisitions inside the park.

In the Adirondack Mountains themselves, a new series of events was heating up, one that would provide at least one good visual for a "60 Minutes" report on Wise Use.

In 1989 the Department of Environmental Conservation (DEC) had blocked a mile-long dirt road into a wilderness area and popular picnic site called Crane Pond, converting it into a hiking trail. In June 1990 a group of masked Liberators using a logging crane removed the boulder blocking the road. They labeled the barrier the "boulder of shame," put it on a truck, and drove it down to Albany in a protest caravan. Later, with members of the Mohawk Warrior Society from the Akwesane reservation on the Canadian border, they held a rally and meeting in nearby Schroon Lake. The Liberators, the Solidarity Alliance, and the Warrior Society exchanged pledges of support in their common struggle against the New York State authorities.

"It would have been real scary if the Warrior Society and ASA had formed some kind of serious common front. That could have led to some real bloodshed," says a state police official who had begun monitoring the property rights militants around that time. The Warrior Society has been involved in a series of shootouts with antigambling Mohawk traditionalists who oppose casino operations on the reservation. Members of the Warrior Society are also suspected of having been involved in—along with gun running, cigarette smuggling, and other illegal activities—the shooting of a New York State National Guard medivac helicopter that flew over the reservation. The chopper was hit by seven rounds from an AK-47 rifle, which disabled the main rotor and seriously injured a doctor on board.

After a three-day stand-off between DEC police, the Solidarity Alliance, and the Schroon Lake townspeople who demanded the right to drive to Crane Pond, the DEC agreed to leave the road open to motor traffic. Don Gerdts and other activists began passing out leaflets for a Fourth of July victory celebration. The leaflets advised people to "bring your deer rifle in case rabid animals should be in the area."[15]

On September 3 a small group of Earth Firsters and their supporters—including Jeff Elliot and his wife, from New Hampshire—decided to protest the DEC's decision to reopen the wilderness area to vehicle traffic by blocking Crane Pond Road.

"We went there, camped overnight, and next morning a dozen of us stood in the road," Jeff recalls. "By 8 A.M. there were forty to fifty local men and some women drinking and shooting guns nearby. The only state trooper there said, 'It looks like trouble. I'm going to get reinforcements,' drove off, and that was the last we ever saw of him. Then the locals backed up a pickup and revved the engine like they were going to run us over. We decided it was time to leave, which is when we realized we were being held hostage. They'd blocked the only road out with their cars. Don Gerdts was real nervous about the gunfire. He got up on a pickup and tried to get his people to clear the road so that we could just leave. We were in our cars waiting to get out of there from about 9:30 A.M. to 1 P.M. That's when I left my car to take a leak and saw this TV guy arriving and began to talk to him."

At that point Elliot, the reporter, and his cameraman were approached by Warrensburg Town Supervisor Maynard Baker, a stocky, sixty-year-old ex-marine with a reputation for getting into bar fights.

"This old-timer comes over and he's screaming about his road, shaking with rage," Jeff recalls. "I tell the TV guy that we think the road should stay open, that it should have access for the disabled and for flying squirrels, raccoons, silkworm moths, and any Homo sapiens willing to walk instead of drive. And the old guy screams, 'You heard them, they're a bunch of homosexuals.' I say, 'Look, whatever your special interest group is . . . ,' and that's when, pow, he hits me. I went down and, I admit, kind of hammed it up. I mean, he had a good punch but it didn't connect all that well." Jeff's wife gives him a skeptical look.

Eventually the dramatic video of Baker punching Elliot and then being pulled away by his friends as he shouts, "Go back to wherever you came from but get out of here, out of our lives and our business!" was included in a 1992 "60 Minutes" report titled "Clean Air, Clean Water, Dirty Fight," which examined violence against environmental activists and the growth of the Wise Use movement. After its broadcast, Baker told the *Adirondack Daily Enterprise* that he'd been misquoted by Leslie Stahl, who told viewers he had regretted his action. What he'd actually told a researcher for "60 Minutes," he insisted, was that he was sorry he had had to punch Elliot but that, given the same circumstances, he'd certainly do it again.[16]

On July 8, 1991, shots were fired at an occupied APA truck near the town of AuSable Forks. Three park agency staffers had just finished talking to a property owner about permit requirements for a subdivision. There were a number of people on the scene, including some members of the ASA. As the park agents were backing out of the drive, someone fired about a dozen shots at them. The truck was hit in the right front fender, hubcap, and tire.

"They drove out of there on their flat and called in to the police as soon as they got safely away and could reach a phone," says Lt. Pete Person of the State Police Bureau of Criminal Investigation (BCI), whose agents have investigated the shooting and other incidents in the park. "We found .22 long rifle shell casings at the base of a tree some distance across the road. There were also some cigarette butts and tire tracks. It looked like someone had been waiting there for some time and a second person had picked him up in an all-terrain vehicle. We'd had some uniformed officers patrolling nearby who were able to interview sixteen people from the scene. We polygraphed five people, and the two we suspected tested untruthful, but we couldn't get a confession and can't use that as evidence. There's two theories at this point: one that they were after the park agency for their own reasons and another is that these two were paid to do this."

In the early morning of November 14, 1991, the Ticonderoga dental office of Dr. Dean Cook, board secretary of the Adirondack Council and an outspoken critic of toxic discharges from a local papermill, was gutted by fire. Fire inspectors ruled the fire an arson but refused to speculate on whether it might have been politically motivated. Dr. Cook is certain he was targeted because of his work with the council and his outspoken opposition to discharges from the International Paper mill in Ticonderoga.

A short time later Elizabeth McLain, commissioner of Environmental Conservation for the state of Vermont, went to a public meeting in Ticonderoga to explain her state's concerns over the papermill's releases of dioxin into Lake Champlain.

"Someone took a gallon of yellow paint and poured it over the roof of my car while I was in that meeting," she says. "I don't even think I was singled out. I think this could have happened to any car parked there with a Vermont plate. I wasn't scared. I was angry that political debate had sunk to this level."

In the fall of 1991, the Adirondack Solidarity Alliance joined up with the Alliance for America at their founding meeting in St. Louis, Missouri. David Howard, a property rights activist from the Adirondack hamlet of Bleeker, became the national group's first president, and Harry McIntosh, from the hamlet of Caroga Lake, became vice president for administration. McIntosh owns the computers that the alliance uses for its database and national networking. The first time I called the national alliance, identifying myself as a reporter, McIntosh immediately started to tell me about an article he'd read in *New American*, the John Birch Society magazine. "It's about this woman who helped prevent the New York schools from teaching homosexuality to schoolchildren. You know what they had in these textbooks for little kids? They teach you about sucking cock in school. That's what was in there." I told him I had a hard time believing that. "Me too. You wouldn't think this sort of thing could go on in America!" he replied indignantly.[17]

Don Gerdts and fellow activist Carole LaGrasse, who'd also attended the St. Louis meeting and D.C. Fly-In for Freedom, set up a short-lived public access cable TV show out of Plattsburgh, New York, partially funded by the John Birch Society. However, LaGrasse complained that the Birch Society was too intellectual, not activist enough.[18]

"Personally, I was shocked when my minister handed me an article on the Adirondacks from the Birch Society magazine," says Adirondack Council Administrator Donna Beal. "I didn't know they even still existed."

As the militancy of the property rights movement increased, its active support among park residents faded. On June 15, 1992, the state assembly voted 104 to 35 to pass a bill giving the APA control over development on shorelines, on roadsides, and in the park's undeveloped backcountry, the first attempt by the legislature to put into effect any of the Twenty-First Century Commission's recommendations. Ron Stafford promised to kill the bill in the senate. A pro-Stafford rally was organized by the Solidarity Alliance, Bob Flacke's Blue Line Council, and other property rights groups from the park with backing from the Adirondacks' paper industry that supports them (Flacke sits on the board of Finch, Pruyn & Co., a paper company with 154,000 acres of holdings in the park). Despite weeks of massive prepublicity, only about two hundred Adirondackers showed up for the rally. They carried professionally printed placards reading, "We Support AdiRONdacks STAFFORD."

"There is nothing in this bill but slavery for the Adirondacks," Calvin Carr shouted to the small crowd gathered on the steps of the capitol. "Cuomo," another speaker insisted, "could not be more socialist if he'd been educated in Moscow." After Ron Stafford was introduced, he promised the cheering crowd that "no bill proposing stricter zoning in the Adirondack Park will pass in the Senate."[19]

"The ridiculous thing is there's tougher zoning in suburban Albany than in the Adirondacks," claims John Sheehan, the Adirondack Council's state lobbyist in Albany.[20]

After listening to the Stafford rally, Sheehan went inside the statehouse to look for a reporter. There he was confronted by ASA member Norbert St. Pierre, of Crown Point, who said, "When we come gunnin', we're gonna come gunnin' for you." Sheehan asked him what he meant. "I mean we're going to shoot you," St. Pierre replied. When Sheehan walked back outside a few minutes later, Calvin Carr came up to him, threw a bottle of orange juice against his chest, and then punched him in the mouth. Much to Carr's surprise, Sheehan punched back. The police arrested Carr, bleeding from his ear, but later released him without filing charges. Sheehan believes Carr's attack on him was calculated to draw attention away from the rally's small turnout.

Two months later, on the night of August 7, Park Agency Commissioner Anne LaBastille's attached barns were burned to the ground in an arson fire that also destroyed her Chevy pickup truck, motorboat, riding tractor, and thousands of dollars worth of tools. A few hours later someone used a hand-carried pump sprayer to do several thousand dollars of damage to the Adirondack Council building, covering its front walls and windows in turquoise latex paint.

Anne LaBastille is a well-known author, whose books include *Woodswoman; Women and Wilderness; Mama Poc,* which recounts her unsuccessful twenty-four-year effort to save the great grebes of Lake Atitlán in Guatemala; and *Beyond Black Bear Lake,* the first popularly written account of the impact of acid rain on the lakes and forests of the Adirondacks and upstate New York.

"I'm a woman alone, so I'm a great target," she says, when asked why she thinks she was singled out for attack. "What's happening in the Adirondacks today reminds me a lot of the death squad stuff in Central America [where the game warden she worked with was murdered]. Luckily, I was away the night of the arson. Otherwise I might have run out to the barn to save my truck and been blown up with it."

Ten months after her $30,000 barns were burned, Anne La-Bastille retired from the APA commission. "It was primarily for professional reasons. I'm traveling a lot, lecturing, and working on my books. But it was also a high-risk position. If they had caught these people and had them behind bars, I might have reconsidered," she admits.

"Anne became a symbol to these people," says Bob Glennon, the director of the APA, who captured Brian Gale trying to burn down the APA office back in 1976. "They'd point to her as a world conservationist and say she didn't represent the Adirondacks' point of view, meaning theirs. Truth is, we're a much better agency for her having served. I joked to Anne that 'If you want to catch an Adirondacks arsonist you have to do it yourself,'" he grins. "She wasn't amused."

Gordon Davis is the attorney and landlord for the Adirondack Council. His yellow and brown chalet-type office building sustained $4,500 in damage. "I'm geared for the traditional type of political activity Americans get involved in, where you divide and argue and find agreement, not this South American revolutionary type of violence these other people are practicing." Davis is a large, red-faced Irishman with sharp blue eyes, a flowing crescent of gray-white hair, and a Kennedyesqe accent. His law office is on the top floor of his Elizabethtown building. The ground floor is divided between the storefront Adirondack Council offices and the Essex County Industrial Development Agency. Above the council offices hangs a carved wooden plaque of a loon, splattered with the blue-green paint from the 1992 attack.

"I was woken up that morning by a guy I knew was a member of the Solidarity Alliance and also happened to be a house painter. He called me at home about 8 A.M. and said, 'Sorry about your office building.' I asked him what he was talking about. He said, 'They painted your building last night' and then offered to clean it up for a fee. I told him to forget it.

"After I found out that they'd also burned Anne LaBastille's barns, I called a press conference in front of my building to condemn the violence. I asked the D.A. to join me, but he said he was otherwise engaged. I called Joe Boone, the county supervisor. He also wouldn't show up. So I went down to Albany to see Cuomo and said, 'Can't you put some of these guys in jail?'"

After Davis's visit, Governor Mario Cuomo ordered the state police to step up their investigations and wrote a pointedly open letter to Ron Stafford suggesting that "the first thing you can do, as the North Country's most prominent leader, is to speak out against these injustices and to let those who are responsible know that their actions will not be tolerated."[21]

"Stafford called me back all bent out of shape," Gordon Davis recalls with a wicked smile. "He's saying, 'You know, I'm against violence,' and I said, 'No, I don't know that, Ron. You haven't condemned this politically oriented violence in public.' He said he certainly would and he did, the night of the next election, three months later. After the results were in and he'd been re-elected, he gave a quote to the press condemning the violence."

I ask Davis about rumors that have circulated among county officials of a plan to blow up his office building. "I've heard rumors of such a plan," he says but won't go into detail. "Look," he says, "this violence has affected the whole debate over the future of the Adirondacks. I myself am more circumspect, realizing there are a bunch of crazies out there, so if I'm affected, a blabbermouth like me, then how do you think it affects the average person living up here?"

Although a $10,000 reward has been offered for the arrest and conviction of the arsonists and vandals involved in the 1992 attacks, no one has come forward to date with any information. Word among anti-enviro activists is that whoever claims the money won't live to spend it.

"Most of their activity at the moment is kind of teenage stuff, like spray painting all the state park signs, which still costs a tremendous amount of money to clean up," says State Police Investigator Rich Cybeck, who keeps track of the ASA, "Liberators," and other property rights militants. "We just had $700 to $800 damage to a sign across the road from Dale French's house that's been hit three times before. Sometimes I'll notice a sign that's been graffitied with aquamarine paint and figure that person's still active. Their linkups with the national Wise Use groups is kind of interesting when you look at all the problems they've been creating. What I really worry about is that everybody here hunts, and with access to hunting weapons, what's a lot of high school sophomoric stuff now could in a heartbeat turn into my having a homicide case on my hands."

After several tries I'm unable to reach Don Gerdts or Carole LaGrasse. Activists tell me Gerdts has lost credibility and dropped out of the political scene but that Calvin Carr and the ASA remain committed to the cause.

I agree to meet the retired lieutenant colonel, Calvin Carr, and his aide-de-camp, Dale French, at Frenchman's Family Dining in Crown Point just north of Ticonderoga. It's a mounted-fish-and-antlers kind of a place, a prefab log cabin diner with wagon-wheel lighting fixtures, half-thawed salads, and hot coffee. Carr, French, and his wife, Jerris, are sitting at a back table drinking their coffees when we arrive.

Carr is much the way I expected him to be, a little bigger than average, with a long, rugged face, hairline mole, battleship gray eyes, thin lips, a squared-off chin. He's potbellied but with an erect posture. Dale French is red-faced and tubby with thin hair, long sideburns, and a reddish blond mustache that droops slightly below his lips. He's wearing jeans and a too-tight red cotton short-sleeved shirt. His wife, Jerris, is rail thin with shiny black hair and a lined face. She's dressed in jeans and a pink sleeveless blouse.

Carr tells me he owns a small seven-worker paper factory that produces specialized resin-treated pulp papers, called foils, that are used for institutional furniture, restaurant trays, and dishes.

Dale says he was a nuclear power plant design engineer but returned home to Crown Point in 1983 because he wanted to be left alone. "Then Mario Cuomo started all this stuff up with his 1990 report."

"I was sweeping up at my warehouse when Dale brought me the preliminary paperwork and I thought it was a joke," Cal Carr recalls. "I said, 'This looks more like a plan for the Ural Mountains than the Adirondack Mountains.'" He gives me an appraising look before launching into an extemporaneous rap on free-market environmentalism. "I don't think there's anything to indicate that some subsequent generation is any more deserving than this generation," he says. "So when people talk about preserving the Adirondacks, preserve it for what? Save it for what? There's no shortage of anything in this country. There are more trees, iron, copper, oil than ever. There's no validity to saying there's a finite supply of oil. Oil is being produced constantly. All the copper or iron we've taken out of the ground could be recycled. Nothing disappears. People talk about 1 percent of the world's water is freshwater. All the water in the world is potential freshwater. It's a natural system of recycling. There's no scientific basis for what they're doing, so the only rationale must be to take us to utter socialism. The mentality driving the park agency is designed to eliminate people and jobs from this area."

"We're fortunate to have Cal here. It's hard to attract industry to our towns," Jerris says, finishing her coffee.

I ask how living in the park has hurt them personally, trying to get to the origin of their anger.

"Well, like with my factory. If I wanted to expand it, any building over forty feet high [four stories tall] needs an APA permit,"

Carr complains. "Outside the hamlet it's harder still. I own a two-hundred-acre farm. It's producing a third less income than three years ago and government regulation is at fault."

"What do you farm?"

"You can't make money at farming today the way the system is set up. My intention in buying that farm, like any businessman, was to make it a performing asset." Dale nods his agreement. "But that farm is costing me because I can't sell off a portion of it at a normal market price, even though it's on a road."

"You mean you can't get a permit from the APA?"

"I'm not going to allow the park service to say what I can and can't subdivide on my land. I wouldn't go to them for a permit. The moment you ask them to permit you, you acknowledge their jurisdiction."

"We simply subdivide our land and tell them to go to hell," says Dale, who now earns his living assembling prefab log homes. "We've got three buildings up the road we did that way and the APA has backed off. The APA won't challenge us. We've rubbed their nose in it."

"The only power the APA has is the same as we citizens, except the attorney general is their lawyer," Cal claims.

I ask how politically effective they think their I-87 highway blockade was, but Cal gives me a tactical response.

"We created a fifty- to sixty-mile traffic jam. I organized the activities from the air. The state police got sent to the wrong exits. They didn't know what was going on."

"Didn't Don Gerdts organize that blockade?"

"Gerdts is very good at self-promotion, very bad at organizing. Dale and myself and Jerris did the primary organizing. Personally, I felt that Gerdts wasn't ethical, that he wasn't in the conflict for patriotic reasons."

He explains that from his helicopter (a Hiller bubbletop that he hires out for commercial seeding contracts) he can see well beyond the houses along the roadsides of the park. "There's no over-development in this park. There's a vast wilderness for fifty miles. So what do they think they're saving? If everybody'd just be honest we could talk to the environmentalists, but their lies and deceptions make it impossible to discuss anything with them. Their grand plan is to control people by locking up resources. The environmental grassroots are shills for the people they think they're fighting. Once the government owns it all, it will all be developed. It is socialism, and what's going to happen in this revolutionary process is the poor slobs doing the footwork will be the first into the meat grinder."

"We know some of them are just dupes, but we have to look at all of them as the enemy because we're at war," Dale pipes in. "We don't take prisoners. We hammer their hides. If their beliefs impact our lives then it's war, and like Calvin says, 'All's fair in love and war.'"

"So are you a member of the John Birch Society?" I ask Calvin.

"No, the John Birch Society was part of a list of groups I swore not to join when I became an officer of the U.S. Army."

I ask him about his career.

" I was ten years in the army, twenty-two in the reserves. I retired as a lieutenant colonel." (A number of his followers, however, have since promoted him to "general" of the Adirondacks campaign.)

Calvin was an instructor pilot in Vietnam, flying combat missions with new trainees. Later he worked on developing night-vision flight programs for helicopters with DARPA, the Defense Advanced Research Projects Agency. He was the first to recognize and report on the "exaggeration of performance" phenomenon related to night-vision fighting, the perceptual distortion pilots experience that leads some to crash into the sides of mountains or plow into the ground thinking they've still got time to pull out. He also flew the first Chinooks without mechanical linkages, admitting that relying on fly-by-wire electronics took some getting used to. "As a combat soldier I always look at calculated risk," he says, which seems to invite the question of how he views the use of violence to achieve political ends.

"People have approached me to do things. I've said just keep that thought for use at some future point when it may become necessary," he claims.

"What about all the vandalism to the Adirondack Council office and people's property?"

"Dirty tricks is just the kind of stuff that comes with organized resistance," he shrugs.

"Yeah, so what?" Dale mumbles before deciding to speak out on behalf of the vandals.

"If those people don't have that outlet, what recourse do they have? The hills are full of angry, ignorant people who might do anything. I told an investigator you may attribute their anger to what we say, but we're not going to compromise the truth of what we're saying. We're educators and informers. We'll tell the truth, that's all."

"Didn't you also punch John Sheehan at a rally in Albany?" I ask Carr.

"John Sheehan and his friends came looking for trouble and they found it. We were having this get-together in support of Ron Stafford and he wasn't welcome there. As I understand it, a fight broke out." He smiles, pleased with himself.

"But then he hit you back?" Nancy asks.

He laughs. "Sheehan got a piece of my ear. He's a big guy but he doesn't have much of a punch."

I ask about the park agency shooting.

"Forget it in connection with us," Dale snaps. He's been through a couple of interviews with the state police and clearly didn't enjoy the experience.

"If we're going to have a civil war, we're not going to put our people in the line of fire," Cal argues. "Three of our people were standing there when the APA vehicle got shot. They were in harm's way."

I ask about other incidents, such as the burning of Anne LaBastille's barns.

"She resigned from the APA because she was terrified after her barn burned, and all I can say is good riddance," Dale smiles ferally. "I'm not sorry for her. I don't have any sympathy. She deserves everything she got."

"If it wasn't for us there would be a real civil war going on here," Cal Carr claims, implying a level of control, if not re-straint, that seems credible. The Adirondack Solidarity Alliance and the Liberators probably function in a rudimentary way as a two-tiered political/military organization, the kind of setup that someone like Cal Carr, who brags of being trained in counter-guerilla warfare, would be familiar with.

"I spent most of my adult life affiliated with this government and now I find it so repugnant I can't believe I'm an American. We may need a new form of government to replace what they've given us now," he says, sounding very much like a right-wing rev-olutionary.

"It's a changed world. We work quietly with computers and fax now," Dale French adds. "With the Alliance for America, we've connected with the grassroots. We've found out about the shrimpers and loggers and others under assault like us, this as-sault on rural America, and we're going to take a stand. We will not allow our children to be forced into urban cesspools like New York. We may have to become survivalists in the end."[22]

In the meantime, as part of their new multimedia approach to organizing, they've begun producing a radio show, "Reality Check," broadcast on two local stations. They give me a tape of a recent broadcast.

Most of the program consists of Rush Limbaugh–inspired ban-ter between Carr and French, with a long sendup of the APA as reported by "Ray Brook Rose" (a woman, probably Jerris, putting on a fake Japanese accent, trying for the Tokyo Rose effect).

"Parents," she wheedles in an exaggerated singsong, "it is your duty to instruct your children in the ways of the earth mother. Teach them that cutting trees is forbidden. Using hairspray, shampoo, soap and all other chemicals is not natural. Tell them to cast off these evil chemicals and soon they will have a new and unique air about them. Children should be trained to alert the chosen ones when they see or hear anyone breaking the laws of [Earth Goddess] Gaia as written in the gospel according to Bob [Glennon]."

Cal and Dale's major topic of concern is an upcoming confer-ence at the University of Vermont on what they believe are plans

for declaring the Adirondacks and Lake Champlain a U.N. biosphere reserve. The symbolic designation for areas where people
and nature function in sync was actually granted in 1989.

"We can stop this thing cold if we create sufficient controversy
surrounding its creation. And we better do it or one morning
you're going to wake up and people with blue helmets are going
to be deciding what you do with your life," Cal warns his listeners.
"There are treaties in place that allow for the United Nations to
enter into a country for the purpose of controlling biosphere reserves."

The June 22, 1993, Biosphere Reserve Conference, which was
to have been addressed by Governor Howard Dean of Vermont,
is cancelled at the last minute owing to concerns over possible disruption and vandalism after the ASA announces plans to stage a
protest. "We just couldn't afford the $5,000 to $6,000 we would
have needed for security—to have people protecting the cars in
the parking lots from having their tires slashed, for example," says
Rose Paul from the State of Vermont Natural Resources Agency,
one of the groups that had planned the meeting.[23]

"The meeting would have gone on if there was no chance of
anyone getting hurt. But these guys have a history of carrying
concealed weapons into meetings, not of using them but of having pistols on them," adds Carl Reidel, director of the environmental program at the University of Vermont.[24]

Overlooking a three-quarter-mile-long pond is a rustic brown
cabin with green-trimmed shutters. Three overturned canoes lie
in the shade of a cedar tree down by a short wooden dock. On the
cabin's porch, a birdfeeder is attracting a crowd of finches, chick-
adees, red-breasted nuthatches, and a big blue jay, who's bullying
the others back from the seed. In the distance a woodpecker is
clacking away, searching deadwood for grubs and other tasty insects. At a different time or season, one might catch sight of loons
on the pond or great blue herons and sharp-taloned ospreys fishing for their dinner. The Adirondacks are, among other things, a
birder's paradise.

The Audubon Society's Dick Beamish and his wife Rachel step

out on the cabin porch to greet me. He's a bald, wistful looking man, with a Caesar comb of silver-brown hair and soft blue-green eyes. She's a thin, healthy blond with classic Nordic features. He's wearing a checked chambray shirt, jeans, and moccasins. She's in stylish but practical sand-colored cottons. Seeing them standing by their cabin by the lake, I'm reminded of an L. L. Bean ad. But the swarming blackflies don't allow us much time for reflection. Dick and Rachel wave me inside their screened porch, flapping their hands frantically to discourage the biting flies from following us in.

"They go after the weak. They're really the scum of the earth," Beamish declares a few minutes later, talking not about the black-flies that infest the Adirondacks every June but the anti-enviro activists who occupy the park year round.

"Conservationists tend to be too meek and subdued in responding to these prodevelopment forces," he argues. "We don't like confrontation. We think it's in bad taste. I run into people all the time who like the letters I write to the newspapers and tell me how much they agree with them but don't want to write letters themselves. They're afraid to get into a pissing match with these skunks. So a few hundred people end up setting the agenda for 130,000. This whole Wise Use movement is tiny compared to those who want to preserve our environment, to the eighteen million New Yorkers who value the Adirondacks and could easily swat them down. But instead, this tiny faction has set the terms of the debate these last three years and will continue to do so until we decide to get out there and be as forceful as we have to in order to stand up to them."

I'm climbing a mud-slick trail up the side of Mount St. Regis. Unlike the well-maintained switchbacks of the West, Adirondack trails are no-nonsense, straight-over-the-top bushwhacker paths through streams and over tangles of root systems, rocks, and boulders. Moving up the mountainside, I startle a six-point buck, who bounds off into the thick vegetation. Small, brown, mottled treefrogs appear underfoot hopping clear of my sneaker treads just in time. The blackflies are taking a more aggressive stance, willing to sacrifice themselves if they can get a good taste of blood before they die. By the end of the day the back of my neck will look like a terminal case of acne, with some forty swollen, red bite marks.

After two hours climbing nature's answer to Stairmaster, I reach the scenic payoff. The 2,873-foot Mount St. Regis's granite round top provides a spectacular vista of dark green mountains, forested valleys, and wild, island-studded blue lakes stretching out to the horizon below a shifting pattern of cloud shadows. I have a good hundred miles visibility across the great northern forest dome of the Adirondacks and can see a scattering of small settlements and a high-peak wilderness to my west. This was the western frontier two to three hundred years ago, when white settler culture was new to the continent. This forested land provided game for generations of Mohawk and Algonquin people, beaver pelts for Huguenot fur traders, rich loamy soil for Dutch farmers, and a place of refuge for loyalists displaced by the American Revolution.

From my high vantage point, the summer green canopy contouring these low rugged mountains and scattered hamlets also bears an uncanny resemblance to a tropical war zone. Cal Carr, the veteran of helicopter warfare in Vietnam, has noted this similarity in his talk of civil war and counterinsurgency. When Carr speaks of flying his helicopter over the Adirondack wilderness and asks, "Save it for what?" you can hear echoes of the American major who, after the 1968 battle of Ben Tre, said, "We had to destroy the town in order to save it." What Lt. Col. Carr and his followers don't seem to realize is that, like the Vietnam War, their war against the wilderness is the kind of venture whereby even if you win you lose.

Roadkill an Activist

*If the preservationists have their way, this country will be nothing
but one big national park.*
JOHN HOSEMANN, CHIEF ECONOMIST,
AMERICAN FARM BUREAU FEDERATION

*From the age of the dinosaurs / Cars have run on gasoline /
Where, where have they gone? / Now, it's nothing but flowers /
There was a factory / Now there are mountains and rivers / You got it,
you got it / We caught a rattlesnake / Now we got something for dinner /
We got it, we got it / There was a shopping mall /
Now it's all covered with flowers*
"(NOTHING BUT) FLOWERS," TALKING HEADS

"David, let me be frank. That's a LaRouchite magazine you're
holding, but it also happens to be one of the best science magazines being published in the U.S. today." Dixy Lee Ray, zoolo-
gist, former head of the Atomic Energy Commission (AEC)
under Richard Nixon, and one-term governor of Washington
(1977–1981), goes on to explain how the National Science Foundation, National Academy of Sciences, American Association for
the Advancement of Science, and the rest of the scientific establishment have fallen victim to the politically correct dogma of the
environmentalists. This is not the case, she continues, for followers of jailed neo-Nazi Lyndon LaRouche, who publish *21st Century Science & Technology*. "I'm not interested in their politics,"
says Dixy, "but they're doing some of the best work on cold fusion

and other technologies frozen out by the science establishment. I read their magazine regularly."

As governor of Washington, Dixy Lee Ray named a litter of pigs after statehouse reporters. Later she had the pigs slaughtered, packaged, and served at a capitol press conference.[1] In the winter of 1993, less than a year before her death at the age of seventy-nine, she remains as feisty as ever. Appropriately shaped like a bomb, with a thick neck and close-to-the-scalp helmet of gray-white hair, Ray is experiencing something of a popular revival, having recently published her second anti-environmentalist book and worked as Rush Limbaugh's radio correspondent during the 1992 Earth Summit (which she labeled "the flat-earth summit"). She has become the unofficial standard bearer for an emerging counterscience that attempts to discredit as "environmental hysteria" commonly accepted research on acid rain, pesticides, ozone depletion, climate change, toxic waste, radiation, and all other human-originated sources of pollution.

"I find that most of the people I respect work outside the accepted wisdom," says the nation's one-time chief advocate of atomic power. "Because of that, many of them have been unable to get their work published." Although she is unappreciated by the peer-review-based science establishment, the many people who have heard Dixy speak at anti-enviro conferences around the country consider hers to be the voice of plain-spoken scientific enlightenment.

I am at a three-day Environmental Conservation Organization (ECO) conference in Reno, Nevada, where Dixy Lee Ray is to speak along with a number of other prominent anti-environmentalists. The ECO conference, which has the feel and fervor of dozens of other anti-enviro conferences that have taken place in recent years, is being held in conjunction with the annual meeting of the Land Improvement Contractors Association (LICA). LICA is a construction-industry group involved in water diversion, reclamation, dam building, and other development projects likely to be affected by wetland permit requirements of the Clean Water Act. In 1990 LICA demonstrated its opposition to these government regulations by establishing ECO. ECO lit-

erature explains that the organization seeks to "optimize the balance between environmental protection and economic vitality"
by opposing "hastily drawn reactionary legislation that fails to
adequately protect our human resources."[2] ECO is run out
of LICA's Maywood, Illinois, office by LICA Executive Vice-
President Henry Lamb.

Despite winter storms that threaten to close down the Reno
airport and Interstate 80 at Donner Summit, more than a hundred people have arrived for the ECO conference and are being
directed to the far end of a hallway off the main casino floor inside
the candy-striped, copper-tinted high-rise Hilton. Some three
hundred developers and contractors have also arrived safely at the
plush hotel/convention center for their annual meeting. After
picking up ECO conference materials and copies of *The New
American* and *21st Century Science & Technology* from the stacks
on the registration table,[3] I enter a large, carpeted conference
room with moveable walls where ECO's first session is under way.

"There are market solutions to the environment. My answer is
to make the right to pollute a property right and tradeable issue,
which is what's beginning to be done on a limited basis. We have
to appeal to mainstream environmentalists like ourselves against
the lunatic fringe. Pollution permit trading is the way to get them
turned our way." John Hosemann, the rotund chief economist for
the American Farm Bureau Federation, is speaking to about
eighty-five mostly middle-aged and older white people arrayed in
several rows of straight-backed chairs.

"The government once encouraged the draining of swamps.
Now it calls them wetlands and punishes the farmer who wants to
turn them into productive land," he continues.

Since World War II more than 50 million acres of agricultural
land have been converted to urban/suburban use by real estate
developers, while another 53 million acres of swamp have been
converted to agricultural use. This was long considered a reasonable trade-off, but that was before the role of wetlands in groundwater filtration, aquifer purification, flood prevention, and
fishery, waterfowl, and wildlife regeneration was fully understood. Given the choice of protecting ag land from development

or continuing to drain and fill wetlands, the Farm Bureau has come out strongly in favor of continued wetlands development.

"The Endangered Species Act is another big problem," Hosemann warns his audience. "It's ruled by biologists and botanists. There's no economic consideration given in its application. The West and South will be hammered the most, because the Northeast killed their animals long ago. So that's where all our national industry and agriculture will have to locate, according to an economist I know. Our national parks will be renamed biosphere reserves, and the only thing left in them will be these small trails where, if we agree to only take so many steps and not wander off or leave anything on the ground, we'll be allowed to look at these endangered animals."

He goes on to talk about the need to form an anti-environmentalist alliance with labor and to describe recent discussions he's had with the Teamsters in Arizona. "I mean, we'll never get [AFL-CIO Director] Lane Kirkland on our side," he admits, "but we can cut away at the AFL's components, like the New Jersey construction unions who came out against this wetlands nonsense when they saw it would mean less building. . . . So if you can throw some white gas on the problem and someone else comes along and drops a match, we got something going. Let's get this revolution under way."

During the first break, Clark Collins from the Blue Ribbon Coalition walks up and introduces himself to Hosemann, who says he's never heard of Blue Ribbon. "But I'm open to be educated."

The next speaker is Bill Hazeltine, a retired mosquito-abatement director and chemical company employee who begins his presentation with an attack on Rachel Carson's 1962 book *Silent Spring*. "Carson should be looked up in the fiction section of the library," he suggests to amused snickers. He goes on to talk about "ethnic groups" in Mississippi who threw rocks at mosquito spray trucks because they thought they were part of a plan to commit genocide against Blacks. As a result, he claims, four people died of mosquito-borne encephalitis. He warns of a similar "strange alliance" forming in California between hunters and wildlife advocates who are paying farmers to create wetlands.

These will only increase insect nuisances and create new health threats, he asserts, unless fish and game agencies can be convinced to return to their old practice of insecticide spraying in wildlife refuges.

Henry Lamb gives his welcoming speech on behalf of ECO. He's a slim, fastidious, silver-haired gentleman in a red tie, white shirt, and blue suit. He explains how free enterprise capitalism is superior to any other form of capitalism, and then sets up a question-and-answer session for himself, Hazeltine, and Hosemann.

Hazeltine talks about a proposed ban on methyl bromide (an ozone depleter) and explains that because it is used to protect grain in transit, its absence may expose grain supplies to deadly microtoxins.

Rogelio Maduro, associate editor of *21st Century Science & Technology,* stands up to talk from the floor. Rogelio, who has a bachelor of science degree in geology, is the coauthor of *The Holes in the Ozone Scare,* a book published by the LaRouchites that has provided most of the ammunition used by Dixy Lee Ray, Rush Limbaugh, and other science critics who deny that human chemicals are causing atmospheric ozone depletion.[4]

"How many people have died as a result of environmental policies like the banning of DDT?" the LaRouchite asks rhetorically. "I'd say millions, because it was the most effective weapon against malaria. Right now methyl bromide is supposedly being banned for ozone depletion, but I think this is really an attack on refrigeration, because that's what CFCs and methyl bromides are used for: the storage and transportation of food. If you look at the environmentalists' policies, they say they want to reduce world population to 500 million, to between 500 million and 2 billion, and the best way to do that would be to destroy the world food system. That would create mass starvation. That's the way to achieve their aim."

"I'd say about 40 million people have died as a result of this banning of DDT, and I have to agree that if there is a conspiracy attacking food production this is a way of achieving it," Hazeltine agrees. He goes on to suggest that with the reduced use of insecticides, "we're also vulnerable to AIDS, because although mosquitoes have been eliminated as carriers, the stable fly could still become a vector for spreading HIV virus."

"I don't know about any apocalyptic scenarios," says the Farm Bureau's Hosemann. "My prediction is we'll just rot. Our country will just deteriorate into a Third World situation. I know of one analyst who estimates our gross domestic product losses as $1 to $2 trillion a year because of regulations, about a third of our total production. We're down to a population that's scientifically illiterate. We'll end up like Argentina, sitting on all these resources and not doing anything with them."

The highlight of the first day's sessions is a talk by James Catron, attorney and activist from Catron County, New Mexico. In 1990 Catron County, a rural district larger than Connecticut but with a population of only 2,600, gave birth to what has come to be known as the counties movement, an offshoot of Wise Use claiming that county commissioners have the right to establish land-use plans that preempt federal authority on federal lands within their county borders. Seventy-five percent of Catron County is federally owned land. This includes the Gila National Forest, where most of the county's ranchers graze their cattle. The plans and ordinances would make it a criminal offense for federal employees to enforce environmental laws if they are in conflict with county plans.

"The ordinances scared the hell out of us," Mike Gardner, a Forest Service district ranger in Catron admitted to a reporter in 1992. "I've got small children. It would be tough to tell my kids why I'm being arrested. It was intimidating."[5] As the counties movement grew, the departments of Agriculture, Interior, and other government agencies felt compelled to remind Catron and other county sheriffs of the felony provisions of the U.S. code relating to interference with or assault on federal agents.

As legal justification for county movement ordinances, Jim Catron, former Mountain States Legal Foundation attorney Karen Budd, and other Wise Use lawyers have cited the National Environmental Policy Act (NEPA), which states that important cultural aspects of national heritage must be preserved in carrying out environmental regulations. These attorneys claim that ranching, mining, and logging represent the "local custom and culture" of rural counties in the West. While the ordinances would almost certainly be overturned in federal court, where the supremacy clause of the Constitution (establishing the primacy of federal law) would come into effect, activists such as Catron and Budd have been careful to try and avoid court fights, keeping their *posse comitatus* (power of the county) arguments in the political realm. Dozens of counties in the West have now passed anti-environmental ordinances modeled after the original Catron County regulations, often with the aid of the National Federal Lands Conference, a Utah-based clearinghouse for the movement. But the counties movement suffered a major setback on January 28, 1994, when Idaho District Judge James Michaud ruled that an ordinance asserting local control over federal and state lands in Boundary County, Idaho, violated both the state and U.S. constitutions and had no real basis in law.

Former Bureau of Land Management Director Jim Baca agrees. "It's pretty simple to understand that if you look at any of the counties that have done this and look at the make-up of their county commissioners, every single one of those members who voted for those ordinances are in one way or another in conflict of interest. They're ranchers, or they're feed store owners, or they're somebody who's been exploiting land, and they just don't want to be knocked off the gravy train. These ordinances are unconstitutional, so we tend to ignore them as the rantings and ravings from the county commissions. I think the one thing that they do point out, though, is we need to do a better job of trying to work with the local folks and trying to mediate some of these land disputes out in these rural areas."[6]

Jim Catron is not one of the local folks Jim Baca has in mind when he talks about dialogue and mediation. Dressed in a white windbreaker and white Stetson, Jim Catron has the kind of wiry nervous energy, animated angular jaw, and brown-eyed predatory gaze that resembles deceased Death Squad leader Roberto D'Aubuisson of El Salvador. "We are not in a struggle with environmentalists but with tyranny. There is no moral difference between Earth First! and Stalin. If the radical environmentalists took power you would not live, you would not be left alive. . . ." Catron warns his audience. "The feds were managing us out of existence. So we began reading laws and regulations and found that the law protects our local customs and culture and economic base," he continues. "Our custom is we believe in the value of production. It is our cultural use of the land to mine, timber, hunt, fish, and graze.

"Eighty percent of the people in Catron County have Scots-Irish last names," Catron continues. "The Scots-Irish were a warrior people, at home on the frontier, a warrior race too wild for the civilized East. So they were pushed to the frontier, where they confronted the Indians, who they understood, because they were another warrior people. They'd kill or marry the Indians, made no difference, any way you could pacify them. That's our customs and our culture. When they set up the Forest Reserves in 1890 and said we couldn't cut our trees, we set fire to the forests all across the West until they reconsidered things in light of our needs. Maybe today the feds have more respect for county sheriffs and jails than they do for their own laws. . . . But understand, we're working within the law. It's the federal agencies like the Forest Service who are the criminals. They have to go around in body armor with M-16 automatic weapons. They say it's because of drug running, but we know it's the people of Catron County they're afraid of. We're also working with Indian tribes and Hispanic villagers," he claims. "They realize the radical environmentalists' agenda means an end to traditional ways of life. Until now greens have wrapped themselves in the American Indian cloak, but the Indian lived free, the Green party was founded in Germany on the ideas of Nietzsche, Engels, and Marx."

Northern Arapaho journalist Debra Thunder disagreed in an opinion piece in the *Salt Lake Tribune* in the spring of 1993. "By describing local custom and culture in purely economic terms, the movement's proponents preclude the West's numerous but poverty-stricken Indian tribes," she wrote. "How, I wonder, can a nation that claimed this sacred and beautiful land in the name of God love the Creator but not the creation? How can a 'culture' survive when its very existence is defined by the consumption of the finite resources that give it identity?"

"The ranchers haven't been here in the American West long enough to establish a set of cultures or customs within the meaning of federal laws that are intended to protect culture," adds Walter Echo-Hawk, a Pawnee attorney with the Native American Rights Fund in Colorado. "Furthermore, the grazing and timbering special interests are being rapidly supplanted by changing American values—environmental and recreational. So it's impossible to say what local culture [in the West] may be, because it's in a period of rapid social change."[7]

Still, Jim Catron remains confident that the conqueror race holds the superior customs and culture. He recommends that I read *Albion Nation* by David Fisher Hacket. "It explains how four of the five peoples who settled America were from the British Isles," he says. I ask him if it isn't true that the Spanish mission padres introduced cattle culture to the Southwest. "The Scots-Irish settled the country and started ranching cattle," he answers sharply. "Hispanics are village people. They liked to stay close to town. They were afraid to ranch. They didn't have the initiative."

At the end of the first day of the conference, Henry Lamb pitches ECO's new direct-access phone net.

"Using it you can send faxes to your congresspeople that will be delivered with only your name and address attached, no organizational ID," he tells the crowd. "You can send twenty faxes for thirty dollars or you can select prewritten messages by phone. A mainframe computer in New Jersey will determine who your congressman is if you're not sure and where to send your message if you don't have the address. We have a wide selection of other information on our phone menu, including status reports on wetlands, animal rights, property rights, protests. And you can voice-access them," he smiles, and then demonstrates on the jury-rigged phone/tape setup on the table in front of him. We hear a dial tone and a recorded ECO ID as his call connects. Then he says, "Property rights," and a canned voice begins reporting over a loudspeaker on an NHLA rally in New Hampshire. "We're hoping to develop a state-level ECO information system in the near future," beams Lamb as he hangs up. Sales reps from the company that set up the system privately explain that they've installed similar voice-activated networks for the Democratic party, the American Foundation for AIDS Research, and the Tropicana Orange Juice Company.[8]

The second day of the conference begins in the LICA exhibit hall with helium-filled balloons and a free buffet of juice, rolls, and muffins. High-heeled chorus girls in skimpy, sequined red bikinis and red feather boas walk among booths promoting laser leveling, grading and robotic excavation systems, Biosol Fertilizer, John Deere construction tractors, and job-site insurance coverage.

ECO's morning session is given over to political strategies. Candace Crandall, a former PR person for the Saudi Arabian Embassy, is representing the Science and Environmental Policy Project (SEPP), a mainstay of the counterscience movement. She says they want scientists to write commentaries for them, but more importantly they want to influence journalists in how they write about environmental science. They're planning a conference with a panel of scientists who are highly skeptical of the "environmental alarmism" that has become so popular. "A very important reporter from a major newspaper I was talking to was very excited about this conference and what we're doing. I'm real optimistic we can bring the press over to our side," she says.

"Was that Keith Schneider?" I ask her, referring to the *New York Times* environmental reporter who's been questioning the cost and benefits of environmental regulations.

"Yes, isn't he great?" she gushes.

Mike Colburn from the Political Economy Research Center, a think tank in Bozeman, Montana, explains how the center does academic research on free-market environmentalism but also tries to influence congressional staffers and national reporters by hosting three-day wine-and-dine seminars at the Lone Star Ranch outside Yellowstone National Park.

Kathleen Marquardt, of the anti–animal rights group Putting People First, a stylishly dressed woman with a broad, intelligent face, complains that the 1992 Clinton campaign stole her group's

name for their campaign slogan, but admits that she was still
pleased to see all the furs worn at the inaugural ball. She explains
that it is important to understand that animals don't have rights,
they have instincts. Animal rights activists, she says, believe that
rats and cockroaches are equal to or better than humans, but in
truth "they don't care a hoot about the animals. They are just using them to attack humans."

She began fighting the animal rights groups, she recalls, after
her daughter came home from public school and said there'd
been a speaker there from PETA (People for the Ethical Treatment of Animals) who called her mother a murderer for hunting.
Putting People First, Marquardt asserts, initially represented
"average Americans who drink milk and eat meat and benefit
from medical lab research . . . but quickly expanded from anti–
animal rights to combating all environmental extremism because
it's all the same." PPF's latest campaign is in defense of Norway's
decision to return to commercial whaling. "We support the consumptive use of marine resources, including marine mammals for
human benefit," she smiles thinly. "Whales are not these ge-
niuses Greenpeace makes them out to be. Whales are the cows
of the sea. Their meat's lean and full of protein. If we ate whale
meat we'd be much healthier."

"The difference between an environmentalist and a greedy developer," lectures Michael Greve from another conservative think
tank, the Washington-based Center for Individual Rights, "is an
environmentalist already has his mountain cabin. Environmentalism is a cause for the wealthy, for the haves against the have-
nots." Greve has a clean-cut manicured look about him, speaks
with a European accent, and wears a hand-tailored three-piece
suit that has to have cost at least $600. "The term *environmen-
talist* is going the way of *feminist*—no one wants to admit they are
one. But the environmentalist drivel is still seeping into the national psyche," warns the angry young conservative. "It's like
women who say, 'I'm not a feminist,' but when you try and have
a sex or gender discussion with them it's just impossible."

After lunch I talk with Gerald Stram, an older farmer from Wisconsin with a gray crewcut and a rough complexion. He owns a

350-acre beef cattle farm that he bought after retiring from the railroad twenty-five years ago. Now he raises seventy-five head of cattle in what's known as a cow/calf operation. "I raise them from erection to resurrection," he jokes. He's attending the conference with his friend Gene Leubker, of Landowners of Wisconsin, a small group the two helped establish.

"The state set up a protected zone along ninety miles of the lower Wisconsin River," Stram explains, "from Baraboo to the mouth of the river, where it feeds into the Mississippi at Prairie du Chien. That restricted our land use because of the view from the river. For twenty-five feet back from the river, I can't cut my own trees. Beyond that I have to get permission for a ways," he explains. "The law went into effect at the end of eighty-nine. Five of us got together and formed our group in ninety. We don't have hit teams like some of those bikers in California,[9] but we were angry enough that if you were DNR [Wisconsin Department of Natural Resources] you wouldn't get out of your car in our area."

In 1992, 250 members of Landowners staged a protest inside the state capitol rotunda in Madison. "This was to protest their plan to fence off all our creeks and streams to keep the cattle out of them and they would have only paid 75 percent of the cost. If they'd have paid for it all, that would have been another thing. When it came to the governor, he vetoed that law," Gerald says proudly. "It showed me we had some political influence. After that fight we got two hundred new members."

"Ask me about my recipes for spotted owls," Kathleen Marquardt jokes, standing behind her display table at the end of the conference's second day. Along with copies of her *Putting People First* newsletter, she has a variety of bumper stickers for sale including, "Don't Steal. The Government Hates Competition," "Save a Skunk, Roadkill an Activist," and "Save a Pig, Roast an Activist."[10]

Jim Catron is standing nearby talking to Bill Moshofsky from Oregonians in Action, part of the Oregon Lands Coalition.

"The big companies sold us out. They took their $1.6 million loss and closed the mill," Catron complains.

"Simpson is the only one of the majors giving our group money.

Mostly we're getting our funds from middle-sized operations," Moshofsky nods sadly.

Someone else comments, "I went to this corporate executive for money and he tells me I can't 'cause my kids are green and my grandchildren are emerald green.'"

I ask Kent Howard, the seventy-year-old president of the National Federal Lands Conference, which coordinates the counties movement, what he thinks about the John Birch Society trying to link up with the anti-environmentalist cause.

"I read the Birch Society magazine every month. I probably should be a member, because I agree with what they say," he answers. "I never got around to joining, but if you look at how the Council on Foreign Affairs [sic] and the Trilaterals run everything it makes sense. Even Reagan was a member."

Howard, who has mottled, weathered skin, thinning hair, and lively silver-blue eyes, recently retired from a lifetime of ranching.

"My place was up on the Idaho border ninety-six miles from Elko, up on the Snake River way past the Independence mine. One of the last bits of paradise on earth," he states as fact, not opinion. "I raised 1,400 head of cattle on 5,000 deeded acres and 160,000 acres of federal land. Two years ago, at sixty-eight, I got out. The value was just going down with the threat of increased grazing fees and enviornmentalist attacks on riparian areas. I sold the ranch to the Rocky Mountain Elk Foundation. In some ways I feel like a traitor, because the taxpayers ended up paying for it. After the Elk Foundation bought it from me, they sold the land to the BLM and the Nevada Division of Wildlife."

Leaving the convention hall, I notice Dixy Lee Ray at a back table. It's after five and she wants "a real drink," not the light beer on sale at the LICA snack bar. Dr. Robert Bolling from Arizona State University goes off to the casino bar to get her a couple of scotch and sodas.

"When I left the governor's office in eighty-one I wasn't vested [time necessary to collect benefits]," she says, explaining her return to activism. "The state requires five years of service for severance, and I only had four. I only had a small pension that I had to augment writing and speaking." Even now, with her book sales approaching 100,000, she can't afford to neglect her paid speaking engagements.

"I try to keep it to four or five a month and don't let them get spread around the country if I can help it. I try to limit my travel. The old bod can't take it anymore."

Bolling returns with her drinks and she begins sipping.

"I've really enjoyed my retirement years, even if Fox Island isn't the center of the cosmopolitan world," she continues.

Fox Island is a rustic haven in Puget Sound south of Seattle. Ray lives there on a three-acre shorefront farm with her sister, six dogs, a few geese, some chickens, 120 fruit trees, and a beehive to pollinate them. "I let the bees keep their honey as long as they do their job," she says, straightfaced.

The last morning of the ECO conference is given over to counterscience, with slide shows and presentations by Bolling, Dr. Fred Singer, and Dr. Hugh Ellsaesser, to be followed later by Dixy Lee's keynote presentation.

Bolling is director of climatology at Arizona State and the author of *The Heated Debate*, an antigreenhouse thesis published by the Pacific Research Institute, a conservative think tank based in San Francisco. S. Fred Singer is president of the once-Moon-affiliated SEPP and former chief scientist for the Department of Transportation. Hugh Ellsaesser is a meteorologist and guest scientist at California's Lawrence Livermore nuclear laboratory. All three argue that human impacts on the atmosphere and climate are either vastly overrated or, in the case of industrial carbon dioxide buildup, actually beneficial to humans.

"The way to cope with the greenhouse effect is to enjoy it," Ellsaesser suggests, going on to postulate that lower coronary rates since 1950 may be linked to increased CO_2 in the atmosphere. "CO_2 stimulates the biosphere like a fertilizer," he claims. "Unfortunately, scientific literature has a bias. Anything we call pollution is considered morally wrong. Any beneficial effects are filtered out. We are failing to consider the cost versus benefits of CO_2 buildup. We should listen to Ronald Reagan, who says government is part of the problem, not the solution. All these bureaucrats, scientists, and environmentalists gain from disaster scenarios. Only whistleblowers like me and Bob don't benefit from telling the truth. It takes courage standing up to the preferred wisdom and having to publish wherever you can."

Dixy Lee's speech focuses on energy. "Energy is the life blood of industrial western civilization, and environmentalists and greenie radicals hate it," she instructs her listeners. "We're being told we must conserve electricity, when we in fact have an assured and affordable supply of electricity. What is so noble about conserving energy? We know how to use it and produce it and with little impact on our environment."

Among the list of environmental problems she reviews and finds of no real consequence is the population explosion that has seen the number of people on the planet more than double since 1950, from 2.5 to 5.5 billion. "The population problem is based on present trends continuing into the future, which they never do," she assures her audience. "Population growth goes up and down like global warming. If you looked at the growth rate of racquetball courts in the 1970s and extended it, the whole country would be covered by racquetball courts today."

Less than a year later, on January 3, 1994, Dixy Lee dies of a bronchial ailment at her Fox Island home. She was fighting "the greenies" to the end. Three days before her death, she criticized as alarmist media reports about secret cold-war radiation experiments conducted on some eight hundred Americans without their knowledge during the 1940s and 1950s. The experiments included injecting patients with plutonium and feeding mentally retarded teenagers, pregnant women, and Washington State prisoners radioactive milk and other tainted substances. "Everybody is exposed to radiation," Dixy Lee told the Associated Press just before she passed on. "A little bit more or a little bit less is of no consequence."

Following Dixy Lee's presentation to ECO, Retired General Richard Lawson, president of the American Coal Association, arrives from Washington, D.C., just in time to give a short but impassioned presentation to the group. He is a large, bushy-browed man with a bulldog visage and dark slicked-back hair.

"When I was the commander of U.S. forces in Europe, it infuriated me to hear long-haired dirty demonstrators carrying placards and smoking whatever they smoked at night called peace marchers. The troops guarding the wall were the peace marchers. The environmentalists remind me of the same thing, of those people," he declares to a hearty round of applause. "The strangest thing you hear now is that this planet is not for people. We must go back to wigwams and loincloths because that's clean. I wonder if they ever saw what the Sioux nation left behind after they went over the hill. . . . There are going to be nine billion people in forty years, and in the real world the issue is how we feed and clothe and house those people or you're going to need more generals than you've ever seen."

"I commend you for being on the front lines of freedom. The efforts of groups like yours are rocking the establishment to its foundations," adds John Fund, an editorial writer for the *Wall Street Journal* and one of the last speakers at the conference. Fund, a sleek, pale-skinned conservative who collaborated on Rush Limbaugh's book *The Way Things Ought to Be,* tells the group that his friend Rush sends them a ditto—and that Bill Ellen, one of the movement's "political prisoners," sends his solidarity from the Petersburg, Virginia, federal prison. "If we can get Bill's story out we can get the American people to realize that if the bell tolls it will toll for them as well. After our editorials in the *Wall Street Journal* asking President Bush to pardon Bill Ellen [just before Bush left office], the U.S. attorney in Maryland held a press conference to denounce the *Wall Street Journal*, and the law enforcement community closed ranks and said Bill Ellen has to stay in jail. I attribute this to their unwillingness to go after violent criminals. . . . They don't want to go after violent criminals but they have to go after somebody, so they go after environmental criminals. I mean, who are these people? Are they really criminals, developers, big business, or your neighbors? I just want to tell you you have allies you don't realize. The *Wall Street Journal* is very interested in this struggle, because if they get to you they're going to go after investors, and they're going to go after business, and they're going to go after all of us. That's why I say, your struggle is our struggle."

After a big round of applause, Henry Lamb presents the *Wall*

Street Journal writer with the first access card for ECO's new telephone information network. He then asks Ocie Mills to stand up
in the audience. A burly fellow rises slowly to his feet. "Ocie has
completed his twenty-one-month sentence for precisely the same
offense that Bill Ellen went to jail for, offending the bureaucrats,"
Henry announces to another round of applause.

Bill Ellen and Ocie Mills are two of a handful of convicted vi-
olators of the wetlands-permit provisions of the Clean Water Act
whom the property rights movement has adopted as martyrs and
political prisoners. Bill Ellen served six months for destroying
federally protected wetlands while building a series of duck
ponds for a private hunting club on the eastern shore of Maryland
not far from Peggy Reigle's investment property. According to the
Wall Street Journal, Ellen met with state and local officials and
secured thirty-eight permits for his worksite. He claimed that his
conviction was based on an expanded definition of *wetlands* developed for a 1989 federal manual that was applied retroactively
to an area he'd filled in 1987. In what the *Wall Street Journal*
pointed to as the biggest irony of the case, Ellen actually created
forty-five acres of wetlands and enhanced habitat for ducks and
geese in developing the preserve.

The U.S. Department of Justice, which prosecuted Ellen's
case, countered that the U.S. Army Corps of Engineers issued
three cease-and-desist orders between 1987 and 1989 ordering
Ellen to stop all construction. Ellen ignored the orders and failed
to obtain any federal permits. The department also insists that the
wetlands he destroyed in 1987 were core wetlands, which qualified for full protection under federal regulations going back to
1976. Although Ellen created forty-five acres of wetlands, the
Justice Department insists that in the process he also destroyed
eighty-six acres of tidal marshes and forested wetlands, habitat
and breeding grounds not only for a variety of waterfowl but also
for two endangered nongame species, the Delmarva fox squirrel
and the American bald eagle.[11]

What the Justice Department, in defending its case, failed to
mention but many wetlands ecologists are quick to point out is
that the Army Corps of Engineers, which reviews wetlands proj-

ects, routinely approves between 80,000 and 100,000 fill permits a year—even though the last two Washington administrations have both pledged "no net loss of wetlands."

The bearded, white-haired Ocie Mills of Milton, Florida, stands about six foot two. He seems friendlier in person than on the cover of the *New American* magazine, where he appears behind black prison bars with his son Carey above a cutline reading, "Eco-Villains? No—Just pawns in the federal land-grab scam."[12] Ocie's attending the ECO conference with his wife, a short, pleasant woman with frizzed yellow hair.

"I've been arrested and arrested and re-arrested," he says almost proudly. "In 1976 two DER [Florida Department of Environmental Regulation] agents wanted to come on my property without a warrant. A fight broke out and I made a citizen's arrest, had these two guys laying on the ground, and that was the beginning of my troubles. They came back later and arrested me for assault and brandishing a weapon, which was my .38 revolver.

"Another time they said they wanted to look at a ditch I was clearing out with a backhoe. It was snake-infested and we had five kids."

"We were worried about those snakes," his wife confirms.

Mills goes on. "The DER claimed jurisdiction on the ditch. I went to trial, was found not guilty, and then I sued them. I was awarded damages and settled on appeal for $15,000. That was a six-year battle. Then, up around eighty-seven, eighty-eight, we had a fight over cleaning out another ditch and hauling fill to build a house. This time DER got the EPA and the Corps of Engineers involved. They told me, 'We're bringing in the big boys,' and then declared it a wetland. I ended up on trial with an eighty-six-year-old judge who misdirected the jury. I challenged the judge after the transcripts were changed by the court reporter to cover up the fact that the man was deaf. I defended myself against seven government lawyers and ended up spending two years at Souflee Field penitentiary along with my son."

He suggests I contact the *Pensacola News Journal* if I want details on the case not covered in the Bircher *New American*. "They ran some fair coverage for the liberal media," he concedes affably.

I take his lead and call the *News Journal*. I detect an audible groan coming from the other end of the phone line when I mention Ocie Mills's name. "This is like one of those stories that will never go away, and I've tried to pass it off to the political correspondent and others but they keep passing it back to me," says Ginny Graybiel, the reporter who's been covering the case for the last seven years.[13]

"It's a very confusing case because of the different state and federal charges," she explains. "You could say that the DER were out of control. Ocie probably violated environmental laws, but it's hard to know what to do with him. He's one of these people who will break the rules just to show he doesn't respect them. Meanwhile we have major papermills polluting the region and the DER has spent millions on this one little case. The first federal judge who was involved was not senile like Ocie makes him out to be. He was just an old-time autocratic judge who was hard of hearing and maybe should have resigned a few years earlier. Ocie was sentenced to twenty-one months in federal prison, which he served, along with his son—largely, I think, because he insisted on representing himself. Then he appealed his conviction. A new Reagan-appointed federal judge upheld his conviction but went on to question whether DER or the feds should be enforcing what he called these 'Alice in Wonderland' environmental regulations. You can't really make too much of this in terms of Pensacola," she adds. "We're basically dealing with two small lots where supposedly he put clean sand on his property, and I'm not that familiar with the wetland laws, but the DER has been considered really lenient towards Champion Paper and their big mill on Eleven-Mile Creek, which has been polluting Perdido Bay for years. It makes them a target of suspicion around here when you see how they've gone after this small businessman while being so favorably disposed to a major polluter. As far as Ocie himself, I think he should get a life. He's this obstreperous guy with a little band of followers, fringe-type people, not unlike John Burt, the anti-abortion preacher down here in Pensacola [who led a protest on March 10, 1993, during which one of his followers shot and killed Dr. David Gunn]."

Ocie and Gene Lilly, a dredge suction miner with a Klondike

Pete mustache and gold-nugget ring from Happy Camp, California, get into a discussion on drugs and the temptations they can generate for your average working man in terms of the money that could be earned for one night's transportation work. "Drugs is just an excuse to build prisons," Ocie suggests. "If they legalized it that would take the profit out of it."

"Sure, look at the Weaver killing in Idaho," says Lilly, referring to the 1992 shootout in the mountains of northern Idaho between white separatist Randy Weaver and federal agents that left three people dead. "That was just an assassination using drugs and weapons charges as an excuse."

"They killed Scott in California and claimed that was a drug raid too, but he was a property rights activist," Ocie claims.

Donald Scott, a reclusive sixty-one-year-old millionaire rancher in Malibu, California, was killed in a drug raid on October 2, 1992. The raid was carried out by thirty agents from a drug task force led by the L.A. sheriff's department but including LAPD, DEA, National Guard, and National Park Service agents with support from the border patrol. Scott was killed when he came out of his bedroom and aimed a pistol at the armed intruders. The search warrant used in the raid claimed that fifty marijuana plants had been spotted from the air, but none was found on the two-hundred-acre spread. A follow-up investigation by the Ventura County district attorney indicated that a sheriff's deputy might have lied in obtaining the warrant and that the raid itself may have been prompted in part by a desire to seize the $5 million property under federal drug forfeiture laws.[14] Because the National Park Service had participated in the raid and before that had tried to hold discussions with Scott about incorporating the ranch into the adjoining Santa Monica Mountains National Recreation Area, property rights activists, including Chuck Cushman, demanded an investigation to determine whether the killing had been inspired by the Park Service's "land-grabbing" policies. But the L.A. sheriff's department, which led the raid, and the widespread and potentially abusive use of drug-forfeiture laws by law enforcement agencies became the primary focus of subsequent investigations, lawsuits, and media coverage.

Given its industry origins, the ECO conference might have

been expected to represent a moderate or centrist position within the anti-enviro movement. Instead it reaffirmed the lack of a political center among the antigreens and their inability to reach beyond the Far Right in forming core alliances and coalitions. The defining political division within the movement, then, appears to be not between the center and the fringe, but between those who believe they can achieve their goals working through the established political process and those who see intimidation and violence as legitimate tools in their war against the preservationists.

"We have our own way of doing things. We have a dozen activists and eighty to ninety other people to get things done, as long as we keep them somewhat under control," brags Rick Sieman, leader of the southern California–based Sahara Club, the group Wisconsin farmer Gerald Stram was referring to when he spoke of California biker "hit teams."[15]

By "getting things done" Sieman is referring to threats, occasional assaults (by club members who are said to be armed with "baseball bats and bad attitudes"), and the lists in the Sahara Club newsletter and on the club's computer bulletin board, called Borderline, of environmentalists' names, addresses, phone numbers, and license plate numbers. The lists are usually followed with this admonition: "Now you know who they are and where they are. Just do the right thing and let your conscience be your guide."[16]

Dozens of environmentalists throughout the country have reported receiving obscene phone calls, death threats, and "Dear Faggot" letters following Sahara Club's publication of their names and numbers. Sieman admits taking pleasure in causing grief for the "limp-wristed faggots," "queers," "butch bitches," and "eco-terrorists" of the Bureau of Land Management, Sierra Club, Greenpeace, Earth First!, and other perceived enemies of homophobic outlaw dirt bikers.

Sieman and "Phantom Duck" Louis McKey founded the Sahara Club in the fall of 1990 after the Bureau of Land Management shut down the famous Barstow-to-Vegas motorcycle race, which had been drawing as many as three thousand entrants a year and damaging sensitive desert terrain while threatening the endangered desert tortoise. Sieman announced that the newly formed club would stage a protest race, and that he and his supporters would come armed to protect themselves against ecoterrorists.[17] About a hundred people turned out for the Thanksgiving-weekend protest, as did a large contingent of law enforcement troopers. Ten people, including Sieman, McKey, and Barry Van Dyke, son of actor Dick Van Dyke, were arrested after some chasing around the desert. Sieman was packing an unloaded .22 revolver. Another rider had a loaded .38.[18]

"Sieman argued that they had to bring guns to defend themselves," BLM Law Enforcement Agent Felicia Probert tells me, "because Earth Firsters might appear disguised as BLM agents, which we found pretty unlikely. I think we might have noticed imposters in our midst and arrested them if we had. We've seen a shift in their focus since that time from opposing the BLM to opposing environmentalists as they became part of the Wise Use movement."

The Sahara Club, along with more mainstream recreational biker and four-wheel-drive clubs, independent miners and mining companies, and the NRA, are active in a Wise Use campaign to oppose the California Desert Protection bill first proposed by ex-Senator Alan Cranston. Sahara Club protestors disrupted several public hearings where Cranston appeared. During 1992 hearings in Beverly Hills, Sahara Clubbers physically harassed several women from the Sierra Club who were trying to testify. Later, after Senators Dianne Feinstein and Barbara Boxer were elected to office, the Sahara Club newsletter warned its members that the desert plan was alive and being pushed forward by "these ultra-liberal bitches."[19]

The Sahara Club has taken particular delight in going after Earth First!, which it sees as its counterpart on the environmental side. Sieman happily recalls the night an Earth First! spokesman came to speak at an L.A. area college. "We showed up with ninety to one hundred members [others put the number at thirty] with black tee shirts under our shirts showing a large muscular arm choking an Earth Firster. We took off our shirts and went up on the stage and took the mike from him and refused to let him speak. Pat Martin, who's a big 275-pounder, got in his face and I had to restrain Pat from getting violent and maybe going to jail. They called in the cops but they couldn't do much. This went on for about an hour. We had a wild time. I was telling the students that this guy was a terrorist. The college president asked us to leave and when I saw that there was no time left, that the time they'd booked the hall for was almost up, I said we'd leave if we got our money back. So we filed out and I had our guys coming back in a side door and collecting the money again. We made $360 profit that night."

A similar event took place in northern California after Earth First! began organizing against the logging of redwoods in 1989. Candice Boak, whose husband worked as a logging contractor in Humboldt County, decided to take a stand on behalf of timber. She recalls how Chuck Cushman came to town "and helped us form a group, choose the name Mothers Watch, and so forth." Once Mothers Watch was established, it received support from local timber companies in organizing proindustry/antienvironmentalist demonstrations and rallies. Millworkers were given days off to attend Yellow Ribbon protests. Boak was invited to the home of John Campbell, Pacific Lumber's president, and they soon became friends. Mothers Watch also videotaped environmental demonstrations and, according to Boak, sent dubs of the tapes to the police and the FBI.

In 1990 Mothers Watch and WE CARE, one of the first "grassroots" groups set up by the California Forestry Association, organized a "dirty-tricks" workshop put on by Rick Sieman of the Sahara Club.

"It was just harmless stuff that added some humor to the summer," Candy claims, without elaborating on the content of the workshop.[20] The next day Tim Haynes, one of her husband's logging employees, was arrested and charged with making a bomb threat after he tossed a box wrapped in duct tape and containing a stack of Sahara Club newsletters into the Arcata Action Center, the local environmental storefront, shouting a warning as he ducked out the door.[21]

Siemen claims that he has conducted thirty to thirty-five dirty-tricks workshops around the country for "logging groups and logging companies" in the Northwest, hunters in Arkansas, and Wise Use activists in Texas, New Mexico, Illinois, and Pennsylvania.

"I offer eighty to one hundred things you can do to stop the human debris," he says. "We're talking some gray stuff here," he chuckles when asked to cite a few examples. "Say I heard of something I'd never use in one of my workshops," he laughs, indicating that of course he would. "Like, say you put wrong year stickers on the license plates of long-haired filthy doper types. You could whip them off on your computer and with a good color copier on sticky-backed paper and give law enforcement a reason to stop them and search them for drugs or weapons or whatever." Other dirty tricks include what are referred to as "pizzas and turds." "Pizzas" are any mail-order merchandise you have delivered in the name of an environmentalist or organization you're targeting. "Turds" are mailings using their return postage to send them heavy and/or offensive objects, ranging from anvils to human and animal waste. Trying to solicit funds in the name of a group such as Earth First! as part of a "sting" against other environmental groups such as the Sierra Club is a dirty trick that's also called mail fraud and has resulted in at least one postal investigation of the Sahara Club.[22]

"See, if you try and go through the system, you get involved in this convoluted bullshit process," Sieman complains. "I teach people how to go after the person responsible for your grief. Like this Forest Service guy closed down a road that should have stayed open to the public. What's the easiest way to find out where the guy lives? Follow him home. I mean, you can't reason with eco-freaks but you can sure scare them."

Ed Knight recalls a different effort to stop Earth First! in northern California. "You reach an agreement up front. You don't expect that someone's going to come forward and say, 'Yeah, I paid him to shoot those people.' You understand you're on your own. We were told if we killed any of them there was $40,000 that was there to defend us in court or to help us get away." At sixty-four, Ed Knight looks like a biker version of Santa Claus. A large, white-bearded ex-logger and one-time Galloping Goose turned Hell's Angel, he lives in Willits, California, a wide spot on Route 101 in the logged-out interior of Mendocino County. This is just south of Laytonville, where local Yellow Ribbon activists tried to get the school board to ban Dr. Seuss's *The Lorax* from the elementary school reading list, calling it antilogging propaganda.

"I've heard everything, from out-and-out murder to torture," Knight says of vigilante plans to counter feared Earth First! "monkeywrenching" (vandalism of logging equipment) during Redwood Summer protests in 1990. "There was a general consensus that anyone caught spiking a tree would be crucified and the tree'd go to town with them attached," he continues, referring to armed meetings that took place in bars and on worksites during the protests. Knight was one of a number of guards who got hired by independent gyppo loggers to set up ambushes in the woods near their equipment, work that differed little from guarding the area's marijuana plantations during harvest season except that the loggers provided better armament. "They gave me this Uzi that was just a beautiful weapon. I'd never handled one of them before," the old biker recalls with a note of wistfulness.[23]

Periodically, the media has associated the movement with political cults as well as violence and intimidation, forcing a scramble among Wise Use and property rights activists to distance themselves from some of their less reputable allies. In attempting to avoid being labeled a fringe element, anti-enviro leaders such as Peggy Reigle of Maryland have publicly insisted that any attempt to connect their "grassroots movement" with Birchers, La-Rouchites, or Moonies is a preservationist smear.

"Preservationists in our area accused us of being Moonies. That's Ron Arnold and his crowd. We don't have or want anything to do with them," explained Joan Smith of California Women in Timber and the Alliance for America. She then went on to compare the environmental movement to the Chinese Communist party.[24]

For first-timers attending anti-enviro events, receiving a flier about a "government land takeover" emblazoned with a bald eagle perched on a clutch of flags above the John Birch Society logo can prove somewhat disconcerting.[25] Founded in 1958 by candy manufacturer Robert Welch, the John Birch Society subscribes to a paranoid conspiracy theory claiming that most of the world's governments are controlled by a small group of "insiders" made up of international bankers, politicians, and atheists (possibly Freemasons) determined to achieve world conquest through the many levers of power they control, including the Council on Foreign Relations, Trilateral Commission, United Nations, and World Bank. Communism, according to Bircher theory, is just one of the insiders' many scams for achieving world domination.

The Birchers reached their zenith of power during the midsixties, organizing precincts during the 1964 Barry Goldwater presidential campaign and later working to counter the civil rights movement. With a hundred thousand secret, selectively chosen members and a string of bookshops, they promoted a number of campaigns to "Impeach Earl Warren," "Expose the 'Civil Rights' Fraud," and "Support Your Local Police." The Birch Society also supported J. Edgar Hoover's FBI, sharing information on civil rights and antiwar protestors through freelance spies such as John and Louise Reese, publishers of a private newsletter called *Information Digest*. The Birch Society, using a technique made famous by one of their heroes, Senator Joe McCarthy of Wisconsin, claimed that there were 154 known Communists working for Dr. Martin Luther King to advance the "Negro revolution," a claim that soon became an article of faith among white conservatives and racists. The Birch Society also believed the civil rights movement to be part of a "proletarian plot" by the UAW's Walter Reuther and his "stooge," Bobby Kennedy, who together formed a dangerous pair of "insiders." By the 1970s Welch had passed the mantle of leadership to a younger generation of paranoids. These included, for a time, Congressman Larry McDonald of Georgia, an old-style states-rights radical who was convinced that the insiders had gotten to Gerald Ford. In divorce proceedings filed in Washington, D.C., in the mid-1970s, McDonald's wife pleaded alienation of affections after he told her they could no longer make love until the Communists were driven out of the capital. In a coincidence that no self-respecting Bircher believes was anything less than an insider plot, Larry McDonald was among the 269 people killed when Korean Airlines Flight 007 was shot down by Russian fighter jets after straying over Soviet airspace on September 1, 1983. By 1989 the Birch Society's membership was down to 25,000 members, mostly older people, despite an attempt to stay contemporary by linking up with the Christian Right and attacking AIDS funding, gay "perversion," and sex education in the schools. In a bid to keep itself afloat, the society restructured its finances and, after thirty-odd years, moved its national headquarters from Belmont, Massachusetts, to Appleton, Wisconsin, Joe McCarthy's hometown. The fall of communism turned out to be an easier adjustment for the Birchers than for many others on the Right, since, according to their world view, communism was only one of many cloaks worn by the insiders. Among the new disguises they were quick to identify and combat was George Bush's "New World Order" and environmentalism. "If it's not stopped, the bandwagon of environmentalism could lead to the scrapping of our nation's form of government and the destruction of our liberty," warned *The New American* in a June 1992 special issue on the environmental threat.[26]

"Greenpeace, Shock Troops for a New Dark Age" was the headline cover story in one of Lyndon LaRouche's publications, *EIR— Executive Intelligence Review*. Other articles included, "Fusion Advances Augur Economic Revolution," "Kissinger 'Insane and Morally Dangerous,'" and "The Debt Plans: Only LaRouche's Will Work." The Greenpeace article accused the environmental group's members of being saboteurs for "a green fascist New World Order," "shock troops of the Green Comintern," murderers of seals and kangaroos, and an "irregular warfare force."[27]

This seems funnier than any parody of the Far Right *Spy* magazine could have come up with until one considers that *EIR* is distributed to dozens of corporations, right-wing groups, and intelligence agencies throughout the United States, Europe, and

Asia and that the LaRouche organization itself has a history of un-predictable violence and cultlike behavior.

Most Americans who've heard of Lyndon LaRouche remem-ber him as the peculiar third-party presidential candidate who bought network air time to expostulate his economic theories during the 1984 and 1988 presidential primaries (predating if not predicting H. Ross Perot's 1992 campaign). In 1986, when two of LaRouche's followers won Democratic nominations in Illinois for lieutenant governor and secretary of state, party gubernatorial candidate Adlai Stevenson III removed himself from the party ticket, saying he couldn't run on the same slate with neo-Nazis.

A 1989 analysis of LaRouche by Political Research Associates, a Cambridge-based think tank that studies right-wing move-ments, reported that his "paranoid and conspiratorial view of his-tory involving racial bigotry, cultural intolerance and a large dose of anti-Jewish hysteria, and . . . LaRouche's idea that his follow-ers will someday evolve into a master race of latter day Platonic 'Golden Souls,' qualifies him as a Neo-Nazi."[28]

Although LaRouche recently served five years in prison for mail fraud and tax evasion involving $30 million in unpaid cam-paign loans, his multimillion-dollar business and intelligence net-work continued to function in his absence, turning out *EIR*, *The New Federalist*, *21st Century Science & Technology*, and reams of other publications, all asserting that the world is dominated by a secret cabal led by the British oligarchy and its Jewish backers, including "Soviet Agent" Henry Kissinger. His followers claim that Queen Elizabeth controls the world's drug cartels, that Prince Philip and Prince Bernhard of the Netherlands pull the strings on the environmental movement, and that drugs and en-vironmentalism are key tools in a plan to bring on a New Dark Age, a descent into madness that only Lyndon LaRouche has the political genius to prevent.

LaRouche's own evolution from Far Left to Far Right to Far Side of the looking glass has included a string of assaults and lawsuits directed on his behalf, accusations of brainwashing and sexual aberrations taking place within his organization, and

documented ties to armed racists, anti-Semites, government intelligence agencies—even a couple of national security officials in
the Reagan White House, until the media got hold of the story.
Now seventy-one, he was raised in New Hampshire and served as
a noncombatant in World War II. After the war he joined the Trotskyite Socialist Workers Party. In the late 1960s he split with the
SWP and became the guru of the Labor Caucus of Students for
a Democratic Society—until the SDS expelled him in 1969. Under the name Lynn Marcus, he then formed the National Caucus
of Labor Committees (NCLC) and preached the need for rapid
industrialization to build the working class (his belief in the power
of industry is one of the few constants in his political evolution;
the cover of a recent issue of *21st Century* promised to "Save the
Earth with Technology").[29] In 1973 LaRouche went through a
transformation after his wife left him for one of his followers (a
man LaRouche later browbeat into confessing he'd been "psychosexually brainwashed" by the CIA, KGB, and Britain's MI 5).
Shortly after the break-up, LaRouche decided to establish "hegemony" on the Left, ordering his followers to attack members of
SWP and other leftist groups with baseball bats, chains, and
karate nunchucks, thereby sending dozens of people to the
hospital. Those who remained loyal to him during "Operation
Mop-Up" became the inner core of his increasingly cultlike organization. In 1974 police broke into a New York apartment and
arrested six LaRouchites who were holding a woman against her
will and attempting to "deprogram" her after she tried to leave
the group. LaRouche developed increasingly bizarre theories of
sexual impotence, homosexuality, and brainwashing, dividing the
world among his followers, their enemies, and the common
"sheep and beasts." Beginning in the mid-1970s LaRouche began
to establish contacts on the extreme Right, attempting to infiltrate and co-opt the American Conservative Union, Young Americans for Freedom, the John Birch Society, and the KKK.
Through Mitchell WerBell, the inventor of the Mac-10 silenced
submachine gun, he developed additional contacts with mercenaries and CIA contract agents and decided to go into the intelligence business for himself. He began to publish *EIR* reports on

the activities of liberals and leftists. *EIR* got wide dissemination among the less discriminating members of the law enforcement and intelligence communities. The LaRouchite reports were liberally sprinkled with outlandish claims—for example, that the antinuclear movement was actually fronting for armed nuclear terrorists and that the Soviet KGB was behind environmental groups including Greenpeace. Reagan advisor and National Security Council Senior Analyst Dr. Norman Bailey would later tell NBC that the LaRouche network was "one of the best private intelligence services in the world," a claim that inspired snorts of derision among intelligence professionals.

By 1984 LaRouche had aligned his group with the very hard Right, which includes Holocaust revisionists and the Aryan Nation. Then, in one of his mercurial turns of inspired megalomania, he decided to run for president. His organization was put through what its members called "the cultural revolution."

"We transformed from an intelligence-gathering and -reporting operation to a full-time fund-raising apparatus," testified campaign Finance Director William Wertz at LaRouche's 1988 tax-evasion trial.[30] Using long-established mind-control techniques, the organization subjected members who failed to meet financial quotas to merciless ridicule and accusations of sexual impotence. Fundraisers were instructed, "If you're talking to a little old lady who says she'll lose her house, get the money. If you're talking to an unemployed worker with kids to feed, forget it—get the money. Most people are immoral anyway." An IRS expert testified that between 1983 and 1986, LaRouche's organization borrowed $33.2 million, of which only $3.2 million was repaid.

On December 19, 1988, an Alexandria, Virginia, jury convicted LaRouche and six of his supporters of conspiracy, mail fraud, and tax evasion. At his sentencing the aging political cult leader claimed that he was a victim of a British intelligence plot, a claim the judge dismissed as "arrant nonsense."

With LaRouche in jail, his followers sought out new areas in which to exert their influence. They have gone on-line, placing "press releases" on the Internet computer system accusing Greenpeace of financial mismanagement and terrorism.

In Europe, LaRouche-affiliated groups like Patriots for Germany and the European Labor party have disrupted meetings of Greenpeace, the Greens, and other environmental groups.

In the U.S., the LaRouchites' most successful campaign has been the promotion of anti-environmental counterscience through publication of *21st Century Science & Technology*, meetings, seminars, congressional testimony (against the banning of methyl bromide), and their common collaboration with the Wise Use and property rights movements.

On January 26, 1994, Lyndon LaRouche was released from federal prison having served one-third of his fifteen-year sentence. At a press conference organized by his followers, he announced that he would again run for president.

On New Year's Day, 1987, the Reverend Sun Myung Moon, self-styled Messiah, founder of a multibillion-dollar international business empire, and publisher of Ronald Reagan's favorite newspaper, told his disciples that he desired "the natural subjugation of the American government and population"[31] under what he described as "an automatic theocracy to rule the world."[32]

His long-time chief aide, Colonel Bo Hi Pak, would later tell conservative activist David Finzer, "We are going to make it so that no one can run for office in the United States without our permission."[33]

Back in the 1970s, Moon—or "Father," as his five to ten thousand U.S. followers call him—used his female church adherents to influence male members of Congress and secretly purchased a D.C. bank for the Korean CIA, actions that resulted in the congressional "Koreagate" hearings of 1978. Bo Hi Pak then accused Congressman Donald Fraser, who headed the hearings, of being a Communist plant.[34]

In 1982, the year Moon performed a mass wedding ceremony for two thousand randomly chosen couples in Madison Square Garden, he also established the *Washington Times*. The right-wing tilt of the *Times* appealed to President Reagan, who said it was the first paper he read in the morning. Several of its columnists, including Pat Buchanan and Bill Rusher, soon began appearing on national television. The *Washington Times* was part of a billion-dollar U.S. media investment by the church. Although Moon's vanity press, *The Times, Insight* magazine, the *World & I*, and several video production and publishing houses have lost an estimated $300 million in revenue during the last decade, they've also brought Moon tremendous access to conservative sectors of the U.S. establishment. The creation of the *Times* as a kind of right-wing *Pravda*, along with millions of dollars directed to various New Right causes and individuals such as Terry Dolan and Richard Viguerie, won over most of the nation's conservative critics. By the early 1980s they had stopped calling Moon a cult leader and begun speaking of him as a dedicated anticommunist.

"Look at the facts. Father is not even a citizen of the United States, yet when he goes to Washington, they say, 'You are the number one conservative leader in this country!'" Moon told his disciples in 1988, referring to himself in the third person.[35]

In 1983 the church set up a U.S. chapter of CAUSA, the Confederation of Associations for the Unification of the Societies of the Americas, which quickly became an active player on behalf of Reagan administration policies in Central America. CAUSA worked closely with Lt. Col. Oliver North, providing support to the Contras after Congress cut off aid to the anti-Sandinista guerillas. CAUSA also gave $50,000 to General Gustavo Alvarez Martinez, the U.S.-backed strongman in Honduras whose internal security forces established that nation's first death squads. But when Bo Hi Pak arrived on the scene and began advising Alvarez on how to set up his own one-man political party, lower-ranking Honduran officers decided things were getting out of hand and staged a coup.[36] CAUSA's U.S. student arm, CARP, the Collegiate Association for the Research of Principles, also worked with the FBI, spying on and disrupting a Central American protest group. At Southern Methodist University and elsewhere, CARP members threw rocks and got into fist fights with speakers from CISPES, the Committee in Solidarity with the People of El Salvador.[37]

In 1987 the church established the American Freedom Coalition following a meeting at the Miami Intercontinental Hotel of

Bo Hi Pak; Robert Grant, the chairman of Christian Voice, a right-wing fundamentalist lobby; Grant's advisor, Gary Jarman, a loyal ex-Moonie and former activist in the American Conservative Union; Moon-funded conservative leader David Finzer; two executives from the *Washington Times;* and the CEO of a Moon-controlled Washington PR firm.[38] Pak and Jarman conceived the AFC as a fifty-state lobby for right-wing causes that would gradually evolve into a pro-Moon third party. Grant would function as the AFC's presidential figurehead. The church got the AFC going with a $5 million loan and a contribution of seventy full-time staffers.[39] The AFC's first successful effort involved the distribution of *Ollie North: Fight for Freedom*, an hour-long video tribute to the indicted Iran-Contra figure, which aired on some one hundred television stations around the country and raised more than $3.2 million for the organization.[40]

Alan Gottlieb, who knew Jarman through the American Conservative Union, agreed to write a fundraising letter for the AFC's North program. He also agreed to hold one of his fundraising seminars for the group, perhaps hoping to snag it as a client (his friend and competitor Richard Viguerie ended up with the direct-mail contract for both the AFC and the *Washington Times*). Gottlieb and Ron Arnold had earlier met with Bo Hi Pak at the *Washington Times* headquarters building in D.C., not to discuss anti-environmental issues, according to Arnold, but to persuade Moon's lieutenant to let them reprint *Washington Times* columnists in Gottlieb's syndicated news service.[41] Ron Arnold was also listed as a speaker with CAUSA during this period.

At its launching in 1987, the American Freedom Coalition broke up into several task forces, including one on the environment headed by Merrill Sikorski, a former Alaska state assemblyman and advocate of opening up Alaska's Arctic National Wildlife Refuge (ANWR) to oil development. Arnold and Gottlieb invited Sikorski and the AFC to attend and help sponsor the 1988 Wise Use conference in Reno, incorporating the AFC's proposals for ANWR into the Wise Use agenda and acknowledging them in the Wise Use book for providing "additional funds or in-kind services."[42] Following the Reno conference, the AFC held a number of early Wise Use organizing meetings in the Northwest. "We organized conferences with local groups in Oregon, Washington, and Idaho, where the CDFE was also active," recalls Merrill Sikorski, who quit the AFC several years ago to return to Kenai, Alaska. He now directs an environmental awareness program in the local high schools sponsored by Unocal. "I started getting disenamored with the AFC because of their focus on the Unification Church," he says. "Their involvement with the church was too overriding. . . . The AFC also lacked a strong leader, lacked someone like Jerry Falwell."[43]

When I called and asked about AFC's role in the founding of Wise Use, Robert Grant, still the nominal head of the organization, hung up the phone.[44]

The American Freedom Coalition opened its Washington State office in Alan Gottlieb's Liberty Park office building, sharing space there with a number of other right-wing groups, including Accuracy in Media, which also had extensive links with Moon's network.[45] According to documents on file with the state of Washington,[46] Ron Arnold was AFC chapter president from 1989 to 1991, and Gottlieb was an AFC state director in eighty-nine and ninety. In a February 1989 cover story written by investigative reporter Walter Hatch, the *Seattle Times* identified Gottlieb as one of six key contacts in a Unification Church–affiliated network in the Northwest that included the AFC, CAUSA, and the American Constitution Committee (which fought to secure a presidential pardon for Sun Myung Moon after he was jailed in 1984/85 for tax evasion). The article also detailed how the church functioned as a multinational business/political empire and discussed how in Japan a high-ranking church defector and journalist, Yoshikazu Soejima, was repeatedly stabbed in a near-fatal attack while preparing an exposé on the church. The article reported that in the United States the *Chicago Tribune* had been picketed for referring to church members as "Moonies."

"In Washington State, where the Unification Church is building a local network of conservatives, Moon's allies have threatened more than just a protest," the *Seattle Times* added. "Ron Arnold, executive director of the Center for the Defense of Free

Enterprise, said one of the center's activities is filing lawsuits. 'If you wrote something that was a smear against the Unification Church,' Arnold warned, 'you could count on seeing us in court.' "[47]

"Resource-Use Conference Had Links to Moonie Cult," read the headline of the *Vancouver Sun* that July.[48] As first the western media and then the environmental media picked up on the story of the Moonie connection to Wise Use, not only CDFE, but the entire anti-enviro movement found itself on the defensive.

When Clark Collins, of the Idaho-based Blue Ribbon Coalition, wrote to the Montana AFL-CIO suggesting an alliance, James Murry, the executive secretary, replied, condemning Wise Use's antilabor connections in Idaho along with its newly revealed ties to the Unification Church. When Clark wrote back suggesting that Murry respect other people's freedom of religion, Murry exploded.

"Your knee-jerk defense of the Moonies because of religious freedom doesn't wash," he wrote. "The Moonies' religious cult practices have nothing to do with this issue: the question here is the Moonies' political practices and their hidden political agenda. The Moonies' political actions are a legitimate concern of every citizen who believes that America's destiny should be controlled by the American voters, not a Korean cult leader."[49] The Montana AFL-CIO under Murry and his successor Don Judge soon developed into a center of opposition to Wise Use activity in the West.

"Wise-Use Promoter Denies Church Ties," the *Idaho Falls Post-Register* reported a few months later. The article quoted Ron Arnold as saying that Wise Use was not associated with the Unification Church but would welcome its support. Gary Glenn, executive vice-president of the Idaho Cattle Association, was not happy with that response. He made it clear that his group would withdraw from Wise Use if the Unification Church became an open member. "The movement has been weakened by the perception that it might be involved with Moon," he explained to the *Post-Register*.[50]

Four years and many Moon articles later, Ron Arnold is still threatening to sue, but no longer on behalf of the Unification Church.

"We've sent notices to these environmental groups that unless you want to contest it in court, watch the rhetoric. They're saying we consorted with a known felon [Moon served thirteen months for federal income tax evasion, four and a half more than Alan Gottlieb]. They've toned down their rhetoric and now talk about our alleged links with Moon. . . . Personally I think there's an element of religious/racial prejudice on the part of these environmentalists. Like, 'Who is this slanty-eyed gook preacher?' They pick anyone way out in right field and use them against us. It's a smear and we don't like it. Why would a religious movement from Asia be interested in environmental issues anyway?"[51]

"Forget that religious stuff. I think the Unification Church is a foreign operation that's got entanglements at the grassroots level involving timber exports to Japan and Korea, oil, and other resources," says Eric Nadler, the reporter on a 1991 PBS "Frontline" documentary titled "The Resurrection of Reverend Moon." "AFC chapters campaigned heavily for continued logging in the Northwest and Alaska. And unlike their previous political work in Central America, here you have them [Moon] involved in an issue without a Communist in sight, and it seems to boil down to a basic economic issue, with foreign economic interests driving their actions."

Tracing the Moon operation back to its origins, as author Dan Junas does in the forthcoming book *Moon Rising*, helps to explain how foreign economic interests came to dominate the work of the church. The seventy-four-year-old Sun Myung Moon first established his Holy Spirit Association for the Unification of World Christianity in 1954 in a shack made of U.S. army ration boxes on the outskirts of Seoul, South Korea. After the Korean War, several young military officers, including Bo Hi Pak, converted to his cause. By the late 1950s, the Unification Church had begun overseas missionary work, gaining its largest following in Japan. According to Moon's home-brewed theology, Korea is Adam to

Japan's Eve. The two nations are destined to join together to form the true nation to which all must bear allegiance when the Second Coming (of a Korean-born Messiah) is affirmed.

In the early 1960s, Moon's followers in Japan became politicized, taking to the streets to fight leftist demonstrators opposed to the U.S.-Japan security treaty and rioting on behalf of Japanese businessmen with close ties to the church. The three most influential of these businessmen were all convicted war criminals and Japanese ultranationalists: Yoshio Kodama, a Yakuza (Japanese organized crime) leader; Nobusuke Kishi, a former prime minister; and Ryoichi Sasakawa, who controls Japan's $14-billion-a-year speedboat racing industry and once referred to himself as "the world's wealthiest fascist."

Together they helped establish the World Anti-Communist League, of which CAUSA would eventually become an integral part, and also helped bankroll Moon's expansion into the United States. Among Moon's earliest political activities in the U.S. were attempts to counter the peace movement with pro–Vietnam War demonstrations coordinated with Young Americans for Freedom (the group in which Alan Gottlieb got his start) and the Nixon White House. While the U.S. media (and many parents of runaway teens) grew concerned about the mind-control techniques being used by the Unification Church to recruit young "Moonies," Moon himself was speaking to his followers about what he considered a far more urgent issue: "America has trouble with Japan regarding the devaluation of the dollar and the yen, and also trade," he told his followers in 1971, "but the United States must hold Japan on its side. America must open the way to aid Korea through Japan. . . . we have to put an anchor in America not to withdraw from Asia."[52]

Attempting to understand the multibillion-dollar international business empire that Moon has created in the twenty-five years since he arrived in the U.S. could give an IRS auditor an aneurysm. In 1990, *U.S. News & World Report* estimated that at least 335 international companies were affiliated with Moon's church, producing everything from heavy weapons to machine guns, computers, clothing, and soft drinks. In the United States, the church has at least 150 companies involved in media, real estate, and commercial fishing, including boats, canneries, processing, wholesaling, distribution, and sixty-five Japanese sushi restaurants.[53] Much of the fish that the church processes in Alaska is sold to Japan, while its media operations seem more oriented towards influence peddling than bottom-line profit taking. Business analysts who have tried to follow the financial dealings of the church say that its U.S. operations lose money and its Korean operations earn only modest profits. Its major profit center is reported to be Japan, home to Moon's largest flock, and to Sekai Nippo (*World Daily News*), Japan's answer to the *Washington Times*.

In 1984 a Japan national bar association report found that church-organized high-pressure sales schemes had bilked consumers out of $165 million.[54] Ex-church members in Japan say the church's mobile sales force was in fact far more effective at raising funds than the bar association reported, but that the real money came from partnerships and investments with Japanese banks and industry. Two officials at Sekai Nippo told the *Washington Post* that at least $800 million in church-controlled money had been transferred from Japan to the United States between 1975 and 1984.

"If they're using substantial amounts of the Japanese money, they're not only running a Korean agenda, but they're also serving as political mercenaries for the Japanese, and it should be a matter of great concern," Pat Chote told the makers of the PBS "Frontline" documentary. Chote is the author of *Agents of Influence*, a book that examines Japan's attempts to shape U.S. policies.

By the 1980s Japan, a resource-poor nation, had established what many observers describe as a neocolonial trade pattern with the United States, selling America finished products such as cars, TVs, and other electronics and in exchange purchasing raw logs, fish, coal, beef, and oil. A Japanese-owned pulpmill in Sitka, Alaska, had been the main beneficiary of below-cost logging in the Tongass National Forest until late 1993, when the mill closed. Much of the Tongass's unfinished timber had been exported to Japan and South Korea. In 1988 Alan Gottlieb's Free Enterprise Press published *People of the Tongass*, a 360-page defense of below-cost logging and mining in the Tongass National Forest. Also, the Mitsubishi corporation has been the main purchaser of raw logs from Weyerhauser, which now finds itself losing market share to finished paper products from Japan. The Japanese are also grazing beef cattle on public lands in Montana and are the main purchasers of Alaskan fish, including haddock and other species facing commercial extinction owing to overharvesting. The Unification Church owns several large fish-processing plants in Washington and Alaska, including International Seafoods in Kodiak, that export to Japan and Korea. In Japan it would also be considered criminally insane to run an off-road vehicle through a park, but Japanese ORV manufacturers are financing efforts to open up U.S. public lands to ORV use.

The Moonies' efforts to help get Wise Use off the ground and their ongoing editorial support through the *Washington Times*, *Insight*, and other Moon-owned publications seem designed to advance the economic cause of Moon's "true nation" of Korea/Japan. If anti-enviros who have worked with the American Freedom Coalition and other Moon-funded groups on the Right have failed to understand this by now, it just goes to show, as Bo Hi Pak told a meeting of the AFC, "what a great sense of humor God has."

The Media Is the Message

*Preservationists are a multi-million dollar industry
and they are using the media to tell slanted stories
and fill their coffers.*
CHARLIE JANZ, OREGON LANDS COALITION

*I make my living off the evening news.
Just give me something, something I can use.
People love it when you lose, they love dirty laundry. . . .
Got the bubble-headed bleach blond comes on at five
She can tell you 'bout the plane crash with a gleam in her eye.
It's interesting when people die. Give us dirty laundry.*
DON HENLEY, "DIRTY LAUNDRY"

The February 1992 "Nightline" report opens with Peggy Reigle saying, "Radical environmentalists have taken what was once a noble cause and made it their own platform for power and control." She is followed by Ron Arnold standing out in the woods: "They want to prevent the people from coming out here and actually using the land. I think that the environmental movement has had the intent of eliminating private property rights all along."[1]

"They call themselves the Wise Use movement, and they're mad," announces Ted Koppel in voice-over.

"We intend to destroy the environmental movement once and for all by offering a better alternative," continues Arnold.

"The growing movement which says it's the environmentalists

who are wrecking the country. Tonight, conservative commentator Rush Limbaugh faces off against Senator Al Gore," intones
Koppel before the "Nightline" theme music and fly-through logo
appear. "It has been, for a good many years now, one of those
motherhood-and-apple-pie kind of issues. There was more or less
universal agreement with the old sixties slogan that 'It's not nice
to fool with Mother Nature.' Even those who did not necessarily
agree with that premise found it prudent to disagree quietly."
Koppel appears, seated behind his studio desk. "Senator Al Gore
tried to place environmental issues at the center of his presidential campaign four years ago, and watched in dismay as the public's
eyes glazed over, and we in the media paid little or no attention,"
he goes on to explain after noting that environmental issues "are
regarded as something of a bore." He then compliments Rush
Limbaugh for "breathing new life and controversy into the subject" before cueing the set-up segment. "While his may be the
most widely heard voice on this subject, he is certainly not alone,
as Michael Guillen now reports."

"Nightline" reporter Michael Guillen does a voice-over as the
camera pans an irrigated farm scene: "Northern California. For a
hundred years, farmers in Glenn and Colusa counties have been
using the Sacramento River to water their crops, valued at millions of dollars a year. But the water pumps are sucking in and
killing Chinook salmon, an endangered species, so the federal
government wants to turn the pumps off this summer, a move that
could endanger the livelihood of Sue Sutton and thousands of
other farmers."

Sue Sutton: "The Endangered Species Act right now is not taking into consideration any of the impact on human needs and/or
the economic impact."

Guillen's voice: "Across the country, in Cambridge, Maryland,
Peggy Reigle and her husband invested their life savings in a 138-
acre farm, but now they can't do anything with it, because the
government has suddenly declared it wetlands, a move that has
soured her attitude towards environmentalists."

Peggy Reigle: "I think the environmental movement started

out with a very noble cause, and—but any good idea carried to an extreme becomes a very bad idea."

Guillen's first stand-up is set against a scenic backdrop. "For a lot of people in this country, the environmental movement has gone too far. Wide open spaces like these, they say, are crowding out their rights as Americans. What's more, they're organizing into a powerful nationwide coalition, and their battle cry is, 'The environmental movement has become an environmental disaster. . . .'"

The camera pans over Wise Use demonstrators in Las Vegas.

First demonstrator: "The best thing for the resources is us being out there."

Second demonstrator: "The Wise Use movement represents individual people, individual rights, the private individual."

Guillen explains how Wise Use represents "a hodgepodge of organizations, everyone from . . . Exxon, which would like to use the land for oil drilling, to ordinary citizens like Peggy Reigle, who simply want to use the land to build their dream houses."

Ron Arnold: "We intend to destroy the environmental movement once and for all by offering a better alternative, the Wise Use movement. We think that people really want man and nature to live together in productive harmony, and not to be subservient to nature or somebody's idea of nature."

"Three years ago, Arnold helped write the Wise Use agenda, which spells out the movement's top twenty-five goals," Guillen continues. "For example, they would allow oil drilling in Alaska's Arctic National Wildlife Refuge, so long as it's done 'carefully. . . .'"

More than two minutes into the set-up piece the Sierra Club's Bruce Hamilton, the first and only environmental voice, is introduced.

Hamilton: "You know, you look at the agenda, and it says, 'Graze everywhere, mine everywhere, log everywhere. The only good endangered species is a dead endangered species.' And I really can't believe that that is what the American people that they claim they represent are in favor of."

"In recent years, major environmental groups, including the Sierra Club, have become big business, with seven million members and $500 million in assets," Guillen explains in voice-over. "By comparison, the Wise Use movement is puny. They claim about three million members and a combined annual budget of $5 million to $10 million. Still, they talk big."

Ron Arnold on screen: "The environmental movement is the establishment now, and now we are the rebels coming to tear them down. Now they're Goliath and we're David, and we intend to put the stone in their head."

During the studio-to-studio segment, Al Gore and Rush Limbaugh debate a range of environmental topics. Limbaugh condemns the "environmental doomsday machine" as "the new home of socialism" and denies that there's a human-made ozone hole. Gore, clearly more at ease in a debate format, explains that there is scientific consensus on the link between chlorofluorocarbons and the ozone hole, comparing the "one one-hundredth of one percent of the scientific community who disputes it" to scientists who work for tobacco companies and insist there is no link between smoking and cancer.

Rush insists that volcanoes are the major source of atmospheric chlorine and that the Arctic ozone hole is the result of the sun going below the horizon for a long period of time. "There are a number of people who will tell you that," he says, "such as Dixy Lee Ray, the former president [*sic*] of the Atomic Energy Commission and governor of the state of Washington and a respected scientist, and she has her own book out called *Trashing the Planet*, which debunks a number of these myths, and I've talked to her about it and I . . ."

"All right, let us . . ." Koppel tries to interrupt.

"And I happen to prescribe [*sic*] to her theories."

"Let us give Senator Gore a chance to respond," Koppel suggests.

Gore asks Limbaugh why he thinks it is that Japanese business has established tougher environmental standards than U.S. law requires.

"I don't know that they have, Senator," Limbaugh replies.

"You don't?" Gore asks skeptically, before going on to suggest that waste in the form of pollution is also economic waste and that those American companies trying to be responsible towards the environment are the ones that will profit in the long term.

"Senator, I don't disagree with that at all in any way, shape, matter, or form," Limbaugh responds. "But you must understand that there are those who seek to blame American business for causing these problems, this movement that was highlighted in the set-up package for the show tonight . . . and I consider it an assault on the American way of life and I think that set-up piece was brilliantly put together and it's about time that kind of thing was exposed, because the other side, quite frankly, has had its way with a willing media."

"Well, actually, you've just confirmed my worst fears, because I saw Al Gore wincing throughout the set-up piece," says a slightly embarrassed Ted Koppel. "So . . ."

"Well, it was good!" Rush insists.

"When I saw that set-up piece I said, 'Great, it plays into your hands, Rush.' They think Gore's the nut case here," admits Kit Carson, Limbaugh's chief of staff.[2]

If the anti-environmentalist movement, with its extremist views and violent tendencies, often gets portrayed in the media as just another campaign of middle-class Americans frustrated with government bureaucracy and needless regulation, it may have more to do with the media's own self-imposed limitations than any machinations on the part of Wise Use propagandists. While critical reports on the anti-enviros have appeared on "60 Minutes," in the pages of *People* magazine, and on the tabloid show "Inside Edition," they have also garnered quite favorable play in media outlets ranging from "Nightline" to the *New York Times, Forbes*, Fox television, and of course the *Washington Times*. Articles written from a Wise Use/Property Rights perspective have appeared in *Reader's Digest, U.S. News & World Report*, and *Fortune* magazine as well as on the editorial pages of the *Wall Street Journal*. Media advocates or admirers of the movement philosophy at present include beefmeister talk jock Rush Limbaugh, ex-Watergate burglar and radio personality

G. Gordon Liddy, columnist/commentators George Will and Pat Buchanan, *Wall Street Journal* editorial writers John Fund and David Brooks, and *New York Times* environmental reporter Keith Schneider.

While the *New York Times* remains the medium of record for America's governing elite, television and talk radio now set the popular standard for commercial media, with 75 percent of Americans identifying television as their primary or only source of news. The electronic media's hunger for conflict and "color," often at the expense of context and content, is typified by the "fully involved" five-alarm fire that can make local TV news hounds appear to be of the Dalmatian breed. Street crime and political confrontations fill out the nightly network news broadcasts along with international "bang-bang," as field producers across the world's war zones have come to refer to the requisite twenty-second shots of blood and combat. These are usually packaged in half-hour news programs (twenty-three minutes plus commercials) and cable news rotations that provide the viewer little in the way of background or analysis. At the same time, *USA Today*, with its seven-hundred-word news stories, digital color photography, and splashy graphics, has set a disturbing trend for print media, piloting financially strapped daily newspapers away from the depths of enterprise and investigative reporting and into the shoals of style and gossip. Even the so-called populist media, talk radio, which has become a potent force in national politics since the 1992 elections, is, according to a survey done by the Times Mirror Center for the People and the Press, heavily overrepresented by political conservatives among both its listenership and its callers. (This tendency reflects the medium's domination by conservative white-male talk jocks such as Rush Limbaugh, Pat Buchanan, Paul Harvey, and G. Gordon Liddy.[3])

The 1980s also saw a consolidation of media ownership and loosening of regulatory restraints on the industry that broke down many traditional barriers between corporate management and news production. The Cap-Cities takeover at ABC established a pattern for network television of making news divisions "pay for themselves" by cutting back on regional bureaus and investigative teams and increasing news tie-ins with the networks' entertainment divisions.

"They've got us putting more and more fuzz and wuzz on the air—cop-shop stuff—so as to compete not with other news programs but with entertainment programs, including those posing as news programs, for dead bodies, mayhem, and lurid tales," complained Dan Rather in a September 1993 speech to the annual meeting of the Radio and Television News Directors Association.[4]

At local news stations, a similar shift is reflected in the increasing reliance on sex and sensationalism during November, February, and May Sweeps, when local viewership counting systems such as Nielson and Arbitron determine future advertising rates and revenues.

Despite the belief of such right-wing critics as Reed Irvine of Accuracy in Media that the U.S. broadcast and print media have a liberal agenda, those media have the same bottom-line business agendas as other highly competitive industries. By the late 1980s, twenty-nine corporations controlled more than half the media outlets in the United States, down from fifty only six years earlier.[5] To keep their competitive edge, they have had to maintain broad consumer acceptance for their news product by eliminating controversial language, opinion, even regional dialects among their network newscasters. Unlike Europe, Latin America, and other parts of the world, where different media outlets are understood to represent different political perspectives, the major U.S. media strive to present themselves as politically neutral and objective. Some historians trace this journalistic "objectivity" back to the 1920s, when mass-production industries and mass-circulation newspapers came into being and the Associated Press used objectivity as a marketing strategy to sell uniform news copy to politically diverse newspapers across America.[6] Objectivity has since become a standard by which the media judges itself, so key to industry credibility that even a highly politicized news organization like the Moon-owned *Washington Times* will insist, against all evidence to the contrary, that its news coverage is objective and unbiased. In the seminal study of modern news making, *Deciding What's News,* sociologist Herbert Gans shows how the news media's stance of objectivity and detachment is rooted in certain shared values, specifically values inherited from the turn-of-the-century progressive movement. These values include ethnocentrism, altruistic democracy, responsible capitalism, individualism, moderation, and the small-town pastoral ideal (a recurring theme in American political culture from Thomas Jefferson to Bill Clinton's designation as "The Man from Hope" [Arkansas]). Gans identifies the media's two overriding shared values as the desirability of maintaining social order and the need for a strong national leadership to maintain that order.[7]

During the 1960s and seventies, much of the media's coverage focused on threats to society's existing structures, what Gans labeled "social disorder" and "order restoration" news. With society being tested by an unpopular war, race riots, generational conflict, student protests, and a president who challenged the constitutional limits of his office, the emergence of a broadly based environmental movement in the 1970s was seen, through the prism of the media, as proof that the United States was still capable of accommodating change. Environmentalism was quickly incorporated into the media's arc of values by being identified with small-town pastoralism, moderation, individualism (Greenpeacers ducking Russian harpoons, local housewife-activists fighting city hall), and responsible capitalism (exemplified by industry's "Keep America Beautiful" antilitter campaign, which focused blame for pollution on individual consumers).

While environmental events and disasters—for example, Earth Day, Three Mile Island, the Santa Barbara oil spill, Love Canal, Bhopal, Times Beach—guaranteed that eco stories got regular news play, for ambitious journalists trying to rise through the industry's ranks the environment would remain a "boring," low-prestige beat so long as the nation's political leadership, who were the primary subject of news media coverage, saw issues such as pollution and species extinction as less exciting than foreign summitry, tax bills, or flag burning. The buffoonery of a James Watt might draw national press attention for a time, but only because of the media's inherent interest in individuals rather than groups. Once Watt was forced from office, the Washington press corps quickly lost interest in the destructive environmental policies carried out by his less colorful successors at the Department of the Interior.

The dramatic elements of conflict and disaster that play well on the news also guarantee a certain level of distortion in its environmental coverage. The *Exxon Valdez* oil spill got extensive play, particularly on the electronic media, in part because it provided such stark visual contrasts: images of Alaska's pristine Prince William Sound played against the apparent ravages of crude oil and its effect on shorelines, birds, bears, and otters. Bioaccumulation of toxics, loss of biodiversity, or depletion of marine resources, while potentially far more disastrous in their consequences, were incremental problems and therefore harder to illustrate.

"How do you show soil or groundwater contamination? How do you illustrate important decision-making processes such as risk assessment and budgeting? . . . Sometimes there is no solution, and good stories go unreported because it is too difficult, time-consuming, or expensive to illustrate them," admits Barry Serafin,[8] whose "American Agenda" segments on the ABC evening news often deal with hot-button environmental issues.

Sometimes attempts to illustrate environmental problems do more to illustrate the nature of the media. A bikinied woman sunbathing on a beach quickly became TV's visual shorthand for "concern over ozone depletion," perhaps making chlorofluorocarbon production a "sexier" issue than it might otherwise have been perceived to be.

There are other reasons the media rarely follow through on stories such as industrial chemical releases or dolphin die-offs that may be symptomatic of larger problems. One is the investment of time and resources required in the investigative reporting of complex subjects. In a time of corporate downsizing, a shrinking news budget is more likely to go into investigating the nepotism of a local politician than studying the necropsy of a dead dolphin. Managing editors and executive producers are also reluctant to let journalists get into the kind of analysis that becomes "proscriptive," something hard to avoid when dealing with the cumulative effects and scientific uncertainties of environmental impacts. When reporters are told that they're "getting too close to the story," it is generally understood that they are being warned that they are losing their "detachment" and putting their professional status at risk.

The Winter 1992 newsletter of the Society of Environmental Journalists, a professional association with some one thousand members, carried an article about a backlash aimed at reporters who cover the environment. Cited among the examples were a Santa Fe, New Mexico, reporter fired by his publisher after producing a well-researched investigative series on the Los Alamos Nuclear Lab (the lab is a major employer in the area); another newspaper reporter in a timber-dependent area of Montana who quit after his stories on logging practices on private land got him bounced off the environmental beat; and an Idaho reporter who was accused of having a "pro-environment" bias because he was an outdoorsman who liked to kayak, fish, and hike.[9]

Despite its generally favorable coverage in the late 1970s, it didn't take the environmental movement long before it came to see itself as mismatched to the demands of the mass media. One response was the development of specialized environmental media that mixed open political advocacy with nature writing, ecological perspectives, and factual, well-researched exposés. Today the Sierra Club is involved in magazine, calendar, and book publishing. Audubon has a mass-circulation magazine and television documentary division and is expanding into interactive media. Greenpeace produces videos, books, and calendars. The National Wildlife Federation puts out two popular magazines, *National Wildlife* and *International Wildlife*. A number of environmental magazines unaffiliated with organized groups have appeared on newsstands, including *E, Earth Journal*, and *Garbage*. Magazines listed under Nature, Conservation, and Ecology in the 1993 *Writer's Market* show a combined circulation of more than four million readers, not counting local publications, organizational newsletters, or the many recreational magazines such as *Outside* and *Field & Stream*, which regularly carry stories or columns on conservation and the environment.[10] At the same time, *National Geographic* has committed itself to expanded environmental coverage, and TBS television produces a weekly half-hour program called "Network Earth" for both U.S. and international broadcast. PBS has "Green Means" spots, and NPR broadcasts "Living on Earth." There are also green video, radio, and wire services as well as book clubs and computer networks.

If the environmental movement has been able to build a substantial specialized media, the anti-enviros' failure to create their own media may reflect just how fragile is their claim that they function as an independent social movement. The two largest circulation anti-enviro publications being put out today are the tabloid newsletters of People for the West and the anti–animal rights group Putting People First, both of which claim press runs of around twenty thousand. Blue Ribbon puts out fifteen thousand copies of its newspaper after the failure of an earlier attempt to boost ad rates by printing fifty thousand copies almost bankrupted the organization. The Alliance for America, which claims to have a million active members, distributes twenty-five hundred copies of an eight-page, desk-top-published newsletter. The *Property Rights Letter*, the most authoritative anti-enviro publication, put out by Ann Corcoran, a vivacious former lobbyist for the Audubon Society (and briefly for the NRA before that), was approaching a circulation of a thousand when she temporarily shut down production in the fall of 1993 to seek new funding sources.

The anti-enviros' attempt to put out a slick national magazine foundered after one year. *Our Land* was premiered at a February 1989 Washington, D.C., press conference attended by the Farm Bureau, National Inholders, CDFE, Blue Ribbon, MSLF, AFC, and a handful of other groups.[11] Two months later six Republican senators sent out a fundraising letter to promote the magazine. Senators Steve Symms and James McClure of Idaho, Conrad Burns of Montana, Jesse Helms of North Carolina, Strom Thurmond of South Carolina, and Ted Stevens of Alaska wrote that "advocates of environmental paranoia, locked-up resources and costly regulation have never lacked a forum for their views, and this imbalance must be corrected." Despite this senatorial en-

dorsement, *Our Land*, which was published out of Idaho by Blue
Ribbon cofounder Darryl Harris, never managed to get off the
ground. Ron Arnold says he tried to get *Our Land* on airport
newsstands, but a minimum print run of sixty thousand was required for placement and Harris could only manage to get out
thirty-five thousand. The magazine's fourth and final issue came
out in the fall of 1990. It included a cover story written by Wise
Use attorney Karen Budd accompanied by a cover photo of a
mother grizzly bear and her three cubs with the tag line, "Endangered Species Act: Preservation Boom or Conservation
Bust?" Other articles included one on ecoterrorism by Pacific Legal attorney Jim Burling, an attack on The Nature Conservancy
by Grant Gerber, and stories on the benefits of offshore oil drilling and the dangers of national park expansion.[12]

Anti-enviro attempts to create footholds in other media have
proved equally anemic. Grant Gerber's Wilderness Impact Research Foundation has worked with Louisiana-based sports producer Dick Davis on some thirteen video documentaries
produced for around $15,000 each. Several tapes, including one
on wetlands and one on Prince William Sound, have aired on
Davis's "Outdoor Magazine" show on cable's Prime Sports Chan-
nel. The most popular tape among anti-enviros, however, is "Big
Park," a short country-and-western music video by Teddy Canady
and the Rough Ranger that portrays an evil band of National Park
Service rangers taking over a family's home, disarming Pop as he
goes for the rifle over the mantel, tying him and Mom up in red
tape, and then carting the whole family, including Grandma and
Sissy, off in a horse trailer as they convert the home into a ranger
station. "God bless all the animals, the forests, and the streams,
and we'll say goodbye to humankind and build a big park of our
dreams," the rangers sing as the kidnapped family is driven off.
Then the chorus kicks in: "We don't answer to the taxpayers or to
your congressman and we don't take no from anyone. We just
want to take your land."[13]

In New Mexico the head of the Cattle Growers Association set
up "Minutemen Media" to run pro-grazing videos on TV but soon
found radio spots on western rock and country-and-western sta-

tions a more cost-effective means of getting out the message. "How would you feel if I told you your children were being taught the foundational beliefs of nature worship and Eastern mystic religions in school?" asks one ad. "Have you ever heard of the web of life? Intrinsic value? Or animal rights? These are all terms used to describe New Age religious beliefs and they have crept into our schools."

"Are wolves or bears essential to nature? Not according to natural history or science. The fact is, species extinction is a very normal natural process," another spot explains. "When was the last time you saw a living brontosaurus or a woolly mammoth?"

"The Nazis, with their massive slaughter of Jews, Poles, and Gypsies, suggest they shared the argument of Ingrid Newkick, director of the People for the Ethical Treatment of Animals, who said there is no rational basis for saying that a human being has special rights," declares a third Minuteman ad, one of several that compare animal rights advocates and environmentalists who oppose trapping to Adolf Hitler and the Nazis.[14]

CDFE has also run a number of its own anti-enviro radio spots on Alan Gottlieb's small media network, but their main outreach effort has been through the production of "battle books" put out by their Free Enterprise Press. Along with *The Wise Use Agenda*, other Free Enterprise books include *Ecology Wars, Storm over Rangeland, Fear of Food, Stealing the National Parks*, and *Trashing the Economy*.

A number of other anti-enviro books, with titles such as *Toxic Terror, Science Under Siege, Environmental Overkill, The Heated Debate, Eco-Scam*, and *Apocalypse Not*, are finding their way onto the nature and environment shelves of the nation's bookstores. Mostly expositions on counterscience, they are published either by right-wing foundations such as CATO and the Pacific Research Institute or by the once well-respected conservative D.C. publishing house Regnery Gateway, which in recent years has passed down a generation from Henry to Alfred Regnery. Its published list includes Dixy Lee Ray's books *Trashing the Planet* and *Environmental Overkill; Animal Scam* by anti–animal rights activist Kathleen Marquardt; Ron Arnold's New

Right–subsidized Watt biography; and *Inquisition*, a book released in 1991 that purports to be an unbiased investigation of Sun Myung Moon's federal tax-evasion troubles. In a letter obtained by PBS's "Frontline" program, Moon aide James Gavin wrote to Moon assuring him that he had reviewed and suggested revisions for the book before publication and that "in addition to silencing our critics now, the book should be invaluable in persuading others of our legitimacy for many years to come." Former *Washington Times* editor James Whelan told "Frontline" that Alfred Regnery was told that the Moon organization would purchase one hundred thousand copies of the book if it was released, a claim Regnery denied.[15]

A handful of anti-enviro authors are also finding outlets with larger commercial publishers looking for controversial approaches to environmentalism. Among this group is Michael Fumento, whose *Science Under Siege*, published by Morrow, attacks the environmental science "establishment." Fumento established his own journalistic reputation with an earlier 1990 book, *The Myth of Heterosexual AIDS*, which was widely criticized by AIDS activists and public health officials after it was excerpted in *Penthouse* magazine.

While the anti-enviros have lacked the capacity to create their own effective media operations, anti-environmentalism as a cause has flourished in the right-wing press. As the communist world teetered on the edge of collapse at the turning of the decade, American conservatives, facing the prospect of losing a single, unifying enemy for the first time in forty-five years, suddenly discovered the green menace. In 1990 George Will, Pat Buchanan, *National Review, Human Events, Conservative Digest,* the *Washington Times*, and other right-wing publications and pundits lashed out at environmentalism with surprising fury. It was either "a green tree with red roots," as George Will labeled it, or else the third wave of messianic movements in western civilization, "the first being Christianity, the second modern socialism," as reported by Pat Buchanan.

"As the Cold War thaws, we may be entering an era in which

government, industry and the media substitute the Green Menace for the Red Menace," warned Greenpeace USA board chairman David Chatfield that summer.[16]

On April 22, 1990, tens of millions of people in the United States and around the world observed the twentieth anniversary of Earth Day in an impressive if not quite messianic show of concern. Both the world's ecological problems and the public's response seemed to have magnified since the first Earth Day protests of 1970. Instead of hundreds of thousands of gallons of oil spilled on the beaches of Santa Barbara, millions had spilled in the Alaskan wilderness. Concerns over localized and regional effects of pollution, such as smog and acid rain, had expanded to worries over global problems such as the greenhouse effect, loss of biodiversity, and ozone depletion. Where once conservation newsletters and college papers had promoted awareness of "ecology," *Time* magazine now ran its "Planet of the Year" cover story. And while students, sportsmen, and housewives had mobilized by the millions on April 22, 1970, by 1990 a Gallup poll found that 76 percent of all Americans called themselves environmentalists.

"Make no mistake. Earth Day is a creation of the Left, a pagan holiday devoted to fashioning a Socialist/Marxist world," warned the national conservative weekly, *Human Events*,[17] setting the tone for the right-wing's response to Earth Day. Patrick Buchanan gave over his quarterly report, "From the Right," to "An Anti-Environmentalist Manifesto" by Llewellyn H. Rockwell, Jr., which labeled environmentalism "an ideology as pitiless and messianic as Marxism," and wanting nothing less than to return the world to "a godless, manless Garden of Eden."[18] *National Review*'s Earth Day issue classified environmentalists as ideological perverts or managerial elitists.[19] In a pre–Earth Day *National Review* article, David Horowitz, a Far-Left writer who had evolved to a far more profitable position on the Reagan Right, identified greens with a "consciousness alien to all that is human, rejecting the historically given needs and desires of ordinary people."[20]

The Heritage Foundation celebrated Earth Day with the release of a "Backgrounder" report entitled *Ecoterrorism: The Dangerous Fringe of the Environmental Movement*, and Richard

Darman, President Bush's director of the Office of Management and Budget, told a Harvard audience that environmentalism was the "green mask" under which "competing ideologies will continue their global struggle."

Clearly the Republican Right and its captive media, losing the devil they knew with the breakup of Soviet communism, was testing out a new devil in the form of the green menace, seeing if preservationist pagans could rally the troops as effectively as the Russian bear once had. As Alan Gottlieb told Timothy Egan of the *New York Times,* it helps to have "an evil empire" to raise potential contributors' fears and open their wallets. "For us," Gottlieb said, "the environmental movement has become the perfect bogeyman."[21]

However, recent schisms between the Christian Right and free marketeers who worship Adam Smith, between "interventionists" and "isolationists," and between pragmatists and loyalists within the Republican party suggest that the United States may be entering a period of growing turmoil on the Right.

While the green menace hasn't lived up to the red menace as a unifying principle for the Right, it has at least won a place of honor in the pantheon of Rush Limbaugh's evil-doers. Writes Rush, in the introduction to his 1992 *The Way Things Ought to Be,* "There are people out there—Communists, Socialists, Environmentalist Wackos, Feminazis, Liberal Democrats, Militant Vegetarians, Animal Rights Extremists, Liberal Elitists—who will try to prevent you from reading this."[22] Luckily for Mr. Limbaugh, 2.5 million readers braved this hairy horde in order to put down twenty-two dollars for a compilation of his radio commentaries and recorded thoughts assembled for print by *Wall Street Journal* editorial writer John Fund.

Risen up from the Sacramento radio market in 1988 like some great whale destined to defend the Reagan legacy, Rush Limbaugh, whose fifteen million listeners make him the biggest thing on talk radio, insists he's just an entertainer. But for politically challenged white males along with out-of-power Republican pols and conservative true believers—be they anti-enviros, Right-to-

Lifers, or America Firsters—Rush has become the Father Coughlin of the nineties, loved both for his right-of-Attila politics and a sense of humor that cannot be faulted for its subtlety.

"You think I could pass as a woman?" he joked on one of his shows, after reading of a seminar on sexual harassment with an all-female panel. "I could pass as a feminist woman. I'll bet you I could. Bella Abzug's cousin, long lost from Outer Mongolia, or some such thing. Just put on a hat, don't shave my legs for a couple of days—I do that, you know—wobble in there on high heels, and spy on this bunch."

He's also strong on visual humor. "Everyone knows the Clintons have a cat. Socks is the White House cat. But did you know there is also a White House dog?" he asked on his syndicated TV show before holding up a picture of thirteen-year-old Chelsea Clinton.

However, Rush's three-hour-a-day political monologues, late-night TV show (produced by former Reagan media consultant Roger Ailes), books, newsletters, and $25,000 speeches are more than the musings of an artful entertainer. A 1992 *Vanity Fair* article on Limbaugh written by Peter J. Boyer described his Wise Use "Nightline" appearance as an early and critical sign that he was beginning to cast a wider shadow across the political landscape. "Gore sounded his warning that 'We now face a global ecological crisis that is more serious than anything human civilization has ever faced,'" the article reported. "But Limbaugh was invited, too: his message that 'there is no ozone hole over the United States,' and that the 'crisis' has been manufactured by 'the doomsday industry, typified by members of the Hollywood acting community who say that we've only got ten years left,' was treated with equal weight. It was a major breakthrough for Limbaugh, whose views, in another time, from another source, might have been regarded as the latest rantings of the Flat Earth Society."[23]

When Rush Limbaugh urged his listeners to vote for Pat Buchanan in the 1992 New Hampshire Republican primary, it was clear that he intended to be a player in national politics. "Rush Limbaugh's gonna be director of communications in Pat Buchanan's White House!" Buchanan later announced to a cheering crowd in Atlanta, Georgia. Following the Republican convention in Texas, when President Bush feared that many hard-core Buchanan supporters might sit out the election, he went on Limbaugh's show, hoping, with Rush's support, to win over the party Right for a final push against Clinton and Perot. By late 1993 party conservatives, inspired by a *National Review* cover story,[24] were seriously talking about "Rush in ninety-six," although Limbaugh himself continued to insist that he wasn't interested in political office, that he only wanted to continue his soliloquies on his Excellence in Broadcasting radio network and TV show.

"Right now Rush is the only voice for our commonsense point of view," says David Howard of the Alliance for America. And despite Ron Arnold's dissent that "Rush is only in it for Rush," it could easily be argued that Rush Limbaugh has done more to spread the anti-enviro message than the Alliance for America, Center for the Defense of Free Enterprise, PFW, NIA, OLC, AER, ECO, and the whole alphabet-soup collection of Wise Use/ Property Rights groups combined.

"Environmentalists," Rush explains, "fall into two categories, Socialists and enviro-religious fanatics. . . . With the collapse of Marxism, environmentalism has become the new refuge of socialist thinking. . . . What better way to control someone's property than to subordinate one's private property rights to environmental concerns. The second group that has latched on to the environmental movement are people who believe it is a religion. Actually, it is a form of pantheism, where nature is divine. . . . They want to roll us back, maybe not to the Stone Age, but at least to the horse-and-buggy era." Never afraid to belabor a point, Rush goes on to suggest that "these people care. They care so much that caring becomes a crutch that makes them feel special and more noble than the rest of us."[25]

As a political commentator, he's also unafraid to be proscriptive in his approach to environmental issues. "If a spotted owl can't adapt, does the earth really need that particular species so much that hardship to human beings is worth enduring in the process of saving it?" he wonders in *The Way Things Ought to Be*. "Thousands of species that roamed the earth are now extinct. Do you hear anyone making the case that the earth would be better off if dinosaurs were still roaming the planet?"[26] ("Children under eight excluded," he might have added, particularly as the only contemporary media figure with a following as large and loyal as his is that of Barney, PBS's purple dinosaur.)

In the chapter of the book titled "Sorry, But the Earth Is Not Fragile," Rush argues that "Mount Pinatubo in the Philippines spewed forth more than a thousand times the amount of ozone-depleting chemicals in one eruption than all the fluorocarbons manufactured by wicked, diabolical, and insensitive corporations in history. . . . In other words Mother Nature has been attacking her own stratospheric ozone for millions of years and yet the ozone is still there, and in sufficient quantities to protect Democrats and environmentalist wackos alike from skin cancer."[27] He goes on to suggest that NASA is running a "scam" in its reporting on the problem in order to increase its funding and that the "agenda-oriented scientific community" is practicing "junk science."

He tells his readers that the best way they can arm themselves against "junk scientists" is to read Dixy Lee Ray's book *Trashing the Planet*. "I used it for much of my source material on ozone in this chapter, . . ." he explains. "I urge all readers to get her book if you want to understand the con job the environmentalists are trying to pull on us."[28]

Limbaugh's counterscience arguments led to a major paper in the June 1993 issue of *Science* magazine, the publication of the prestigious American Association for the Advancement of Science. In an unusual four-page article titled "The Ozone Backlash," the magazine, which usually concerns itself with cutting-edge developments in microbiology, chemistry, physics, and other fields of science, reports that "while evidence for the role of chlorofluorocarbons in ozone depletion grows stronger, researchers have recently been subjected to vocal public criticism of their theories—and their motives."

The article traces Rush's ozone argument to Ray's book, in which she cites two sources for most of her information on ozone depletion: Fred Singer and Rogelio Maduro, the coauthor of the

LaRouchite book *Holes in the Ozone Scare*, who told the ECO conference it was all an environmental plot to depopulate the world through mass starvation.

Atmospheric chemists and other leading climate researchers interviewed for the *Science* article described Maduro's work as "based on a selective use of out-of-date scientific papers, and an equally discretionary choice of scientific results, often taken out of context." In this article, chemist Sherwood Rowland (who helped develop the theory of chlorofluorocarbon impacts in 1973) is quoted as describing the LaRouchite book as "a good job of collecting all of the bad papers [in the field] in one place."

The basic argument made by Maduro and his coauthor is that 600 million tons of chlorine enter the atmosphere annually from seawater, 36 million tons from volcanoes, 8.4 million tons from biomass burning, and 5 million tons from ocean biota. In contrast, CFCs account for a mere 750,000 tons of atmospheric chlorine a year.

Linwood Callis, of NASA's Langley Research Center, points out one crucial problem with their argument: "Chlorine from natural sources is soluble, and so it gets rained out of the lower atmosphere. CFCs, in contrast, are insoluble and inert and thus make it to the stratosphere to release their chlorine" (which destroys ozone molecules).[29]

Surprisingly, Rush Limbaugh makes a similar argument in his book. Nine pages after discussing all the chlorine Mount Pinatubo released into the atmosphere, he attacks Carl Sagan's pre–Gulf War prediction that igniting the Kuwaiti oil wells could have catastrophic impacts on the global climate. "Smoke must rise high enough in the atmosphere and stay there so strong winds can circulate it in order for there to be any chance for global impact," he points out. "But—and I love this—the Kuwaiti smoke was not in the atmosphere long enough to rise very high. Why? It was dissipated by rain and clouds! Rain! It just came along and just cleaned it right up!"

As for questions of scientific peer review and journalistic accuracy, Rush Limbaugh's claim that Mount Pinatubo spewed out a thousand times the amount of chlorine produced by industry was shown to be a misreading of Dixy Lee's claim regarding chlorine emissions from the 1976 Mount Augustine eruption in Alaska. Dixy Lee based her estimation on a 1980 *Science* article by deceased vulcanologist David Johnston, but she also confused his figures for Mount Augustine with his much larger theoretical estimate of releases from a California eruption that occurred 700,000 years ago.

Still, counterscience, like other anti-enviro causes, continues to get wide play not only on Rush Limbaugh's show but also in the *National Review*, on the editorial pages of the *Wall Street Journal*, and on the news pages of America's newspaper of record, the *New York Times*. For anti-environmentalists perhaps the most sympathetic and certainly the most influential journalist to favor their cause is *New York Times* environmental reporter Keith Schneider. Schneider, who helped expose the Burford/Lavelle scandal at the EPA in the early eighties and mismanagement of the government's nuclear weapons plants in the late eighties, today refers to Wise Use/Property Rights as "the third wave" of environmentalism, a term first coined by his predecessor, Philip Shabecoff, in writing about mainstream environmental action groups.[31]

In the first of a controversial five-part series on environmental regulation called "What Price Cleanup?" Schneider described "a new third wave of environmentalism that is sweeping across America. It began in the late 1980s among farmers, homeowners, and others who were upset largely by the growing cost of regulations that didn't appear to bring any measurable benefits. Corporate executives had long been making similar arguments but had gone unheeded, even during twelve years of Republican rule, because often they were seen as interested only in saving money." The article then went on to quote Monsanto chemical company CEO Richard Mahoney, who suggested that the nation was finally ready to start listening to industry.[32]

"This is the third and most important work of my career, covering the risks and benefits of environmental regulation, who benefits and who loses," Keith Schneider explains in a phone interview from his new farm home in rural Michigan. "Rural America as such has become a target for environmental regulation, a target of new big industrial facilities for incinerators and large landfills, and what the property rights movement is saying is there's a risk here. The people I'm talking to are raising the specter of intrusiveness. Who's the best manager of these lands that people have been on for generations, me or the government? And if you look at the way the government's handled Superfund, nuclear waste disposal, military bases, you can see they're raising good questions.

"Meanwhile," he continues, "the national environmental movement is raising funds with uncertain science—global warming, the ozone hole. But what I'm finding in Congress is a much more skeptical view of the national environmental agenda."[33]

"Journalists are coming around. Keith is only the first on the 'let's-beat-up-the-environmentalists bandwagon,'" declares Ron Arnold.

"Keith Schneider I think is really fair and balanced," grins Chuck Cushman, who has been favorably quoted in several Schneider articles. "I'll take my hits because I know that overall he's doing good, balanced reporting."

At a workshop panel on Wise Use at the annual convention of the Society of Environmental Journalists in November 1992, Schneider first stated that he didn't want to be seen as a supporter of the Wise Use movement and then went on to explain his sympathetic view of it. "I think that the movement is maybe one of the most important and interesting movements to arise in environmentalism in a long time," he said, "because they are prying into the environmental issues that we've all grappled with for two decades. 'Is there really a global warming? Is there really an ozone problem? Does toxic waste cleanup really represent the best use of public financing? What are the best uses of public lands?' These are the kinds of questions I'm asking, and they were brought to me in large part because of the multiple layers of the movement. It is not a heterogeneous movement. I find it almost laughable that in the environmental press the rap on the Wise

Use movement is that it's corporate funded, while the largest corporate donation I know of in the environmental movement is the million dollars that GE gives the Audubon Society to support their Audubon Society TV specials [GE terminated its funding after Audubon produced a pair of documentaries on logging and grazing that generated Wise Use boycott threats]. The property rights groups I know of have no corporate funding at all. They're basically mom-and-pop-type community environmental groups," Schneider continued. "I think this year [1992] the movement reached a real pinnacle. The Bush administration developed a strategy for piggybacking on this movement, particularly in the West. . . . This movement has attracted considerable attention at the top levels of the government and the Republican party, and I think they're gong to continue to piggyback on this movement. What we have to be mindful of is the fringes of the movement, is not where the Wise Use movement is going to move. I don't think the Ron Arnold view of things is going to be paramount. The property rights view is the real strength of the movement. They now call themselves the Alliance for America, the Peggy Reigles of the world. . . . She and others like her have organized themselves through computers and faxing and a tremendous amount of use of technology to stay in touch, and that's where the real movement is going, because it's the restrictions on property and constitutional issues [like takings] that's driving the heart of the movement."[34]

Whether the Republican party has "piggybacked" on Wise Use or simply used Wise Use to create "manufactured negative public comments" on behalf of resource industries, as stated in the July 1993 *Congressional Report* on the Yellowstone vision document, Keith Schneider clearly believes it's the hottest thing since in-line skates.

And because of his position on the *New York Times*, Schneider's opinions can influence reporting nationwide. A June 1993 article in the *American Journalism Review* highlighted this by showing how a 1991 story Schneider wrote headlined "U.S. Officials Say Dangers of Dioxin Were Exaggerated" changed the national tone of dioxin reporting—at least twenty major newspapers reprinted the piece and many other papers followed up with similar reports and editorials based largely on Schneider's work.

The *Review* article also suggested how faithfully, if not accurately, the press can play follow-the-leader by tracking a metaphor Keith made up, ran past a couple of his sources, and then attributed to "some experts": that exposure to dioxin was no more harmful than a week of sunbathing. The *Arizona Republic* attributed the claim to "top federal scientists." The *Newark Star-Ledger* attributed it to "some health experts." The *Financial Times* of London thought it came from "a U.S. report," while the *Sacramento Bee* believed "a widening group of scientists" thought dioxin exposure was no more dangerous "than a week at the beach."[35]

Keith Schneider's "mainstreaming" of the Wise Use movement in the pages of the *New York Times* has had a similar effect: legitimizing the anti-enviros with the mass media, particularly the eastern media establishment, which is unfamiliar with the history, associations, and core beliefs of Wise Use.

Sympathetic stories on Wise Use/Property Rights penned by Schneider include "Environment, Inc., on the Defensive," "When the Bad Guy Is Seen as the One in the Green Hat," and a May 1993 piece on Catron County, New Mexico, titled "In Cattle-Raising West, a County Wants to Help U.S. Manage Federal Lands," which depicts the radical "mining-as-culture" counties movement as an attempt "to make environmental protection less costly."[36]

"In terms of the media food chain, we've elevated Wise Use to this large alternative movement, which I don't really see on the ground," says Tim Egan, the *Times* Seattle correspondent, who covers natural resource issues in the West. "Keith and I have differed on this a lot. I probably travel more in the West than any other national reporter, sixty to seventy thousand miles a year to all these small towns and rural communities, and I just don't see any signs of a real environmental backlash. I don't see it at town hall meetings or in local elections or in all these other venues for popular sentiment. If I did I'd write about it more, but really all I see are the same old faces."[37]

There's a fine line a journalist risks crossing when he or she goes from admiring a social trend, as Schneider clearly admires the anti-enviros, to promoting it by giving it greater weight than it deserves. He may have crossed that line in a 1992 article he wrote on environmental policy changes being hammered out during the last days of the Bush administration when he sought reaction from "leaders of environmental, industrial, and property rights groups."[38]

It would undoubtedly raise editorial red flags at the *Times* if their Mideast correspondent, while covering Israel and the occupied territories, began soliciting the responses of Israelis, Palestinians, and Druze Arabs, or if their Washington correspondents reported on a civil rights bill by getting responses from the administration, civil rights leaders, and white separatists. But Schneider's pro–Wise Use reporting, tied as it is to his savaging of environmental regulations, had won the backing of Max Frankel, the *Times* recently retired executive editor and former editorial page chief. When Frankel ran the editorial pages, his concern over the costs of environmental regulation and recapitulation of shopworn "jobs versus environment" arguments stood in marked contrast with the environmentally friendly editorial stances of his predecessor, John Oakes.

"It's sad to see the *New York Times* use its news pages to stake out an editorial position, but that's what I see happening," says ex–*Times* reporter Phil Shabecoff, who served as the paper's environmental reporter for fourteen years before being pulled off the beat and reassigned to cover the IRS in 1990 (he retired a short time later). Shabecoff is a short, tanned, avuncular New Yorker who looks somehow out of place in the sterile mall culture of suburban Falls Church, Virginia, where he now edits *Greenwire*, a five-day-a week environmental news service that goes out to some five to six hundred subscribers, ranging from the White House, ABC, and CNN to small college newspapers.

"Growing up in New York, all I ever wanted was to be a foreign correspondent for the *New York Times*, and I did it," he grins before catching himself, his smile fading. "You know that Chinese saying: Be careful what you wish for, it may come true."

During thirty-two years with the *Times*, Shabecoff hit many of the high points of a career in journalism. He covered labor and economics, served a stint as a European correspondent, and was the *Times* White House reporter during the Nixon and Ford administrations before being given the position he'd sought to create since 1970 as the paper's first environmental journalist.

"Abe Rosenthal [*Times* former executive editor] was supportive. He wasn't happy with all my coverage, but he never kept any of my stuff from getting in the paper," Phil recalls. "Like, I remember when I first wrote about radon. He'd never heard of it, which made him nervous, but that radon story still ran on page one."

Asked if things started to change when Frankel took over as news editor, he shakes his head wryly. "Well, it certainly ended with Max. As far as I'm concerned, he didn't have a clue on these issues. Howell Raines, the D.C. bureau chief [now editorial page editor], told me New York was concerned I was writing too many stories about environmental problems and not enough about the economic impact of environmental regulation. That was the editorial position the *Times* wanted staked out on the news pages. The *New York Times* I joined in 1959 wouldn't have done that, and I wouldn't do what they wanted me to do, so they claimed my coverage was too pro-environment. I asked them to cite examples. The only example Raines came up with was, 'You used the word dolphins being *slaughtered* instead of dolphins being *killed*.' My perspective is, yes, there was bias and ignorance, but it was on the part of my editors, particularly my national editor."

Phil rummages around his office before pulling out a Balance in Journalism award from the National Environmental Development Association, an industry lobby. He then suggests a list of names a reporter could contact, including past Republican heads of the EPA, who would confirm his record for fairness and accuracy. He mentions how he sits on the corporate advisory council for Dow Chemical and the board of directors of the Institute for Cooperation in Environmental Management, not the sort of positions normally open to someone perceived to be biased or far out. He pauses, realizing what he's doing. "You can see I still get upset by this. I feel embarrassed." It's obvious: after thirty-two years with the *New York Times*, Phil Shabecoff's sense of betrayal remains painfully close to the surface.

"Environmental journalists need to push the envelope more, need to challenge the environmental orthodoxies," says Keith Schneider. "I joined the *Times* in 1985 after an eighteen-month effort to get myself hired. Before that I was a freelancer. I've written across the board. I wrote for *California Farmer* and *Mother Jones*. I was having good success. I was running and gunning. I wrote for *Reason* and *Inquiry*, the CATO Institute magazine. I wrote for Manhattan, Inc. I wrote across the spectrum. . . . I won two Polk Awards, one I shared with *Amicus* journal in 1984 for a report on faked data on toxicity testing by industrial labs. The second one I won, in 1989, for a *New York Times* series on deterioration of weapons in atomic factories at Rocky Flats, Hanford, and elsewhere. . . . I was covering the environment and agriculture when Phil left the *Times*. I don't know what happened in terms of his losing his job. He was a pioneer in the field, although I think we differed on how we viewed our jobs."

Shabecoff is more forthcoming in his criticism of Schneider, particularly regarding the articles he wrote for the "What Price Cleanup?" series on regulation that ran in the spring of 1993. "I found his series to be shocking," Phil says. "It was an editorial position planted in the news column. It was certainly one-sided, with brief and skeptical statements on the other side of the issue."

The five-part series reviewed toxic cleanup, animal testing for human risk assessment, ocean dumping, and the high costs of eliminating pollution-caused cancers, hammering away at the expenses involved in government programs and for corporate cleanup. In Keith's opening article (he wrote three of the five stories), "New View Calls Environmental Policy Misguided," he quoted some twenty-five unnamed officials and experts, all of whom seemed to back up his contention that "much of America's environmental program has gone seriously awry." Surprisingly, at no point in the series' almost 250 paragraphs of copy is pollution prevention mentioned as a cost-effective remedy for America's environmental waste problems.

The dramatic contrast in reportorial perspective between Shabecoff and Schneider recalls an earlier changing of the guard at the Great Gray Lady. During the 1980s the *Times*'s Central American correspondent, Ray Bonner, under attack by the Reagan administration for reporting the 1981 El Mozote massacre of hundreds of civilians and other army-led human rights abuses in El Salvador, was reassigned and later replaced by Shirley Christian, a pro–U.S. policy reporter. Christian had enhanced her reputation among conservatives with a *Washington Journalism Review* article attacking reporters who covered the Nicaraguan revolution for being dupes of the Marxist Sandinistas. The effect of the changeover was that the *New York Times* coverage shifted from being out front in breaking news from Central America and into step with Washington's official line on why the U.S. had to support military regimes and organize rebel armies in the region.[39]

Similarly, the shift from Shabecoff to Schneider has seen the *Times*'s coverage move from broad-ranging exposure of environmental problems to a cost-benefit downplaying of the dangers of toxic chemicals and advocacy of regulatory "reforms" long favored by industry.

"I know a lot of people on the outside take a conspiratorial view of the *Times*'s coverage, but it really doesn't work that way," claims Tim Egan. "Remember, while Keith Schneider has been in Washington covering toxic waste [L.A. Bureau Chief] Bob Reinhold and I have also been getting page-one stories dealing with environmental land-use issues like water rights, grazing, and forestry. We've helped make how these public resources get used into a national topic of debate, where before they were seen as only regional concerns. I go back East for editorial meetings on a regular basis, and if there was some kind of environmental agenda on Max's part I would have encountered it, and I haven't. This is much more a reporter-driven thing. An individual reporter's coverage can change the paper's perspective on an issue, and because it's the *Times*, that reporter can impact how that topic gets covered nationally."

The first article on which Keith Schneider seems to have staked out his position as the hard-eyed critic of misguided environmental cleanup policies was published on August 15, 1991. Titled "U.S. Backing Away from Saying Dioxin Is a Deadly Peril," the page-one story opened, "In a rare official reassessment, several top Federal health authorities are backing away from the position that the chemical compound dioxin is toxic enemy No. 1. Exposure to the chemical, once thought to be much more hazardous than chain smoking, is now considered by some experts to be no more risky than spending a week sunbathing."

Having set the tone with his sunbathing metaphor, Schneider quoted EPA Director William K. Reilly, who said, "I don't want to prejudge the issue, but we are seeing new information on dioxin that suggests a lower risk assessment for dioxin should be applied." The article went on to report that Dr. Vernon Houk, the CDC official who ordered the evacuation of 2,240 residents from the dioxin-contaminated town of Times Beach, Missouri, in 1982, had, by May of 1991, decided that the order had been unnecessary, and that if dioxin was a carcinogen, it was only "a weak carcinogen."

The article also quoted Marilyn Leistner, the former mayor of Times Beach, as saying, "If dioxin is less dangerous, that should be good news. The truth is, it's not. People have been hurt, their lives ruined by what happened in the area. One minute it's bad. The next it's good. It's a roller coaster that just won't stop."

Without introducing any new information or studies on dioxin, the story concluded with Laverne Baker standing on a barricaded bridge across the Meramec River from the quarantined town. Laverne's husband, Leroy, had committed suicide after the couple was forced to evacuate their Times Beach home of almost thirty years. "It's all a mistake?" Keith quotes her. "They took our homes, our lives, and now they say it's a mistake?"[40]

Apparently it wasn't a mistake, according to a story that ran in the news section of the *Wall Street Journal* six months later. "The current reappraisal of dioxin, an industrial byproduct ubiquitous in the environment, is as much a result of a well-financed public-relations campaign by the paper and chlorine industries as it is a result of new research," reported *Journal* staffer Jeff Bailey on February 20, 1992.[41]

One example he cited was a conference of dioxin experts sponsored by the Chlorine Institute at the Banbury Center on Long Island. Along with the three dozen experts in attendance was scientist George Carlo, a $150-dollar-an-hour observer for the chlorine industry. Carlo reported that the conference reached a consensus that there was a safe threshold beneath which dioxin exposure was not dangerous. This was news to the other scientists at the conference, and a Chlorine Institute official later conceded to the *Journal* that the claim was "a botched publicity effort." But apparently not so botched that the chairman of Georgia-Pacific and three other paper company executives weren't able to get a meeting with EPA chief Bill Reilly, who a short time later cited the "safe threshold" claim from the Banbury meeting as the basis for his suggestion that a lower risk assessment might be needed.

The other key figure in Schneider's article, Vernon Houk, who announced his "reversal" on the danger of dioxin in May 1991, had actually begun reevaluating his approach to dioxin in the mid-eighties, when CDC was studying the effects of Agent Orange on Vietnam veterans. Retired U.S. Admiral Elmo Zumwalt, whose son was among those affected, accused Houk of manipulating scientific data to downplay the harmful effects of dioxin. Houk accused the admiral of being "crazy." Houk went on to play a key role in the Bush administration's denial of disability benefits to dioxin-exposed vets (a ruling that was later reversed for those suffering from a number of cancers, liver disorders, and other maladies found to be related to dioxin exposure). In 1988 Houk wrote to the Canadian government, urging it to lower its dioxin standards, and saying that dioxin "may be without consequence even in very high dose exposure to humans," a claim he later repudiated, although he admitted having written the letter. In 1990 Houk was called before a congressional committee to answer charges of improperly aiding the paper industry's campaign to loosen restrictions on dioxin pollution in water. During his testimony he admitted he'd drafted relaxed water standards for the state of Georgia copied from reports given him by the paper industry. None of this information was included in the laudatory sidebar on Houk that accompanied Schneider's dioxin article.

"I think a lot of us were really excited when we saw this major story in the *New York Times* and then kind of disappointed to see that there was nothing new there, that it was based on the same industry studies and claims that had been floating around for some time," says Jane Kay, an award-winning environmental reporter with the *San Francisco Examiner*. Also missing from Schneider's dioxin article and the next day's *New York Times* editorial titled "Downgrading Dioxin" was any reference to the *Times*'s 80 percent interest in a Maine papermill and 49 percent interest in three Canadian papermills. On August 12 two Canadian Indian tribes had sued Kimberly-Clark and the *Times* for $1.3 billion, charging that one of their Canadian mills had polluted tribal rivers with dioxin and other toxins. This apparent conflict of interest (papermills being a major source of dioxin pollution) first surfaced in a *Village Voice* column written by James Ledbetter on August 27.[42]

"I did not even know it. Didn't think to ask, was not aware of it. The first time I heard of it was when I read it in the *Village Voice*," says Keith Schneider, who doesn't believe the suit or the *Times* interest in papermills has had any effect on the *Times*'s coverage. The *Times* had in fact reported the suit in a small article inside its business section on August 14, the day before Keith's front-page story ran. On the fifteenth, the *Times* and Kimberly-Clark agreed to sell off the papermill named in the suit. The author of the "Downgrading Dioxin" editorial, deputy editorial page editor Phillip Boffey, told the *American Journalism Review* that editorialists "are supposed to cite financial interests, however tangential. . . . I just failed to do it in this case because frankly I was unaware of the lawsuit."[43]

While almost all new research on dioxin since 1991 has tended to bolster its reputation as one of the most toxic elements created by industry, Keith Schneider's coverage has continued to downplay the risks. "The amount of dioxin we produce in this country as opposed to chlorine is literally an eyedropper in Lake Michigan, a leaf's worth in the whole United States," he suggests with his ready command of metaphor.[44]

In September 1992 an EPA panel of independent scientists held a four-day meeting to review dioxin. In a variation on "Is the glass half full or half empty?" *Newsday* reported that the panel found "the chemical's effects may be broader and more troubling than previously thought." "Dioxin's Health Risks May Be Greater than Believed, EPA Memo Indicates" was the headline on a *Wall Street Journal* story once the panel's findings were reviewed and found to indicate that dioxin could have reproductive, behavioral, and immune-suppressive effects on humans at close to existing background levels of exposure. The headline on Schneider's story tried to accentuate the positive. "Panel of Scientists Finds Dioxin Does Not Pose Widespread Cancer Threat," it read.[45]

In July 1993 the National Academy of Sciences, after reviewing thousands of studies, released a report concluding that exposure to dioxin can cause three types of cancer and two other diseases and may be linked to three additional cancers and a number of other health problems. An August 1993 report based on a 1976 chemical-plant explosion that released a cloud of dioxin in Seveso, Italy, also found higher than normal rates of leukemia, lymphoma, and liver cancer among people who had had low to moderate exposures.[46]

The *American Journalism Review* and its New York cousin, the *Columbia Journalism Review,* are the only national magazines dedicated to reporting critical media issues, ethics, and performance stories from a professional perspective within the field of journalism. As a result, the views and conclusions reached in the pages of *AJR* and *CJR* tend to define the new thinking or reinterpret the common wisdom within the profession. Given its influence within the media, Keith Schneider was understandably upset with the dioxin story *AJR* ran in its June 1993 issue.

"See No Evil," read the orange and black boxed headline on the magazine's cover, set against a purple halftone aerial shot of Times Beach. The story opened by quoting from Schneider's kickoff piece on the "What Price Cleanup?" series, suggesting that billions of dollars are wasted battling problems, like dioxin, that are no longer considered especially dangerous. "Schneider's conclusions about dioxin's risks have a major flaw," states the *AJR* article, written by freelance journalist Vicki Monks. "They're wrong."

Monks went on to quote a number of scientists, such as Dr. William Farland of the EPA, saying there was no basis for thinking dioxin was less dangerous than previously thought, that it might in fact be more so. The article then tracked the Schneider sunbathing metaphor, compared various publications' coverage of dioxin, quoted additional scientists, and, in a rather pointed dig, quoted Times Beach ex-Mayor Marilyn Leistner as saying, "Our lives were not disrupted for no reason. We had to move because the dioxin was causing real health problems. To see a child born with cancer and then die after a few months . . . another [baby] born with kidneys on the outside of its body. . . . All I can say is that I'd take a week in the sun anytime over moving back to Times Beach."

"The coverage of dioxin is a glaring example of the danger of blindly accepting facts as reported by any other news organization," the *AJR* article concluded, "even if it's the *New York Times*."[47]

"I'm an enemy now of the environmental movement. The national environmental community has targeted me. The *American Journalism Review* put me on the cover with a scientifically dishonest attack. It's an unblemished hit piece, a dishonest, selectively chosen account. It was designed to knock me out of the box, but I don't think it's going to," Schneider says, clearly stung by the criticism.

In a letter to the *AJR*, he declared, "I am a reporter, not an ideologue. I follow the facts and new knowledge about the environment where they lead. I report the results as fairly, accurately, and with as much gravity and honesty as I am capable."

With his move to the Midwest, Keith Schneider hopes to spend more time finding stories in the heartland, outside the Washington beltway, where he's been based for the last several years. "I notice that both sides at the local level, the property

rights groups and anti-toxics activists, are asking where the national environmental groups are at. Both sides are aiming their
critiques at six or seven big groups with clout in Washington who
are lobbying for programs that are having bad results in the field,
lobbying for these regulations that are questionable in terms of
their impacts on policy and on life in rural America," he claims.

"He has a view he's bought and it affects his coverage," counters
Tim Egan. "As a westerner, I see that the big change is not in the
backlash but in a nascent environmentalism that you find in all
these small towns and cities across the West. It's coming from new
wealth and people. It's gotten so that even in Alaska you're beginning to see the change. There's plenty to criticize with some
of these Washington-based environmental lobbies that have
grown fat and lazy, and I think a lot of local groups do criticize
them and a few of them are responding, but I don't buy this parallel between local environmental activists and Wise Use. People
who don't live in the West tend to pump them [Wise Use] up and
make them more powerful than they are. I mean take [Secretary
of Interior] Bruce Babbitt. The anti-environmentalists tried to
make him their poster boy, hoping he'd do for them what James
Watt did for the environmentalists, but it's not happening. This
great countermovement is just not there."

Except in the media. The anti-enviro cause has gained high visibility in the media through the support of the conservative press
and a few key figures such as Rush Limbaugh and Keith Schneider. But unlike the Christian Right, with its millions of grassroots
followers, Wise Use/Property Rights lacks the membership base
to parlay that coverage into effective local action without resorting
to confrontational tactics, intimidation, or violence. If its organizers are thrilled that the national press believes they're leading
a big parade, they also have to realize that as time goes on more
skeptical members of the press may ask to see more than a rifle-
carrying drill team.

If it's less than shocking to see how pro- and anti-
environmental politics have divided journalists and affected media institutions ranging from television to talk radio to the *New
York Times*, that may be because most people have come to ac-

cept that the media are also a subject and players in the American political drama.

For a sense of constitutional stability and sustaining principles unmarred by the buffeting winds of political conflict, many citizens are more likely to turn towards our legal system of jurisprudence.

Up Against the Law

*The law, in its majestic equality, forbids the rich as well as the poor to
sleep under bridges, to beg in the streets and to steal bread.*
ANATOLE FRANCE, 1894

*The Constitution does not guarantee
that land speculators will win their bets.*
PACE UNIVERSITY LAW PROFESSOR JOHN HUMBACH, 1993

On July 23, 1993, the state of Alaska sued the United States of
America for $29 billion. It was the latest volley in an environ-
mental war launched against the U.S. from "Wally's World,"
which is what local critics call Alaska under the administration of
seventy-five-year-old Governor Walter Hickel. In 1990 Hickel
was elected as the candidate of the Alaskan Independence Party
with 39 percent of the vote in a three-way race. With decriminal-
ization of marijuana also on the ballot, it wasn't long before
bumper stickers appeared reading, "Pot Got More Votes Than
Hickel." Aside from his desire to get the feds to open up the Arctic
National Wildlife Refuge for oil development and his plan to shoot
enough wolves to increase the moose and caribou herds, turning
the Alaskan plains into a "hunter's paradise," Hickel has also proposed building major freeways and rail lines into the wilderness,
piping Alaska's water south to California, and putting state funds
into a feasibility study on the mining of asteroids.

In its suit, filed with the U.S. Claims Court in Washington,
D.C., the state of Alaska argues that the establishment of national

parks and wilderness areas in Alaska is a breach of contract and a legal "taking" in that it denies the state revenue. According to its 1959 statehood agreement, Alaska is to receive 90 percent of all revenues from oil, mineral, and gas leasing on federal lands, a multibillion dollar windfall that has given state residents an annual cash bonus in lieu of taxes. But many Alaskans still see themselves as a colony of Washington. They resent the extensive system of parks, wildlife refuges, and wilderness areas established by the federal government, which they accuse of trying to turn Alaska into a "museum." The get-rich-quick frontier mentality of Alaska's older, "territorial" generation finds legal expression in State Attorney General Charles Cole's complaint that while national parks and wildlife refuges may attract tourists, they should not be kept off-limits to mining and oil drilling. According to Alaska's legal-takings theory, if the United States insists on protecting wild and scenic tracts such as Denali National Park by excluding extractive industry, it must compensate the state 90 percent of the value of the oil, gas, and minerals it leaves buried in the earth.[1]

Although legal experts say the suit doesn't have much chance, they acknowledge that it falls within the bounds of a growing school of anti-environmental legal theory that has gained credence in recent years as part of a broader judicial backlash against environmental law. Where once Supreme Court Justice William O. Douglas argued that parts of nature and its "environmental wonders" are entitled to be represented in court, today Supreme Court Justice Clarence Thomas insists that any protection of nature that affects the dollar value of real estate must be financially compensated by the government.

One of the notable changes in the teaching and practice of law over the last thirty years has been the emergence of environmental law as a major current in the legal mainstream. Almost every law school in America now includes a survey course on the subject, and many schools offer specialized instruction and degrees in it. Lawyers familiar with the nuances of environmental law can be found in most government offices and corporate suites, a development that reflects both the rapid growth of protective environmental legislation and the ongoing legal clashes over how these laws are to be interpreted. Environmental advocacy groups have learned to use lawsuits as effective weapons in their battles to prevent the development of wilderness areas or compel government agencies to enforce antipollution laws where industry or the government itself has placed communities at risk. Small businesses and corporations have had to hire teams of lawyers to interpret the growing and often contradictory environmental rules and regulations promulgated at every level of government, and polluters and other environmental lawbreakers have become the target of "green cops" working out of U.S. attorneys' offices, natural resources agencies, and local jurisdictions. Unlike bank robbers and muggers, however, these criminals have responded to their indictments, fines, and convictions not with feigned contrition but by attacking the laws they've been convicted of violating. During the Reagan and Bush administrations, when Congress refused to gut certain key environmental laws unpopular with industry, the executive branch developed what became known as a "train-wreck strategy" to undermine those laws they didn't like. When 213 counties failed to meet a 1982 Clean Air deadline, the Reagan administration proposed enforcing a never-used provision of the law to ban all new construction of homes and offices in those communities, hoping (in vain, it turned out) to provoke an anti–Clean Air Act backlash.[2] Refusal by the EPA, Department of the Interior, and other agencies to enforce laws governing toxic cleanup, clean water, wilderness protection, and the Endangered Species Act seemed designed to provoke environmentalist lawsuits, forcing stringent court rulings that left no room for compromise or conciliation. Administration spokespeople and their conservative backers would then point to "judicial gridlock" as proof that environmental laws didn't work.

Almost all sides in the northwest timber wars agree that by using this kind of intentional inaction the Bush administration pushed the spotted-owl controversy into the courts, where it resulted in rapid closure of U.S. national forest lands to logging and left long-term economic and forest ecology issues unresolved. In June 1993 the Clinton administration announced its own "Option

Nine" northwest forest plan, which, although disliked by all sides, was nonetheless seen as a step away from use of the courts as a tool of political sabotage by the government.

Moving well beyond the government's ability to create legal train wrecks, some corporations and developers discovered that they could use the law as a tool of intimidation, going after their opponents with what came to be known as SLAPPs—Strategic Lawsuits Against Public Participation.

In West Virginia the DLM Coal Corporation filed a multimillion-dollar libel action against Rick Webb and his small nonprofit environmental group after they requested an EPA hearing on pollution of local rivers by mine runoff and wrote an editorial in their newsletter criticizing strip mining.

In Squaw Valley, California, stunt skier Rick Sylvester was slapped with a $75 million lawsuit for speaking out and writing letters to the editor against a planned development.

In Louisville, Colorado, a developer sued local activist Betty Johnson for unlimited damages after she organized a petition drive for a growth moratorium. According to a survey in Florida, 15 percent of all growth-management advocates in that state have been the target of SLAPP suits.

In Alaska the Shee Atika timber company sued the Sierra Club for $40 million when the Sierra Club took up the cause of Alaskan natives who wanted to keep logging off their traditional hunting grounds.

According to Penelope Canan and George Pring, the two University of Denver professors who first coined the term in 1988, SLAPPs are used by corporations and developers to silence public opposition by dragging people into court with spurious suits. The goal is not to win settlements but to intimidate critics and create a "chilling atmosphere" designed to discourage other would-be citizen activists.[3] Of the hundreds of SLAPP suits being filed every year, Professor Canan reports, about 60 percent are directed against people and groups protesting unchecked growth and other environmental abuses. "Right now we're seeing a rapid increase of cases involving landfills and toxic waste sites," she says, citing examples in Fort Worth, Texas, and Terre Haute, Indiana.[4]

"As a tactic it's designed to make environmentalists get scared and go away," says Joe Brecher, a private attorney who works with the Sierra Club Legal Defense Fund. "It targets local ad hoc neighborhood groups, people who don't expect to be sued for speaking their mind. I've had a few cases where it's worked, where the clients couldn't stand the heat and got out."[5]

Victor Monia, a SLAPP victim in a suit involving a California citizen's group that had won a one-year moratorium on hillside development, described how, after a developer sued them for $40 million, "people melted away . . . people who had been very active just sort of disappeared."[6]

Although 83 percent of SLAPPs are dismissed before they reach trial, they can still cost defendants tens of thousands of dollars in legal expenses and tremendous amounts of personal time and energy.

Rick Sylvester compared the impact of a SLAPP suit to "having a monster move in with your family." Another SLAPP victim described how "I became so preoccupied by the suit that it changed my whole focus and direction in life. This case was an overhanging cloud. Even though you may prevail, you'll spend a ton of money fighting it. You can win and still lose."

The SLAPP suit that probably deserves top honors for pure chutzpah was filed not against an environmentalist but against Vietnam veteran and antiwar activist Brian Wilson. Wilson, protesting arms shipments to Central America in 1987, sat down on a railroad track to blockade an ammunition train at the Concord Naval Weapons Station in suburban Concord, California. He expected to be arrested for civil disobedience. Instead he was run over by the train when it failed to slow down and he was unable to scramble out of its way in time. He lost both legs and had part of his skull crushed in. Before he'd even been fitted for artificial legs, he was sued by the military train's engineer, brakeman, and conductor for having inflicted great emotional stress and trauma on them.

In recent years several SLAPP victims, including Rick Sylvester, the Squaw Valley skier, have fought back with countersuits for
civil rights violations and malicious prosecution. As early as May
1991, a Missouri woman won an $86.5 million settlement against
a waste-incinerator corporation that had sued her for criticizing
them.

Despite these "slapp-backs" and legislative efforts in California, Washington, New York, New Jersey, and several other states
to discourage SLAPPs through early judicial review and recovery
of attorneys' fees, many polluters and developers continue to find
it easier to use the court system as a weapon of intimidation than
to try making their cases with the public. Still, SLAPP suits are
by nature reactive and involve a certain level of risk both in terms
of public relations and the possibility of countersuits against
plaintiffs. Today's property rights advocates, working through a
network of right-wing nonprofit law firms and legislative think
tanks, have hit upon a more proactive legal strategy for the 1990s.
They are pushing for a radical reinterpretation of the Fifth
Amendment "takings" clause that they hope will lead to the effective dismantling of environmental legislation and ultimately to
the Holy Grail of conservative wish fulfillment, a rollback of the
regulatory state established during Franklin Delano Roosevelt's
New Deal.

Most people are familiar with the First Amendment of the Bill
of Rights, the first ten amendments to the U.S. Constitution,
which guarantees them freedom of speech and assembly, religion, and a free press. They also know the Second Amendment,
which reads, "A well-regulated militia being necessary to the security of a free state, the right of the people to keep and bear arms
shall not be infringed," as well as the Fifth Amendment—but
only that clause heard regularly in gangster movies and on tele-
vised congressional hearings that protects a defendant against
self-incrimination. However, the Fifth Amendment also states,
"No person shall be . . . deprived of life, liberty, or property
without due process of law; nor shall private property be taken
for public use, without just compensation."

Today, when the government condemns land to build an interstate highway or commercial airport, the Fifth Amendment guarantees that the landowner be paid market value for his or her lost property. In 1887 Kansas brewer Peter Mugler argued the first case for a "regulatory taking," claiming that a prohibition law passed in his state meant he had in effect been denied his property rights under the Fifth Amendment because his brewery had lost its value. The Supreme Court ruled against him, stating that "a government can prevent a property owner from using his property to injure others without having to compensate the owner for the value of the forbidden use." This "nuisance clause" has enabled governments to establish health and safety regulations, labor codes, and environmental protections that limit what an individual owner can do with his or her property without having to pay that owner compensation.

In 1926, in a case titled *Village of Euclid* v. *Ambler Realty,* the Supreme Court confirmed that zoning ordinances, which establish agreed-upon beneficial land uses for a community, are another form of legitimate government restriction on property that does not constitute a taking.

These precedents, which recognize that democratically determined social values may limit the unrestricted use of property—so that, for example, a riverfront property owner might not be allowed to dump manure upstream from his or her neighbor's property—would not be seriously challenged for the next sixty years. The institutional forces that would launch this next major challenge began taking shape in the 1970s.

In 1971 the U.S. Chamber of Commerce hired attorney and future Supreme Court Justice Lewis Powell to advise it on how to counter environmental and consumer activists. He recommended the formation of a business-sponsored legal center that would not hesitate to "attack the [Ralph] Naders . . . and others who openly seek destruction of the system."[7]

In 1973 the Pacific Legal Foundation, the first of a chain of business-sponsored "public interest" law firms, was established in Sacramento, California. According to an early profile in *Barron's* magazine, PLF's founding mission was to "stem the rampage" of environmentalists and welfare advocates. Its earliest cases included the defense of DDT spraying in national forests and legal challenges to environmental impact reports. The PLF has gone after antinuclear activists, rent-control advocates, affirmative action programs, and more recently the slow-growth initiative process, arguing in the latter context that "growth can bring about complex and varied land-use problems that must be carefully addressed. But resorting to the ballot box for solutions is not appropriate."[8]

Two years after the inception of the PLF, the National Legal Center for the Public Interest was founded to assist in the creation of additional probusiness nonprofit law firms. Since then twenty-two of these "free-enterprise" law firms have appeared, including the Mountain States Legal Foundation, New England Legal Foundation, Federal Lands Legal Foundation, and Washington Legal Foundation.[9] Every year the Heritage Foundation holds a conference where the directors of these firms come together and strategize. While all the firms share a common conservative free-market philosophy, PLF and Mountain States have been at the forefront of the anti-environmentalist movement, acting as the main legal advocates and advisors for Wise Use/Property Rights activists.

Free in-kind legal services to anti-enviro groups doesn't come cheaply. The probusiness nonprofits are funded by tens of millions of dollars from right-wing foundations, including Coors, Olin, Scaife and Bradley, and such major corporations as Exxon, Ford, Union Carbide, Georgia-Pacific, and Phillips Petroleum. Pacific Legal Foundation operates on a $4 million annual budget, whereas according to its IRS filings, the smaller Mountain States Legal Foundation received $3.25 million between 1986 and 1990 and paid its president, William Perry Pendley, $130,000 a year.[10]

In 1984 the *Yale Law Journal* dedicated most of an issue to an analysis of the probusiness law firms by Tulane Law Professor Oliver Houck, who wondered whether they rightfully qualified for 501(c)(3) nonprofit status as "public interest" charities. He examined two IRS requirements: their cases could not be substantially directed to insiders, and could not be "economically feasible" for the private bar.[11] Houck found that 70 out of 132 cases filed by the Pacific Legal Foundation were invalid by the terms of the IRS requirements and another 16 were questionable. "In questions bearing upon nuclear power and the regulation of utilities, PLF's ties to the benefited corporations were remarkably close," the report noted.[12]

"In at least twenty-four cases on the docket, the position MSLF [Mountain States Legal Foundation] was advocating directly benefited corporations represented on its board of directors, clients of firms represented on its board of litigation, or major contributors to MSLF's budget,"[13] noted Houck in his case-by-case analysis. The report detailed how the law firms provided insider profits to their sponsors while pursuing causes whose beneficiaries—including oil companies, utilities, and mining corporations—could just as easily have hired private attorneys.

Applying the IRS criteria, Professor Houck found that the work of the probusiness nonprofits "stretches the concepts of charity and public interest practice beyond meaningful definition." The *Yale Law Journal* report produced many raised eyebrows in the legal community but no discernible action by the IRS under President Reagan.

In the early 1980s the Federalist Society, a conservative legal forum, began to establish itself at various law schools around the country as a counter to the left-of-center National Lawyers Guild. "We had all these professors influenced by the New Deal saying everything was supposed to be an improvement since Roosevelt packed the court [*sic*], that property and economic rights were somehow lesser than social rights," recalls Jim Burling, a takings expert working out of the Pacific Legal Foundation's Sacramento office. "We were being told that Chief Justice Rehnquist's rulings were some kind of reactionary throwback to a retrograde era before FDR. I wasn't aware there was an influential alternative intellectual tradition in conservatism until groups like the Federalist Society got going," says the blue-eyed, curly haired lawyer.[14]

A stronghold of the Federalists and other New Right thinkers was the University of Chicago, home to Milton Friedman's "Chicago School" of economics and the revisionist "law and economics movement" that looks at the law in terms of economic costs and benefits rather than "abstract" concepts of right and wrong.

While Friedman's free-market economic theories would be the major contribution of this university to the Reagan Revolution, Richard Epstein, a professor at the law school, was also destined to play a role with the publication of his 1985 book, *Takings: Private Property and the Power of Eminent Domain.*[15] There he argued that under the Fifth Amendment the government must pay property owners whenever environmental regulations, health and safety rules, or zoning laws limit the value of their property. He went on to suggest that even income taxes could be seen as a form of takings. The same year Epstein's book came out, President Reagan appointed Loren Smith chief judge of the U.S. Claims Court, a relatively obscure judicial backwater where cases involving government contracts, patents, Indian claims, and federal pay disputes are settled. Smith, a veteran of the Nixon Watergate legal defense team and a 1980 Reagan campaign attorney, numbers among his heroes conservative scholars Robert Bork and Richard Epstein.[16]

That Epstein's interpretation of the Fifth Amendment was also being read by higher-ranking officials in Washington is confirmed by Charles Fried, the U.S. solicitor general from 1985 to 1989, who, in his 1991 book, *Order and Law: Arguing the Reagan Revolution*, wrote, "Attorney General Meese and his young advisors—many drawn from the ranks of the then fledgling Federalist Society and often devotees of the extreme libertarian views of Chicago Law Professor Richard Epstein—had a specific, aggressive, and, it seemed to me, quite radical project in mind: to use the takings clause of the Fifth Amendment as a severe brake upon federal and state regulation of business and property."[17]

"I'm glad to see Charles nailed it right on the head in seeing where we want to go with this compensation clause," says Nancy Marzulla, president of the Washington, D.C.-based Defenders of Property Rights, which she founded with her husband Roger.[18] In the mid-eighties Roger Marzulla was assistant attorney general under Ed Meese and Nancy an attorney in the Justice Department's much-criticized civil rights division. Toward the end of the Reagan administration, Marzulla directed Mark Pollot, his special assistant on land and natural resources, to draft Executive Order #12630, which President Reagan signed on March 15, 1988. The presidential order, which followed Epstein's radical theories rather than existing case law, required government agencies to evaluate the private property takings implications of any regulatory actions they conducted.[19]

While the courts had not yet accepted this type of "regulatory takings" arguments, they were becoming more open to a politicized, or "activist," approach to the law as Ronald Reagan and George Bush filled the courts with growing numbers of conservative federal judges—including Supreme Court Justices Anthony Kennedy, Antonin Scalia, Sandra Day O'Connor, David Souter, and Clarence Thomas. By 1992, 60 percent of all federal judges had been appointed during the Reagan/Bush years, including all sixteen judges on the U.S. Claims Court (recently renamed the U.S. Court of Federal Claims).[20]

Two things lawyers familiar with the Court of Claims tend to agree on is that the court conforms to the conservative "ideological litmus test" that became a standard part of the judicial selection process during the 1980s and that its Chief Judge Loren Smith puts on a swell magic show. Whether performing for the anti–New Deal Federalist Society, the libertarian CATO Institute, or an ABA/Pacific Legal Foundation conference in Seattle, the stocky, cigar-chomping jurist, with his full beard and waxed mustache, seems to relish center stage. He's shocked attorneys with his spring-loaded gavel trick, tied up bureaucrats with fancy rope tricks, and illustrated the bankruptcy of his opposition with a bag that keeps changing colors every time he turns it inside out. "Some people think I'm doing a good job as chief judge," he told the Federalist Society meeting in Washington, D.C., in March of 1992, pulling a wad of cash out of his pocket. "But my critics think all I've done is this," he smiled before lighting the fake money with a match, holding the blazing flash paper aloft as if holding Lady Liberty's torch.

"His slight-of-hand isn't limited to parlor games," reported the

Legal Times. "A few listeners . . . concluded that in his takings rulings, Smith is more than capable of pulling questionable interpretations of the law out of his hat or making precedents vanish."[21]

Following the philosophical lead of Professor Epstein (whose most recent book argues that civil rights legislation protecting workers against job discrimination is a breach of contract law), Judge Smith has ruled favorably on a surprising number of regulatory takings claims. In *Loveladies Harbor* versus *United States,* he ruled that denial of a permit to a New Jersey developer seeking to fill tidal wetlands for luxury homesites was a taking, and awarded the company $2.7 million. In *Florida Rock Industries, Inc.,* versus *United States,* he supported the takings claim of a company that wanted to quarry limestone in a wetlands area, awarding it a million dollars after its mining permit request was turned down under the Clean Water Act. And in the largest takings case to date, *Whitney Benefits, Inc.,* versus *United States,* he awarded $150 million to a coal mining company prevented from mining private lands in the Powder River area of Wyoming after the 1977 Surface Mining Control and Reclamation Act went into effect (a legislative rather than a "regulatory" taking, if one wants to get technical). Ironically, one of the strongest advocates for property rights, the National Cattlemen's Association, had favored this federal protection of surface lands from mine-company abuses.

While Smith's cases all face a strong likelihood of reversal by the U.S. Court of Appeals, the possibility of winning a "regulatory taking" at the Court of Claims has set off a spate of new property rights litigation, as have a couple of Supreme Court decisions.

In 1987 Pacific Legal won a U.S. Supreme Court ruling on a potential "regulatory taking" in *Nollan* versus *California Coastal Commission.* Antonin Scalia, writing for the majority, ruled that the state coastal commission was wrong in demanding an expanded public beach in exchange for a building permit. The commission had reasoned that since the Nollans' new, larger beachfront home would block the public's view of the ocean from a passing road, the Nollans should mitigate that impact by giving up a third of their property to provide the public with extra space on the state-owned beach itself. The court failed to see the commission's "mitigation" reasoning, given that the view from the road would still be blocked.

A more significant and potentially far-reaching case argued before the Supreme Court was that of *Lucas* versus *South Carolina*. In 1986 developer David Lucas bought two lots on a barrier island off the coast of South Carolina for $1 million. In 1988 the state passed the Beachfront Management Act, designed to curb development in ecologically sensitive (and storm-threatened) areas. Lucas, prevented from building on his lots, claimed he'd suffered a total loss on the value of his land and sued for compensation. Lucas won in trial but was reversed by the State Supreme Court, which ruled that the state had "legitimate police power" in protecting public safety in the storm zone (Lucas's lots had been at least partially underwater 50 percent of the time since 1949).[22] He and his lawyer then petitioned for a hearing before the U.S. Supreme Court, which was granted during the 1991–92 court session.

Although the property rights movement that quickly rallied to Lucas's cause has portrayed itself as representing small homeowners confronted by "land-grabbers" and acquisitive government bureaucracies, a review of some of the briefs filed in support of the *Lucas* case suggests who is most likely to benefit from any court decision that recognizes this type of regulatory taking. Among the sixteen groups filing *amicus curiae* briefs were the Pacific Legal Foundation, Mountain States Legal Foundation, American Farm Bureau Federation, National Cattlemen's Association, National Association of Homebuilders, International Council of Shopping Centers, Land Improvement Contractors Association, American Mining Congress, National Coal Association, National Forest Products Association, and U.S. Chamber of Commerce.

Among the briefs in support of South Carolina's right to regulate beach development were those from the Chesapeake Bay Foundation, Coast Alliance, Audubon Society, U.S. Council of

Mayors, Council of State Governments, twenty-six states, Guam, and Puerto Rico.[23]

In a split decision on the last day of the court's calendar year (a day on which the court also had to decide on an anti-abortion challenge to *Roe* versus *Wade*), the justices filed a five-vote bare majority opinion in favor of Lucas. Antonin Scalia, the Court's leading conservative, again wrote the majority opinion, which argued that since Lucas had suffered a total loss of value, and since building on the island was not prohibited prior to 1986, when he purchased his land, the case should be remanded to South Carolina for a financial settlement. In a footnote Scalia also indicated the Court's willingness to consider future cases involving a partial loss of value due to regulation.

While the *Lucas* finding was too narrow to have much application in other cases, property rights advocates were hopeful that the Court's conservative majority would soon agree to expand the definition of regulatory takings to include a partial loss of value. This in turn could open the way to massive compensation claims against the government and the subsequent unraveling of most environmental regulations. However, in June of 1993 the Court upheld a lower court ruling in a case known as *"Concrete Pipe . . ."* that rejected a partial takings claim under the Fifth Amendment. Since then, the Court has refused to review any additional takings cases.

The 1992 presidential election also dramatically shifted the likely direction of the argument. After Bill Clinton became president, Justice Byron White, one of the five majority votes on *Lucas*, resigned, and Ruth Ginsburg, a sharp legal mind with a reputation for not letting ideological agendas predetermine her judgments, took his place.

Takings has become a hot issue for debate within the country's law schools and legal journals. In the spring of 1993 both the Stanford and the University of Vermont law reviews printed a number of selected symposia and law conference papers on the subject.[24]

"The intellectual impact of *Lucas* is greater than its practical impact," claims John Echeverria, a gray-eyed, casually confident attorney who represents the National Audubon Society on takings issues. "The question is, is *Lucas* the foundation for rewriting the Fifth Amendment or only an oddity? At this point I'd have to say it's pretty much of an oddity."[25]

Wise Use advocates in the West seem to agree. Says Ron Arnold, of the Center for the Defense of Free Enterprise, "I advised the Pacific Legal Foundation not to go with the *Lucas* case, because he's a developer building homes for rich people and won't get much public sympathy. Wayne Hage is different. He's a family man, a cowboy, and a rancher—all these great images. We've been doing his direct-mail fundraising and getting a great rate of return. We've rallied actors to his cause—Hollywood actors like Sam Elliot in Carmel Valley. Michael Martin Murphy, the country-western singer, has done a benefit concert. We've gotten piles of media."

If the *Lucas* case is an oddity, ex-rancher Wayne Hage's takings claim is more frontier theater than jurisprudence, even if it does get argued in front of Judge Loren Smith, with his magical-realism approach to the law.

Represented by Mark Pollot, author of Reagan Executive Order #12630, Hage sued the U.S. Forest Service for $28.4 million, claiming that when they reduced the number of cattle he was permitted to graze on his 240,000-acre allotment in the Toiyabe National Forest, they took his property from him. Actually "permitted" is too polite a term for the running battle Hage and the Forest Service have conducted over several years across the desiccated rangelands of southern Nevada. In the summer of 1991, armed Forest Service employees rounded up seventy-three of Hage's cows after he refused to move them from an area they said he'd overgrazed and damaged. Rather than reclaim his cows by paying the cost of the roundup, Hage decided to sell the rest of his two thousand head of cattle, claiming that he could no longer run a profitable enterprise because of Forest Service harassment.[26] He then filed suit, claiming a regulatory taking. Historically, the courts have ruled that a permit to graze, log, or otherwise operate commercially on public lands is a revocable license, like a driver's license, a privilege and not a property right.

Hage argues that the government's restriction of his grazing permits constitutes a taking because of the "preexisting" property rights of early white settlers, a claim he expostulates in angry, numbing detail in his 1989 book *Storm Over Rangeland*, published by CDFE's Free Enterprise Press.[27] Arizona State University Law Professor Joe Feller, one of the country's top experts on public lands law, uses Hage's book as a teaching tool for his students, letting them write papers dissecting the "legal nonsense" he says it contains.[28]

"When you really look at it, what's being said," says Jim Baca, former director of the Bureau of Land Management, which oversees most federal grazing lands and permits issued, "it's that you've given us something for so cheap for so long that we now own it and we have to be paid for it. I mean it's a bizarre way of thinking."

One of the more imaginative claims in Hage's suit argues that the introduction of elk into Nevada's Toiyabe National Forest constitutes a taking, because the wild elk eat grass and drink from watering holes that his cows might otherwise have used. This claim convinced Nevada Attorney General Frankie Sue Del Papa, whose state Department of Wildlife had first introduced the elk, to join the suit on the side of the Forest Service. When she hired an attorney from the National Wildlife Federation to represent Nevada, a mini-brouhaha exploded among the state's Wise Use advocates, with the cattlemen and Farm Bureau attacking her as a preservationist and she herself countering that the state had a legitimate interest in preventing rulings favoring "permittees who abuse the land."[29] In 1992, in a separate case, Wayne Hage was tried and convicted in Las Vegas on charges of cutting down and removing mature piñon and juniper trees from the public lands where he'd held his grazing permits, a felony conviction he's now appealing.

"You can ask, is ranching a legitimate use of public lands, which is what this argument is really about, but that's a political, not a legal, issue," argues Audubon's John Echeverria. The environmental lawyer recalls reaching a similar conclusion at a conference on property rights he'd attended in 1993. "When I got there

I said, 'The first thing people need to agree on is what the Fifth Amendment really means,' and this farmer replied that he didn't care what it meant; if a government regulation hurt his value he'd oppose it. I think property rights is really part of a broader focus on rights that's taking place in our society today: people talk about their right to live, their right to die, their right to privacy. It's not being balanced with a sense of responsibilities to society. Unless you act with some sense of responsibility to your neighbors, any possibility of maintaining community is destroyed, and that's what I see happening in America today."

While attempts to redefine the meaning of the Fifth Amendment through the courts seem to have reached their limit, legislative efforts continue at both the state and federal level. In 1990 Senator Steve Symms of Idaho sponsored a bill that would have codified into law Executive Order #12630, requiring the attorney general to certify that all government regulations were in compliance with private property rights as defined by Professor Epstein.

"The National Environmental Policy Act [NEPA] was one of the most powerful acts in history, passed by both houses and signed by President Nixon. Yet all it does is review environmental impacts," says former Symms aide Trent Clarke. "Once it went into effect, the feds always made decisions, siding with extreme protection rather than face legal and other challenges from the environmental community. Private property rights legislation uses the same mechanism, a review process to determine the need for compensation, as a counterbalance to NEPA."[30]

The Symms proposal was originally rejected by the Senate. In 1991, attached as a rider to the surface-transportation bill, it passed the Senate and was killed in conference with the House. The next year it again passed the Senate as a rider to a bill proposing EPA be raised to cabinet rank, a bill that failed to go anywhere. Before Symms left the Senate in 1992, he asked Senate Republican leader Bob Dole of Kansas to act as sponsor for future takings bills, which Dole agreed to do.

"It's an important issue, private property," explains Dole's deputy chief of staff, James "Witt" Wittinghill, who is overseeing the bill for the senator.[31] "This legislation says you can't put blinders on and charge ahead denying people use of their property for the environment or any other cause."

The legislation, S. 177, cosponsored on the House side by conservative Democrat Bill Condit of California, didn't appear to be making any progress during the 1993–1994 congressional session. "We'll go ahead with it when we think we have fifty-one votes," Wittinghill smiles coolly, crossing his legs and freeing his black cowboy boots from the pants cuffs of his black, chalk-striped suit. "It won't survive as stand-alone legislation with Democratic control of the House, but we could always add it to an appropriations bill. Senator Dole has long supported cabinet rank for the EPA, provided it went through as a clean bill. So although many people were encouraging us to again add this as a rider, it wouldn't have made sense in terms of the senator's position that this should be a clean bill."

"Dole was going to offer it on the EPA cabinet level proposal but backed off when he saw he didn't have the votes," counters Bill Klinefelter, the legislative director of the AFL-CIO's Industrial Union Department. "If they thought it had any chance of passage they would have pushed it. We successfully beat back this last takings attempt with better education in the Senate. We demonstrated that takings is far broader than it was being portrayed," the pugnacious union man claims. "It wasn't just about wetlands. It's really aimed at all regulation, and could be used to attack OSHA as easily as environmental regulations. Plus, it would set up its own regime, an antiregulatory bureaucracy."[32]

Klinefelter lobbied the senators as part of an environmental/labor/consumer coalition that included the steelworkers, National Wildlife Federation, and Consumers Union. "We also got letters supporting our position from Attorney General Janet Reno and other members of the administration. I'd say that for the time being, at the federal level, we've beat this thing down," he smiles firmly.

But in statehouses across America, from New York to California, the number of takings bills continues to expand and diversify. Two versions of takings bills have been introduced in most of the states. The first type is the assessment bill, based on the Reagan order requiring state agencies to set up reviews of the regulatory takings implications of virtually all government actions.

The more radical type is the "compensation bill" developed by Mark Pollot for the American Legislative Exchange Council (ALEC) and based on a bill first introduced in Vermont by Republican State Senator McLaughery. This version would automatically pay compensation to any property owner whose property value declines 40–50 percent or more as the result of a government rule, regulation, or program.

"The best I know, this is 100 percent grassroots activity by all kinds of people that have property interests," says John J. Rademacher, general counsel for the American Farm Bureau Federation (AFBF), the multibillion dollar not-for-profit insurance company and farm-advocacy organization. The AFBF—which lists support of regulatory compensation payments as one of its 168 policy positions, along with opposition to "one world government," U.S. withdrawal from the World Court, abolition of most civil rights legislation, and revision of the Child Labor Act for Agriculture—has been one of the primary forces behind the introduction of statehouse takings bills.[34]

"The Farm Bureau was very active in getting these bills introduced in Arizona and Utah [where they passed]. If you ask most politicians at the state level, they'll tell you that the Farm Bureau is behind them," brags Andy Neal, chief lobbyist (or research analyst, as he prefers to be called) for the California Farm Bureau Federation.[35] *Forbes* magazine also credits "the Farm Bureau's lobbying clout" for whatever success takings bills have had to date. Still, some critics worry that the Farm Bureau's lobbying on this issue may have a long-term negative impact on agriculture.

" 'Takings law' to limit the power of government may result in environmental anarchy," warned Drake University Law School Professor Neil Hamilton at a recent Soil and Water Conservation meeting in Kansas City also attended by Farm Bureau President Dean Kleckner. "If the farm community stakes its response to public desires for environmental protection on an extremist position which in essence says, 'If the public wants me to protect the environment on my land then pay me,' . . . farmers may risk a political and social backlash which may cause the public and lawmakers to re-examine support [subsidies] for agriculture."[36]

Aside from the Farm Bureau and other anti-wetlands lobbies, such as the Homebuilders Association and International Association of Shopping Centers, takings has also become a legislative centerpiece for ALEC, the American Legislative Exchange Council, a think tank made up of 2,500 conservative state legislators that is based in the Heritage Foundation building in Washington, D.C.

In 1990 *Detroit News* columnist Warren Brookes warned ALEC's annual convention in Boston that "if the flat-earth environmentalism that now dominates the U.S. Congress and the Bush Administration . . . continues to be enacted at its present pace, nothing less than the future of the American dream and freedom itself are on the line."[37]

Since then, ALEC has pushed compensatory takings bills as part of an anti-enviro legislative package along with "no net loss of private property" bills, which would require states establishing new parks to sell off their old parks. ALEC is also lobbying for "greater than" bills, which would prevent states from passing any environmental regulations tougher than the already established federal standards.

"ALEC is a little more big business oriented than we are," confesses John Shanahan, environmental analyst with the Heritage Foundation. This is like a Roman Catholic cardinal calling the Greek Orthodox Church "a little more godly." At least 350 corporations contribute a minimum of $5,000 each to work with ALEC and have access to its legislator members. They also provide recreational opportunities for these elected officials. A recent ALEC convention included a skeet shoot sponsored by the NRA, golf tournament by R. J. Reynolds, tennis match by Philip Morris, and hospitality suite by the Distilled Spirits Council.[38]

By the end of 1993, four states had passed ALEC and Farm Bureau-sponsored takings bills: Arizona, Delaware, Washington, and Utah. Twenty-nine other states had defeated or failed to act on the bills. With a tight economy and strapped budgets, many states rejected the bills because of their potential cost. In Maryland the state treasurer estimated takings assessments would cost $10,000 for every commercial property studied. The New Mexico Fish and Game Department figured it would need $1.5 million a year to review its own actions. In Utah the "Cowboy Caucus" was allowed to claim a property rights victory, and the governor signed a takings bill only after a "black-widow" provision was added exempting every state agency from having to file reports. Arizona, which passed its takings bill in 1992, delayed implementation after opponents collected more than 71,000 signatures to put it up for a referendum vote in 1994. In Wyoming, a conservative ranching and oil state, a takings bill was defeated after the only witnesses to testify in its favor were lobbyists from the Farm Bureau and Mining Association.

And opposition to "takings bills" has been growing, as environmentalists have begun linking up with organized labor and consumer groups. Both the AFL-CIO and the National Governors Association have now adopted policies against takings. "After receiving a call from environmentalists, we called our people in Wyoming to help defeat it out there," says the AFL-CIO's Bill Klinefelter. "We just now called Missouri to try and get the governor there to veto a takings bill. This is radical stuff and in some ways almost ridiculous, but it'll be with us for a long time because it's a good organizing tool for the other side," he says. "Takings has become the visible symbol of Wise Use."[39]

"It is important to recognize the property rights movement is laden with individuals and organizations whose larger goal is promoting a conservative political agenda to limit the power of government," adds Drake University's Professor Hamilton. "The 'property rights' debate is not just a question of constitutional law but a clash of political ideology over the direction of national resource protection policy."[40]

"Government does and has done and always will do scores and scores of things that affect people's property positively and negatively. Government can't function without doing that," says Jonathan Lash, an attorney, president of the World Resources Institute, and cochairman of the President's Council on Sustainable Development. "Everyone agrees that part of the legitimate role of government is to regulate and adjust relationships among members of society who don't have equal power in society, and you can't do that without affecting wealth. So when you build a new school, when you build sewers, when you build roads or fail to build roads, you affect property. If you regulate industrial pollution, you affect someone's property, and if you don't regulate it you affect other people's property. So the simple formulation that government is using environmental regulations in a way that deprives people of their property rights simply ignores the full range of what is going on in the world."[41]

For anti-enviro radicals and the many industrial hardliners who support them, that may sound like so much liberal obfuscation. They know who their enemies are and, with their moral absolutism, they believe that if the legal system doesn't serve their needs, they have the right to "defend" their property by any and all other means necessary.

The Green P.I.

"Do you see that red dot on your chest?"
"Yeah. What about it?"
"It's a night scope from a rifle."
WEST VIRGINIA ENVIRONMENTAL ACTIVIST FAITH REILLEY
being warned to leave a protest demonstration.

Do not take chances. Plan for the worst: work and hope for the best.
COMMON SENSE SECURITY

The private investigator stood by the rubble and ash pile in the wooded clearing eight miles outside of the old resort town of Eureka Springs, deep in the Ozark Mountains of Arkansas. The dank smell of charcoal still permeated the humid air a month after the flames had consumed Pat Costner's cedar-shake home of seventeen years. Pat, a small-framed country woman with dark hair pulled back in a bun, tried to describe the layout of the three-bedroom house that she'd built herself, now reduced to a cracked cinderblock base surrounded by a grove of singed walnut trees. A dozen chickens wandered through the ash, leaving gray clawprints behind them. The arson team the detective had hired out of Tennessee had proved its worth. After lifting up the building's collapsed tin roof, which the local fire inspector hadn't bothered with, they'd discovered the metal fuel can used to torch the building. But even before locating the can, they'd known the fire had been deliberately set. The average house fire will not exceed 300 to 500 degrees Fahrenheit at floor level or 1,800 degrees at ceiling level. But in the left front corner of Pat's house they'd found melted bedsprings, indicating temperatures exceeding 2,700 degrees F. And in the office area the aluminum bases of two chairs had melted down into a puddle, indicating floor-level heat of at least 1,300 degrees F. These superheated temperatures could only have been generated by a flammable liquid or other accelerant. The arson investigators collected debris from different parts of the house in four one-gallon cans and sent them to a private forensics lab in Hendersonville, Tennessee, for analysis. Using gas chromatography and mass spectrometry, the lab determined that the debris in two of the cans contained "components identifiable as evaporated gasoline." These samples included ash and charcoal taken from the office/library where Pat Costner, Greenpeace U.S.A.'s director of toxics research, had kept her critical files, records, and reports.[1]

Reluctantly, Pat approached the private investigator to find out what had come of five days of follow-up interviews in and around town.

"It looks like there was a man asking about you just before Christmas. He returned with another man after New Year's. They were stocky, white guys. People described them as kind of thuggish. A night watchman overheard them talking about having trained at Quantico [a Virginia Marine base that also houses the FBI's training academy]. They wanted to know where you lived but no one at the bar and restaurant where they had dinner would tell them anything." The P.I. paused, waiting. Pat shook her head in bewilderment. Then she said, "I remember someone calling saying they thought it was the FBI asking for me, and I just didn't think anything else about it at the time. I figured they knew where I was if they had anything to ask me."

The P.I. nodded, not surprised. Eureka Springs was the kind of place where people left their doors unlocked when they went out at night and told their kids to be polite to strangers. There was a moment of awkward silence broken only by the monotonous two-note refrain of cicadas and the occasional clucking of Pat's chickens.

"Are you all right?" the investigator asked, squeezing her hand.

"I'm fine, thanks. Just nerves," Pat answered. "I really don't know what I'd have done without your help."

"That's what I'm here for," replied Sheila O'Donnell, her face briefly lighting up with a smile as fresh as a Donegal breeze.

Five foot seven and solidly built, with shoulder-length salt-and-pepper hair, broad cheeks, and wide (but not innocent) eyes, forty-nine-year-old Sheila O'Donnell is not your typical private investigator. She's nonviolent, progressive, and lacks a law enforcement background, but this granddaughter of Irish immigrants still has all the hallmarks of a good detective: tenacity, toughness of character, and an unflinching willingness to engage difficult problems head on. To environmental activists under siege from Maine to south Texas, Sheila has become known as the Green P.I.

"Right now I'd say about half my cases are environmental," she explains over cappuccino on a warm spring day near her home in Mill Valley, California. "I've got ten cases involving violent attacks on environmentalists. I've talked to activists in twenty-five or thirty similar cases. I turned copies of those cases over to the Center for Investigative Reporting [an award-winning journalism project based in San Francisco] and they've been able to develop another 120 examples and it's continuing to expand. I'm sure the real numbers are well into the hundreds—thousands if you count vandalism, phone threats, and harassing letters. My worry is that there's really no place for people to go when they get a threatening call in the middle of the night or find their dog beheaded on their front steps. I mean they can call me but I'm only one person."

On an "Eye on America" news segment about the problem that aired March 3, 1993, CBS correspondent Eric Hayes reported, "Most of these [cases] are not high-profile environmentalists; they're not out sabotaging industry. They're more likely to work within the system to protect the environment. They're finding, though, that the system can't protect them."[2]

"Right now the FBI won't touch this," says Linda Chase, a staff aide to Congressman George Miller, chairman of the House

Committee on Natural Resources, who has looked into some of the incidents. "They think ecoterrorism, tree spiking, attacks on logging equipment, that sort of thing, is a national problem, but reports of environmentalists being physically attacked they just want to pass on to the local sheriff."[3]

With neither the FBI nor local law enforcement agencies showing much interest, the investigative effort has fallen to a small group of reporters and activists around the country along with private detective Sheila O'Donnell. Sheila's background, she admits, has given her a somewhat cynical view of how much help environmentalists under siege can count on from the people who collect their taxes.

"It's like the early days of the civil rights movement in terms of the escalating violence," she says. "Unfortunately, a number of these incidents come after a long period of threats and intimidation that law enforcement has tended to ignore. There's a definite feeling that the enforcement agencies, particularly the FBI, are not on the side of the activists."

Sheila herself was raised in a large Irish Catholic family in the town of Newton, outside of Boston. Her father was a professional gambler who played the horses. Her mother stayed home to take care of a sick older brother, who died of a rare bone disease when Sheila was sixteen. A graduate of a private girls' school run by Irish nuns, she had a hard time adjusting to college life, trying several schools before dropping out to take a job as a secretary at McGraw-Hill. At twenty-three, restless and disturbed by all the young men she knew who were going off to a war that didn't make any sense to her, she left her family and moved to Washington, D.C., where she found work with the New Mobilization Committee to End the War in Vietnam. "I was so naive I went to their office in a dress and heels. They told me to go home and change," she recalls with a smile. "They found out I could type and got me a job with a mobe committee lawyer. It was a period when the D.C. cops were being very aggressive because there were these almost constant protests going on. There were the big moratoriums, and people took to the streets after the Cambodia invasion, Kent State, the mining of the harbors, all these different incidents. In May seventy-one we had over fourteen thousand arrests in the course of a weekend. People would write lawyers' numbers on their arms with ballpoint pens, and I'd be the one answering the phone when they called from jail. The FBI began following us to legal strategy meetings. I'd go into the women's room and see a man's shiny leather shoes and white socks in the next stall."

Sheila's transformation from antiwar liberal to legal skeptic came during the trial of Daniel and Philip Berrigan, two Jesuit priest brothers accused of conspiracy to blow up heating ducts under the capitol and kidnap Henry Kissinger. "I was amazed that the government could bring these charges against these two antiwar priests without proof," recalls the former parochial schoolgirl. "When the government rested their case, so did the defense. The jury went out just long enough to select a foreman, coming back with a not guilty finding. To see the government involved in this kind of misconduct just shocked me."

Sheila became active with the leftist National Lawyers Guild, getting work as a paralegal investigator. "The first case where I began to work as an investigator was looking into a right-wing spy operation," she recalls. "There was this woman calling herself Sheila O'Conner, who'd infiltrated the D.C. office of the National Lawyers Guild for the FBI, and she had a boyfriend named John, and *I* had a boyfriend named John at the time, and naturally people started confusing us. There was some suspicion about this woman, particularly after she borrowed somebody's car and disappeared. I got a call from an investigator with the New York state assembly trying to figure out who these people were. We found out their real names were John and Sheila Louise Reese and they were putting out a newsletter called *Information Digest*, a very unreliable intelligence brief on the Left for corporate and governmental clients, including the John Birch Society. I began tracking their work and found documents tracing him back to the Newark riots of sixty-seven. He'd been mixed up with these riots where over thirty people were killed. Shortly thereafter, a small group of us started a magazine called *Public Eye* to publish research we were developing on John Reese and the Birch Society,

Lyndon LaRouche, and other extremists.[4] There were links we
were discovering like the LaRouchites were targeting the antinuclear movement, claiming people opposed to the Seabrook Nuclear Power Plant in New Hampshire were terrorists and using
Information Digest as their source to scare the hell out of the New
Hampshire state police. Their talk of nuclear terrorism frightened the cops, and we worried they were likely to overreact and
hurt someone."

At about the same time, Sheila began doing street work to improve her investigative skills. Her criminal defense cases ranged
from medical malpractice to drugs and homicides but no divorces
or child custody disputes. "My ancestors did enough domestic
work," she jokes. One case she took on involved a fourteen-year-
old busboy accused of the torture-murder of his mother's friend.
"His mother and the victim both worked as waitresses at this
restaurant/pub, and there was a question if the owner might have
offed the woman," Sheila recalls. "She had lent him money and
then threatened to go to a lawyer when he wouldn't repay it. That
night she was tortured and killed by a right-handed assailant, and
our young client had lost his right arm in a childhood accident, so
we were pretty sure he wasn't the perpetrator." Sheila got a job
as a waitress at the pub to try and develop more information on
the owner. She found that the other waitresses were both scared
and suspicious of the man. When the case finally went to trial, the
defense argued that the pub's owner had better cause and opportunity to have committed the murder than the accused boy, winning an acquittal for their client. Shortly thereafter the bartender
at Sheila's regular hangout began referring to her as "Dickless
Tracy."

In 1985 Sheila moved to California. "I'd just turned forty, and
this journalist from the Bay Area asked me to move in with him,
and so I decided to leap without looking and moved to Marin. And
while he and I didn't work out, everything else proved worth it."
She got work with a couple of San Francisco detective agencies,
later becoming a one-third partner in Ace Investigations, opening
a small office within sight of the municipal pier on the wide crescent beach at Pacifica just south of the city on Route 1.

In 1988, while back in Washington on a civil litigation case, Sheila met a couple of people working with Greenpeace. Later they invited her to a camp in Maine, where she held a workshop for their international toxics campaigners, teaching them how to trace documents, conduct interviews, and other investigative techniques. "I was very impressed with these folks," she recalls. "They were young, bright, really high energy, and highly motivated. They loved the earth and knew how to have a good time as well as how to work. Many had come to their activism through their play—surfers who'd seen their beaches polluted or hikers who found clearcuts where they liked to trek, that sort of thing."

Judi Bari is not that kind of an activist. A former postal union organizer, carpenter, and single mother of two young girls, Judi Bari has always been a tireless political advocate for the disenfranchised. She identifies with the plight of working people, including loggers and millworkers, as much as she identifies with the redwood forests whose protection has become a major cause in her life. Even the folk music she writes and plays with fellow Earth Firster Daryl Cherney has the didactic politics (if not always the lyrical polish) of a Woody Guthrie or Phil Ochs. Art, she believes, should be socially responsible. In the late 1980s, when Judi began organizing Earth First's campaign to save northern California's redwoods, one of the first projects she took on was defending the rights of Georgia-Pacific workers exposed to PCBs during a chemical spill at the Fort Bragg mill. Other Earth First! leaders whose backgrounds were in wilderness protection were uncomfortable with her mixture of worker and feminist politics and radical environmentalism. Still, they chose not to argue with one of their more effective organizers—that is, until she renounced the controversial tactic of tree spiking in order to focus on nonviolent civil disobedience: people sitting in trees, chaining themselves to mill gates, and blocking logging trucks and bulldozers with their bodies.

Judi was driving in her car with a friend and their children in August 1989 when they were run off the road by a log truck they'd blockaded the day before. She recalls that the truck driver came up to her afterwards, looking shaken and saying, "I didn't know there were children in the car." No charges were brought against the man.[5]

Over the next nine months, as she worked to organize the Redwood Summer protests that she hoped to model after the nonviolent Mississippi Summer protests of the 1960s civil rights movement, Judi received a growing number of death threats, including a clipped newspaper photo of herself playing the violin with a rifle's cross-hairs superimposed over her face.

On May 23, 1990, Judi and Daryl Cherney headed south to the Bay Area to meet with Redwood Summer supporters. On May 24, after stops in Berkeley and Oakland, they took off again for Santa Cruz, a college town a few hours south of the Bay Area where they hoped to recruit students for their demonstrations. They didn't get far. Just before noon on a busy street in the city of Oakland, a pipe bomb exploded beneath the driver's seat of Bari's 1981 Subaru station wagon, shattering her pelvis and dislocating her spine. Cherney, riding in the passenger seat, suffered facial lacerations and eye damage from flying glass and metal. Within minutes of the explosion, even as firemen and paramedics were working to save Judi's life and rush the two victims to Highland Hospital, the FBI's domestic terrorism squad, working with the Oakland police, had commandeered the investigation from the Alcohol, Tobacco and Firearms agents on the scene. That night, based on information provided by the FBI, the Oakland police obtained a search warrant, telling a judge that Bari and Cherney were "members of a violent terrorist group involved in the manufacture and placing of explosive devices."[6] OPD and FBI agents then raided Seeds of Peace, a seedy collective house in the flats of Berkeley whose young pacifist communards had met the previous night with Bari and Cherney to discuss providing logistical support for the Redwood Summer protests. The raiders were looking for a bomb factory but instead found a portable kitchen, cooking utensils, sacks of brown rice, and a couple of Portasans in the backyard. Nonetheless, the next morning homicide Lieutenant Mike Sims of the Oakland PD held a press conference to announce the arrest of Bari and Cherney for possession and transportation of an explosive device. "The decision to arrest was based on, uh, the placement of the device in the vehicle, the, uh, nature of its construction, physical and other evidence that was, uh, developed by the investigators." The tall, blond cop hesitatingly read his statement in front of dozens of reporters, minicams, and microphones.[7]

"I remember hearing about the bombing and arrests on the radio and thinking, that doesn't sound right. I've never heard of environmental activists getting involved with bombs," recalls Sheila O'Donnell. A short time later she got a phone call from Greenpeace U.S.A. Executive Director Peter Bahouth, asking her to look into the bombing for them. Greenpeace had been the victim of a 1985 terrorist bombing in New Zealand that had sunk their ship, the *Rainbow Warrior,* and cost the life of one of their volunteers, photographer Fernando Pereira. The bombing turned out to be the work of French secret agents bent on preventing the *Rainbow Warrior* from leading protests against France's nuclear weapons testing in the South Pacific. Greenpeace hated terrorism and wanted to know the truth on the Oakland bombing. "If Judi and Daryl were involved they wouldn't support them, but people who knew the two of them were convinced they wouldn't be involved in something like this," Sheila recalls.

It was more than a week before Judi was able to stay conscious and pain-free long enough to meet with the private investigator in the intensive care unit of Highland Hospital. An armed police guard stood at her door although she was in traction and still too weak to have the explosive powder washed out of her matted brown hair. On her second day in the hospital, after extensive surgery and blood loss, the police had moved Judi's bed to the jail ward. Her surgeon, on discovering what they'd done, had it rolled back up to the ICU, instructing the police to keep their hands off his critically injured patient.

Judi recalled the moment of the bomb blast. With a strangely disjointed clarity, she'd known instantly that she'd been bombed, that this was a political assassination attempt, and that she might die. Then, as they'd pulled her from the wreckage, the pain had struck in a sickening, overwhelming wave. She'd begged the paramedics to give her something for the pain, but they'd told her they couldn't, that if they did she might die. She wanted to die anyway it was so bad. To give herself a reason to live, she tried to visualize her two daughters, but was unable to conjure up their faces.[8]

Sheila and Judi spoke for some time until Judi tired. Impressed with Judi's courage, determination, and even flashes of humor in the face of what was obviously still intense pain, Sheila left the hospital committed to working on the case. "You don't want to be gullible, but after a while in this business you develop an instinct for when people are lying to you and when they're telling the truth," Sheila said. "And I had the feeling Judi was honestly frightened that someone was out there who wanted her dead, and not having succeeded might try again and that the government just wanted to blame it on her."

The government's charges against Bari and Cherney, although widely reported in the media, would prove grossly misdirected. Immediately after the bombing, police told the press that Bari must have known the bomb was in her car because she'd put her guitar case on top of it. But the guitar case was barely damaged. An affidavit filed by Police Sergeant Robert Chenault claimed that an FBI agent at the scene of the explosion told him the bomb was on the floorboard behind the driver's seat. But Judi Bari's surgeon, Peter Slabbaugh, said that the injuries to her pelvic area and buttocks indicated that the force of the blast had come from below, not behind, an impression confirmed by an Oakland fire captain on the scene. When the FBI released the car to the defense team, it didn't take the expertise of the Silicon Valley bomb expert Sheila had hired to recognize the obvious. The car's roof was bowed out above the driver's seat. Where the driver's floorboard should have been was a jagged hole (part of the flooring had been removed by the FBI). The front seat was shredded down to exposed and heat-seared cushion wires, one of which had punctured Bari's colon. The passenger's seat was less severely damaged, and the rear bench seat and floorboard were more or less intact, with only minor shrapnel damage. A fist-sized hole, like that left by a rocket grenade, was punched out of the driver's door panel where one of the screw-on endcaps of the pipe bomb had shot off. If the bomb had been better constructed, with the end-caps properly sealed, it would have done its intended job, killing both passengers. After six weeks of claiming that the bomb had been in plain sight behind Bari, the police finally conceded that the bomb was hidden out of sight under her seat. Immediately following that admission, however, they announced that finishing nails taped to the outside of the bomb matched finishing nails found in an FBI raid of Bari's Mendocino home (where she worked as a carpenter). FBI bomb expert David Williams told Oakland Police Sergeant Michael Sitterud he could testify that the nails found in Bari's house matched the bomb nails to within a batch of 200 to 1,000 nails, a claim quickly leaked to the *Oakland Tribune* and other local media.[9]

On investigating that claim, Sheila and her team talked to several highly skeptical nail manufacturers. The manager of one Bay Area nail plant had been visited by the FBI and had told them that finishing nails are basically indistinguishable from each other. He explained that most nails, particularly finishing nails, are now manufactured overseas. The nail-press machines that are used are often of a common type, such as the German-made "Wafios." A wire is fed into the machine where it is cut at a rate of 1,200 to 1,400 nails a minute. The machine stamps the head and shapes the point. The gripper holding the wire leaves marks that can later be matched to that gripper. Gripper dies wear out and have to be replaced every four or five weeks. Cutter dies are machined in the plant and changed every day, meaning that theoretically a finishing nail could be matched to a single day's production on a single machine, one out of a batch of between 576,000 and 672,000 nails. Without being able to match the nails more precisely, the government did not have much of a case. On July 17, the Alameda County District Attorney decided not to press charges.[10] Several months later, in an interview with a local PBS producer, the FBI admitted that its nail evidence was inconclusive.[11]

"With the FBI, I think they had Earth First! terrorists dancing like sugarplums in their head. I don't know that they ever for a moment asked, 'Are these people victims?'" Sheila says.

Sheila's skepticism seems well placed in light of an additional FBI crime-lab analysis of the pipe bomb conducted shortly after the explosion. The bomb consisted of an eleven-inch piece of galvanized pipe attached to a piece of wood paneling and packed with an explosive mixture of potassium chlorate and aluminum powder. Nails were taped to the outside of the pipe to create additional shrapnel. There was a light switch safety device, a nine-volt Duracell battery to provide an electrical charge, and a cheap Bullseye pocketwatch timer.[12] In addition there was a crude motion-trigger device made up of a ball bearing and two bent wires that would had to have been jolted together to complete the bomb circuit, meaning that the car would have to have been in motion for the bomb to explode. Bari remembers cutting through Oakland traffic and then hitting her brakes hard just before the explosion.

But the FBI report refers to the ball bearing and wire fragments as "a booby trap device." Experienced IRA bombmakers occasionally will "booby trap" time bombs with parallel motion switches in order to kill army bomb technicians who try to move the bombs. But such booby traps are not likely to be found in crudely built homemade pipe bombs, and not even a suicide bomber would arm a motion-trigger device while driving to his target.

Still, for the FBI to correctly identify the ball bearing and wires as a "motion trigger" rather than a "booby trap" would have meant acknowledging that the car's driver, Judi Bari, was the intended target of the bomb—a victim rather than a terrorist.

"If you come to the scene of a crime with your own theory of who's responsible and you refuse to turn that around, you build a house of cards that will come crashing down around you," says O'Donnell.

The FBI and OPD continued to try and build a case against Bari and Cherney, even after the would-be assassin sent a letter to a local newspaper taking credit for the crime. On May 29, five days after the bombing, Mike Geniella, a reporter covering timber issues for the *Santa Rosa Press Democrat*, received a three-page typewritten letter signed "The Lord's Avenger."

"I remember saying to myself, now we've got the real nuts involved," Geniella recalls of his first reading of the letter. He says he put it down for a minute and returned to a story he was working on but suddenly stopped typing to look at it again. "And I thought, God, this letter describes a bomb. And it not only describes a bomb, it describes a second bomb. And then it was that kind of—like when the adrenaline starts pumping. . . ."[13]

Written in a rambling manner that mixes hellfire and brimstone fundamentalism with an army manual's precision of language, the letter provides detailed descriptions of both the car bomb and a second pipe bomb, which had been left at a Louisiana Pacific lumbermill in Cloverdale, California, two weeks earlier. That bomb had been set on the porch of the mill office next to a five-gallon gas can but failed to penetrate the can and start a fire after one of the bomb's screw-on endcaps blew off. After receiving the Lord's Avenger letter from the *Press Democrat*, the FBI quickly keyed in on that case.

"Four or five suits arrived, very high energy. They took the evidence, said they'd be in touch, and that's the last we saw of our bomb," recalls Rich McComber, the Sonoma County sheriff's deputy who'd first investigated the LP incident.[14]

After examining the letter and the LP pipe bomb, the FBI concluded that the Lord's Avenger "either built the two bombs or knew how they were built."

The Avenger claimed that the LP bombing was meant as a provocation to be blamed on Bari. A cardboard sign left near the bomb site read "L.P. Screws Millworkers," an R-rated sentiment not completely in keeping with Judi's occasionally X-rated exhortations. When the LP bombing failed to draw much notice, the Avenger decided to use a more direct method.

"The Lord had shown me that his Work needed no Subtergufe [sic] and must be clear and Visible in the eyes of all. I was his Avenger. The demon must be struck down."[15]

The Avenger claimed to have planted the second pipe bomb in Judi's unlocked car while she was meeting with loggers in the Mendocino County town of Willits to try and negotiate a nonviolence agreement for the Redwood Summer protests. He also claimed that the assassination attempt was a response to her pro-abortion activity at a "baby-killing clinic," where he saw "Satan's flames shoot forth from her mouth her eyes and ears."

Judi had organized a counterprotest against a group of Right-to-Life demonstrators at the Ukiah Planned Parenthood Clinic in November 1988, where, to the tune of "Will the Circle Be Unbroken?" she and Daryl Cherney sang a lusty chorus of "Will the Fetus Be Aborted," which included these lines:

> Betty Lou, she got pregnant, and was addicted to fifteen drugs,
> She went down to the abortion clinic, and was accosted by right-
> wing thugs.
> Will the fetus be aborted, bye and bye, lord, bye and bye?
> There's a better world awaiting, in the sky, lord, in the sky.[16]

"We were really outrageous," Judi later admitted. "In retrospect I probably would have done it differently, but because of the way that they were acting, we decided if they were gonna be bullies, we'd show them what their tactics were like."[17]

The Lord's Avenger letter went on to suggest a second reason for the bombing. "All the forests that grow and all the wild creatures within them are a gift to Man that he shall use freely with God's Blessing to build the Kingdom of God on Earth. They shall be never ending because God will provide . . . Judi Bari spread her Poison to tell the Multitude that trees are not God's Gift to Man but that Trees were themselves gods and it was a Sin to cut them. My Spirit ached as her Paganism festered before mine eyes. I felt the Power of the Lord stir within my Heart and I knew I had been Chosen to strike down this Demon."

"If law enforcement had used all their resources from the time of the bombing to track real leads like this letter instead of trying to nail Judi and Daryl, I think we might have been able to catch the bomber early on," Sheila O'Donnell contends.

A 1991 documentary on the bombing that aired on PBS stations KQED in San Francisco and KCET in Los Angeles profiled several possible suspects who were never seriously investigated by the FBI. There was Bill Staley, the six-foot-three ex–Chicago Bears tackle and born-again fundamentalist who led the antiabortion protests at the Ukiah clinic. On camera he denied a clinic staffer's charge that he'd threatened to rape her and make her have his baby. The documentary also aired an interview with Steve Okerstrom, a logging contractor from Willits who lost a $700,000 Fellerbuncher tree-cutting machine in a fire that he believed had been set by Earth Firsters even though the state fire marshal ruled it accidental. "I know there wasn't a whole lot of effort put in to checking to see whether it was set," he told producer Steve Talbot. "I know they spent a whole lot more time trying to figure out what happened to the back end of Judi Bari."

The documentary also examined Irv Sutley, a long-time left-wing activist and gun lover who posed Judi and Daryl with his Uzi assault rifle for photos they considered and then rejected for the cover of one of their music tapes, "They Don't Make Hippies Like They Used To." Shortly after Sutley's photo session, a print of Judi with the Uzi was sent to the local police along with an anonymous letter signed "Argus," claiming that Earth First! had begun automatic weapons training and offering to spy on Bari. The Willits police later matched the typing of the informant's letter to the type used in one of the death threats Judi had received before the bombing. And the documentary reported on Mike Koepf, a former political ally of Judi's and ex-Green Beret with a history of domestic violence who'd become a harsh critic of hers after she developed a friendship with his ex-wife. It also profiled Judi's own ex-husband, Mike Sweeney, who had had financial conflicts with her during their divorce and was also a suspect in an earlier electrically triggered arson fire at an airport whose expansion he'd opposed.

However, Judi Bari categorically rejects the idea that the bombing might have been personally motivated. She believes that the timber industry was behind the attempt on her life (although no solid proof of this has surfaced). In 1992 she and Daryl Cherney filed a civil suit charging the FBI and Oakland police with false arrest and violation of their civil rights. On May 24, 1993, the third anniversary of the bombing, Judi held a press conference on the steps of the San Francisco federal building to pass out photos taken at the time of the bombing by the Oakland police and released to her attorney through the discovery process. The photos show a large bomb blast hole in the floor of the Subaru directly below where the front seat had been. "From the very first the FBI and the police knew exactly where the bomb had been placed and they deliberately lied and tried to frame us," she charged.

The FBI refuses to comment because of the pending suit but did tell Mike Geniella of the *Press Democrat* that they've closed the case for lack of evidence. Today, Judi Bari, although still handicapped from the bombing—her right foot paralyzed, her pelvis, nerves, and coccyx damaged beyond surgical repair—has returned to the political frontlines. Among her proudest accomplishments is the Mendocino Real Wood Co-op which she helped found with several out-of-work loggers. The co-op produces value-added wood products from the selective cutting and milling of second-growth trees.

Back in 1990, when the government dropped its charges against Bari and Cherney but failed to pursue other leads in the case, Sheila O'Donnell came to fear that law enforcement's attitude might be taken as a signal by anti-enviro militants that terrorist attacks against environmentalists would be tolerated or at least not actively investigated by the authorities. She was relieved when she didn't hear of any new attacks. Then, on March 2, 1991, Pat Costner's home was torched.

"I went to this environmental law conference in Eugene, Oregon, in the early spring of ninety-one," Sheila recalls. "A number of people came up to me there and said, 'Did you know Pat Costner's home was burned?' I said, 'Has anybody investigated?' Nobody had. When I got home two days later, more people called me, but still no one had investigated. So I called Pat, even though I barely knew her—I'd just met her briefly at that camp in Maine. She was really devastated. She was blaming herself, saying it might have been the wood stove, which she'd left burning when she went out. It turned out she'd been leaving that stove burning for the past seventeen years. Then she told me she had a major Greenpeace report on hazardous waste incinerators due out in two weeks, and I knew we could have something serious here."

On first meeting Pat Costner, you wouldn't guess she's a fifty-three-year-old scientist with three grown children. About five foot six, rail-thin, with round owl-like glasses, and an Arkansas accent as thick as honey butter, Pat has a country simplicity that could almost be taken for severe until she smiles and a pixielike grin lights up her face. The daughter of cotton farmers from the state's northeast delta, Pat divides her time between her home in the rural Ozarks and places like Geneva, Switzerland, where she recently represented Greenpeace on a working committee of the Basell Convention on Transnational Movement of Hazardous Waste, and Moscow, where she's attended a U.S.-Russian conference on chemical weapons disposal.

Pat has a master's degree in organic chemistry and was working towards her doctorate in the late sixties when, following her first divorce, she had to go back to work. "When you're divorced and with a two-year-old to raise, childcare can suddenly become the most traumatic issue in your life," she remembers. She spent several years working for Shell Oil developing methods of labeling catalysts and studying kinetics in the oil-refining process using radio nucleoids. After her second marriage didn't work out, she found herself with three small children to raise. This time she took work in Colorado as a research chemist for a division of Syntex synthesizing industrial quantities of organic specialty compounds.

"I was living in Boulder with my three kids and didn't like raising them in an urban environment. I became convinced it wasn't healthy," she says. "So I moved back to Arkansas in 1974 and got a lab going in Blytheville, near where I was born. I was doing wastewater analysis, simple stuff like that, but it supported me and my kids. I bought some land near Eureka Springs and started building a house, settling into a rational and healthy lifestyle. We raised beans and chickens and rabbits. Eureka is an old, turn-of-the-century resort community in the hills famous for its springwater, but by the time we got there all the springs were contaminated by sewage. We tried to have meetings and figure out how to clean it up. The city and this big engineering firm out of Little

Rock were developing a wastewater-treatment plan. Some local people gave me a copy of the plan, and I could see right off it was a pile of dreck, that it wasn't going to provide a solution. So I teamed up with some local people and we presented the EPA with evidence to stop the project and to identify the main sources of pollution, which included the central waste-treatment facility in town. Something like 80 percent of the town's sewer lines were leaking, contaminating not only the springs, but wells and creeks throughout the area."

Pat helped found and became chief scientist for the Eureka-based National Water Center, setting up a new lab in town and later publishing a book on waste disposal problems called *We All Live Downstream*. In 1987, after her book came out, she went to a meeting in Washington, D.C., of the Citizens' Clearinghouse for Hazardous Wastes, where she met Greenpeace Toxics Campaign Director Dave Rappaport. Following a series of meetings, Rappaport asked her if she'd be interested in taking his job while he was off on sabbatical.

"The kids were getting older and spending their summers with their dad, who lived in Houston," Pat recounts, "and they wanted to spend more time in the big city. So I agreed to live in D.C. and work for Greenpeace for a year while the kids were off with their dad in Texas. After that I stayed on with Greenpeace, working out of my home in Arkansas."

Pat goes on to describe the house that was her home and "lifestyle" for seventeen years. "It kind of grew up around me and the kids," she says, talking about the additions they had built onto a common living room/kitchen area with attached sleeping loft and bedrooms. "We used a lot of recycled materials in building out, and a lot of care. First we added a big greenhouse. The greenhouse glass helped warm the house in the winter. Then, the year before the fire, we added a fourteen-by-thirty-foot office/library for all my files and reference books and also a back porch that looked out onto all these trees. We kept forty chickens, bees, and rabbits. The chickens kind of went wild and roosted in the trees, got to acting more birdlike. I'd just feed them some grain or corn I'd throw out in the yard. The house sat here in an east-west valley, with creeks on two sides at the end of a one and a half mile gravel road." She pauses, reflecting. "I used to feel so safe and good coming down my little bitty road that just me and my neighbor used. Coming home, this was my little spot of sanity, serenity, and peace."

The winter and early spring of 1991 was not a time of peace and serenity for Pat Costner. She and Greenpeace coauthor Joe Thornton, in Seattle, were working overtime to complete a sixty-four-page report on toxic incinerators titled *Playing with Fire*, which was due out that May. The ironically named report would examine a network of 1,100 incinerators, kilns, and industrial boilers across the U.S. that burn more than 7.6 billion pounds of hazardous waste a year. The report was expected to name names and ascribe blame for illegal toxic releases and to identify corporations that targeted poor rural areas for new waste incinerators. The hazardous-waste industry and its backers at the EPA were not looking forward to its publication.[18]

A week before Christmas, Pat went to Oklahoma to meet with Native Americans and speak at a public meeting, where she countered the claims of a Nebraska-based firm called Waste Tech that the toxic incinerator it wanted to install on the Kaw tribal reservation would only release carbon dioxide. After listing the toxic materials its stacks might release, Pat went on to argue that incineration plants were not the answer to hazardous-waste disposal, and that industry had to move towards zero discharge of toxics through new methods of production. A week later the tribal council pulled out of its deal with Waste Tech and the first of the two strangers arrived in Eureka Springs asking where Pat Costner lived.

Pat was also active in a number of other conflicts—monitoring a PCB incinerator in El Dorado, Arkansas, and the Vertac Agent Orange plant and Superfund site that was burning dioxin waste in Jacksonville, Arkansas (where local antipollution activists were being harassed and receiving death threats). ENSCO, the owner of the El Dorado incinerator, hoped to open a larger regional incinerator in Mobile, Arizona. Pat took a number of trips to Mobile to testify and present data against that proposed facility. The previous May, hundreds of local citizens opposed to ENSCO's incinerator had staged a noisy protest during a public meeting. The police cleared the hall, arresting eighteen people and shooting five of them with electric tasers. The detainees were held, handcuffed, at a nearby airfield until the hearing was over. Later it was learned that three of those arrested had been identified from videotapes provided to the Arizona police by the Environmental Protection Agency, which supported ENSCO's toxic incinerator plan.[19] The plan was eventually defeated, one of six multimillion-dollar incinerator projects that were defeated with the help of Pat Costner's expert testimony in the year before her house burned down.

While Pat was working on the final draft of her Greenpeace report, the EPA made several attempts to secure documents on the Vertac Superfund site from an *Arkansas Gazette* reporter, Bobbi Ridlehoover, who'd been running a series of investigative articles on Vertac, the EPA, and its cleanup contractors. The EPA argued that the sensitive documents, which had been removed from the Agent Orange plant by disgruntled workers, were actually dioxin-tainted hazardous waste. Ridlehoover, with the support of her editors, declined to turn the reports over to the EPA, and the government agency backed down. The former plant operators threatened to use the FBI to recover similar documents from a lawyer representing the workers.[20]

By March 2, 1991, Pat Costner couldn't help but be aware of the rising tensions over the toxics-incineration issue and industry interest in her upcoming report, but she didn't consider that she herself might be under observation. "I was at home that Saturday night," she recalls. "I had a friend in from D.C. who was doing a piano concert in town, so I left for that at a quarter of eight and couldn't have been gone more than three hours. I remember driving home from the concert and seeing a glow in the mist. By the time I got to my house, it was burned to the ground. I mean it was totally destroyed. The only thing standing was a couple of cedar posts, my stove, some burned-up office equipment, and some two-by-sixes where the back porch had been. It was one of those times you're just fully in the moment. Sheila later asked me where my dogs were, and I remembered the dogs tried to get in the car with me as I headed back to town, which was something they normally wouldn't have done. I went to a local hangout and a friend Jim said, 'How are you doing?' and I said, 'I'm doing all right but my house just burned down,' and he thought I was joking. Then some other friends came by and asked, 'Is there anything we can do for you?' and I said, 'You could get me a sleeping bag,' and they actually came back with one. Then I had to get out. I hate being emotional in front of people, and so I went back to my place and there were people there standing around looking at the ruins, which I didn't like at all, and Larry Evans, an old local, asked me where I was going to sleep and I said, 'In my car,' but he wouldn't let me. He made me come over to his place and use the sofa, and I couldn't sleep all night. All I could see in my mind over and over is this box. I'd gathered this box of family pictures and set it in the door between the living room and my office, so I could sort through them, and I could imagine those pictures burning up one by one." She pauses. "The next day I poked around in the ashes and the first thing I found was this ceramic chicken that my daughter . . ." She begins to cry. "Hold on, let me get into my tough pragmatic mode. I don't usually talk about this. . . . It's just amazing how it can still crush and hurt my heart, all this time later."

After a moment she recomposes herself and goes on, smoothing out her features, her eyes just a bit more shiny than before.

"There wasn't much left to find—an earring, the strings to my Gibson Hummingbird guitar. If they were trying to sabotage our report, they failed. It still came out in May like originally planned. I was working on the final draft when the fire happened but the prior copy was with my coauthor in Seattle. What was lost that could take years to reconstruct was my reference library. This fellow in the D.C. office [of Greenpeace] kept calling me after the fire saying maybe they could recover the inventory or something from my hard drive. He wouldn't listen when I told him my computer was just a lump of plastic and metal, so I finally put it in a box and mailed it to him, and I heard they placed it in the front of the office with a sign attached, 'Back up your hard drive.'

"Within a relatively short time, friends lent me an Airstream trailer and I moved it out on the property on a Sunday afternoon and ran a phone line into it," she continues. "On Monday when I came back from town the phone line was just dangling there and I just looked at it and found the other end in the trailer and it was obvious it had been cut. I went back to town and called Sheila, and she told me to find a safe place to stay, not to go back out to my land. And that really frightened me in a way the arson had not.

"That Thursday the arson team arrived and took pictures, and about fifteen minutes later, after moving the roofing, they called me over and pointed out this square, empty fuel can where the living room had been," she recounts. "They said the arsonists had probably doused the office and then laid a fuel trail to the stove, which would have given them five minutes to get away. I remember I'd been replaying that in my mind—the stove door being open after the fire. The stove had fallen about ten inches when the floor gave way, but it had a latch handle that shouldn't have come open, and all my office file drawers were also opened in the office after the fire, and it just hadn't sunk in at the time."

Today Pat has built herself a new house where her old one once stood.

"I'd never advise anyone to get burned out and rebuild in the same year," she says. "Sometimes when that new house was going up I'd stop and just hate it 'cause it wasn't my house. I'll be real with you. My son Mason was appalled I was building it there till I explained that you can't build a new old house. I don't have the time to build it over twenty years like I did before."

Three years after the fire Pat continues to carry on her work directing Greenpeace's toxic research program. "I'll assure you it's not bravery or bravado that keeps me going. It's just that this is what I do, and I vacillate between being afraid and insecure and just not accepting it as a reality. But I have to keep functioning the way I feel comfortable. I can't imagine doing anything else. There are very few scientists who aren't obligated to industry and government, and I feel privileged that I get to take what I believe is a really fair and objective view of things from my position."

The closest Pat comes to bitterness is when she reflects on the official response to the fire.

"The city fire marshal came out the day after the fire and said he didn't see any obvious signs of arson. Later he explained he'd meant he didn't see any arson trail as such. The local sheriff didn't come out the day after the fire when I asked him to. Later, after Sheila and the arson investigators got involved, he said he was impressed that it was a crime and if we found out who did it he'd be there to arrest them.[21] Greenpeace asked the FBI to come in on this and they said it didn't meet their criteria for getting involved. I think Sheila was the only person who actually understood what had happened and the implications of it. She was my strength and stability throughout."

In April 1992 several attacks were aimed at Diane Wilson, a shrimper protesting expansion of a Taiwanese-owned plastics plant near her home in Seadrift, Texas. In the first attack, on April 9, three shots were fired at her mother-in-law, who lives in a trailer on the same land as Wilson, her husband, and five kids. The next day a helicopter landed near their isolated homestead and someone shot the family dog, hitting it twice. One bullet went through its neck, a second .22 round was removed from its leg. The dog, a young Dalmatian, recovered but died suddenly the following spring, possibly from poisoning.

In October 1992 Diane's shrimp boat, the *SeaBee*, was sabotaged and almost sank beneath her six miles off the Texas coast. Although she works her forty-two-foot boat alone, Wilson has never learned how to swim.

This was not the first time Seadrift had experienced violence linked to social controversy. A little more than a decade ago Vietnamese immigrants and Anglo shrimpers clashed over the control of fishing grounds on the seafood-rich bays and estuaries of Texas's central Gulf Coast. The Ku Klux Klan got involved, one man was killed, and several homes and boats were burned before peace was restored. "I always put the blame on no one being willing to get involved in the dispute," says Diane Wilson. "There was no communication between the Vietnamese and the Anglos, and the state and federal agencies refused to deal with the situation in its early stages before it got out of control."

It's a critique that could as easily be applied to today's growing incidents of anti-environmental violence and intimidation.

"My father and grandfather were fishermen and his father too," says Diane, who's also married to a fisherman. "I was brought up on the bay, and I got a dear love for the water and the natural way down here."

It is that love of the rich brown bays and blue Gulf waters of the Texas coast that has turned forty-five-year-old Diane Wilson, a thin but muscular woman with curly dark hair, almond-shaped eyes, and a friendly, determined manner, into an environmental activist and anti-enviro target. Aside from its protective network of barrier islands, looping bays, and marine-rich estuaries, the Texas coast south of Galveston is also home to an extensive network of oil refineries, petrochemical plants, and other industries. In 1989 the Associated Press carried a story on the nation's first toxic-release inventory for industry. Point Comfort, twenty miles across Lavaca Bay from Seadrift, was rated the nation's worst site for land disposal of toxic waste. The source of the problem was a chemical factory run by the Formosa Plastics Corporation of Taiwan, which was in the early stages of expanding its facility. It was planned as the largest chemical factory expansion in the United States in over a decade.

"When I read that AP story, it made me react. When I know something is wrong I do something," says Diane. "So what I did, I formed an environmental group. We called ourselves the Calhoun County Resource Watch. Calhoun is part of the tri-county area along with Victoria and Jackson counties. Down here there aren't a lot of people or jobs, and industry is totally infiltrated in the whole power structure so there was an immediate backlash to us. I'm not a socialite. I'd never talked to a banker or a mayor of a town in my life," she says. "Suddenly they're coming up to me on the street saying, 'You're getting involved in something you don't know anything about.' When I tried to have our first meeting in city hall, they wanted me to put it elsewhere. I should have been at home with my kids, they told me. All our county and state officials who were invited backed out of that meeting. We had about seventy people at the Seadrift school, since they wouldn't let us meet at city hall. At the second meeting all these chamber of commerce people showed up. There were about fifteen of them. They were so rude and sat apart from everyone else and started attacking me, asking who the hell was I to run down industry. I finally got so fed up with how rude they were, particularly the head of the chamber of commerce and the mayor of Port Lavaca, I finally told him to shut up. It got wild. When they realized I wasn't coming around, they started saying I was a spy working for the attorney general of Louisiana, or that I was a union organizer, which is the same as saying you're a Communist around here."

Y. C. Wang, Formosa's owner, had earlier established a bidding war between Texas and Louisiana to determine which state would get his plastics factory expansion, with its projected fifteen hundred full-time jobs. After Republican Senator Phil Gramm put together a package of tax breaks and incentives that included a $26 million grant to dredge the harbor and build docks and bulkheads for Formosa at Port Lavaca, Wang finally went with Texas.[22] The factory there produced ethylene dichloride (EDC), a toxic substance used in plastics production; polyvinyl chloride (PVC); and bulk plastics used for everything from PVC piping to grocery bags. According to *Chemical Week* magazine, Formosa is also planning on becoming the major U.S. producer of chlorine once its additional plants go on-line. Called the "Big Daddy of chemical plants" by the *Houston Press*, Formosa's expansion has also been facilitated by a Texas Air Control Board permit for an annual release of 420,000 pounds of dangerous volatile organic compounds (VOCs).

"Formosa brought fifteen reporters in from Taiwan to show them this new plant they were building, and Y. C. was coming with them and I found out about it and was going to show up," Diane recalls of her first protest in 1990. "So they put out a notice inside the plant saying no one was to harm me and then sent someone to the fish house where I worked to say if anything happened to me they certainly weren't going to be responsible since they'd put this bulletin up.

"In October of 1990 they had three hundred construction workers demonstrate at the Baher Community Center, where this big event took place, and they were paid an hour overtime to come down there and picket in support of Formosa. So there it was: the most powerful elite in three counties out to meet Y. C. Wang and his people, and me and my ten supporters and three hundred construction workers. And there were also three police cars and six police, which is a big force for around here. People were afraid to be seen with me. This woman from the chamber of commerce told me there'd be trouble there. I think it was totally set up for trouble, but we were extremely peaceful so there wasn't any."

Aside from bringing Taiwanese reporters to Texas, Formosa also took tri-county politicians on all-expense paid tours of their facilities in Taiwan. They hired a former area congressman as a consultant (his wife sits on the Texas Air Control Board), contributed to local charities, schools, and a hospital; bought ambulances for the paramedics, a computer system for the sheriff's department, two vehicles for the Point Comfort police, and paid for a new deputy for Jackson County. According to the *Texas Observer*, Formosa executives also contributed thousands of dollars to Senator Phil Gramm's 1990 re-election campaign.[23]

In 1990 and 1991 Lavaca Bay, already suffering chemical run-off from three area plants—Union Carbide, British Petroleum, and Alcoa (which fishermen blame for mercury dumping)—had a major dolphin die-off that killed more than a hundred of the protected marine mammals. In 1991 the EPA fined Formosa Plastics $3.4 million for contaminating the soil and groundwater in Point Comfort, but at the same time issued a draft "Finding of No Significant Impact" on the bay from Formosa's $1.3 billion expansion program, which would require pumping millions of gallons of chemically laden discharges into the bay.[24]

"It was an outrage," Diane says. "I'd read about this guy, Mitch Snyder, this homeless activist getting this shelter by fasting, and that got me going. I'd always liked Gandhi and Cesar Chavez. I realized for everything I did I'd have to count on myself, so I decided to do my first hunger strike, protesting the EPA decision not to ask for an Environmental Impact Report. I stayed on the fast for two weeks and threatened to go to the EPA in Dallas and continue it on their doorstep, and they got someone to talk to me and realized maybe an impact report was necessary. Six months later they demanded an EIR [Environmental Impact Report] and the Texas Water Commission and Formosa volunteered to do it, saying they wanted to assure the community it was safe."

In early 1991 Formosa also hired a video crew and stenographer to begin recording Diane Wilson's statements at public hearings.[25] At the same time the Taiwanese Environmental Protection Association invited Diane to visit Taiwan, where they were leading a campaign against Formosa's local plants. These plants were causing major pollution problems in that nation.

"They flew me over there, and while I was there I met a number of dissidents, both environmentalists and prodemocracy types, some of whom were in hiding in the countryside. Some of the people over there told me the Taiwanese government was putting up the money for Formosa to expand," she says. "So on my return home I went to this county judge to ask him about industry and how these things worked, and he kind of joked to me about meeting with the chamber of commerce and local bankers and all these people who were upset with me, saying, 'Now I've told these fellers no matter how upset you get, you can't kill her.'

"I went on a second hunger strike after they went ahead and built the plant, spent a billion dollars without waiting for the EIR to be completed," she continues, "and I was hearing things about the way the plant was being rushed to completion, without a general contractor or anything, and so I fasted for an investigation on the plant's construction problems. And by then I had got an environmental attorney from Houston, Jim Blackburn, and we sued them."

On the thirteenth day of her fast, Wilson and Blackburn negotiated a twenty-four-page agreement with Formosa secured by a handshake between Wilson and Pamela Giblin, Formosa's attorney.

"I'd talked to workers at the plant and added workers' right to organize to our list, so then the OCAW [Oil, Chemical and Atomic Workers] came in and I was smeared as a union organizer," Diane recalls. "I'd ended my hunger strike and agreed to pull back my public opposition but within three or four days Formosa started reneging on the agreement."

Pam Giblin told the *Texas Observer* that the company did not renege because "there never was an agreement." Joe Wyatt, the ex-congressman Formosa had hired as their lobbyist, claimed the deal was just a union ploy anyway and that "we don't just shove the union down our workers' throats."[26] It was around that time that Diane Wilson began receiving threatening phone calls at her home.

In early 1992 the Texas Water Commission gave Formosa a permit allowing them to discharge up to fifteen million gallons of chemical wastewater a day into Lavaca Bay once their factory expansion was completed. The wastewater could include cancer-causing chemicals such as chlorine, benzene, chloroform, ethylene dichloride, and vinyl chloride. The State Health Department announced that as soon as the discharges began they would close Lavaca Bay to oyster harvesting. Shrimpers figured their industry couldn't be far behind. Diane Wilson began organizing among her fellow shrimpers and went on a third hunger strike, traveling to Dallas with a woman from Greenpeace to seek publicity. While she was there her home was attacked.

The Wilsons live on twenty acres at the end of a dead-end road in a remote willow-and-brush-forest area of Calhoun County, "way out in the boondocks," as Diane describes it. Her mother-in-law lives in a trailer beside the main house. She was going out to get the mail at 8:30 in the morning on April 9 when three shots were fired and hit the ground around her. She didn't see anyone and wasn't sure what to make of it. The next morning the kids missed their bus and Leslie Wilson, Diane's husband, drove them to school. Leslie had served as a helicopter mechanic in Vietnam and had recently given up on shrimping to run a crew boat that took men to and from the area's offshore oil platforms. This familiarized him with the sounds of the newer Coast Guard helicopters that patrolled the coastline. When he returned home from dropping the kids off at school, his mother came to him and said that the dog had been shot. The dog, covered in blood, had run to her door, and she'd heard a helicopter and seen a man with a gun in the front yard, she told him. He went inside to try and calm the dog and stop its bleeding when he heard a helicopter hovering somewhere in front of the house. He called the sheriff and told him he thought the helicopter was there to pick up whoever did the shooting. The sheriff was reluctant to send a deputy out until Leslie threatened to shoot at the chopper himself.

More than an hour after he called, a sheriff's deputy arrived and told him that the Coast Guard was flying in the area and that that was probably what he'd heard. Leslie insisted it wasn't a Coast Guard helicopter he'd heard. When he went into the house, the deputy asked his mother if he suffered from post-Vietnam stress syndrome. The deputy also suggested that Diane might get sick from her fast and have to go into the hospital or be institutionalized. When Leslie took the dog to the vet later that day, the vet (whose father worked in the bank where Formosa does all its local business) suggested it had probably been in a dogfight. Only after Leslie insisted that he X-ray the animal did he find and remove the bullet from its leg and identify the second through-and-through neck wound. Around midnight that night the helicopter returned, hovering over the Wilsons' house a second time.

"As soon as my attorney heard about the shooting, he thought it was the federal government 'cause we were suing the EPA and all these other agencies," Diane recalls.

Greenpeace contacted Sheila O'Donnell and she gave Diane a call on her return to Seaview. Sheila suggested that the Wilsons contact the local Coast Guard stations and secure a copy of the police report on the incident. Diane and Leslie called all the Coast Guard stations within several hundred miles and discovered that there had been no helicopter overflights anywhere near their home on the morning or evening of April 10. When they got a copy of their "assignment report" from the Calhoun County Sheriff's Department, there was also no mention of a helicopter.[27]

"Sheila called me a couple of times and gave me some suggestions and sent me some information that was helpful," Diane says. "Thing is, you have to do your own protection down here. The local mayor and justice of the peace all have contracts with the company" (as does her local state senator, who manages Formosa's security company, Triple-D).

Among the materials Sheila sent Diane was a six-page brochure she'd written called "Common Sense Security."[28]

"Popular consciousness of environmental issues," states the brochure, "has seen tremendous growth in the past few years. People organizing or speaking out against environmental degradation in this country and abroad are facing an escalating pattern of harassment. Increasing also is the number of arsons, robberies, burglaries, and attacks on environmental activists, especially on women. . . ." The brochure goes on to suggest that activists "spend a few minutes to assess your work from a security point of view."

Next are listed fifty-four tips categorized under ten headings. Some of the suggestions under "Office" are: "Keep mailing and donor lists and personal phone books out of sight. Always maintain a duplicate at a different location: update it frequently. . . . Keep a camera, loaded with film, handy at all times. . . . If you are the last person to leave the office late at night, leave the light on when you depart. Do not advertise your departure."

"Common Sense" reminds recycling-minded activists that looking through their office trash could provide a treasure trove of information for an anti-enviro vigilante. And here are two of the tips under the heading "Telephone": "If you receive threatening calls on your answering machine, immediately remove and save the tape. . . . Keep a pad and pen next to the telephone. Jot down details of threatening or suspicious calls immediately. Note the time, date and keep a file." (Some phone companies offer Caller ID, a service that provides the number of incoming calls to their customers, and most have call-trace codes to help law enforcement agencies investigate harassing calls.) Under "Mail," the brochure suggests, "Get a mail box through the Post Office or a private concern. Be aware that the United States Post Office will give your street address to inquirers under certain circumstances. . . . If you receive a threatening letter, handle it as little as possible. Put both the letter and the envelope in a plastic bag or file folder. Give the original to the police only if they agree to fingerprint it. Give them a copy otherwise because you may wish to have your own expert examine it."

Other advice follows: "Automobiles—Keep your automobile clean so you can see if there is an addition or loss. . . . Put your literature in the trunk or in a closed box. . . . Keep your car locked at all times. Police—Report any incidents to the local police and ask for protection if you feel it is warranted. . . . Report threats or harassment to your local police. Demand that they take a report and protect you if that is necessary. Talk to the press and report the police response as well as the incident(s). . . . Report thefts of materials from your office or home to the police: these are criminal acts."

Among "Common Sense Security" suggestions for countering surveillance: "Brief your membership on known or suspected surveillance. Be scrupulous with documentation. Do not dismiss complaints as paranoia without careful investigation. The opposition can and frequently does have informants join organizations to learn about methods and strategy. . . . Photograph the person(s) following you or have a friend do so. Use caution. If someone is overtly following you or surveilling you, they are trying to frighten you. Openly photographing them makes them uncomfortable. If you are covertly being followed, have a friend covertly photograph them. . . . If you are being followed [by car], get the license plate number and state. Try to get a description of the driver and the car as well as passengers. Notice anything different about the car. . . . Debrief yourself immediately after each incident. Write details down: time, date, occasion, incident, characteristics of person(s), impressions, anything odd about the situation. . . . Keep a 'Weirdo' file with detailed notes about unsettling situations and see if a pattern emerges."

Under "Break-ins," the brochure suggests to "Check with knowledgeable people in your area about alarm systems, dogs, surveillance cameras, motion sensitive lights, deadbolt locks and traditional security measures to protect against break-ins."

In general the brochure reflects O'Donnell's lack of sympathy for the FBI as an impartial investigative agency. One of its tips, for example, is, "Do not overlook the fact that government agencies sometimes share information within the government and with the private sector, particularly right-wing organizations.

This has been documented." The brochure concludes by suggesting that "if you feel something is wrong, trust the feeling. Your instincts are usually right. . . . None of this advice is intended to frighten but to create an awareness of the problems. . . ."

Unfortunately "Common Sense Security" lacks a heading for "Fishing Boats."

"In October of ninety-two I was out on the bay hauling my nets and I noticed the boat was listing," Diane recalls. "I ran and throwed the hatch up and the water is almost over the engine and it was coming in around the filling box [containing the rotor shaft] and the wires were all gone from the electric pump and so I hand-pumped like crazy for a while and later found some wires and hooked up the pump directly to the battery. The wires had been jerked loose. I couldn't figure how it could have happened, but then it happened again three or four weeks later. The filling box is usually tight down so there's not enough room for water to be leaking in. Someone had to loosen the filling box and pull the wires on the pump, but the first time it happened, you know, you just have a hard time believing someone would really do something like that intentionally, you kind of deny what's before your eyes. And I don't swim at all, even though I'm a shrimper. And also my radio'd been swiped some time before, so I'm out there five or six miles all alone with no radio and think I could of died if that boat sank."

In April 1993 Diane heard a police scanner somewhere in the woods near her house. "It's not something you'd hear normally 'cause we're way out here away from everything," she explains. A short time later her dog came into the yard, laid down, and died. "We just buried him. We don't have the money to go have a dog's body tested or anything. We barely have $15 dollars between us. But he was only four years old and recovered from the shooting, so it was pretty suspicious."

Rather than retreat in the face of ongoing harassment and intimidation, Diane decided to go on another hunger fast that spring, protesting Formosa's chemical wastewater-release permits, which were scheduled to go into effect by the end of September 1993. At thirty days, this was the longest of her fasts; it ended in May after state officials persuaded Formosa to work with an independent commission to find ways to reduce or recycle its wastewater. Diane, although still a minority voice within her job-poor county, was beginning to pick up support.

"Diane's done a lot more good than she realizes. Formosa's expansion is much more scrutinized because of her," says Charles Spiekerman, regional director of the Texas Air Control Board in Corpus Christi, eighty miles south of Seadrift.[29]

By the winter of 1993/94, legal suits, opposition from the U.S. Fish and Wildlife Service, and organized protests by the $200-million-a-year shrimping industry had temporarily delayed Formosa's discharge permit.

"Matagorda and Lavaca and Spirit Center and San Antonio bays are all hooked together in about a hundred miles of these waters I grew up on," Diane says. "The coziness is unreal. Plus, it feeds a lot of families. I take the bay real personal. It needs protecting. It has to last more than just this one generation."

Diane admits that the campaign of harassment and violence directed against her has taken a toll. "I've been called a prostitute, a lesbian, a racist, a bad mother. My parents, sister, and brother are upset with me. My husband and I are nearly on the verge of getting a divorce, but I will not stop. They will not get that bay."

I ask Sheila O'Donnell why she thinks so many anti-environmentalist attacks have been directed against women.

"Women are the backbone of the environmental movement, particularly the anti-toxics movement, so that's one reason they're targeted," she says. "But I also think there's something else going on here. Women get targeted and men feel guilty they weren't there to defend them. It's a terror tactic. It raises the fear level, and frightened people are less effective organizers. It has a kind of sub rosa effect. People don't get involved as readily. But I think it also strengthens those people who choose not to be intimidated."

Sheila herself seems unintimidated, even though she's encountering a growing number of cases like those of Judi Bari, Pat

Costner, and Diane Wilson. I ask her why she doesn't carry a weapon when she's investigating this kind of attack.

"I don't want that kind of energy around me," she explains. "I go into situations where people are armed and if I feel uncomfortable I leave. Otherwise I might stay and engage in something I don't want to be a part of. To carry a weapon you have to be convinced that you're willing to take another person's life, because you don't want to wound an armed person, you have to kill him. And I think to carry that gun you really have to be fresh, to be practiced. Cops are fresh because that's what they do with their lives. But I feel that my work is really about supporting life, not taking life."

Casualties of War

If the troubles from environmentalists cannot be solved in the jury box or at the ballot box, perhaps the cartridge box should be used.
FORMER SECRETARY OF THE INTERIOR JAMES WATT, 1990

*Fighting to save the environment could put you
on the endangered list.*
DAN RATHER, CBS EVENING NEWS, MARCH 3, 1993

"I'm going to blow your fucking brains out," said a Pecos, New Mexico, logger and member of People for the West to Sam Hitt as Sam set up his slide projector at an environmental open house in the Pecos high school gym. "Yeah, and he deserves it too," chimed in a PR flack from the U.S. Forest Service. Hitt and his Santa Fe–based environmental group Forest Guardians had been trying to stop Forest Service plans for new logging on nearby Elk Mountain.

Since that incident in 1990, Hitt has received a number of death threats on his telephone answering machine.[1] Pat Wolff, another Forest Guardians activist, who led a campaign against the trapping and shooting of coyotes, mountain lions, foxes, and other predators, received an anonymous letter in August 1992. The letter read, in part, "I am definitely spreading the word that Patricia Wolff should be quieted. . . . Shooting individual offenders [is] justified, including the two-legged offender you."[2]

In Bend, Oregon, some twenty timber-worker members of the Oregon Lands Coalition crashed a meeting of the Oregon Natural

Resources Council at Central Oregon Community College. One of the timber workers pointed to Andy Kerr, director of the state-wide environmental group, and launched into a harangue comparing him to Saddam Hussein. "I will kill you," another man shouted at Kerr. "I will kill you if you don't get out of here."

"Death threats come with the territory these days," Kerr shrugs, recalling a number of similar incidents.[3]

"Intimidation can also be subtle," says Scott Groene of the Utah Wilderness Alliance in Moab, Utah. "People fear being blacklisted, fear losing their jobs if they speak out as much as they fear the violence." In July 1992 Groene found a death threat taped to the porch of his home that concluded, "Utah will have harmony when Scott has a fatal accident in the environment!" He also received a number of harassing phone calls that ended after several months. He figured out why when he read a letter in the *Moab Times Independent* on March 3, 1993: "Editor, My wife and I have found ourselves in a very awkward situation. Our phone number is mistakenly listed in the local directory under the name Scott Groene. As a result we get a great deal of unnecessary calls. We also get a great deal of hate calls. The irony of this situation is that my wife and I try to keep an open mind on most issues and normally we don't harbor any resentment against someone that might have a different point of view. Unfortunately, I am finding it harder all the time to keep an open mind when I get calls at 7 A.M. telling me to 'drop dead.'"[4]

In November 1991, two southern loggers went beyond threats, assaulting and hospitalizing river guide Bruce Hare outside a Long Creek, South Carolina, restaurant. Hare was a founding member and spokesman for South Carolina Forest Watch, an environmental group that had succeeded in halting timber operations in parts of the Sumter National Forest. A civil jury later found logger David Phillips liable for $1,800 in medical bills and $30,000 in malicious damage to river rafts that belonged to Hare.[5]

Castle Bunch, a fifty-seven-year-old resident of Windrock, Tennessee, and the head of Save Our Cumberland Mountains, was beaten up at a town council meeting in September 1992 because of his opposition to a proposed landfill that was supposed to bring new jobs into the area. His main attacker was a man he'd known his whole life, a friend who'd married his wife's cousin.[6]

"Take that, you faggots and environmentalists!"

" 'That' was a fusillade of bullets from a high-powered rifle, one of which ripped through the scrub surrounding our desert campsite . . . ," reported a pair of Associated Press journalists who'd been camping in southern Utah in the fall of 1991. "Instantly prone and breathless, we watched the four-wheel-drive pickup move up the main road and then veer off toward Grosvenor Arch, its powerful spotlight bouncing beams across the sand and sage. The crack of rifle fire continued."

A few minutes earlier the two reporters had had a tense conversation with three beer-swigging cowboys in the pickup who'd been spotlighting and shooting at jackrabbits. After driving off a hundred yards, the cowboys started shooting at them.

"At the time we saw the incident as a maddening example of what can happen when alcohol and loaded guns wind up in the same hands," they wrote. "But upon reflection, the episode seemed to underscore tensions in Utah between urban north and rural south over such long-simmering issues as grazing rights, wilderness, development and the environment."

The local sheriff agreed. "Some cowboys can see some people that are obviously from the city out enjoying nature, and they're all of a sudden labeled faggots and environmentalists."[7]

Mike Jackson is an outspoken environmental attorney in Quincy, California, a logging town of about five thousand people in the Sierra Nevada. On the night of the town's first Yellow Ribbon rally, shots were fired into his storefront office on Main Street and a death threat was left on his office answering machine. "This was not the most brilliant terrorist act—leaving their voice on a recording machine," Jackson laughs. "I took the tape across the street to KPCO [the local radio station] and they played it for a couple of days. We all thought we recognized the voice as that of a midlevel manager at a local timber company. I'm sure when his wife heard his voice on the radio it had the desired effect, 'cause we've never had any more incidents since then."[8]

In Kenova, West Virginia, Diana Bowen, a member of the

Ohio Valley Environmental Coalition, was videotaping yellow sulfur smoke rising from one of the stacks at the Ashland Oil refinery across the Big Sandy River in Kentucky when a car pulled up a short distance behind hers. Two men got out and walked down the riverbank. She tried to ignore them. Ever since area residents had begun videotaping suspected illegal emissions from the refinery, there'd been threatening phone calls and shouted warnings. Cars had followed people along the rivershore and a woman had been run off the road.

"The first gunshot was at a distance. The second and third were closer, and I realized something was wrong," Bowen recalls. "The fourth shot they fired at me was real close, and with the fifth shot a tiny branch fell out of a tree just across the road. I was thinking maybe I should turn the video camera around and get a picture of them, but then I thought, no, that's not a good idea. I got back to my car just as those two gentlemen got into their car and took off. I was terrified. My knees were knocking together. I was shaking all over."

A spokesman for Ashland Oil later told a reporter that the company was doing some pile driving that day and that Bowen may have mistaken the piles being sunk into the ground for gunfire. "I grew up around guns. My father was a policeman and my husband is a hunter, and there's a big difference between the sound of a pile-driver and being shot at," Diana retorts. A journalist from the Huntington, West Virginia, *Herald-Dispatch* and others who have watched and listened to the videotape agree that there are shots being fired "from a handgun or small-caliber rifle," according to the newspaper reporter.[9]

"It's the worst thing that ever happened to me in the woods, having a man with a gun pointed at my chest with his finger on the trigger calling me an environmentalist and saying I'm stealing his forest and he's not going to take it anymore. It was a terrible, sickening feeling," recalls Lamar Marshall, a member of the Sierra Club and publisher of the *Bankhead Monitor,* a colorful environmental magazine in northwest Alabama. Marshall has been the subject of threats and accusations from EAGLE, a local Wise Use group, for some time. In November 1992 he and two friends were taking photos in the Bankhead National Forest when a drunken hunter held them at gunpoint and began ranting about environmentalists locking up the forest. The armed drunk was with a teenage boy carrying a twelve-gauge shotgun who was clearly terrified by the situation. The hunter wanted to lead his hostages to an abandoned well but they refused to go. He ordered the boy to pull the slide back on his shotgun. Lamar and one of his friends were carrying concealed handguns (many environmentalists in Alabama travel armed for self-defense). "My friend Darryl had squatted down on the ground about twenty feet behind me and had his pistol down by his side. Later he said if the boy had cocked that shotgun he figured there'd be a firefight and that would sure spoil his day. I said if there'd been a firefight it would have spoiled my life," Lamar recalls.

After about twenty minutes the gunman, still ranting, handed the boy his rifle to hold as he tried to squat down. When he fell over backwards, the environmentalists took off at a run. They got his license plate number and later gave it to the police. The authorities questioned the man before releasing him, saying they didn't consider him dangerous. Five months later he killed himself with a high-powered rifle.[10]

Community-based environmental groups from New York, New Jersey, Alaska, California, Florida, Texas, Arkansas, Louisiana, New Mexico, Montana, North Carolina, South Carolina, Tennessee, Ohio, Missouri, Michigan, Utah, and a number of other states have become the targets of intimidation and violence directed against their offices and members. Where no local environmental groups exist, individuals perceived as being "preservationists" are often targeted.

The most common incidents occur in rural communities and low-income industrial areas dependent on a single industry or resource base for their economic survival, areas that for reasons of class or location get little notice from the national media or the major national environmental groups. The Lower Price Hill neighborhood of Cincinnati is that kind of a place. Heavily industrialized and polluted, local hospitals report that children living in Lower Price Hill are up to five times as likely to suffer from respiratory diseases as children in other parts of the city. In 1989 Paula Siemers, a divorced mother of five, lost her only son, Aaron, to a rare form of leukemia. Suspecting that his death was linked to the area's polluting factories, she began attending meetings and helping to organize protest marches directed against nearby plants. These included the Queen City Barrel Company, a plant that reconditions toxic waste drums and that was cited forty times for hazardous-waste violations in one two-year period.[11]

Soon after Paula started a petition campaign she began receiving hang-up calls and death threats. The harassment quickly escalated. Hate notes were left on her porch, including one that called her "the pollution bitch." Rocks were thrown through her windows, one hitting her little girl, Rachel, as she lay in bed. In the spring of 1991, Paula was walking through the neighborhood taking hamburgers home for her kids when a gang of young thugs yelled at her that she was a troublemaker and began throwing rocks. One hit her in the back of the head, knocking her unconscious. After she was treated and released from the hospital, someone fed poisoned meat to her Doberman, killing it. Crushed cats and other roadkills were thrown into her yard. Her house was twice set on fire, and someone left a small pile of .38 bullets on her front porch. In the summer of 1992, Leslie Stahl and a "60 Minutes" camera crew visited her for a segment they were doing on Wise Use and environmental victims of vigilante attacks. Stahl suggested that the people attacking Paula might be afraid that her efforts to clean up the environment would shut down their companies and cost them their jobs. "It comes down to feeding your children," Paula agreed. "It's economic blackmail. They're put into a corner where they have to choose one or the other, or they feel they have to." Despite the harassment, violence, and threats, Paula said she was going to stay on and fight to clean up her community. A few weeks later she was attacked, beaten, and stabbed by two men. "They didn't say anything. They ran up behind me and they punched me and hit me. They just came out of nowhere. I didn't even know I was stabbed. I just thought they had beat me, and then someone screamed and said, 'You're bleeding,' and I don't remember much after that," she later recalled from hiding.[12]

The single stab wound, from a switchblade or stiletto-type thin-bladed knife, just missed her kidney. The men who attacked her were never caught. After she was again treated at the hospital and her wound sewn up, she decided it was time to get out. In late 1992 Paula Siemers took her children and moved to the Pacific Northwest. When Sheila O'Donnell spoke to her six months later, she found her nervous, anxious, and depressed, showing all the symptoms of post-traumatic stress syndrome. A short time after that conversation, Siemers moved again, cutting off most of her contacts with friends, journalists, and environmentalists.

Rather than originating with a single organized group, the anti-enviro violence spreading across America seems to have three primary sources. There are spontaneous outbursts of violence, like the drunken cowboys' shoot-'em-up in Utah, or Ocie Mills's decision to make his "citizen's arrest" of two Florida Department of Environmental Regulation officials at gunpoint back in 1976.

More common are the campaigns of escalating harassment leading to violence that seem to accompany the political organizing efforts of Wise Use/Property Rights groups such as Yellow Ribbon, Sahara Club, People for the West, and the Adirondack Solidarity Alliance. In one example, in rural Ringwood, New Jersey, conservation-oriented Mayor Craig Siegel resigned after receiving anonymous hate mail, harassing phone calls, and physical threats that came in the wake of Wise Use fliers labeling him an ecoterrorist, leftist, and leader of an antigrowth religion.[13] Delaware Valley, New York, publisher Glenn Pontier points to the night Wise Use organizer Chuck Cushman came to town to "scare the hell out of people" as the start of two years of escalating confrontations, threats, and militancy that led to the burning down of his house.

Still, some of the worst violence seems to go beyond the logistical capabilities of local anti-enviro groups, developers, or low-paid workers indoctrinated with the idea that environmentalists want to steal their jobs. A number of attacks—such as those directed against Pat Costner, Diane Wilson, Kansas housewife Lauri Maddy, Georgia computer programmer Tony Winters, and fish camp operator Stephanie McGuire in Perry, Florida—suggest a third source of violence: professional security agents familiar with terrorist tactics. The security industry refers to such agents as "cowboys," hired gunmen who in the past might have busted unions, burned African American churches, or broken into offices of Central American refugee centers, but who today are available to do the dirty work of some of America's dirtiest industries.

The private security industry is itself one of the fastest growing and least regulated sectors of the U.S. economy. In the last twenty years it has grown from a $2-billion- to a $20-billion-a-year business employing more than 2.5 million people, more than twice the number of all public-sector police. According to the *FBI Law Enforcement Bulletin*, "The future police community will separate into three distinct strata, public, private and corporate."[14] In recent years the private and corporate sectors have been involved in a range of politically and constitutionally dubious activities, including union busting, workplace drug "stings," the kidnapping of fugitives in violation of extradition treaties, and the kidnapping of children at the center of custody cases. A number of government intelligence agents from the CIA, FBI, and DEA have "retired" into more lucrative private-sector police work, bringing their knowledge of terrorist tactics and "dirty tricks" along with them.

Certainly there are strong indications of dirty tricks operations being run against U.S. environmentalists. Jeremy Rifkin is a well-known social critic and author who works out of Washington, D.C. His most recent book, *Beyond Beef*, is an environmental critique of the cattle industry that calls for a 50 percent reduction in consumption of beef. The Cattlemen's Association has denounced the book as "fiction" and, in concert with the food-marketing industry, has set up a "Food Facts Coalition" to counter *Beyond Beef*.

In the spring of 1992, Rifkin's national book tour had to be canceled after it was repeatedly sabotaged. Melinda Mullin, the book's publicist at Dutton Books, says she received calls from fictitious newspaper and TV reporters trying to get Rifkin's itinerary. After someone managed to get a hold of it, radio and TV producers who'd scheduled Rifkin's appearance began receiving calls from a woman claiming to be Mullin cancelling or misrepresenting Rifkin's plans. Finally, Mullin had to begin using a code name with the producers. Liz Einbinder, a San Francisco–based radio producer who had had *Beyond Beef* on her desk for several weeks, was surprised to receive angry calls and an anonymous package denouncing Rifkin within hours of placing her first call to Mullin. This led to speculation that Dutton's New York phones might be tapped.[15]

In July 1992 the U.S. House Committee on Interior and Insular Affairs released a report titled *Alyeska Pipeline Service Company Covert Operation.* The report documented how, in the wake of the 1989 *Exxon Valdez* oil spill, the North Slope pipeline company (owned by a consortium of oil companies) paid Wackenhut, one of the country's largest private security firms, more than a million dollars to spy illegally on suspected whistleblowers, environmentalists, and critics providing congressional investigators with evidence of environmental violations at the oil-tanker terminal in Valdez.[16]

One of the main targets of the private security spies was industry critic and retired oil-tanker broker Charles Hamel. According to the report, "Wackenhut agents watched Hamel's home, picked through his trash, obtained his personal credit, banking, and long-distance telephone records as well as information about his divorce, his family, his ownership of property, his business disputes with Exxon, and virtually all his activities in the environmental area." They also had their agents infiltrate and spy on environmental meetings and demonstrations.

On March 24, 1990, an agent from Wackenhut's Special Investigations Division (SID) took photos of "key members" of an Anchorage demonstration commemorating the first anniversary of the *Exxon Valdez* oil spill. He also took down license plate numbers of cars parked in the area and later, after getting the names and addresses of the cars' owners from Alyeska's corporate security chief, added them to an "index" SID was keeping of oil-industry critics.

Other targets of the spy operation included Alyeska employees, state officials and scientists, a Fairbanks radio-talk-show host, disgruntled fishermen, and a public interest law firm. Wackenhut agents even discussed mounting a spy operation against Congressman George Miller, chairman of the House Interior Committee (later to become the Natural Resources Committee), which was investigating the *Exxon Valdez* oil spill.

In West Virginia, a fly-by-night security outfit called OSI turned a water cannon on peaceful demonstrators outside the gates of a solid-waste dump in Hedgesville. OSI's fatigue-clad guards paraded around the dump's perimeter with Dobermans and were repeatedly charged with trailing after and trespassing on the private property of local environmental activists. The dump's owner was finally forced to let the firm go, noting that "they were not effective in minimalizing conflict."[17]

In New York, someone hired a private detective to investigate the background of Kathy Kellogg, a reporter from Colorado who had moved back home to rural southeastern New York, where she had become active in leading local opposition to a planned waste dump. Integrated Waste Systems (IWS), the Buffalo-based company trying to establish the dump, had bought a 423-acre site half a mile from Kathy's family's farm. The broker who had bought the land from a widow and a farmer had told them he planned to turn it into a campground. After Kellogg helped form Concerned Citizens of Cattaraugus County, a Buffalo-based private investigator made a series of calls to her former editor at the *Durango Herald*. He claimed he was a potential employer for an environmental organization in New York City and asked for any references and political or personal information they might have on her. The editor became suspicious and later contacted Kellogg.[19] When confronted by a reporter for the *Buffalo News*, the detective, Roger Putnam, explained, "Basically, it's what any corporation would do when they're trying to find out what the enemy is all about."[20]

In an editorial titled "Stop Farmersville Snooping," the *Buffalo News* suggested that "it's alarming—downright scary—that an

ordinary citizen cannot step forward and become involved in a
community issue without someone snooping around about her
past. . . . Stop it. Let's argue the Farmersville dump on its merits
without further conspiratorial snooping."[21]

In 1987 Tony Winter and his wife Rosemary, then six weeks
pregnant, moved to a rural subdivision near Albany, Georgia, a
short distance from a Merck & Company pharmaceutical plant.
Later Rosemary gave birth to a baby girl they named Jordan.
Within weeks of her birth Jordan developed respiratory problems and had to be put on a breathing machine. Along with her
respiratory disorders, doctors found that the baby had a compromised immune system and unexplained skin rashes. Meanwhile,
Tony developed blinding headaches, numbness in his extremi-
ties, breathing difficulties, nausea, and fatigue that eventually
forced him to resign his job as a computer programmer. Among
the complications his doctors diagnosed were chronic demyeli-
nating polyneuropathy (CIDP), a disease in which the protective
sheaths around the nerves deteriorate, causing them to die. Winter was at a loss to explain his family's sudden health problems until he saw a 1990 TV report based on the national Toxics Release
Inventory. The report identified Merck as the number one industrial source of chemical emissions in the state of Georgia. An
earlier 1987 state report showed that Merck had emitted 1.7 million pounds of dichloromethane, a suspected carcinogen, and
800,000 pounds of toluene, a chemical that can damage the pul-
monary and nervous systems, into the local air and water. The
Georgia Environmental Protection Division also had found four
contaminated areas within the plant fenceline. Groundwater at
one location contained 927,000 parts dichloromethane per billion; state regulations allow 5 parts per billion. Toluene had been
found in concentrations of 183,000 parts per billion in the groundwater. The legal limit is a thousand parts per billion.[22] Aside from
living a mile downwind from the plant, the Winters were also
drinking the local tap water. What they didn't know was that the
city was pumping its water from a well just behind their house and
close to the plant. After having his family's blood and tissue samples tested, Tony discovered that their bodies contained high con-

centrations of industrial chemicals, including dichloromethane and toluene.

That year the Winter family moved away from the plant. In the summer of 1991, in the eighth month of her second pregnancy, Rosemary Winter's doctor told her that one of the twin boys she was carrying was dead. Because the twins shared the same amniotic sac, she had to carry both fetuses to full term. That August she gave birth. Tony, Jr., the live baby, was healthy but slow to develop neurologically. His immune system was later found to be compromised. The dead twin was sent to a toxicology lab. An autopsy revealed that the stillborn's body contained high levels of arsenic, chromium, and other toxic chemicals. In 1992 Tony and his family filed a lawsuit against Merck, claiming that contamination from the plant killed their unborn child and created their chronic health problems. Tony, a twenty-nine-year-old registered Republican and self-styled conservative, also became active with a community group called CHEER, Citizens for a Healthy Environment, Economy and Resources. A year later, on Sunday, February 28, 1993, the *Albany Herald* published a long front-page article about the suit, chemical contamination at the plant, and the Winter family's health problems accompanied by a photograph of Tony and his doctor, Jack Woodard.[23]

"That's when the harassment started, just after that article ran," Tony recalls. The following Sunday the axle came off the front end of his van as he and his family were leaving their home on a vacation trip to Atlanta. "I hit a pothole and felt the axle separate from the van," he says. "You can see where pins had been knocked out from it. Our mechanic said it had to be intentional—he couldn't figure any other way it could have happened. The cop who came by our house to look at the van said, 'This stuff's way over my head.'"[24]

Jack Woodard, Tony's doctor, was very outspoken with Merck's lawyers during depositions that were taken at his office over the next weeks. He kept hot water for tea and coffee in gallon jugs marked "hazardous waste." "Merck's lawyers were not impressed with his sense of humor," Tony recalls. In March 1993 the doctor's forty-pound mixed-breed dog was stolen, its throat cut, and the blood drained from its body before it was dumped back on his driveway. The local sheriff thought the killing was the work of a cult—until he heard about Woodard's planned testimony in the federal pollution suit.

The doctor's wife had gotten the tag number of the red truck that had dumped the dog's body. "I called the Georgia Bureau of Investigation and they ran the number and told me it belonged to an eighty-year-old man who lived five hours away," Tony Winter says. "I had someone else run the number and it turned out to belong to a guy, an independent electrical contractor, living across town [this was confirmed by the person who ran the license tag check]. So then I called the FBI, asking if they'd investigate, and they said unless it had an international flavor they weren't interested. That's an exact quote."

The sheriff's department placed Dr. Woodard under a protective watch, and Dr. Woodard installed a $6,000 security system around his house and began carrying a pistol.

"After that incident the doctor pulled way back. It scared his wife real bad," Tony says. "The real sad part was the dog had belonged to their son, who died of cancer, so in a way it was their link to him."

Between April and September of 1993, there were eleven reported break-ins at the Winters' home.[25] "Nothing was ever stolen. I have a lot of computer equipment and a TV and VCR that were all still sitting there after the break-ins. There was even about twenty dollars in bills sitting next to my computer on the table one time that was undisturbed. They just wanted to let me know they could get in my house. They'd leave doors open, water running. Some guy even peed on our living room floor, which tells you what kind of people we're dealing with."

It's a story that sounds all too familiar to Lois Gibbs, the executive director of the Citizens' Clearinghouse for Hazardous Wastes, who recalls a similar series of harassing break-ins at her house when she first began organizing pollution protests in the Love Canal area of Niagara Falls back in the late 1970s.

The police put watches on the Winters' house and family. "One night there was banging on our outside wall and we saw this guy

running away at two in the morning. From what I could see he fit
the description of the contractor with the red truck. The cop coming by on patrol saw him running but didn't stop him to ask him
his name or anything. He said he didn't have cause. I said, 'This
guy's running from our house at two in the morning and you don't
think that's suspicious?' I'm not too satisfied with how the local
police have handled our situation."

On August 22, 1993, a Dodge Dakota truck belonging to Rosemary's father and parked on the wide, tree-lined street outside
the Winters' house was sideswiped by a hit-and-run driver. The
family was getting ready to celebrate Rosemary's twenty-ninth
birthday. "We were leaving for dinner when he saw his side-view
mirror laying on the ground, went around to the street side of his
truck and found the damage," Tony says. "It cost him $1,000 to
fix. It just kind of makes you sick, this type of stuff."

Tony admits that the harassment is one reason he settled his
suit in October 1993. "The only condition on the settlement is I
can't disclose the amount I received," he says. "It doesn't prevent
me from continuing to bitch and raise hell or even enter a class
action suit against the company, which is what a number of us are
now planning."

Among seven boxes of company records he received during the
discovery phase of litigation, Winter claims that he found proof
that contamination from the Merck plant, which employs 250 to
300 people, has spread beyond the fenceline into the surrounding
groundwater and now threatens one of two other major employers in the area, a beer brewery. The other big factory in town is a
Procter & Gamble plant that packs disposable diapers made from
cellulose produced at P&G's Buckeye Mill on the Fenholloway
River in Taylor County, Florida.

On April 7, 1992, Stephanie McGuire's cousin, Linda Rowland,
took Stephanie's son to the store while she stayed behind at the
fish camp they managed on the Fenholloway River in Florida. The
Fenholloway, on north Florida's Gulf Coast, was once considered
a fishing and recreation paradise until it was reclassified an "industrial river" in 1947 in order to attract Procter & Gamble's

Buckeye Cellulose pulp mill. Florida's obsolete "industrial river" classification allows companies to dump anything they want into a river. With its right to pollute assured, P&G began operations at its mill in 1954. Forty years later the Fenholloway runs black as oil from 50 million gallons a day of industrial discharge from the Buckeye Mill, which produces more than a thousand tons a day of chlorine-bleached cellulose used in sanitary napkins, tampons, and disposable diapers. Studies conducted by the EPA have found dioxin levels in the Fenholloway to be close to two thousand times what the agency considers an acceptable level of risk. Cancer rates for the county are unreliable, since most people go to Tallahassee or Gainesville for hospitalization, and the counties where they die, not where they lived, keep the cancer death statistics. Anecdotal evidence, however, suggests a high rate of cancer for rural Taylor County, where the mill is located. The county also has disproportionately high rates of leukemia and blood and liver disorders, problems associated with dioxin and other chemical exposures. Also, female fish in the river have developed male characteristics—according to EPA scientists, because of pollution-caused hormonal changes. A number of local wells have been contaminated along with the county's groundwater. The tap water has taken on a yellow-green tint and foul odor. The local newspapers' responses have been to praise Procter & Gamble for providing free bottled water to area residents. P&G dominates the local economy to such a degree that residents refer to the plant as "Uncle Buck," and call the awful odor emanating from its 600-acre facility "the smell of money." *Wall Street Journal* reporter Alecia Swasy, in her book *Soap Opera—The Inside Story of Procter & Gamble*, describes the county seat of Perry as "a company town seemingly out of the 1800s. . . . Locals commonly refer to blacks as 'niggers,' and segregation still exists at restaurants and bars. Some still talk about Dixie 'rising again.' Men joke about using whips to turn women into 'good housewives.' Disputes are often settled with guns."[26]

Ned Mudd, a tough-as-nails environmental lawyer out of Birmingham, Alabama, recalls a two-day trip he took to Perry to represent local residents, including Stephanie McGuire, in a dioxin suit they brought against P&G. "I told my assistant, 'Next time we come down here we're going to rent a fast car with Florida plates and have two shotguns in the back.' It's that kind of a nasty place. I remember saying, 'Somebody's going to get killed in this town.' "[27]

Local rancher Joy Towles Cummings first got into a dispute with P&G in 1989 over a logging lease on her family land. A former ag-chemical saleswoman who took over the family ranch after her grandmother got too old to manage it, Joy quickly began to suspect that the plant's chemical pollution of the river, wells, and local springs was far worse than anybody suspected. She began getting inside information from plant workers about sinkholes below settling ponds and chemical leaks from unlined dumps as well as illegal dumping at the mill itself. By the spring of 1991, she was ready to form a citizens' group and take on the company. About the same time Julie Hauserman, an award-winning journalist with the *Tallahassee Democrat*, wrote an investigative series called "Florida's Forgotten River," exposing the pollution problems along the Fenholloway. In the wake of those articles Joy's group, Help Our Polluted Environment (HOPE), got its first dozen members. Among them was the outspoken Linda Rowland, who had worked at the mill for fifteen years, and her painfully shy cousin, Stephanie McGuire. P&G supporters quickly formed their own Wise Use countergroup, called Defenders of Taylor County. Defenders wrote to state officials denouncing HOPE as a "pseudo-environmental cult." Shortly thereafter the women in the group began receiving threatening phone calls, including one from a caller who told them he would cut out their tongues if they didn't hush. After that Joy Towles Cummings began packing a .38 revolver in her purse.

"I carry a gun with me all the time. It's not safe for me not to," says Joy. "You're pretty much on your own down here. We don't trust the sheriff. His deputies used to follow us around, and more recently he's been covering up like a cat covers its mess. So I just count on my friends and my family. I don't go anywhere alone or without my gun."[28]

After Joy was invited to appear on a local TV show, the show's host, a Baptist preacher, was taken off the air. The small station's owner had been pressured to get rid of him by a major advertiser, a local furniture store owner and former P&G employee. According to Alecia Swasy's *Soap Opera*, the store owner claimed he'd received threats that his store would be burned down because his ads appeared on the program. The station owner also told the show's host that callers had threatened to burn down the TV station after HOPE's founder appeared on his program.

Joy Towles Cummings's fears, and those of other members of HOPE, were realized with the April 7 attack on Stephanie McGuire. Linda Rowland and her cousin Stephanie had been receiving threatening phone calls for some time. After Joy's twenty-three-year-old son died in a car accident, Rowland and McGuire received a call from a man who said, "You know how accidents happen. They can happen to you." Boats at their fish camp had been cut loose and pheasants caged near their house had been poisoned. The two women, isolated at their rural fish camp, had begun keeping handguns and shotguns near them at all times. At about five on the afternoon of April 7, after Linda and Stephanie's son, Shawn, had driven off to the store, Stephanie waited for the last fishing boat to return from the Gulf of Mexico two miles down the Fenholloway. She later recalled hearing a boat pull up to the dock and going outside to greet it. There she spotted a man dressed in camouflage. He told her he'd shot a cow up the road and wanted the owner's name. Feeling uneasy, she began to head back to the house. Before she could get there two other men in camouflage and masks came out of the woods. One hit her on the head with a rock and tossed it into the river. She fell to the ground, managed to get up again, and hit him in the mouth with all her strength. He reached under his camouflage mask, removed a tooth she'd dislodged, and put it in his pocket. The men knocked her back to the ground, stomping on her hand. They burned her skin with a cigar and slashed her throat with a razor. "After they cut my throat they poured water in it from the river and said, 'Now you'll have something to sue about,'" she later recounted to Sheila O'Donnell and another P.I., a former Navy SEAL from Alabama who photographed and videotaped her injuries. The unmasked attacker told her, "This is the last face you'll see." Two of the men then raped her. One of her dogs, a terrier named Boo-boo, may have saved her life, attacking one of the men and biting him in the face. He threw the dog in the river and, bleeding heavily from his cheek, retreated to their boat. The other two followed. One of them lifted and aimed a shotgun at McGuire. "Oh, God, they're fixing to shoot me," she later recalled thinking, but the boat's driver revved the engine so that the shooter lost his balance as they sped off towards the gulf.[29]

McGuire crawled into her house, called her neighbors, and dialed 911. The neighbors, who lived about five miles up the river, arrived before the medics and drove her out from the camp to where they met the ambulance and transferred her. She was then taken to a Tallahassee hospital, where she was treated for her wounds. At the time she was too embarrassed to admit that she had also been raped.

"I think those guys thought they were beating up Linda [Rowland] 'cause she's the outspoken one and they got the wrong gal," says Joy. "It's easy to mistake them. They're two great big heavy women. What I think is these guys were not from Taylor County," she continues. "Three Taylor County men would not show up to beat up one ole fat gal. If they were mad they wouldn't rape and beat and threaten her. They might holler and get in a gunfight but they wouldn't do this kind of thing."

Joy had been reporting earlier cases of harassment to the FBI in Tallahassee, who had assured her they'd come down to Taylor County if something major happened. But after the attack they told her they'd only get involved if the local sheriff blew the investigation.

The Taylor County sheriff's investigation, as it turned out, was not a model of forensic efficiency. Following the attack, sheriff's vehicles drove over the crime scene. Deputies who said there was not enough blood on the ground to conform to McGuire's story never entered the blood-splattered house; nor did they ever interview Stephanie's neighbors, who went to help her and were the first on the scene after the attack. When Stephanie and Linda returned to the fish camp the next day, they found a watch Stephanie had lost during the attack that the sheriff's deputies had overlooked during their quick search of the crime scene. Sheriff John Walker soon began suggesting that her injuries were the result of a lesbian quarrel between the cousins. But Stephanie said she had gotten pregnant from the rape and had suffered a miscarriage. Joy Towles Cummings was there when she took the pregnancy test and confirms that it came up positive.

Stephanie McGuire was interviewed on the "60 Minutes" segment on Wise Use,[30] and after that Walker tried to charge her with perjury for saying that she had had a miscarriage, but the state attorney declined to prosecute. Still, in an unusual move, the sheriff's department made public an affidavit accusing her of perjury.

Phone harassment against the two women also continued for some time after the attack. They moved several times, finally leaving the county. After one move the harassing calls stopped until Joy Towles Cummings accidently mentioned their new phone number during a conversation on her own home phone. Then the calls started up again. The local newspaper also published a story telling its readers where they had moved. One of their Rottweilers was subsequently poisoned with table scraps laced with antifreeze.

"We've got her (and Linda) in a safe place now," Joy says. "They were so afraid and our local papers kept running these ugly stories about Stephanie. They don't have the support system I have with my friends and family around me. No one could get onto my farm without us knowing. I also don't go anywhere without my guns."

"60 Minutes" rebroadcast its "Dirty Fight" report on June 6, 1993. "It had tremendous impact. There was a flurry of activity in Taylor County following the rebroadcast. The Taylor County Chamber of Commerce and Procter & Gamble responded more strongly to the second running than even the first time," says State Attorney Jerry Blair.[31] Shortly after the rebroadcast, stories that McGuire was either beaten up in a bar or by "her girlfriend" were being widely circulated on the national Wise Use/Property Rights fax network.[32]

The private investigator and former Navy SEAL who had interviewed Stephanie McGuire and taken photos and videos of her injuries following the attack (and was convinced she was telling the truth) provided the pictures to the Florida Department of Law Enforcement. A female agent from the FDLE was assigned to the case on the assumption that Stephanie would be more comfortable working with a woman, but they did not get along. "It never was a good-faith investigation," claims P.I. Sheila O'Donnell, who spoke with the FDLE agent before the agent first contacted Stephanie. "She told me about how she'd heard Stephanie was a lesbian and she'd looked at her pictures and seen worse injuries that were self-inflicted," Sheila says. "She didn't know my relation with Stephanie McGuire, but was still willing to make these inflammatory prejudgmental statements, saying she was suspicious of McGuire and didn't trust her."

On July 13, 1993, the FDLE, Taylor County sheriff's office, and Third District State Attorney Jerry Blair put out a report saying that Stephanie had suffered real wounds but that they didn't believe her story.

In her book, *Soap Opera,* Alecia Swasy reports that Jerry Blair, an elected official, was pressured by Taylor County officials to bring criminal charges against Stephanie and that he had received a number of phone calls, including calls from the chamber of commerce and Dan Simmons, the Buckeye Mill's public affairs manager. "They wanted to vindicate the honor of P&G," a source close to the investigation told her. "It is in the best interest of the community and P&G that the attack didn't happen and she be discredited."

Among the findings released was a forensic lab analysis by Dr. Joan Wood of Tallahassee saying the burn on Stephanie's breast was caused by a hot Lincoln-head penny, not a cigar. But, like the profile of Jesus seen on a burned tortilla in Texas, the image of the Great Emancipator may have been in the eye of the beholder.

In an interview with State Attorney Jerry Blair, he admitted that there was conflicting evidence. "Our medical examiner and two of his associates in Tallahassee told us they considered that the burn could have been caused by a cigar or by a heated penny. There would have been a conflict of scientific testimony if we'd proceeded against her. I'm in no position to prosecute anyone or prove that some sort of attack did not take place," he says. "But we have no suspects at this time." When asked about apparent irregularities in Sheriff John Walker's investigation, he's quick to add, "At no time did we investigate the Taylor County sheriff's office. I've looked at all the investigative files and saw no evidence of dereliction."

Perhaps Blair's frankest statement came at the time the report was released in July 1993, a statement he confirms to be accurate. "I think there's been a tremendous interest [in Taylor County] in proving that Ms. McGuire lied and I can't prove Ms. McGuire lied," he told a reporter from the *St. Petersburg Times*. "I think there is a perception down there that if it could be proven in court, that instantly the image for the Procter & Gamble plant would be changed overnight, and that is not going to happen."[33]

Nonetheless, P&G's PR man, Dan Simmons, claimed that the report challenging Stephanie McGuire's account of the attack had "lifted a shadow" from the community. Joy Towles Cummings responded that "Stephanie is being victimized again. I think they never intended to investigate this from the start."[34]

In September 1993 the fish camp where Stephanie was attacked, including a trailer, cookshed, and hundred-year-old log house, was burned to the ground. Joy, a friend of hers, and her friend's father were filming pollution seepage along the riverbank when they saw the smoke. As they drove into the camp, they found Dan Simmons, Buckeye's public relations man, taking photographs of the still-smoking ruins. He appeared nervous as Joy began questioning him about what had happened and why he was there.

"Dan and I usually joke, but I wasn't in a humorous mood just then," she says. "He kept saying I'd lost my sense of humor, but you could see he was nervous. My friend Sandra was making moves like she might just push him into the river, but I figured if anyone was going to do it it was going to be me. Just the week before he'd announced how the water quality of the river was improving and how it was now safe for fishing and swimming. So when he again said how I'd lost my sense of humor, I just shoved him in the river. We were laughing when he came up sputtering and I said, 'Now who's lost their sense of humor?' It's kind of hard to climb out of that river 'cause the banks are all slick from the oil and chemicals the mill puts out. Sandra's dad's an old guy who's kind of bent over and carries a cane, and he extended it to Dan, who reached out to take a hold of it, and when he did Sandra's dad just pushed him back in with it. That really set us to laughing. I expected the sheriff would come and arrest me that night but he didn't. I figure Dan never admitted it happened 'cause if he did the guys at the mill would probably tease him forever about lettin' some gal push him in the river. Later my Greenpeace friends said I shouldn't have done that because it was violence, but I don't think so. I mean, he's the one who said it was safe for swimming and all. Besides, if we didn't have some fun around here I think we'd just about lose our minds."

Because much of the violence directed against environmentalists around the country is aimed at individuals rather than institutions, it makes it easier for Wise Use advocates, industry representatives, even politically compromised members of law enforcement to claim the attacks are personally motivated and unrelated to environmental conflicts, as may have occurred in Stephanie McGuire's case. At other times it can be genuinely hard to know if an attack was politically motivated, the result of a personal dispute, or a combination of factors. In West Virginia twenty-four-year-old Steve Kettering and eighteen-year-old Holly Folden were wounded by buckshot after a local man opened fire on their pickup truck with a shotgun. The man, Richard Beall, was later convicted of assault. Beall had briefly worked as a security guard at a dump that was the center of a local controversy. A second man, a guard at the dump, was charged as an accessory after the fact for hiding Beall's shotgun. Hilda Kettering, Steve's mother, believes it was the antidump protests she'd been leading that prompted the shooting. "Steve had eight shots and Holly was a mess, with thirty-some shots that went through her ears and cheeks. Her head was nothing but blood when I saw her," she told reporter Jonathan Franklin of the Center for Investigative Reporting. Beall and his friends claimed that Kettering had driven his pickup truck onto Beall's property and that fighting words had been exchanged before things escalated. Several area environmentalists claimed the guards from the dump had staged an ambush. The dump president claimed that no one really knew why Beall fired on the pickup. "They got him all excited, and he was the kind of guy who would shoot if he was excited," was the best explanation he could offer.[35]

In April 1993 Charles Dickson was shot, shocked with an electric taser, and had his house set on fire after he confronted two men at his rural home fifteen miles down a gravel road in Seldantna, Alaska. From 1981 to 1991, Dickson had led protests against a nearby oil-industry disposal site. Because of his environmental activities, he had lost work, been threatened, and been almost run over by a car outside a grocery store. But it had been two years since he'd settled his lawsuit against the oil companies involved. Besides, the two men who attacked him also stole his tools, and home burglaries are widespread in rural Alaska.

Asked what he thinks might have motivated the attack, Dickson says he has no way of knowing. "People ask me if I think this is retribution. Everyone I know asks. I don't know why this happened. All I know is I'm lucky to be standing."[36]

Still, despite occasional confusion over motivation, the great majority of anti-enviro attacks are on people—housewives, wilderness advocates, schoolteachers, journalists, mill and factory workers—who had little or no experience of criminal violence until they became politically active around environmental issues.

On June 5, 1993, a historic country store in Lloyd, Florida, fifty miles northwest of Taylor County, was burned to the ground in an arson fire. The boarded-up store was owned by Bob Rackleff, a former speechwriter for Jimmy Carter and leader of environmental opposition to a controversial sixty-four-mile-long petroleum pipeline and Texaco tank farm planned for the area. The Colonial Pipe Company, the pipeline contractor owned by a consortium of oil companies, had run TV and radio ads attacking Rackleff. Someone was also distributing "Just Say No to Rackleff" bumper stickers.[37] Over a four-year period, Rackleff received a number of threatening phone calls. Three months before the arson, a "fact sheet" put out by Colonial suggested that "one benefit from the pipeline and [oil] terminal Mr. Rackleff might welcome is Texaco's promise of a fire truck and training for Lloyd's volunteer fire department. With that truck at the ready, Lloyd residents could respond more effectively if Mr. Rackleff's store catches fire again [the store, which was in need of restoration, had been partially damaged in a 1984 fire]."[38] Following the arson fire, Colonial Pipeline offered to match the state fire marshal's $1,000 reward for information leading to the arrest of the arsonist, going on to suggest that while "there is no link between our proposed project and this criminal act," the "dangerous and unsightly" appearance of Rackleff's store had "generated a strong reaction from local residents."[39]

On August 30 a lumberyard owned by Bill Addington was torched in Sierra Blanca, Texas, a poor, predominantly Hispanic town, population nine hundred, ninety miles east of El Paso. Addington has been a leading opponent of a huge 128,000-acre sludge dump that receives forty to seventy railcar loads of New York City sewage sludge every day. Someone had tried to burn down his lumberyard in July 1993, but that fire was spotted and contained. The August blaze, which "was kind of spectacular," according to Addington, generated flames sixty to seventy feet high, took six hours to bring under control, and smoldered for two days before finally dying out. The fire destroyed about $20,000 worth of hardwood lumber along with piping, tin, and other materials Bill stored for his family's Guerra and Company general store across the road. He also lost a number of antiques from the days his grandfather ran the store, including a cast-iron Detecto penny scale with a round glass face that Bill remembers being weighed on as a child. "Money can't replace my granddad's stuff," says the fast-talking activist with the west Texas twang. "This fire was fueled by hate and fear. It was really meant for anyone else who speaks out, or is thinking of speaking out, because they know they're not going to stop me."[40]

"It worries me sometimes, because we don't know who did it

and might do it again," Carolina Bustamante, another member of Save Sierra Blanca, the local antidump environmental action group, told the *El Paso Times.*[41]

MERCO, the company that runs the dump, responded to Save Sierra Blanca by setting up its own Wise Use group called CARE, Community Action for Resources and Environment, made up of dump employees and their families. MERCO sent two busloads of CARE protestors to the state capital when Texas Attorney General Dan Morales filed a suit against the company that's also been the target of an influence-peddling investigation in New York.[42] After the arson fire the Texas attorney general sent a couple of his people to meet with Addington.

"We're a sacrifice zone," Bill Addington claims. "I hate to use buzzwords, but it really is environmental racism the way they've placed this dump out here in a poor Hispanic area and the way the stench coming through town is making people sick. They've spread this web of money from New York City to Sierra Blanca, and they've damaged my hometown by turning us into a garbage-based economy, by dividing the community, and by turning people against each other. Aside from the violence I think it'll take a generation just to fix the distrust they've spread."

"This is Silkwood country," says Kansas activist Lauri Maddy, a four-foot-eleven, hundred-and-fourteen-pound blond dynamo who in the course of her ten-year campaign against a Wichita area chemical company has twice come close to death in high-speed highway confrontations.[43]

"I was coming home from a Vulcan [chemical company] Community Involvement Meeting, where I'd confronted the plant manager about water quality," she recalls of a December 1991 incident. "After I got a burger, I noticed I was being followed for about seven miles, so I sped up, and this white pickup truck came up and tapped my bumper at 60 mph. It pulled up next to me and I could see they had tinted windows. I slowed down but they wouldn't go ahead of me so I could see their tag. We were on I-35 speeding through Wichita, and I decided to get onto K-15 where there were more [police] officers, and they slid up next to me again and hit my side panel, where we were, sixty feet up on this overpass, and they tried to bump me up and over so that I'd flip off this viaduct, and that scared the hell out of me. It was so sudden and intense where I had no place to get away from them. For a mile after that overpass, they stayed side by side with me, trying to force me into this canal that runs along the side of the road through Wichita. I finally spotted this cop up ahead, and they did too, because they slammed on their brakes and did a complete turnaround, spinning their truck with all this smoke from their tires and heading back up this one-way street." Scared as she was, Lauri was also impressed by the evasive 180-degree "hand-brake" or "Rockford File" turn that's taught in police and private security antiterrorist driving courses. It requires that the driver turn the wheel hard to the left while hitting the emergency brake to lock the rear brakes and spin out the vehicle, and then shifting back into drive just before the end of the spinout. An electric solenoid switch could have also been installed, so that the regular brake pedal would lock the rear brakes.[44] "It was real Batmobile type stuff," Lauri says. "I'd never seen anything like it." Unfortunately when she asked the policeman if he'd also seen it, the answer was no. She filed a report with the Highway Patrol but nothing came of it. "I got home and I guess I was still ashen. My husband said, 'What happened to you?' and then my kids began to cry."

Lauri Maddy had just been released from a month's stay in the hospital when she was interviewed about this and other incidents. She had had a tumor removed from her bowel, bladder, and spine during this, her eleventh hospitalization in a decade. "It was horrid but I'm getting back on my feet," she says.

Since moving in the early 1980s to a neighborhood near the Vulcan and Alvedo chemical complexes, a pair of adjacent plants that produce pentachlorophenol and feedstocks for chlorofluorocarbons (CFCs) and agricultural fumigants, Lauri and her family have suffered a series of debilitating health problems. Her husband developed brain lesions and suffered a stroke at age thirty-eight. One of her three children also began suffering seizures, as did the children of seven other residents among the group of twenty-eight Haysville, Kansas, citizens who formed Neighbors Against Pollution (NAP) in 1984.

Six years later, when Lauri was protesting increased production of pentachlorophenol and expansion of the Vulcan facility, one of her dogs was shot and another drowned. "It was a very active period," she recalls of the early spring of ninety-one. "Greenpeace was in and out of the area, helping us with our campaign. Then one day the police notified me that my dog Bear had been found in a field three houses away from us, shot in the back with a .357 magnum. We still have the bullet," she adds. "Bear's a big hundred-pound Australian blue. We put him into doggie surgery and doggie rehab, which cost us a fortune. His spine was damaged so that he was paralyzed in his hindquarters but we've worked with him over time. His spine's healed now so that he can get around pretty good." A few weeks after Bear was shot, her other dog, Rup, was found drowned in their pool. "She was a blue/Labrador mix, about four years old and eighty-five pounds. I'd gone to the grocery store and my friend went out to clean the pool and found Rup floating in the middle of the water. Normally if one of the dogs fell in they'd claw along the side to the ladder and pull themselves out, but there were no claw marks or anything like that. It was very creepy."

Lauri has been told that Vulcan has shown videotapes of her to its employees, numbering between seven hundred and a thousand, saying that she's responsible for layoffs and the added costs of pollution-prevention equipment they've had to install over the years. A former plant manager joked that he was also allowing derogatory cartoons of Lauri to be hung on the company bulletin board.[45]

"I'm not targeted as highly as I used to be. I've become more high-profile, nationally active, and they know not to mess with me a lot," she claims. Still, in August of 1992, someone felt confident enough to take a shot at her.

"I'd been down at Strother Field [a Superfund site] talking to a couple of workers who were unhappy that they were not being provided with bottled water while working in this polluted zone and also some rural neighbors of the cleanup site," she says. "I was on K-15 heading home, traveling north, when this red Mustang started following me. It followed me for a long time. I was driving a sports car, a Fiero, and we were probably going ninety-five mph. I was looking for a cop because this guy was really spooking me—he was coming right up on my bumper. I finally figured enough is enough and hit my brakes, and he went speeding around me. And I remember the blast from the gun and sparks from my windshield and they just kept going. I don't know why I did what I did next, but I pulled over to the side of the road, stopped the car and bawled like a baby, I was that scared."

When she exited at the next town, the police examined the dime-shaped hole and fracturing of her windshield. It appeared that a small caliber round like a .22 had creased the windshield. They suggested it might have been fired as a warning. "It's hard to accept that maybe they've tried to kill you," the forty-year-old activist admits.

Even more reminiscent of the mysterious 1974 death of anti-nuclear activist Karen Silkwood was the autumn 1993 death of New Mexico Navajo activist Leroy Jackson. Leroy, forty-seven at the time he died, was a founder and leader of Dine Citizens Against Ruining the Environment—Dine CARE—an antilogging group on the Navajo reservation. Dine is the Navajo-language term for the tribe, which operates on the largest Indian reservation in the United States, covering parts of Arizona, New Mexico, and Utah. On October 9, eight days after Leroy was first reported missing, his body was found by New Mexico state police on State Highway 64 at the Brazos Bluff Lookout, east of Tierra Amarilla and twenty-five miles south of the Colorado state line. The window curtains of his white Dodge van were closed and his body was lying in the back with a heavy blanket pulled up over his face and some blood congealed under his head. There were no apparent signs of struggle. Because the state police crime unit was at the site of a shooting homicide at the time, no fingerprints or photos of the van were taken at the rest stop before it was towed sixty miles south to Santa Fe for processing. A pack of Camel cigarettes and some loose tobacco were found in the van when it was searched in Santa Fe.

The State Office of the Medical Investigator (OMI) later ruled that Leroy died of "methadone intoxication" and that his body contained traces of Valium and marijuana. Methadone is an orally administered synthetic narcotic given to heroin addicts to curb their craving for opiates (often mixed with orange juice or in a cherry-flavored syrup). An adverse reaction to the drug can cause bleeding from the nose and mouth, which is what the police concluded caused Leroy's blood to pool below his head. Leroy's wife, Adella Begaye, his physician, David Lang, and his friends and fellow activists all insist that Leroy was a healthy individual, a long-distance runner who didn't smoke cigarettes, drink alcohol, or take drugs. "There is no history of his being a drug abuser of any type," agrees state police spokesman Major Frank Taylor. Leroy did suffer from occasional migraine headaches, for which he had a Valium prescription.

As an activist Jackson had received a number of death threats and had been hung in effigy by angry loggers at a 1992 prologging rally. Jimmie Bitsuie, a board member of the Navajo Forest Products Industry (NFPI), the tribal-owned company Leroy was fighting, warned a reporter that "somebody's going to get hurt" if logging was cut back because of Leroy's activities. And at a public meeting in Window Rock, Arizona, on September 28, a few days before Leroy disappeared, new threats of violence were raised by angry out-of-work loggers.

The threats were not taken lightly by Leroy and his friends. The Navajo reservation government had had a long history of corruption and violence under the previous administration of Peter McDonald (now serving fourteen years in prison). There were several unsolved deaths during Peter McDonald's reign, and in July 1989 McDonald's supporters staged a riot in which two people were killed. Before his disappearance, Leroy Jackson was scheduled to travel to Washington to give testimony to Department of Interior officials. He'd planned to protest alleged corruption inside the tribal logging company (which had gotten $14 million in debt selling timber at 45 percent of its commercial value) as well as a Bureau of Indian Affairs proposal to exempt Native American logging companies from laws protecting the Mexican spotted owl, a threatened species. Brenda Norell, a reporter and friend, had discussed with Leroy the possibility that he might be killed because of his work. "I warned him to be careful, to watch his back," Brenda said. "He joked that if he were killed the police would have a long list of suspects to deal with because he had made so many enemies. . . . When I heard he'd disappeared, the first thing I thought was, 'Well, they got him.'"

Dine CARE's President Earl Tulley said that Leroy joked (perhaps prophetically) that the only way his enemies were going to get him was if they put something in his drink.

At the time of his death Leroy Jackson had been an activist for just over three years. He'd become involved in the forest protection cause in 1990 when he'd gone up to his mountain hogan (a traditional Navajo dwelling) in the Chuska Mountains and found the surrounding Ponderosa pines marked with blue paint. Several months later he and his wife returned to the hogan to find that all the marked pines, including many old-growth "grandfather trees," had been cut down. He became concerned that the reservation logging was destroying sacred springs, medicinal herbs, and ceremonial sites of traditionally minded Navajos. These concerns led him to cofound Dine CARE. With his group he fought to reduce logging on the reservation, and his activism brought him into conflict with the Navajo Forest Products Industry. In the summer of 1993 he convinced the Navajo Forestry Department to reduce the size of NFPI's Tohnitsa timber sale on the eastern flank of the Chuska Mountains from twenty-five to fifteen million board feet. NFPI claimed that this reduction caused them to lay off eighty-five of their four hundred employees, although George Arthur, chairman of the Navajo Agricultural Products Industry, later told the *Denver Post* that "mismanagement rather than environmentalists" led to the layoffs.[46]

Still, Leroy was deeply troubled by the prospect of any Native American jobs being lost on the poverty-stricken reservation. "It was a conflict that really disturbed him, that he really agonized over, and I don't think I or anyone else could give him a clear solution to the problem," says Sam Hitt of New Mexico's Forest Guardians environmental group.[47] However, Leroy's wife and

friends strongly deny that he was in a seriously depressed or sui-
cidal state at the time of his disappearance. They point out that
he was looking forward to his trip to Washington, that he had just
purchased a herd of sheep to graze on some land he owned, and
that he had contracted for a new solar-passive house in the woods
below the Chuska Mountains, one of his favorite spots. There,
under a ninety-foot "grandfather tree," one hundred of his
friends and family would later gather to bury him.

Leroy, who traded in Navajo weavings and antiques, was last
seen in Taos, New Mexico, on Friday, October 1. That morning
photographer Richard Spas wrote him a $1,200 check for a
century-old Navajo weaving. In the last reported sighting of him,
Leroy then went to pay a Taos merchant $800 for a rug he'd re-
ceived earlier. The $406 dollars in cash later found by police in his
van closely matched the remaining funds he'd have had from
these transactions.

After his body was found, the state police told his wife that a
witness, a hiker who used the Brazos rest stop as a take-off point,
claimed to have seen Leroy's van parked there on October 2, the
day after his disappearance. But a tow truck operator cruising the
route looking for business says he didn't see it there when he went
by on October 4, and Dr. David Lang also says it wasn't there
when he cruised up and down U.S. 64 searching for his missing
patient and friend on October 6. Leroy's supporters argue that if
the van had been parked there, in one of the poorest parts of rural
New Mexico, for more than a week, it would have either been
vandalized or investigated and reported by local hunters, who are
active in the area and tend to keep an eye out for each other. They
believe Jackson died somewhere else and that the van was then
driven to the rest stop, perhaps to assure that his body would
be discovered and serve as a warning to other environmental
activists.

"We think it was a murder, based on the various discrepancies
that have surfaced," says Sam Hitt.

"It was a professional murder," agrees Brenda Norell, who covers reservation politics for the Associated Press and says she'd

never felt things so polarized as they'd gotten just before her friend's death.[48]

State police spokesman Frank Taylor admits that the police have been unable to resolve the conflict in testimony between the hiker and the other two witnesses, since all three remain firm on the dates they claim they saw or didn't see the van parked in the rest area. After two months, with many questions still unresolved, the state police decided to close the case, ruling it an "accidental death due to methadone overdose."

"The medical investigator told us he died in reaction to a moderate, not a lethal, dose of methadone," Taylor explains. "He didn't have his pain medication with him when he died and his family told us he sometimes took nonprescription medication for his headaches. Maybe a friend gave it to him telling him it was a pain reliever. Or maybe, because he was an activist, someone gave it to him without his knowledge with intent, maybe not to kill him but to discredit him, to make him look like a drug user. Right now there's a lot of speculation like that, a lot of theories but not much to go on."[49]

With the state police having declared the death "accidental," the FBI declined a congressional request from Representative Bill Richardson (Democrat of New Mexico) to initiate an investigation of their own.[50]

Local environmentalists, frustrated by law enforcement's response, have hired a private investigator, hoping he might be able to turn up some new leads. In the meantime Leroy Jackson's wife, Adella Begaye, has testified before the Navajo Tribal Council, which had previously refused Leroy's requests to testify before them. Speaking in Navajo, with an ABC camera crew, several other reporters, and officials from the Navajo Forest Products Industry looking on, Begaye argued against any new logging in the Chuska Mountains. After listening respectfully, the council voted to continue the logging.

In June of 1993 Kansas activist Lauri Maddy was one of some thirty victims of anti-environmental violence and harassment who met at the Highlander Center in New Market, Tennessee.

The center is a conference, meeting, and research facility with a history of social activism that goes from CIO unionism in the 1930s and the civil rights movement in the sixties to environmental justice issues today. "We all realized that what was happening to us was real, that no one believed us, and there was nowhere to turn," Lauri says. Out of that meeting came an agreement to use Lauri's Rose Hill, Kansas, home as a clearinghouse and repository for what was termed a People's Network database on harassment.

"There'll be a hot line for environmentalists who've been harassed and plans for what we call 'healing and dealing' [posttraumatic counseling]," she explains. "We'll try and raise money in 1994 to establish the network as a permanent and ongoing program."

Lauri Maddy and others agree that some of the most disheartening cases of attacks on environmental activists are those that succeed in silencing people. In the Midwest a mother and her daughter were the only ones in a small depressed town to openly oppose an incinerator that brought three hundred jobs to the area. The same day she received a telephone threat, her daughter was run down and seriously injured by a hit-and-run driver. After she was released from the hospital, their protests ended. In southern Indiana a couple won a lawsuit against a coal company that was causing land subsidence. They were later forced to move after threats that they'd be burned out if they didn't. In New Mexico a woman whose dog was killed moved to avoid further violence. In Appalachia a group of people stopped their environmental protests after a series of violent attacks. A man who was harassed and lost his business in southern Missouri after protesting a local source of pollution stopped his complaining and later refused to talk to a reporter about what had happened. A group in Michigan has been the target of a campaign of threats and violence for protesting a plant where a major chemical accident took place but are afraid to go public with their story. In timber towns in Oregon, Washington, and Montana, people who have been labeled "environmentalists" have been forced to move.

"The woman who headed up the opposition before I got here is terrified," says Kathy Kellogg, the ex-reporter who is fighting the IWS landfill in southeastern New York. "She's been so frightened that she doesn't want to do it anymore. A lot of people are keeping silent for fear of harassment even though they don't want the dump."

"They won. They shut me up. I certainly don't see any good that would come from talking to you [a reporter] about it now," is how another victim summed up the feeling of those citizens who have given in to anti-enviro violence and intimidation. Asked if things might have gone differently if there had been better police response, this victim admits that lack of interest on the part of local law enforcement played a role in his decision to surrender his First Amendment freedoms. "It's not worth possibly getting killed over," he explains.

Police response to anti-environmental attacks, particularly the pattern of harassment and threats that usually proceeds overt acts of violence, has been generally weak. In some areas where a single industry dominates the local economy, the police may reflect the biases of that industry, treating environmentalists with greater suspicion and distrust than other crime victims. Many local agencies, challenged by the day-to-day task of combating widespread street crime, have simply decided to leave political and terrorist-related investigations to the "suits" from the FBI who seem to like those kinds of time-consuming high-profile cases. The problem with that occurs if the FBI then turns around and tells local law enforcement that environmentalism is a source of terrorism but that violent anti-environmental radicals are not.

THIRTEEN

Failure to Enforce

*One crazy person calls me at two o'clock in the morning and explains
to me how he is going to blow my brains out with a .357 magnum.
That shook me up.*
PATTY FRASE, NATIONAL TOXICS CAMPAIGN FUND

We don't have the manpower. If you turn up dead,
then *we'll investigate.*
MENDOCINO SHERIFF'S DEPUTY, to Earth First!
activist Judi Bari when she complained of death threats

"On April 6, 1970, Mr. Robert Waldrop, local representative of the
Sierra Club, 235 Massachusetts Avenue, N.E., Washington,
D.C. (WDC), made application for the use of National Capital
Parks to 'peacefully petition the government for immediate action
to preserve the environment and to express citizens' concern for
environmental problems,'" reads a June 1970 FBI intelligence
report that goes on to identify speakers, groups, and individuals
associated with the "coalition of students and conservation organizations" who put together the first Earth Day on April 22,
1970.[1]

Other FBI reports attempt to link the environmental activists
with organizations the bureau has already targeted for surveillance, infiltration, and disruption. One report claims that a leader
of an inner-city antifreeway group "has been publicly identified
in the past as a Communist Party leader." Another report is concerned with "the *Mound Builders Gazette,*" a newsletter out of

Takoma Park, Maryland, that plans to provide "in-depth coverage of the polluters and the protectors of the environment." The FBI report states that the *Gazette's* editor, "according to another Government agency was formerly associated with the Students for a Democratic Society (SDS) at George Washington University, with the Southern Christian Leadership Conference and was one of the prime movers in Action Coordinating Committee to End Segregation in the Suburbs, better known as ACCESS. The SDS is characterized in an appendix page attached hereto."

As twenty million Americans gathered peacefully across the nation on April 22, 1970, for what would later come to be identified as the birth of the modern environmental movement, the FBI ordered its agents into the streets of between forty and sixty U.S. cities to spy on the Earth Day rallies.[2]

In New York they report on the more than one hundred thousand people marching down Fifth Avenue, which has been closed to "internal combustion engine" traffic by order of Mayor John Lindsay.

In Denver, the FBI's surveillance teams record the remarks of Senator Gaylord Nelson of Wisconsin, a founder of the event, as he declares, "Earth Day may be a turning point in American history. It may be the birth of a new American ethic that rejects the frontier philosophy that the continent was put here for our plunder, and accepts the idea that even urbanized, affluent, mobile societies are interdependent with the fragile, life-sustaining systems of the air, the water, the land."

In Washington, D.C., the FBI observes "a contingent of George Washington University students" chanting "'Save our earth. . . . About two P.M., the group, numbering about 750 persons, moved out in the direction of the Interior Department. Some of the signs carried were 'Save Our Earth—Concern, Inc.,' 'Save Our Seas: We Demand a Moratorium on All Off Shore Drilling,' and 'End the Fascist Rape of America.' Some persons wore paper surgical type masks and one had a gas mask." The FBI agents stay with this crowd as it rallies at the Interior Department and then marches on to the Sylvan Theater, where ten thousand demonstrators have gathered to listen to music and speeches.

"Shortly after 8 P.M., Senator Edmund Muskie (D), Maine, arrived and gave a short anti-pollution speech," the FBI report continues. "Senator Muskie was followed by WDC journalist I. F. Stone, who spoke for 20 minutes on the themes of anti-pollution, anti-military and anti-administration. Denis Hays [*sic*], National Coordinator for Environmental Action, WDC, followed and gave a short anti-Vietnam war and anti-pollution talk. Phil Ochs was the next speaker. He made a few anti-war, anti-administration remarks and then introduced Rennie Davis, one of the convicted defendants in the Chicago Conspiracy Trial. Davis spoke for approximately ten minutes . . ."

To understand why federal agents were spying on citizens peaceably practicing their First Amendment rights of free speech and assembly, it's important to recall that the late 1960s was a period of tremendous political and cultural polarization in America. By the spring of 1970, the FBI under J. Edgar Hoover was engaged in a domestic war on dissent. Its COINTELPRO, or counterintelligence program, had targeted Martin Luther King, Jr., Malcolm X, Dr. Benjamin Spock, Abbie Hoffman, Jane Fonda, anti–Vietnam War activists and veterans, student radicals, the Black Panther party, civil rights groups, the National Lawyers Guild, and many other organizations and individuals as enemies of the state. Surveillance, wiretapping, infiltration, disruption, and armed raids were the tools the FBI used to carry out its domestic war under a broad mandate to repress "radicals and revolutionaries" put forward by the Johnson and Nixon Justice Departments. Within that context, the growth of a broadly popular antipollution movement was seen by Hoover's FBI not as a healthy expression of citizen participation in a free society but as another source of dissent and subversion.

In 1971 Senator Ed Muskie called the FBI spying on Earth Day "a dangerous threat to fundamental Constitutional rights," after the D.C. surveillance report was slipped to him by an official from one of the many police and intelligence agencies that had received copies. "If anti-pollution rallies are a subject of intelligence concern, is anything immune?" the Democratic senator wondered.[3] The following year the Watergate burglary of the Democratic National Headquarters would answer his question.[4]

Although the FBI's professionalism and commitment to operating within the law would improve following the death of J. Edgar Hoover in 1972, a similar pattern of abuse may have developed beginning in 1987 as the FBI sent its domestic terrorism squad in pursuit of radical environmentalists. On the last day of May, 1989, FBI agents in full body armor raided a modest house in Tucson, Arizona, pushing past the wife of a suspected terrorist leader and into his bedroom. There they woke him up and arrested him, naked, at gunpoint. The alleged terrorist was former Wilderness Society lobbyist and Earth First! cofounder Dave Foreman. The night before his arrest, a series of red flares in the desert sky had signaled to dozens of FBI SWAT commandos in helicopters, on foot, and on horseback, who swooped down on a couple of Earth Firsters in the process of trying to blowtorch the legs off an electrical pylon that was part of a statewide water project. It hadn't been hard to find them: they had been driven to the spot by their friend and co-conspirator FBI undercover agent Michael Fain.

In press conferences and trial presentations following these arrests, federal prosecutors and the FBI would claim that their two-and-a-half-year-long investigation (involving fifty to a hundred agents and costing more than $2 million) had broken up a "Green Mafia" directed by terrorist mastermind Foreman to sabotage nuclear power plants in three states, a horrific example of "ecoterrorism" that might have resulted in radioactive releases if not for the swift action of the FBI's domestic terrorism squad.[5] Interestingly, it had been only three years since George Bush, as vice president, had overseen a task force on terrorism that concluded that components of the infrastructure such as nuclear power plants and the national power grid might make attractive targets for terrorists and ordered the FBI to anticipate and prevent such attacks.[6]

Foreman's defense attorney, famed cowboy litigator Gerry Spence, who had represented Karen Silkwood's family after her mysterious death, privately argued that what the FBI had were a few disgruntled people on the fringes of Earth First! who had been involved in damaging power lines and a ski lift. What the FBI wanted, he argued, was to implicate Foreman in a major conspiracy to discredit environmentalism.

Spence's defense was helped along by the discovery of a tape of Fain talking with other FBI agents, with his body mike still on, forgotten: "This [Dave Foreman] isn't really the guy we need to pop, I mean in terms of an actual perpetrator. This is the guy we need to pop to send a message. And that's all we're really doing . . . Uh-oh. We don't need that on tape. Hoo boy."[7]

The Earth First! conspiracy case came to trial in the summer of 1991. But after two months of argument and testimony (including that of an Earth First! informant who'd been paid $54,000 by the FBI and confessed on the stand to being a regular consumer of peyote, LSD, heroin, barbiturates, marijuana, and speed) the trial ended not with a bang but a plea bargain. In a compromise agreement that the judge referred to as "a package deal," four defendants pled guilty to one count of vandalizing a ski lift and were given sentences ranging from thirty days to six years in prison, while Foreman pled guilty to a single charge of conspiracy based on his handing the FBI informant two copies of his book, *Ecodefense: A Field Guide to Monkeywrenching*, which describes various ways of sabotaging industrial equipment.

The FBI's domestic terrorism investigation of Earth First! based out of their Phoenix office (with Washington oversight) had, over the previous four years, expanded through several states, including California, Montana, and New Mexico. In the course of their investigation, the FBI established more than sixty phone taps on people in communication with Foreman, including Judi Bari in northern California (the San Francisco office of the FBI has more than six hundred pages of documents on Earth First! in its files).[8] When Bari's car was bombed in May 1990, the FBI declared it a terrorist incident based on the unsubstantiated claim that the bomb was being knowingly transported by the two Earth First! victims. The San Francisco FBI office then seized the telephone records of Judi Bari, Daryl Cherney, and a dozen other environmental activists, and sent 634 long-distance numbers found in them to FBI field offices throughout the United States with requests for subscriber information. Agents from two other federal law enforcement agencies have since confirmed that the FBI was investigating Earth First! as a terrorist group at the time, although the FBI publicly denies this.[9]

"Domestically the FBI may have been a victim of its own success," says a congressional source involved in oversight of the bureau and its $35 million annual domestic terrorism budget. "Real terrorist incidents had declined dramatically by 1990. The left-wing Weatherman remnants, the right-wing Order, the Puerto Rican bombers and the JDL had all been defeated or quieted down. It made the FBI look silly to then be going after environmental crunchy-granola types, but that seems to be what they were doing."

According to files released under the Freedom of Information Act, the FBI's interest in Earth First! goes back more than a decade, almost to the founding of the group in 1980. With its motto "No Compromise in Defense of Mother Earth!" and advocacy of vandalism (what it calls "monkeywrenching"), Earth First! quickly displaced the Zodiac-riding, toxics-protesting daredevils of Greenpeace to gain a reputation as the "bad boys" (and girls) of the environmental movement.

Earth First's guerilla theater actions—for example, running a huge black plastic "crack" down the front of Glen Canyon Dam or dressing up as wild animals at public hearings—and its members' willingness to face arrest to protect unpaved wilderness won the small "nonmovement" widespread respect among activists and nature lovers. Ed Abbey, the famed naturalist writer whose 1975 novel, *The Monkey Wrench Gang*, inspired Earth First's founders (and who himself had been the subject of a twenty-year-long FBI investigation),[10] saw in Earth First! one of his literary notions of a half-mad, half-lovable gang of redneck ecologists come to life. However, Earth First's advocacy of monkeywrenching—which included pulling up surveyor stakes from Forest Service logging roads and burning or disabling expensive logging and mining equipment—made some mainstream environmentalists uneasy. But what really began to isolate Earth First! from its many supporters and provided resource industries a propaganda weapon with which to bludgeon environmentalism was the decision to push beyond vandalism and risk endangering people through the advocacy and use of tree spiking, the driving of saw-shattering spikes into trees on public lands scheduled for clear-cutting.

Earth Firsters insisted that by giving the Forest Service warning of tree spikings, monkeywrenchers avoided violence while delaying or preventing below-cost public timber sales. This sounded suspiciously like the Provisional IRA's rationalization that by giving a twenty-minute warning to the British army before its bombs went off it was providing a safety buffer against civilian casualties.

In May 1987 George Alexander, a worker at Louisiana Pacific's Cloverdale, California, mill was almost killed when his bandsaw exploded after hitting a sixty-penny nail. The "spike" had been countersunk into a twenty-foot log from a small second-growth tree, what timber workers refer to as a "pecker pole." George's throat and face were slashed and his jaw broken as the flat of the bandsaw blade wrapped around his face, knocking out a dozen teeth. He might have bled to death had not friend and co-worker Rick Phillips applied pressure to his jugular vein for more than an hour until emergency medical personnel finally arrived. There had been no warning of any tree spikings or organized protests in the Cameron Ridge Road area near Elk, California, where the young spiked tree had been cut, although LP President Harry Merlo was quick to condemn the incident as "terrorism in the name of environmental goals." The Sonoma County sheriff's investigation led to a suspect, a Los Angeles man with a history of aberrant behavior who periodically set up camp in the Cameron Ridge area. Neighbors described him as "a survivalist type." Unfortunately, the sheriff was unable to develop enough solid evidence to charge the man. Alexander, who had been trying to get his supervisor at the mill to replace the old bandsaw that shattered, was surprisingly equitable about the conflict the timber industry was claiming almost cost him his life. "I'm against tree

spiking, but I don't like clear-cutting either," he told a local reporter from his hospital bed. After his recovery Alexander turned
down an offer to go on an industry-sponsored tour denouncing
ecoterrorism. Although Louisiana Pacific put up a $20,000 reward
for information leading to the conviction of the tree spiker responsible for the near-fatal incident, Alexander had to file a lawsuit to win a $9,000 injury claim against the company and was
subsequently laid off when they shut down the mill.

Despite Earth First's insistence that monkeywrenchers always
marked spiked trees and warned authorities when an area was
spiked (their point being to prevent the trees from being cut in
the first place), the George Alexander incident provided a sober-
ing warning for those willing to heed it. Tree spiking became an
increasingly divisive issue within the group, eventually leading
Judi Bari and other prominent activists to renounce the practice.[11]

In the summer of 1993, two Montana men were convicted of
felony charges growing out of a tree spiking incident in 1989 in
Idaho's Clearwater National Forest. Two other men who had been
with them in eighty-nine pled guilty to misdemeanor charges.[12]
Despite a campaign by Wise Use/Property Rights and the timber
industry to portray tree spiking and other forms of "ecoterrorism"
as common and widespread occurrences, the Idaho case is the
only instance in the United States of someone being tried and
convicted for environmentally motivated tree spiking.

"A lot of monkeywrenching turned out to be much less than
thought. Almost everybody, including law enforcement, overre-
acted to it," says Steve Robinson, director of Fire and Law Enforcement for the Bureau of Land Management. Robinson is in
charge of 250 BLM agents who enforce the law on 270 million
acres of public lands. "In the past few years, anytime a D-9 Cat
got vandalized everyone immediately thought, 'monkeywrenchers,' although often it was just some sixteen-year-old kids," he
says. "We have not had any convictions for ecoterrorism on the
largest existing U.S. land base. From a public relations stand-
point, I think environmentalists realized how counterproductive
this sort of thing was and turned against it. Even Earth First! re-

alized it wasn't working, and are now doing sixties-type protests. This summer they were blocking access to a Forest Service area in Idaho, sitting in roads knowing they'd get arrested. It was very nonviolent. There's been no sabotage of any kind that we've seen." I ask him how he could then explain the FBI's apparent ongoing interest in ecoterrorism and lack of interest in violent attacks on environmentalists. "They're their own unique outfit," he says diplomatically.

"The FBI has not been even-handed in crime prevention," admits the congressional source quoted earlier. "The FBI's underlying mind set is that defense of the status quo is not terrorism but challenging it is, so in that light they may see property damage as more serious than attacks on individuals. I think there's undue attention and a misallocation of resources in this ecoterrorism stuff while the anti-environmental violence could at least be called criminal activity that the FBI is ignoring."

Resource industries have also made a concerted effort to keep the FBI and law enforcement in general focused on environmentalists as the perpetrators rather than the victims of crime. Within months of the founding of Earth First! in 1980, the FBI received its first warning about the group from the Salt River Project, a major southwest utility that was later cited by the EPA for generating much of the smog that obscures the Grand Canyon. In 1982 the FBI sought an extortion indictment against Earth Firsters who handed Secretary of Interior James Watt a letter threatening civil disobedience protests if he continued his environmentally damaging policies.[13] The U.S. attorney in Denver told the FBI it didn't have a case. When Lois Gibbs, executive director of the Citizens' Clearinghouse for Hazardous Wastes, requested her FBI file under the Freedom of Information Act a few years ago, she was told it couldn't be released because she was listed as an "extortionist."

More recently the FBI has been identifying (and misidentifying) Earth First! "spin-off" groups for industry and other law enforcement agencies, creating problems for local environmental activists. In May 1993 an alliance of the National Audubon Society, Wilderness Society, and Forest Guardians of New Mexico was denied a conference room at the Albuquerque Holiday Inn on the day Secretary of Interior Bruce Babbitt was holding public hearings at the hotel on federal grazing fees. Department of Interior officials told the hotel manager that members of the alliance included "radicals," and that one of them had a long arrest record. An internal DOI memo that later surfaced indicated that the FBI had told Babbitt's staff that the Santa Fe–based Forest Guardians was "a radical Earth First! spin-off group" and that one of its leaders, Sam Hitt, had a long arrest record. Neither statement was true. Alliance members have since filed a civil suit against the agencies involved.[14]

The FBI turned down two written requests for interviews for this book. In May 1993 I sent a one-page letter requesting a meeting to discuss, among other topics, "the status of ecoterrorism and related 'special-interest' domestic terrorism . . . how the bureau determines when patterns of crime take on the characteristics of organized terrorism and when this becomes an issue of concern for law enforcement . . . a sense of the FBI's work in the field of domestic terrorism . . . and what impact (if any) political pressure and media concerns play in determining allocation of resources."

Several weeks later Agent Ray McElhaney of the FBI's Office of Public and Congressional Affairs explained that the FBI would decline the interview because "your questions are too broad and would require speculation, and we don't deal in speculation."

In September 1993 I sent a three-page letter to the FBI, again requesting an interview. Among the specific questions I asked this time were these: "On ecoterrorism I would like to know if the FBI has held seminars on this topic at Quantico or elsewhere. . . . Has the FBI participated in joint industry–law enforcement seminars? . . . Is the FBI aware of a pattern of criminal activities directed against environmentalists? . . . Who determines FBI involvement in crimes such as postal death threats, arsons, assaults, and shootings that may be politically motivated? . . . Is there anyone in the bureau looking at anti-environmentalist attacks as politically motivated group violence?"

This time Ray McElhaney was more specific about why the FBI would not agree to an interview. "We as an agency can't comment and won't comment on domestic terrorism or investigative sources, methods or techniques or cases that we're working on or cases that we've worked on in the past. You need to use FOIA [Freedom of Information requests, which take about three years to complete] for that." He did offer to make agents available to discuss the jurisdictional basis under which the FBI investigates environmental crimes such as hazardous waste dumping. "They won't be able to discuss any specific cases, however," he cautioned. Nor would they be available for an interview during the time this reporter was in Washington, D.C.[15]

The FBI, however, has not been the only law enforcement organization whose interest in "ecoterrorists" grew in the 1980s along with membership in environmental groups opposed to the policies of the Reagan and Bush administrations. The Federal Law Enforcement Training Center in Glynco, Georgia, trains all federal agents other than the FBI and DEA. Some seventy-five agencies, from the Secret Service to the Fish and Wildlife Service, send their law enforcement agents to Glynco. Here agents take a survey course on what the trainers call "environmental extremist groups," using the *FBI Bulletin* and Nexus as part of their training curriculum.

"I do some of those terrorist class presentations in Glynco. It's an overview. We lump the different groups: animal rights, Greenpeace, Earth First!, and Sea Shepherd, all those groups with the same kind of confrontational tactics together," says Forest Service Special Agent Carla Jones. Jones, based out of the Forest Service's District Six office in Oregon, is her agency's leading "expert" on Earth First! She takes calls from and exchanges information with "both law enforcement and industry people."[16]

Scott Curley, the training center's senior instructor on domestic terrorism, is a little more careful about distinguishing terrorist from protest activity. "We have a domestic terrorism course which covers the Dave Foreman element of Earth First! and the Animal Liberation Front. Those are the only two groups that fit

the FBI definition of terrorism. We also have environmental activist group instruction, which is part of our 'Demonstrations and
Protests' course. We look at the tactics of particular groups.
Greenpeace might chain themselves to a gate or a building's en-
tranceway, for example. Their tactics would be different from, say,
the Ku Klux Klan. We have a practical exercise at this building
here on the grounds where we role-play a sit-down protest and
our students go up in twos and place them under arrest, take their
booking photos, and so forth. We also look at Greenpeace and Sea
Shepherd as part of our Seaport Security program."

Scott Curley worries that a potential source of future violence may come from (animal rights) antihunter activity and hunters' response. He admits he hasn't heard much about anti-
environmentalist violence or anti-enviro groups. "We're not up to
speed on that," he says. "The first time we really heard of it was
when we saw it on "60 Minutes" [in September 1992]. We ran a
Nexus search on the Sahara Club after they interviewed their top
guy. We do mention them in our course, but we don't have any
materials on them." Curley doesn't see Earth First! as posing a
serious threat to domestic tranquility. "There's more violence in
U.S. post offices than in the entire environmental movement," he
believes. He notes that there has been more Earth First! activity
on the East Coast recently, particularly demonstrations in the
Southeast, "but of the First Amendment, legal-protest type."

Unfortunately, Agent Jones of the Forest Service has developed the bad habit for a law enforcement officer of failing to distinguish between malicious criminal acts, civil disobedience, and
protected First Amendment protest activities. "Probably there's
been a decline of vandalism on the West Coast, but it's increasing
in the Midwest and East Coast. It's all the same stuff: spiking
trees, pulling survey stakes, blocking roads, sitting in trees. We
even had two helicopters burned," she says (failing to mention
that the helicopter incidents took place thirteen and seventeen
years ago). "Now it's going on in Idaho and Colorado, Ohio, Pennsylvania, and Vermont."

I tell her that I've just returned from Vermont, where I'd spoken to state officials. The only criminal incidents they'd mentioned involved a resource agency employee who'd been punched and had his video camera smashed by an angry property owner.

"They [Earth First!] had a demonstration near a logging road with more than a dozen people," she says. "The Forest Service has been dealing with Earth First! for fifteen years now. We know these people," she adds defensively, sounding like someone trapped in a codependent relationship.

In 1986 Congress budgeted specially earmarked funds for a Forest Service force of special agents to counter the cultivation of marijuana on public lands, but the agency has since drafted its "pot commandos" to break up logging protests in the woods. In July 1988 several paramilitary pot commandos aimed high-powered rifles at tree sitters in Oregon's Siskiyou National Forest while sheriff's deputies climbed up to arrest them.[17] Pot commandos have also been used to make arrests and to enforce forest "closures" against campers and hikers where federal timber-sale protests were expected. They were active in the summers of 1992 and 1993 tracking and arresting Earth First! sit-in protestors in the Nez Percé National Forest in Idaho, where the Forest Service has proposed opening up 76,000 acres of land to logging in the largest wilderness area in the lower forty-eight states.

Recent media reports and congressional hearings revealed that during the last decade, while the Forest Service was directing much of its law enforcement resources against Earth First! it was also allowing the timber theft of millions of dollars worth of trees from the national forests by logging companies and independent gyppo loggers. On October 5, 1993, frustrated Forest Service law enforcement agents and a former U.S. attorney from Oregon testified in Washington about "a systematic breakdown of the Forest Service law enforcement program" resulting from the agency's desire to "get the cut out" for industry. One agent testified that Forest Service senior officials often worked with the timber thieves to sabotage investigations.

With documented cases of "monkeywrenching" declining in the 1990s, resource industries such as timber and mining, along with their anti-enviro supporters, have had to work more creatively to try to maintain law enforcement interest in their cause by identifying potential new sources of "ecoterrorism." To that end, Mountain States Legal Foundation, Wilderness Impact Research Foundation, and the Center for the Defense of Free Enterprise have all set up "terrorist hot lines" or hired private security agents to infiltrate Earth First! and other environmental groups, although nothing has come of these donor-funded efforts. Grant Gerber used his background as an army intelligence officer running agents in Cambodia to coordinate the operation. "We set up a sabotage line for reporting acts of terrorism by Earth First! We hired some people to infiltrate the group. We had one guy who got real close to the top guys, was really on the inside but could never give us enough to set up a sting or anything like that," he says regretfully.[18]

Although the Wise Use spy operations were probably legal, the Mountain States Legal Foundation should have been charged with torturing an acronym for their 1-800-TESTIFY hot line: the initials stood for "Tell of Environmental Sabotage and Terrorism Interfering with Freedom—Yours." Many of the line's calls came from environmental pranksters reporting clear-cuts, smog alerts, and toxic spills. Mountain States also sponsored something called "The Intermountain Logging Conference Forum on Eco-Terrorism."

A number of more recent ecoterrorist tales being promoted by the anti-enviros are either highly speculative or made out of whole cloth (or synthetic fiber). Beginning in 1991, a string of murders occurred in the Midwest: eight men were killed in the woods by a sniper using a high-powered rifle. The victims included hikers, hunters, and fishermen. At the time Kathleen Marquardt of the anti–animal rights group Putting People First syndicated her own weekly newspaper column, "From the Trenches," to hundreds of newspapers and publications around the country. In her October 27, 1992, column she wrote that some sportsmen "suspect that these murders are the action of 'animal rights' extremists who have taken 'hunter harassment' to a new and grisly plateau." Later in the piece she admitted that "if these murders are connected, the anti-hunting motive may be unrelated."

"The update is they caught the guy. It had nothing to do with animal rights," Marquardt casually conceded in a June 1993 interview,[20] before going on to suggest that the *E. coli* outbreak at a Jack-in-the-Box restaurant in the Pacific Northwest that left three children dead and hundreds ill may have been antimeat sabotage. "I heard it was sabotage, that somebody planted feces on this meat to scare people off of eating meat," she claimed. Asked for the source of her vegetarian murder theory she said, "I talked to somebody who talked to Jack-in-the-Box."

On April 14, 1991, the *San Francisco Examiner* ran a page-two article from the Newhouse News Service titled, "Tale of a Plot to Rid Earth of Humankind." The tale was provided by ex-CIA Agent Vincent Cannistraro, who claimed that a cabal of "radical environmentalists" were developing a recipe for a virus that could kill humans but leave other species unharmed, a kind of neutron bomb for animal lovers. Next to the story, the *Examiner* ran a large photo of Earth First! cofounder Dave Foreman. Cannistraro had worked with Oliver North on the National Security Council providing CIA funds to Contra leader Arturo Cruz in the mid-1980s. By the time his "Andromeda strain" story ran, he was working for the National Strategy Information Center, a CIA-associated beltway think tank that dabbled in "low-intensity warfare" doctrine and counterterrorism.

Ron Arnold, who has spoken at joint industry/law enforcement meetings over the years and brags of being an FBI "asset"—a CIA term that sounds better than the FBI's own, "informant"—was once caught inventing an imaginary ecoterrorist hit squad for the foreign media. In a 1986 trip to Wellington, New Zealand, sponsored by the Agricultural Chemical and Animal Remedies Manufacturers, Ron alerted the press to the fact that the United States was experiencing a dangerous "upsurge of ecoterrorism. We have had power stations blown up, bridges burned, electrical transmission towers collapsed, forest trails booby-trapped with wired shotguns, attacks on forestry pesticide application crews, Forest Service officers shot to death and numerous other acts of violence in the name of the environment," he was quoted by the *New Zealand Herald*.[21]

Ron was later asked to cite his sources in a deposition taken as part of a lawsuit brought against the government by activists who claimed they were being targeted as marijuana growers because of their antipesticide work (an industry strategy originally suggested by Arnold). Transcripts of the deposition show attorney Paul Merrell questioning Ron:

Q. Could you tell me where any Forest Service officer has been shot to death in the name of the environment?

A. Yes.

Q. Would you do so?

A. Yes. In southern Oregon the case is documented in a General Accounting Office report called "Illegal and Dangerous Activities on the Public Forest" or some title of that effect circa 1986, eighty-five, which is where I got that information.

Q. Does this report identify the persons who shot the Forest Service officer or officers as doing such an act in the name of the environment?

A. As I recall, it was described as what's commonly called a mule or a hired person sitting on a marijuana patch who shot and killed a Forest Service official who happened to stumble across the guerrilla plantation.

Q. What was there about the incident in southern Oregon . . . that links the incident to "in the name of the environment" unquote?

A. A number of documents that have been found on destroyed equipment. Are you familiar with my *Reason* magazine article on this subject?

Q. No, I'm not.

A. Well, that will elucidate it in much more detail and a very stern editor checked out all the information in it. Perhaps it would give you a better basis on which to ask questions.

[Later in the deposition they return to the subject.]

Q. Mr. Arnold, this morning you spoke briefly about an article you had written in *Reason* magazine.

A. Yes.

Q. From the February eighty-three edition entitled "Eco-terrorism."

A. Yes.

Q. Am I missing something? I don't see anything in the article about marijuana. I've just been skimming it rather rapidly.

A. There's nothing in there about marijuana.

Q. How does this connect with a Forest Service official being killed near a marijuana patch?

A. Well, if you'll open that up to the next page from where you are you will see the facsimile and a transcription of a note that was from some group that purported to be an earth-loving group that had just blown up or otherwise destroyed a large amount of logging equipment. Those events and notes are evidently fairly common.

The person who gave me that indicated that that was not the only one that they had ever seen. And the class of types of actions that you see elucidated in that article, all acts of violence, all by people who have various ideological beliefs about the environment and I categorize those the same as people who—of the environmental movement who both use and cultivate their own marijuana to be associated through those links which are shown in numerous arrest cases and such as that. That's the connection.

Q. How does that relate to a Forest Service official being killed on a marijuana patch? I'm still not clear.

A. I just answered the question.

Green P.I. Sheila O'Donnell sees a well-thought-out strategy in the anti-enviros' constant promotion and use of the term *ecoterrorist*. "I see that calling an environmentalist a terrorist sets up a fear dynamic. It makes the police and private security firms begin to worry," she says. "It sets the stage for a counterreaction and makes anti-environmental violence seem like an acceptable response."

The Federal Bureau of Investigation defines *terrorism* as "the unlawful use of force or violence against persons or property to intimidate or coerce a government, the civilian population, or any segment thereof, in furtherance of political or social objectives." Ongoing attempts to silence environmentalists through intimidation and violence would seem to fit this definition more readily than declining incidents of sand-in-the-crankcase vandalism against logging and mining equipment. However, federal law enforcement agencies continue to pursue "ecoterrorists" and spin out low-grade intelligence data on "Earth First! spin-offs" while refusing to address the more violent and potentially deadly attacks against green activists. In 1992, the year Pat Costner's home was burned down, Diane Wilson's dog was shot and boat nearly sunk, Paula Siemers was stabbed, Anne LaBastille's barn was burned, the Adirondack Council office vandalized, and dozens of other environmentalists were harassed, shot at, and assaulted, the FBI reported that "there were no suspected terrorist incidents recorded in 1992."

This double standard can also be seen in law enforcement's response to who is being harassed. Wise Use activist Kathleen Marquardt of Putting People First was delighted with the swift federal response she received after reporting death threats from suspected animal rights extremists. "The FBI and the D.C. Terrorist Task Force worked with us after the threats. A couple of agents came to my house and talked to me about what security precautions to take. They were very concerned. They gave us a set of guidelines to follow. Every once in a while if something comes up in their investigations [of the Animal Liberation Front] they'll call and say take extra precautions for the next four days and I'll wait on the porch with my shotgun when my teenage daughters come home from their dates. It has a side benefit," she smiles engagingly. "I don't think my daughters are going to get into trouble on their dates."

By contrast, most environmentalists who've asked the FBI to help investigate threats or attacks against them have been told their cases don't fall under the FBI's jurisdiction, although local SACs (special agents in charge) of the bureau's fifty-six field offices have considerable discretion in how they interpret the laws under which they're allowed to initiate an investigation. When Tony Winters was harassed and Dr. Jack Woodard's dog killed before they could testify in Winters's federal lawsuit against Merck, there was clearly a legal basis for an FBI investigation of witness intimidation and denial of access to the federal court system. But when Tony Winters called his local FBI office in Albany, Georgia, he was told the feds weren't interested "unless it had an international flavor." Similarly, Greenpeace's request that the FBI investigate the arson that destroyed Pat Costner's home in Arkansas was rejected for failing to meet the FBI's "criteria." Pat Wolff, one of the few environmental victims who has gotten the FBI to look into a death threat (after she approached her neighbor, an FBI agent), was asked to give her fingerprints, questioned about her ex-husband, and left with the impression "that it wasn't a very big priority for them."

If environmentalist victims of terrorist-type attacks suspect that political considerations have limited their ability to receive equal protection under the law, they aren't alone. The abortion rights movement began asking for some form of federal protection of clinics and medical workers in 1983. The fact that none was forthcoming is reflected in statistics gathered by the Bureau of Alcohol, Tobacco and Firearms showing that by September 1993 there had been more than 125 bombings and arson attacks on family planning clinics resulting in millions of dollars in damages.[22] In addition there were more than one hundred butyric acid (nausea-inducing "stink bomb") attacks, burglaries, and trashings. One doctor was murdered, another wounded, and a clinic manager paralyzed for life from a shotgun blast. These terrorist tactics seem to have had their desired effect. Despite prochoice public opinion, 83 percent of U.S. counties now have no abortion providers. Many doctors admit to being afraid to provide this medical service. For those who aren't afraid, Right-to-Life militants are more than willing to offer reminders of why they should be. In February 1993, a month before Dr. David Gunn was shot to death in Pensacola, Florida, 34,000 medical students across the country received an antiabortion magazine called *Bottom Feeder*, which featured such "humorous" suggestions as, "What would you do if you found yourself in a room with Hitler, Mussolini and an abortionist, and you had a gun with only two bullets in it? Shoot the abortionist twice."[23]

Because the FBI refused to define attacks on abortion clinics and providers as "terrorism," most of the clinic bombing and arson investigations fell to the Bureau of Alcohol, Tobacco and Firearms. Although ATF has been successful in catching several abortion clinic bombers in New York and Florida, their much smaller size and limited resources make them a less effective agency than the FBI in battling the growing nationwide campaign of violence and intimidation.

"If you think the fight over abortion, right-to-life versus pro-choice has gotten ugly, wait till you see what the fight over the environment has turned into. When money and jobs are involved it can turn violent, and has," is how Leslie Stahl introduced the September 20, 1992, "60 Minutes" report on Wise Use and anti-enviro vigilante violence. That was before the Pensacola murder of clinic physician Dr. David Gunn. As of January 1, 1994, there was no proof of any environmentalist having been murdered at the hands of an anti-enviro vigilante or private security thug but the possibility, especially in light of Navajo activist Leroy Jackson's mysterious death, remains frighteningly real.

Beginning in 1983/84 the Subcommittee on Civil and Constitutional Rights of the House Judiciary Committee was approached by abortion rights groups who felt that they were not receiving adequate protection from law enforcement. Initially these groups presented committee Chairman Don Edwards and other congressional and staff members documentation of the pattern of attacks, then they provided monthly reports of hits on family planning clinics. The subcommittee made a number of contacts with the Department of Justice and held its first hearings on the problem in 1985. It would take another seven years of lobbying, street-level organizing of "clinic-defense" teams, and the murder of a well-respected doctor before the seriousness of the problem was fully recognized with the passage of the federal Freedom of Access to Clinic Entrances (FACB) legislation in the spring of 1993.

In contrast, by the end of 1993, five years after environmental organizers began encountering violence and intimidation on a widespread scale, none of the big Washington environmental lobbying groups had formally approached the government to request congressional hearings, a Justice Department investigation, or any other kind of legislative or law enforcement response to the problem.

"I watched that '60 Minutes' show and thought, darn, I wish they hadn't run it, it's going to scare people," said Greenpeace Executive Director Barbara Dudley after being introduced to me and told that I was investigating the violence. "I wonder what the appropriate way is to respond to intimidation in a way that empowers people?" she added when asked if the movement wasn't obligated to acknowledge that its frontline people are under attack.[24] The irony is that Greenpeace, which has been a victim of terrorist attacks both at home and abroad, is the only one of the major D.C.-based environmental groups to have taken any action on behalf of grassroots victims under attack. The Sierra Club, Wilderness Society, National Wildlife Federation, Audubon, and other organizations that have done fundraising in response to the Wise Use/Property Rights backlash, had, by the beginning of 1994, failed to commit any of their funds or lobbying resources to defending the lives and safety of locally based activists who are the foundation of their movement.

"Up until now the environmental movement's response to this problem has sucked," says Lauri Maddy, the Kansas activist and target of harassment who is helping organize the "People's Network" hot line and database on anti-enviro violence.

Labor and civil rights leaders, long familiar with right-wing vigilante attacks on their movements, also see serious problems with the greens' response. "The environmental movement has not had a history of grassroots struggle. That's not to say there aren't many grassroots environmental movements, but the national organizations have been very limited in responding to these right-wing attacks," explains Dr. Ben Chavis, executive director of the National Association for the Advancement of Colored People (NAACP). "Of course, part of the Wise Use movement is an attempt to blame environmentalists for the bad economy, just like others blame immigrants or minorities for the bad economy. The Reagan-Bush legacy and the economic situation in our country, the confluence of those two factors, make fertile ground for an increase in right-wing activity not only in the environmental but also in the civil rights arena. We've taken a very strong posture of not taking attacks lying down," he adds by way of example. "Every time one of our offices receives a threat or is bombed, we immediately go on the public record not only to express our outrage, but also to make it crystal clear that the NAACP will not be intimidated by these right-wing and reactionary tendencies."[25]

"It's the responsibility of social and political movements not to let people drop by the wayside," says Chip Berlett of Political Research Associates, a Cambridge-based think tank that studies right-wing movements in America. Berlett is one of a handful of investigators around the country who've followed the growth of anti-enviro violence and its impact on grassroots activists. "For the big environmental groups, violence may be too hot an issue to handle, so they respond by ignoring the problem, hoping it goes away," he believes. "But for many of the people who've been attacked there's an emotional crisis occurring. Many of these victims suffer post-trauma syndrome. They need help. To remain silent may make sense to the fundraisers who don't want to scare people but it's morally unforgivable."[26]

Also bad strategy. Without a strong push from the environmental lobby, public law enforcement agencies—which are facing a rising wave of nationwide crime including antiabortion violence, Islamic fundamentalist terrorism, and escalating hate crimes directed against minorities and immigrants—are unlikely to seek new ways of giving themselves extra work by pursuing anti-environmental extremists.

"Because these investigations involve highly politicized cases is one reason they've gotten the [extra] manpower investment they have," says Lieutenant Pete Person of the Bureau of Criminal Investigation (BCI) of the New York State Police. Person is overseeing the investigation ordered by New York Governor Mario Cuomo after the arson and vandalism of 1992 in the Adirondacks, one of the few instances of law enforcement taking a proactive role in trying to solve these pattern crimes.

"The bottom line in our job is to ensure nobody gets hurt. I wouldn't be comfortable with an organized conspiratorial group operating around here, which is why I believe in preventive maintenance," the state trooper explains, indicating how increased police interest in vigilante activity can reduce violence. "If you know I'm considering you a suspect and questioning you and talking to other people about you and tracking leads, you'll be less prone to go out and commit another crime," he says. Person admits that actually capturing and making a case against the anti-enviro arsonists, vandals, and shooters is "like chasing black flies in the Adirondacks." Still, it's notable that an escalating pattern of political violence seemed to level off when the state police got involved.[28] "I think it would be horrible to be attacked and not have the police there to help you," says Adirondacks park victim Anne LaBastille, describing an experience more common among environmentalist targets of intimidation and violence than the close cooperation she received from the New York State Police after her barns and vehicles were torched.

"It may take someone getting killed" has become a common refrain among frontline environmental activists and investigators of anti-environmental violence. The worry has arisen that, owing to a combination of federal law enforcement bias and movement denial, no one has taken at face value the Wise Use declaration of a "holy war against the new pagans who worship trees and sacrifice people."

"It's like waiting for the other shoe to fall," says P.I. Sheila O'Donnell. "And when it does, there'll be blame enough to spread around."

FOURTEEN

The More the Change

*For civilization as a whole, the faith that is so essential
to restore the balance now missing in our relationship to the earth
is the faith that we do have a future.*
SENATOR AL GORE

Power concedes nothing without a demand.
FREDERICK DOUGLASS

A joint government/industry plan to develop an environmentally friendly car that gets eighty miles to the gallon. A nationwide biological survey to classify America's botany and wildlife. An EPA plan to eliminate harmful pesticides by the end of the decade. New fees for grazing, logging, and mining combined with "eco-management" of tens of millions of acres of public range and forest lands. A quarterly meeting of top officials from government, industry, labor, and the environmental movement seeking new approaches to sustainable development. Global agreements on climate change and biodiversity. The establishment of new national parks and wilderness reserves. From a Wise Use/Property Rights perspective, the Clinton administration, after an uncertain takeoff, has begun to sound like their worst green nightmare come to life.

Environmentalists and long-time political observers, on the other hand, are far from convinced that the administration's low-cost plans and agreements come anywhere near to meeting their forest-green rhetoric. *"Plus ça change plus c'est la même chose,"* says Brock Evans, vice president of the National Audubon Society.

"Excuse me?" I respond.

"The more the change, the more the same thing," he says, quoting Voltaire. "I see this as a hundred-year war and we all play our parts. I said before the election, if Clinton wins we can't expect heaven. We can expect to get maybe 65 to 70 percent of what we want. Well, that's not heaven but it sure beats the hell out of the 5 percent we've been getting for the last twelve years."[1]

"Teddy Roosevelt, FDR, and Carter were gung-ho environmentalists. They were balanced off in this century by the Reagan administration. I think our hope with Clinton was for a Carter with effectiveness, but my gut feeling is this is just another average Democratic administration," says the more skeptical Mike McCloskey, chairman of the Sierra Club. "Clinton is very wary of regulation on industry except for informational purposes—warning label sorts of things. He's fairly conservative on pollution and energy, somewhat better on natural resources. I think there's going to be more symbolism than substance in environmental policy."[2]

Like a steamboat heading towards a precipitous waterfall, the ship of state under the Clinton administration is churning up a lot of water as it maneuvers around in the midstream of environmental policy. What is difficult to tell, however, is if it is trying to come about or just head for the shallows. Either way it has managed to get the traditional Wise Use land barons of the West and property rights developers east of the Mississippi all bent out of shape.

To a reporter returning to the capital near the end of the first year of the Clinton administration, it's clear that something dramatic is happening. Even in the midst of health care reform, the NAFTA debate, and new foreign policy debacles, environmentalism is, if not moving to the front burner, at least heating up the back of the stove. There are stirrings both institutionally and legislatively that have everyone slightly unnerved, a sense of change that justifies both the fears of the present crop of anti-

environmentalists and the skepticism of mainstream environmental activists. It is, as the intellectuals like to put it, a transi-
tional period in America history when the dominant paradigm no
longer applies and a new way of viewing the world emerges. The
utilitarian nineteenth-century approach to nature has run up
against the resource economics of the twenty-first century. Critical issues, largely unaddressed during the past decade, are again
on the political agenda:

· *Population growth.* Three hundred thousand people starved in
the 1992 Somalia famine, but every twenty-nine hours the world
population increases by another 300,000 people.[3] Human population, which rose incrementally over the last 40,000 years, has
doubled in the last 40 years and is expected nearly to double again
in the next 50 to around 10 billion people. Ninety percent of this
growth is taking place in the poorer nations of the Southern Hemi-
sphere, putting tremendous strain on soil, water, and forest resources and adding to such international migration patterns as
those from Latin America and Haiti to the United States. Population shifts within the United States and projected growth in areas
such as southern California are undermining long-term attempts
to clean up that region's air and water quality and protect its natural desert and coastal ecology.

· *Endemic toxic pollution.* American males now have 50 percent of
the sperm count of their grandfathers. Doctors and biologists suspect a pesticide-estrogen link. DDT and "estrogenlike" pesticides
such as endosulfan, which are still in use, are also being linked to
increased rates of breast cancer in American women.[4] A recent
study by the National Academy of Sciences found children to be
more susceptible to impacts from pesticides and other chemical
exposures than adults, but farmers continue to put nearly a billion
pounds of agricultural chemicals on our topsoil every year. Industry emits far more chemical tonnage as nonproductive waste in the
form of air pollution and runoff into the nation's waterways. Of
nearly 70,000 chemicals in commerce today, many synthesized
since World War II, fewer than 2 percent have been fully tested
for human and biological health effects. Often, the downside of
chemicals such as CFCs, PCBs, and DDT are not discovered until
serious (sometimes global) damage has already been done.

· *Loss of biodiversity.* The United States has lost 75 percent of its songbirds since 1968.[5] Migratory waterfowl are steadily declining. An estimated one-third of our Atlantic and Gulf Coast dolphins have been killed in recent die-offs linked to contamination. All major commercial seafood stocks are depleted as a result of overfishing and coastal habitat loss. Wild salmon are taking the place of spotted owls as the indicator species for declining northwest forest and watershed ecosystems. Despite some notable exceptions—for example, the bald eagle, alligator, and California gray whale— most of America's eight-hundred-plus endangered species, both plant and animal, are not recovering. Rather, thousands more species are becoming increasingly threatened by habitat loss and pollution. The American wilderness heritage of wildlife, solitude, and adversity is quickly giving way to a culture of domestication, overcrowding, and conformity. As the chances of encountering a large predator in the American wilds decrease, the chances of being victimized by a predatory member of our urbanized culture increase.

· *A changing atmosphere.* Since the industrial revolution human activity, particularly the burning of fossil fuels, has increased carbon dioxide in the atmosphere by one-third, contributing to a possible heating of the atmosphere known as the greenhouse effect and a more certain acceleration of the carbon and nitrogen cycles responsible for plant growth and decay. A more immediate concern to the world's scientists and policymakers has been the depletion of atmospheric ozone resulting from use of chlorofluorocarbons (CFCs), industrial solvents, and coolants that destroy ozone in the upper atmosphere, increasing the amount of the sun's ultraviolet (UV) radiation that reaches the earth. In February 1994 a report in the *Proceedings of the National Academy of Sciences* reported on the first possible biological impacts of ozone thinning on terrestrial life. Since the mid-1980s there have been worldwide reports of declining numbers of amphibian species such as frogs, particularly in high-elevation wilderness areas. A four-year Oregon State University study found that the hatching failure of frog eggs in the Cascade mountains strongly correlated with their exposure to natural amounts of UV radiation. In addition, frogs lacking the enzyme that helps repair DNA damage caused by UV radiation had the worst rate of egg hatching.

"The implications are much broader than just frogs," said the study's lead researcher, Andrew Blaustein. "We are looking at natural levels of UV and it's killing these eggs. If it's killing frog eggs, it is probably also having an effect on the plants and invertebrates and fish. The implications are pretty broad to other organisms, including humans."

Despite the claims of counterscience and Wise Use rhetoric about environmentalists trying to "lock up" America's productive resources, the environment is no longer seen as a relative value but as a context in which human cultures, economies, and jobs exist, along with a variety of other animal species, brightly colored plants, pesticide-resistant mosquitoes, spotted owls, and spotted cows.

The line forms early in front of hearing room S-128 in the Capitol, where a conference committee of the House and Senate is meeting to discuss a grazing-reform compromise offered by Senator Harry Reid of Nevada as part of the $13.4 billion 1994 Department of the Interior appropriations bill. After the politicians and their staffs fill up the small meeting room, there appears to be no space left for the four beefy cattle lobbyists in Stetsons who have been waiting at the front of the red-rope line. Still, they manage to squeeze in after a Senate Republican staffer comes out to usher them past the two guards at the door.

The Clinton administration, with its reintroduction of grazing reforms, appears to be slowly climbing up the learning curve. After public land reforms were pulled from the first Clinton budget under pressure from western senators, it was decided that Secretary of Interior Bruce Babbitt would announce that the reforms would be carried out administratively. But his announcement, in August of 1993, came before the Department of Interior's funding had passed the Senate, suggesting that the learning curve was still a pretty slippery slope. Western senators, borrowing a tactic Democrats used to defeat offshore oil drilling during the Reagan and Bush years, wrote a moratorium into the DOI budget denying any future funding for implementing grazing reforms. While the Senate passed the moratorium 59 to 40, the House rejected it 315 to 109. This opened the way for Harry Reid's compromise agreement at the October 14 conference committee. Voting along party lines, the House conferees voted 5 to 2 and the Senate conferees 8 to 7 to raise cattle-grazing fees from $1.86 per animal unit month (AUM) to $3.45 per AUM over three years. Babbitt had originally wanted to raise the fees to $4.28.

The AUM is the result of a system the government set up in 1934 to charge ranchers for grazing one cow and a calf or five sheep for a month on the West's 260 million acres of BLM and Forest Service public lands. By 1993 the BLM's $1.86 federal rate was well below the rate most states charged and about a fifth the rate charged for private grazing lands in the West. While the Cattlemen's Association argues that $10-AUM private lands are generally better quality range, most ranchers will admit that if not a "below-cost subsidy" their federal grazing permits are at least a better-than-average deal, which is why there are so many cattle overgrazing public lands today. Even the military, another big landholder in the West, charges three times what the BLM charges for letting ranchers graze on its property.

"In some areas it wouldn't be bad to raise fees, like around where I am. But you have to see the real plan these people are pushing is to get us off public lands, same with the miners and loggers. That's the preservationists' agenda," warns Van Blaricom, an elderly white-haired cowboy and trapper from eastern Oregon who began ranching just after World War II and recently became a member of the anti-enviro Oregon Lands Coalition. After talking about the benefits cows contribute to range ecology and wildlife, he shows me a set of glossy pictures he's just picked up from Safeway. They're of his last winter's trapping and show sixty-one thick-furred coyotes, four bobcats, and five badgers hanging from his low red barn wall. "It just pays enough to cover my [snowmobile] gas and traps and so forth, but I enjoy it, getting out there in the solitude," he explains, fingering the miniature leg-trap pin hanging from his jacket.[6]

As soon as the Senate-House conference committee agrees to

accept the grazing-fee compromise, including most of the environmental protections for rivers, range, and wildlife that Babbitt has proposed, fifteen western senators threaten to filibuster the entire DOI budget, calling Reid a "liar" and "backstabber" for agreeing to the compromise. In late October they carry through their threat. The Cattlemen's Association, which has written an antireform bill for Senators Ben Nighthorse Campbell (D) of Colorado and Malcolm Wallop (R) of Wyoming, goes all out to protect their twenty-seven thousand permitholders, calling in their chits with those western senators whose campaigns they have contributed to over the years. Three votes to end the filibuster fail. Babbitt, in a game of "who blinks first," declares he'll move administratively on his original plan if the Senate doesn't pass the compromise, but decides against a personal visit to the Hill to try and convince undecided senators. In a final head count reform supporters find themselves 4 votes short of the 60 needed to overturn the filibuster and are forced to pull the compromise proposal from the budget.

Senator Alan Simpson (R) of Wyoming and other hard-liners have won out against a majority of the House and Senate with their anti-"preservationist" arguments and warnings that increased fees will destroy the western way of life and "do those old cowboys in." Not everyone is buying their argument, however. An editorial in the Wichita, Kansas, *Eagle* takes Republican leader Bob Dole to task for siding with the permitholders. "Western grazing areas are public lands. They belong to all Americans," the *Eagle* declares. "The American people deserve fair compensation for the use of their property. It's sad that Dole wants to continue subsidizing western ranchers when Kansas has one of the nation's most efficient and productive livestock industries—an industry that does not get government support."[7]

In a *New York Times* article titled "Wingtip 'Cowboys' in Last Stand to Hold on to Low Grazing Fees," reporter Tim Egan points out that the top 10 percent of grazing permitholders control half the public grazing lands. Numbered among this elite are the Metropolitan Life Insurance Company, the Mormon Church, the

Japanese-owned Zenchiku Corporation of Montana, Hewlett Packard's William R. Hewlett and David Packard, and various oil and mining concerns.[8]

At around 12:45 A.M. on October 31, the new range war over grazing and mining seems to escalate dangerously. In the early morning hours of Halloween day, someone tosses a leather satchel or case containing a powerful explosive device onto the flat roof of the Bureau of Land Management building in Reno, Nevada. The bomb blows a three-foot hole in the roof, causing $100,000 worth of damage to the building and six office workstations below. The explosion can be heard from five miles away. Witnesses report a black Honda with an American flag attached and a pickup truck speeding from the scene just after the blast. The FBI and ATF are called in to investigate.[9] A short time later, BLM receives a letter warning, "If you think Reno was something, you haven't seen nothing yet." It is postmarked North Platte, Nebraska, and signed the "Tom Horn Society." Tom Horn was a late-nineteenth-century gunman hired by western livestock interests to kill rustlers and scare off settlers.

The Department of the Interior in Washington has the scale if not the beauty of the arid West whose resources it oversees. Built in 1937, its building consists of six massive rectangular stone boxes with smaller boxes stacked on top of them. The BLM, long disparaged by environmentalists as the "Bureau of Livestock and Mining," takes up a wing on the fifth floor down a long breezy hallway past painted murals of sodbuster settlers and the Oklahoma land rush of 1889.

"If we can pass grazing reform, the rest—mining and other public lands issues—will follow, because the miners don't have the same mystique as the cowboys," says former Bureau of Land Management Director Jim Baca. "It's a new reality to recognize this is public land. Traditionally the livestock industry viewed it as their lands, and they sense a loss of control with these reforms that they didn't expect, which is why you're getting this intense backlash."[10] Hearing this kind of talk from the head of the BLM is not unlike hearing Russian President Boris Yeltsin declaim on the failures of communism.

Baca, formerly New Mexico commissioner of public lands, is a short, rotund man with a thin graying mustache, gray-brown hair, and a western string tie. With the calm assurance of a miscast sheriff, he has staked his reputation on his ability to turn around a federal agency long under the sway of the West's land barons. "One of the most valuable changes we're undertaking is going from livestock advisory boards to resource advisory councils, which instead of just ranchers will include environmentalists and industry and scientists to balance this greater demand for multiple use, meaning more than just ranching and mining now. There's a demand for recreation and scenery and wilderness, and I see a lot of combat ahead and there's always going to be that," he admits.

"Wise Use gives a number of these conservative congressmen and senators a chance to assert their views, to reflect what they want to believe is true," he claims. "I've watched these groups form and spread with the county ordinances and show up in town meetings and I think they've become a force. On public lands they're certainly influential way beyond their numbers. Still, I see us making significant change. I want to see more mediation on the local level. If we do grazing and mining reform, a lot of problems will be resolved."

Four months later Baca is gone, a victim of the environmental backlash he's fought against as well as Secretary of Interior Bruce Babbitt's new willingness, in the wake of the Senate defeat, to compromise with western grazing interests whom he now refers to in private meetings as "this 800-pound gorilla I've got to deal with."

In late January of 1994 Baca was offered a "promotion" to Deputy Assistant Secretary of Interior which would have given him more pay, but less power. His outspokenness on grazing, mining, and other reforms had offended several western politicians, including Governors Cecil Andrus of Idaho, Mike Sullivan of Wyoming, and Roy Romer of Colorado, who had been complaining to Babbitt. "Frankly, my friend, you don't have enough political allies in the West to treat us this shabbily," Andrus had written to the secretary after a disagreement with BLM Director Baca over a proposed air force bombing range (that Andrus favored) in an Idaho wilderness area. When the White House began to ask why Baca was being reassigned against his will, Babbitt's Chief of Staff Tom Collier lobbied the western governors to make their complaints directly to President Clinton in order to deflect any subsequent criticism away from Secretary Babbitt.

In a private meeting on February 3 Babbitt told Baca his services at BLM were no longer desired. Baca responded by handing him his resignation letter. Later in the day Babbitt told a reporter from the *New York Times* that the BLM director's departure "does not reflect any change in public lands policy . . . I am deeply committed to getting grazing rules worked out and also to getting reforms of the Mining Law of 1872 enacted." Other officials at the Department of the Interior backed up their boss, insisting that Baca's differences with Babbitt were a question of management style, not of substance. "He and the secretary just didn't have the same approach to the issues," said one midlevel policymaker.

Neither environmentalists nor Wise Use types were buying that. G. Jon Roush, president of the Wilderness Society, claimed Baca's departure raised "disturbing questions about what direction it [the administration] will now take on mining law and grazing reform."

"Secretary Babbitt is trying to move a reform agenda without alienating the opponents of reform," said Sierra Club Executive Director Carl Pope. "I don't think he can achieve it, and I think it is foolish to try."

Myron Ebell, Chuck Cushman's Washington lobbyist, gloated that Baca had been "an absolutely radical preservationist . . . dedicated even more so than Babbitt, to driving natural resource industries off federal land."

"One down and 99 to go," is how Mike Fusco, field coordinator for the New Mexico Cattle Growers Association, responded to news of Baca's resignation.

"We went out there [to D.C.] to get something accomplished, we didn't go out there to continually fold to the lords of yesterday. And that's what's going on," claims Jim Baca in an interview from

New Mexico a month after his resignation. He's returned home to run for governor against incumbent Democrat Bruce King, a rancher. "Babbitt has no backbone and so he can't stand up for his principles," charges Baca. "I mean he believes in these things, but if he gets pounded on by the governors, pounded by the senators, he backs down every time. I've dealt in these issues a long time and some of these groups who have had sway over the public land use for so long won't compromise no matter how much you try and give them, no matter how much you try and work with them; it's never enough. My message has been let's work with them but when we make a decision let's make it. When I did these things as state land commissioner in New Mexico, when I raised the grazing fees you thought the world was going to end. They bitched and moaned and talked about how I was putting everybody out of work and two weeks later it was like it never happened."

On March 17, 1994, after months of western field-hearings and attempts to find a consensus-based approach to range reform similar to Clinton's Northwest Forest Plan, Babbitt announces his new range-reform program. "There were some who said our [original plan] might threaten traditional resources. In some ways they were right," he concedes before going on to suggest that future decisions on range management and environmental recovery be made by local "multiple resource" councils, made up of ranchers, public officials, and environmentalists recommended by the western governors, which would then develop rules tailored to each state. "Those closest to the land, those who live on the land, are in the best position to care for it," Babbitt declares. Under the new plan grazing fees would be increased over three years to $3.96 per AUM rather than the $4.28 he'd originally proposed. There would also be an incentive fee, a 30 percent discount to ranchers who treat the public lands better than required under the new rules.

"These are not the resource councils we first envisioned," says Jim Baca. "We were trying to do away with the grazing advisory boards. Now they're just renaming them, handing over the man-

agement of the rangelands to these local users through boards
which will be appointed by the governors, who will appoint nothing but these special interest groups."

But the public lands ranchers, having already won significant
concessions with their table-pounding tactics, are not about to
claim a victory. "The secretary's original plan would have killed
western ranching. This proposal leaves us in intensive care," complains Mike Byre of the (Cattlemen's) Public Land Council.

In the midst of his own election campaign Jim Baca identifies
campaign funding reform as the key to any serious public lands
reform. "There's a reason Wise Use's political power outweighs
their actual numbers and that is their political contributions,
their campaign contributions to politicians in the West. I mean if
you're a governor in Wyoming, you will listen to the Cattle Growers Association. It doesn't matter about anything else. You do
what they tell you."

When you enter Congressman Mike Synar's outer office in the
House Rayburn Building, your eye is drawn to the blue- and
black-dyed Cherokee war bonnet hanging on his front wall. It has
a powerful aura of combat about it, not inappropriate to Capitol
Hill. The congressman's private office is decorated with black
leather couches, a red carpet, spiky cactus, and various Native
American artifacts, including a rounded stone tomahawk. Synar
enters, dressed in a dark suit and cowboy boots, happy to renew
an earlier discussion about one of his favorite topics, "wealthy,
whining welfare cowboys." "They're mad," he says. "Any time
you take something away that has been literally a windfall you're
going to have this kind of anger. They'll do anything. They'll use
any tactic they have and they have a number of senators and some
congressmen who don't care what the facts are.

"I think we're still in a good position with this grazing thing,"
he adds with a tight grin. "If you can't win here, you can't win
anywhere. If you can't take on 2 percent of an industry that is basically big companies, you might as well give up on mining and
timber and sustainable growth and offshore drilling and everything else. You're not going to win anything. The thing is, we're
now in a time where this country is going to make decisions that

we will live with well into the next century. We are planting the seeds we are going to come back and harvest somewhere in the year 2010, 2020, 2030, not only in the area of legislation—making progress on safe drinking water, clean air, Superfund, and so forth—but also to change the attitude on how Americans deal with the environment. In the same way the children of this country shamed the adults into recycling, we have to use this moment in time where people of like minds come together and make the progress we haven't been able to make before because of past confrontations. If we can in the next few years get the confrontation level down to where everyone's pulling on the same end of the rope, we will have done more for the environmental movement than we've ever been able to do.[11]

"A lot of this backlash is some of the most misinformed stuff I've ever seen in my life," he snaps in response to another question, losing the Clintonesque consensus-building tone and returning to the more confrontational style he seems comfortable with. "What's interesting is that the opposition to the environmental movement has also gotten smarter. They're changing their rhetoric just enough to where it sounds palatable. A good example is this Fifth Amendment takings thing. They weren't winning on the basis that we were foreclosing and trespassing and stealing land—this canned speech they'd give to the local Farm Bureau or Rotary Club meeting—so they changed their tune to 'this is the Constitution.' 'This is what Rush [Limbaugh] tells us is the intellectual argument.' They weren't winning on the merits, on the science, so they changed the subject."

Although Synar has fought to exempt Oklahoma oil wells from toxic pollution limits, he's still widely regarded as an independent-minded environmental reformer. His ranching and farming district—77 percent white and 17 percent Native American, 63 percent rural with a median income of around $20,000 a year—has the classic profile of a region where the Wise Use antienvironmental backlash could be taking place but isn't.

"When I was a freshman in Congress I was going to take on a Superfund project in my district, and I was warned by Senator Boren that to take this issue on was very dangerous because Oklahomans weren't environmentalists," he recalls. "And during that whole thing I learned something. He was right, they aren't environmentalists, they're conservationists. The ranching community really believes in their heart, as they grew up with 4-H and FHA chapters, that they had to leave it better than they found it. Secondly, the hunters like to have adequate game and good fishing for fishermen. You know, on a Friday afternoon people in a rural area that are not necessarily the richest in the world like to get Johnny and Mary and put them in the car and drive the boat out to a nice clean lake that's free and has good access and they can have the same benefits of recreation as someone who has ten times their income. So when you start dirtying their water and filthying their air and cutting them off to those kinds of opportunities, they're not environmentalists but you have changed their ability to enjoy their life and they'll be first in line to take a stand. I've never found an issue like that that Oklahomans will not embrace as quickly as people from New York City or Los Angeles."

From the Rayburn Building an aide to California Congressman George Miller walks me over to the Capitol. We hike through a large basement tunnel alongside blue, smooth-running congressional subway cars, closed to the public during "members only" rush hour. George Miller, chairman of the powerful Natural Resources Committee, which oversees public lands, minerals, water rights, Indian affairs, nuclear energy, and national parks, meets us in a crowded waiting room just off the House floor.

A big, bluff, outspoken man, youthful looking at forty-nine despite his white mane of hair and clipped white mustache, George Miller is a congressional powerhouse with an in-your-face attitude that has humbled many an opponent. "When Barbara offers a bill, Miller practically laughs at us," complains an aide to pro-mining Congresswoman Barbara Vucanovich of Nevada. Miller did laugh at fellow committee member Republican Don Young of Alaska when Young compared him to a Communist. "I know my chairman is giggling, but listen to my words," Young pleaded as he went on to argue against the committee's attempts "to socialize our natural resources" by reforming the 1872 mining law.

"You have a coalition of people who are trying to raise spurious issues, marginal issues, to try and change the debate but on the fundamental debate, public support, sentiment, and concern is growing on behalf of the environment," Miller insists. "People want their public lands preserved, they want their water cleaned up, they want to be safe from toxics, they want safe food, they want a reasonable rate of return for the public investment in dams or grazing lands or forest lands. Those are very fundamental majority positions. What you have [with Wise Use] is a lot of special interests who are trying to generate some ideological movement to try and disguise what it is individually they want in the name of their own profits, their own greed in terms of the use and abuse of federal lands.[12]

"The fact is, mining reform's going to take place," he continues. "The basic scientific argument for forest preservation or for clean water or clean air—that's growing all the time. The jobs-versus-environment argument they use is not where public opinion is at. It's not supported. That's why neighborhoods, even though it's going to create jobs, fight against incinerators. That's why neighborhoods, even though it's going to create jobs, say we don't want you to mow down our forests. That doesn't mean people don't have compassion for people whose jobs are threatened or rendered obsolete, but they still understand that they can eventually lose both, they can lose the job and the resource. And if you tell me that anti-environmental violence is on the increase, to me that's sort of a sign that they've lost the issue. The fact is, we're seeing more coalitions being formed between ranchers and environmentalists, and commercial fishermen and environmentalists, and small millowners and environmentalists. Those coalitions are forming much faster than the Wise Use movement," he says, "because these people understand, if we can make this resource sustainable I can stay in business but if I just turn it over to the big guys and they mow it down, I'm out of business. If they pollute this river I don't have a commercial fishery anymore. If the wetlands aren't restored and there's no shrimp, then I can't fish in the Gulf of Mexico. So these connections are being made at a much faster rate than this backlash.

"Most of the environmental movement is very local, where people are focused on their own town, their own community, their own region," he concludes, tapping an antique table with his fist for emphasis. "People become environmentalists because they see something in their community they don't like after they've made an investment in their home, their schools, their families. In a derogatory sense, people talk about it as being NIMBY: Not in My Backyard. But it's a logical decision about what you want to go on in your backyard. It's your backyard! And this nation considers the Pacific Northwest its backyard. It considers the Grand Canyon its backyard, the Florida Keys its backyard. The coastline of this nation is our backyard, it's where we all go on weekends, on holidays. So come on, come on. . . ." He laughs, a big dismissive laugh that has deflated more than one anti-environmental witness to come before his committee.

"I'm real excited about the grassroots environmental movement and the way it's expanding," says Lois Gibbs, the former Love Canal housewife who now runs the Citizens' Clearinghouse for Hazardous Wastes, an umbrella for local antipollution groups based out of a three-story townhouse office in Falls Church, Virginia. "We had our tenth anniversary conference with some seven hundred people last May at the Crystal City Marriott," she says. "Forty percent of the attendees were African American, Hispanic, Native American, Asian. The environment is an issue unlike any other. It affects everyone, no matter where they live, their color or income level. You can pull everyone in around something like this. I think on a community-by-community basis the anti-environmentalists are being out-shouted with each passing day. They're angry because they're losing ground and the ability to keep control."[13]

"One of the things the environmental movement does is it gets people to take a long view of life," says Dr. Ben Chavis, executive director of the National Association for the Advancement of Colored People (NAACP). "People are now thinking about this generation and about the next generation and what responsibilities we have in terms of stewardship, and I think that the right wing may have underestimated how the environmental issue penetrates even across lines of race, across lines of socioeconomic circumstance, so that these stereotypic devices the right wing uses to divide people don't work anymore. I've been in a number of communities where whites and Blacks have never marched together, but they're marching together now around the environment," he says.[14]

Chavis, a civil rights activist for the past thirty years, was instrumental in documenting and raising the issue of environmental racism: the placement of toxic dumps, incinerators, and polluting smokestack industries in low-income, minority communities. "There are several growing movements," he explains. "One is called the environmental justice movement—that's primarily people of color. There's another activist environmental movement that's primarily white. Both of these movements are moving towards convergence, which I'd call a sustainable-development movement. In spite of the right-wing vigilantes and the existence of what's known as the Wise Use movement, I'm optimistic, because as I've traveled throughout the United States, throughout all regions, I see a larger movement, a much more credible movement that's really rooted where people live. And I think the emerging environmental justice, slash, sustainable-development movement is going to be one of the bridge movements that will take our society into the next century and that will really transform American society."

The anti-enviros' response to grassroots environmental groups and the movement against environmental racism has been to deny their significance. When pressed to identify any Wise Use links to minority movements, Ron Arnold claims support from Blacks in Energy. Actually called Blacks for Nuclear Energy, this short-lived utility-industry front group claimed several dozen members in the early eighties under the leadership of Clarence Pendleton, the controversial Reagan-appointed head of the U.S. Civil Rights Commission. More recently, Chief Raymond Yowell of the Western Shoshone National Council turned down an invitation to attend CDFE's 1993 Wise Use Leadership Conference in Reno, Nevada, noting links between Wise Use activists Alan Gottlieb, Ron Arnold, Chuck Cushman, county movement attorney Karen Budd, and various anti-Indian groups in Washington State, Nevada, and Wisconsin.[15] In Washington and Idaho, neo-Nazis have tried to link up with the anti-enviro movement and are suspected in at least one protected-owl killing. "Basically, we don't think an owl is worth any white worker's job. The government has betrayed the white loggers of this country," declared Justin Dwyer, Washington State director of the White Aryan Resistance. The adoption of anti-enviro rhetoric by openly racist groups such as WAR has proved embarrassing for established Wise Use/Property Rights groups while at the same time reflecting their narrow social base.

Despite its limited appeal, the anti-enviro movement, backed by the Farm Bureau, ALEC, the International Council of Shopping Centers, the Homebuilders Association, and other developers and developer wannabes, is likely to remain active for some time to come. By focusing on wetlands, the National Biological Survey, and the Endangered Species Act, anti-enviro organizers hope to separate protection of biodiversity from the more easily understood (and widely supported) issues of pollution prevention and public lands reform. One example: just before the grazing debate heated up in October of 1993, congressional conservatives had a field day proposing and attaching "property rights" amendments to the Biological Survey Act.

The act authorizes the first nationwide effort to count and map every species of plant and animal in the United States, an effort widely applauded by the nation's wildlife biologists and conservationists. Secretary of Interior Bruce Babbitt has compared the biological survey to the U.S. Geological Survey of the last century and argues that with the knowledge it generates it will be easier to identify ecosystems under stress and begin finding ways of protecting unique and interconnected natural systems and habitats that harbor life without being forced into last-minute "environmental train wrecks." He says he wants to negotiate habitat-protection plans before the Endangered Species Act has to be invoked and huge sums of money spent on remediation efforts to try and save single species in danger of extinction, as has occurred with the California condor, desert tortoise, manatee, spotted owl, and others. The anti-enviros' response, as first proposed in the 1988 Wise Use agenda, has been to recommend gutting the Endangered Species Act where it interferes with industry.

The vicious tone of the congressional attacks on the biological survey suggest that it is seen as a stalking horse for the Endangered Species Act, which is up for reauthorization some time in the near future. Republican Representative Don Young of Alaska warned Congress that the biological survey would lead to trespassing on private property by "federal goons." "We create parks and refuges and wilderness areas, but they create no dollars for the American worker," he complained. "Mining creates jobs, trees create jobs, farming creates jobs, and American factories create jobs. That is what we should be addressing in this Congress."[16] Republican Jack Fields of Texas argued that the survey would create "an environmental Gestapo" to "confiscate property"; and helped pass an amendment to the bill that would prevent civilian volunteers from participating in the work of the survey.

Another amendment, offered by Democratic Representative W. J. "Billy" Tauzin of Louisiana, would prohibit takings where 50 percent of a property owner's value was lost owing to the use of survey data to enforce the Endangered Species Act or the wetlands provisions of the Clean Water Act. Tauzin also offered an amendment to remove references to *ecosystems* in the bill's definition of *biological resources*. Republican Robert Walker of Pennsylvania claimed that the bill was going to attempt to do a census of all the ants in the country. "What are we going to do? Send out schoolchildren to count the ants on the sidewalk on the way home? Or are we going to have Boy Scouts and Girl Scouts out doing spider surveys?" he asked, straightfaced, in floor debate.[17]

The Moon-owned *Washington Times* quickly joined the fray with an editorial cartoon showing lines of government vehicles marked EPA, OSHA, County Planning and Zoning, and so forth approaching a rural farmhouse. "Did you see the news, dear? Russia tentatively has a new constitution that would abolish the Communist-dominated congress and allow private land ownership!" reads one cartoon blurb coming from the farmhouse. "Gee, maybe we could adopt that in this country," another responds. In an accompanying commentary headed "Masters of All They Survey?" Alston Chase, a former professor who writes a syndicated column about the West from a free-market perspective, rails against the biological survey, labeling it a plot to violate property rights and hinting at dark conspiracies and "an incestuous partnership" between the government and private land trusts, including The Nature Conservancy. Labeling The Nature Conservancy "Uncle Sam's real estate agent," he reports that "in 1992 alone, it received $90.7 million from sales to state and federal governments and other conservation agencies," but fails to note that the wild and scenic lands it sold for public parks and wildlife reserves were valued at more than $109 million.[18]

The National Biological Survey Act, with its "property rights" amendments, finally passed the House on October 26, 1993, on a 225–165 vote. It was a problematic victory for resource-industry representatives like Jack Fields and Billy Tauzin. The week before, the House had approved a conference report on the Interior Appropriations bill which had included a preapproved $163 million for the biological survey. An attempt to send the conference report back to committee with instructions to add the new amendments failed on a vote of 253–174. Meanwhile, the Senate had also fast-tracked $158 million for the survey.

Anti-enviro activists cried foul. Two weeks later Chuck Cushman and his D.C. lobbyist Myron Ebell organized a "Fire Babbitt" call-in, attempting to jam the White House's internal phone lines, including some eighty to ninety lines into the White House offices of the chief of staff, domestic policy council, and the vice president.

The attack on the biological survey could, in one sense, be seen as a rearguard action, a defense of the right to practice environmental abuses on private rather than public lands. Harry Reid of Nevada recognized the shifting balance on public lands when he called on his fellow senators to "reject the demogoguery that comes from those who represent a West that no longer exists." But the approaching end of rapacious logging, mining, grazing, and water abuse may also signal the beginning of a new series of threats. Those who believe in the conquest of nature and the "taming" of the wilderness are giving way to millions of urban refugees who, in seeking to claim a life in harmony with nature, threaten to love it to death. A number of logging companies have begun subdividing clear-cut land for ranchette housing. Cattle ranches are being sold for new developments. Towns such as Bozeman, Missoula, and Livingston, Montana; Boise and Pocatello, Idaho; Moab, Utah; and Jackson, Wyoming, plus just about every nineteenth-century mining town in Colorado are going through construction booms of $200,000 to $300,000 townhouses and "mountain meadow" condo developments. Strip malls are appearing along Idaho's highways. In northern Montana near Glacier National Park, the population around Whitefish, now 70,000, is projected to boom to 200,000 over the next fifteen years. "Suddenly all these county commissioners who used to think zoning was socialistic are scrambling to impose some commercial and residential controls and talking about the need for land planning," says an aide to Congressman Pat Williams of Montana.[19]

While western senators such as Alan Simpson of Wyoming, Larry Craig of Idaho, and Dennis DeConcini of Arizona continue to fight tooth and nail for the rights of multinational mining corporations, beef ranchers, and logging companies on public lands, those who have rallied to the banner of Wise Use are beginning to discover that private property rights cut both ways. Wealthy new settlers such as media mogul Ted Turner in Montana and singer-songwriter Carole King in Idaho have closed off trails and right-of-ways across their private lands, making it harder for long-time residents to reach wilderness areas containing fish, game, and 1872 mining claims. Wise Use organizers are stymied, reluctant to join their constituents in demanding public access across private property but resentful of the environmental ethic being exhibited by far too many of these new, politically savvy property owners. Having also taken on the role of spoilers, sabotaging attempts at job-based compromises between resource workers and environmentalists, Wise Use groups are proving less adept at offering viable alternatives to those workers whose traditional sources of income have disappeared.

In 1991 Montana-based Wise Use activist Bruce Vincent, the Montana chapter of People for the West, and another prodevelopment group, the Western Environmental Trade Association (WETA), sabotaged the Kootenai and Lolo Forest Accords. These accords, drawn up between the state's timber unions and environmentalists, would have allowed for mixed wilderness and sustainable logging zones within the two national forests. At an informational meeting on the compromise held in Libby, Montana, Dennis Winters, a $6,000-a-month consultant hired by WETA (who shared his Helena office with PFW), stood up and told the crowd that the accords would cause 30 percent unemployment in their community and lead to "wife batterment, child molestation, and all the rest of it."[20] Winters, Vincent, and PFW continued their campaign against the accords for several months, linking environmentalists to unemployment, alcoholism, child abuse, satanism, and paganism. As a result of their efforts, the Montana congressional delegation eventually withdrew its support of the logger-environmentalist agreement.

Two years later, in October of 1993, Champion International, the major logging company in Montana (and a strong backer of Bruce Vincent's efforts) pulled out of the state, announcing that it would sell 867,000 acres of land to the Plum Creek Timber Company of Seattle, a firm with a reputation for finishing off dying ecosystems. Champion also sent out lay-off notices to 1,500 millworkers in Libby and other logging towns in western Montana. A recently released university study had found that during the past decade Champion had overcut Montana's forests at a rate nearly three times the sustainable rate of new growth. "I've been in the timber industry since 1951, and this is the biggest single blow I've seen—far worse than any cutbacks from environmental restrictions," said James Hill, a leader of the Western Council of Industrial Workers, which represented the timber unions.[21]

"Environmental blackmail really began in the mid-seventies with state hearings on how to implement the Clean Air Act," recalls Jack Sheehan, legislative director for the United Steelworkers of America.[22] "The steel and smelting industries tried to bring our workers out against it, saying it would cost them jobs. But

I. W. Abel, our president at the time, said we would be, 'a bridge, not a buffer to clean air.' We were part of the national Clean Air Coalition that got the act passed," he smiles proudly.

Sheehan, who looks like a tough old lizard, has been around union politics since before the AFL and CIO hyphenated. He's based out of the Steelworkers' Washington office on the seventh floor of AFL-CIO headquarters just above Lafayette Park and the White House. "When the environmental movement came up with the idea of environmental health concerns, it was embraced by labor," he explains. "You have to figure it's no coincidence that OSHA [Occupational Safety and Health Administration legislation] passed in the wake of the Clean Air Act. . . . Industry was asleep at the wheel when the 1970 Clean Air Act passed but they went all out against it in 1990," he continues. "Of course, over the years we'd established a good relationship with EPA and the environmentalists. At our 1990 international convention, we had three hours of panels on the environment. We had the chairman of the U.N. climate-change study speak and we put out a publication, *Our Children's World—Steelworkers and the Environment.* The theme was jobs and the environment do go together.

"I became aware of Wise Use about four years ago, when the American Mining Congress began approaching our members out West saying increased fees and reclamation would cost jobs," Sheehan says. "I never felt it was a particularly heavy push against the environment. They were more focused on trying to avoid paying any royalties. We had a special session of our national legislative conference on mining. Our fellows were suspicious all along that the companies were trying to roll them into their cause, and our people didn't go for it. I understand they got some miners to go to some public hearings, gave them a box lunch and a day off, that sort of thing. But most of the fervor of this backlash is still with the mineowners and the big landowners."

"The struggle has become an argument between employers and workers," says Bob Wages, president of the Oil, Chemical and Atomic Workers Union (OCAW), "with the companies saying that environmental regulation is anticompetitive, is dangerous, will result in job loss, *ergo* it's important you support our efforts to deregulate. They say if we have to comply with the clean air standards or the timber regulations or the Endangered Species Act you're going to lose your job. That's a pretty Draconian threat. That's when reason falls out the window." Wages, a husky six-footer with a broad reddish face and closely cropped red beard, doesn't buy that argument. "When I was a rank-and-file oil worker, we had 180,000 members in this union; now we're about half that size. This is the result of out-sourcing, use of subcontractors, closure of refineries because of imported product, the fact that there was redundancy in the refining system. It isn't because of environmental regulation; that hasn't cost people these jobs. That's what industry will tell people, but that's not what's going on out there in the real world.

"What's really going on," Wages continues, "is American industry wants to do in the Third World, in Mexico, and Bolivia and Nigeria what they spent a hundred years doing here. That's why we're losing jobs. They're not going to retool industry here, because they can do it elsewhere and make more money, so why should they do it here? There ought to be international labor standards and international environmental standards, but that's not going to happen as long as multinationals run the world. And the politicians won't do anything about it because the Democratic and Republican parties are a bunch of rich Washington lawyers. I've never seen such a collection of gutless wonders as exists in this town. . . . I guess I'm cynical," he admits with a sudden, unexpected smile.[23]

Wages is in D.C. to lobby the Department of Energy to make sure atomic workers being displaced by the end of the Cold War are included among the cleanup forces needed to repair the radiological mess left behind after a generation of top-secret weapons construction at Rocky Flats and other nuclear-bomb factories. Wages understands how workers desperate to feed their families can become involved in covering up radiological and chemical spills, leaks, and pollution problems. He admits he's had personal experience of it.

"One of the most horrifying experiences of my trade union life was having to walk into an auditorium in Toms River, New Jersey, during the debacle over the shutdown of Ciba-Geigy and being put in the position by the local union of having to support keeping that plant open," he recalls. "Now, this plant poisoned a whole county. There's no debate about it. More than one county. It was sitting on a toxic plume. It was seeping into the groundwater. But I was sent in there as the vice president of the union to support the workers to keep it open. Worst detail I ever pulled. What we should have been talking about is making that company make whole all them workers. I mean, the workers admitted that they poisoned all the world, because they were told to, because that's how they operated the goddamn plant for all those years, and they'd been told that if they snitched they'd be fired. We had volumes, to be able to take that company to the mat. They suborned perjury. I mean I had shit on that company. They were telling workers, 'Swear on this affidavit you never did this,' when they'd been doing it for twenty years. 'Well, I could go to jail couldn't . . . ?' 'No, no, no, it'll be all right.' Horrifying stuff. And the community outside the plant was organized around three or four women working with some clean-water groups. These people were spied on. Their automobiles were vandalized. Their utilities were tampered with. I spent three days there and it was the worst three days of my life. I've never been as ashamed of what I do. I came so close to quitting, I said, 'Fuck it! Who needs this?'"

Like an old-time labor radical, Wages believes it's going to take a long-term social movement—including guaranteed incomes for displaced workers, what he calls a "Worker Superfund"—to turn the country around. "Until we have broader options, environmental blackmail will continue," he says. "Most people, what they really care about is getting food on the table and buying sneakers for their kids, and right now they can't make socially responsible decisions because their only decision is to produce the poison or starve to death. When we're confronted with these issues, we tell our people that the enemy is that polluting company that's made its decision to be socially irresponsible and nobody else. We have a heartfelt belief that our natural allies are in the environmental community and the public health community, because we understand that what affects them most kills us first."

The anti-environmentalists' failure to make new friends in organized labor and their feelings of loss following the defeat of their old friends in the Bush/Quayle administration has led a number of them to seek out new political allies. During the 1993 CDFE-sponsored Wise Use Leadership Conference in Reno, Nevada, Chuck Cushman proposed joining Ross Perot's United We Stand organization, a suggestion that one Republican congressional staffer compared to rats climbing aboard a sinking ship. A more innovative proposal was that Wise Use get involved in the growing local government revolt against unfunded federal mandates, such as Medicare, Clean Air, and Clean Water compliances. The problem likely to be encountered in the pursuit of that strategy is that while local and state governments may be desperately seeking ways to cut their spending, the vast majority of the public supports clean-air and -water projects, particularly in the wake of the April 1993 disaster in Milwaukee, Wisconsin, where 50 people with preexisting illnesses died, 370,000 got sick, and more than a million people had to boil their tapwater for a week following exposure to cryptosporidium owing to a breakdown in the city's water-purification system.[24]

"You can talk about cutting unfunded federal mandates, but I don't believe environmental issues are appropriate to the list, not if you accept that one of the roles of government is to protect people's health," says Carol Browner, the lanky and engaging thirty-eight-year-old head of the Environmental Protection Agency. "If you go back to the origin of workplace standards in this country, to that history, when it was first proposed that you couldn't use children in the workplace or that people couldn't be required to work sixteen-hour days, what did the business community say? Oh, we won't make it, we won't be competitive, you can't do this to us. Well, we seem to have survived just fine and in fact we're a better world for that and hopefully that is where we will find ourselves when it comes to environmental protections."[25]

She's asked if she's affected by the Wise Use/Property Rights backlash in her day-to-day efforts.

"I'm not, I'm really not, in terms of the decisions I make or the

THE MORE THE CHANGE

agenda I'm putting forward," she says. "I'm worried about it mainly because Congress has a role to play in my programs. State legislatures have an increasingly large role to play in terms of implementation of environmental programs, and I'm worried that those people feel its impact and what does that mean in terms of what I want to see achieved in this country in terms of environmental protection?"

Browner experiences the environmental backlash more directly on February 2, 1994, when the House votes 227 to 191 against consideration of a bill to elevate the EPA to cabinet rank unless there is debate on cost-benefit risk assessments, unfunded mandates, and property rights. The grafting of these three issues onto any and all environmental legislation during the 103rd Congress gets them dubbed the "unholy trinity."

By rejecting the House leadership's limits on the scope of the EPA debate, members signal their growing willingness to listen to anti-environmental arguments that assert environmental protections weaken the economy (a claim refuted by most studies). While there is a good deal of talk about relative risks, federal impositions, and the Fifth Amendment, the EPA's announcement the previous day that it will begin to examine the possible elimination of chlorine, a toxic chemical used in many of today's manufacturing processes, seems to be an understated factor in the surprise vote. The idea that industry may have to reorganize some of its most basic ways of doing business to assure the country clean air, soil, and water is not an appealing one to PAC-dependent politicians.

"Carol Browner and the EPA announced a big new initiative to eliminate chlorine and chlorinated products in America without a risk analysis, without any cost analysis of what that's gonna mean to the U.S. economy, to jobs, to people," claims Billy Tauzin, who has become something of a "property rights" poster-boy on the Hill. Tauzin's third congressional district in southern Louisiana is an economically depressed and polluted region of bayous and wetlands whose economy is largely dependent on the oil and gas industry and on chemical manufacturing. Among the "constituencies" who help Tauzin, Gary Condit, and others mobilize against EPA's elevation to cabinet rank are the Wise Use/Property Rights network, the Chemical Manufacturers Association, and the Farm Bureau.

"The Farm Bureau's interesting," Carol Browner says. "I met with them recently. You should look at what the heads of the fifty state bureaus do when they're not serving as chairs of the state bureaus. A lot of them are insurance guys. They're not farmers any more, and a lot of them have never been farmers. There's an interesting dynamic about Washington trade associations," she continues. "Trade groups tend to speak at the lowest common denominator, so that what we've found is you can reach around the associations to individual members and you'll find a greater willingness to work together to deal with the issues. Talk to individual farmers. Most farmers will tell you they don't like using chemicals. They're expensive and they do have serious questions about the effects on their own families who live on the farm. Look at the six hundred pesticides that are currently registered in the United States for food use. Almost two-thirds of them have never been subjected to a strict health-based scientific review, but they're on our food products today. So we are dealing with, in almost every instance, public health issues that people feel very, very strongly about."

"There's a growing lobby for organic foods from farmers and consumers. It's the fastest growing force in California agriculture. Farmers are actively looking for biological pest control systems to replace chemicals," agrees Deputy Secretary of Agriculture Richard Rominger, himself a lifelong farmer who once ran California's Department of Agriculture under Jerry Brown.[26] "Most farmers also support wetland and conservation programs where there is some [financial] assistance provided to keep soil and nitrates and phosphates from getting into our water systems. If you look at wetlands, look at the history of this country. You'll see there was this idea that we'd fill them in and make them quote, productive, unquote. When we decided they had great value in themselves things changed. But people haven't all caught up to what science tells us now. . . .

"Whenever things move in a new direction there are some

people who want to put on the brakes," he says when asked about the environmental backlash. "You have an extreme reaction in everything but it's usually only a small percentage," he claims. "Property rights is not an easy issue, but owners don't have unlimited rights to do what they want with their land, and often regulations like zoning or agricultural policies improve their value. So along with takings you also have what some people have begun to call 'givings.' If somebody's dumping in the river, there's a real difference if you're upstream or downstream in how you see your property rights affected. More and more of the population, something like 80 to 85 percent, call themselves environmentalists, and I think farmers feel the same way," the sun-weathered policymaker declares.

While the green rhetoric heard from high-ranking Clinton administration officials contrasts dramatically with Ronald Reagan's claim that trees cause pollution and the antiregulatory pronouncements of Dan Quayle's Council on Competitiveness, in its first year in office the administration shows little stomach for confronting anti-enviro conservatives around takings and other key issues in Congress and the courts, refusing even to rescind Reagan's Executive Order #12630 (which promulgates an extreme right-wing interpretation of the Fifth Amendment). This is seen as a sign of weakness by the anti-enviros who respond by concentrating their fire on public lands issues, the Endangered Species Act, the Clean Water Act, and other key elements of environmental protection.

Willing to invest its political capital and make major trade-offs to advance programs around jobs, free trade, communications technology, deficit reduction, and health care, the Clinton administration fails to take similar risks for the environment during its first twelve months in office. Rather it hammers together a set of mediagenic agreements and ecoinitiatives that draw a skeptical reaction from environmentalists. On the eve of Earth Day 1993, President Clinton announced his intention to sign an international treaty on global warming that George Bush had initially refused to support when he and 118 other heads of state came together for the 1992 Earth Summit in Rio. During his speech in the U.S. Botanical Gardens, Clinton committed the United States "to reducing our emissions of greenhouse gases to their 1990 levels by the year 2000." At the time this was seen as a victory for Al Gore over Treasury Secretary Lloyd Bentsen, Energy Secretary Hazel O'Leary, and other fans of fossil fuel.

The administration's original plan to reduce these greenhouse gases had included a deficit-reducing energy tax in the budget and increased gas taxes of up to twenty-five cents a gallon. But a computer-driven "grassroots" letter-writing and phone-in campaign orchestrated by the National Association of Manufacturers helped kill the energy tax,[27] and congressional timidity kept the gas tax below five cents, guaranteeing that with the lowest fuel pricing in the developed world, alternative energy sources would continue to remain noncompetitive. There was talk of imposing new fuel-efficiency standards for automobiles, but instead Bill Clinton held a Rose Garden ceremony in late September with the CEOs of Ford, GM, and Chrysler to announce a government-industry program to create an eighty-miles-per-gallon "green car" sometime in the future. Clinton promised that the program would usher in "a new car-crazy chapter" in American history. The Big Three automakers immediately began using the agreement as an argument against California and other states imposing mandatory requirements for emission-free autos by the end of the century. The American Legislative Exchange Council complemented this lobbying effort by trying to push "no-greater-than" legislation in California and other states that had adopted clean-air standards tougher than those of the feds. When, in October, the administration finally announced its "Climate Change Action Plan" to reduce greenhouse emissions, it also turned out to be a voluntary effort based on redirected federal spending and the good will of industry. An economist with the Environmental Defense Fund, a moderate group that generally favors "market-based" solutions to pollution, compared the regulation-free Clinton plan to tightrope walking without a safety net.

"The terms of some of these agreements are awfully crude, protecting industry from liability. Deals are being made in haste," complains Michael McCloskey of the Sierra Club. "The whole thing looks like they know they need to touch some bases but don't do it so skillfully. What this really comes down to is business as usual."

Jonathan Lash, president of the World Resources Institute and co-chair of the President's Council on Sustainable Development, disagrees. "Environmental policy in the U.S. has been developed anecdotally. A problem has become a concern, Congress has enacted legislation to deal with that specific problem, and there's never been a coherent national set of goals or strategy to tell us where we want to go as a nation. I think this administration is going to change all that."[28]

The Washington buzzword of the moment, a free-trade import from the Rio Earth Summit, is *sustainable development*, the idea that we can meet our economic needs today without compromising the quality of life for future generations. I hear it used repeatedly by administration officials, environmentalists, trade union leaders, corporate executives, and anti-enviro activists who see it as yet another preservationist plot to undermine the free-enterprise system. In a variation on a theme, Tom Zosel, a manager for 3M, one of the nation's corporate leaders in pollution prevention, explains how his firm's successful twenty-year 3P (Pollution Prevention Pays) program has reduced waste output by more than 600,000 tons and is now being extended into the twenty-first century as part of its commitment to "sustainable growth." The only problem with this concept is that while market growth is theoretically unlimited, natural resources are finite and will always need to be conserved, protected, and restored. Sustainable development, like sustainable growth, may be something of an oxymoron, a consensus-building term that everyone can agree on as long as its implementing language remains largely undefined.

If Wise Use has been successful in any area it has been in subverting the meaning of language in a way seldom seen outside a Pentagon press briefing. Recognizing that the environmental ethic has become entrenched in American life, the anti-enviros have adopted contrarian names such as Alliance for Environment and Resources, Citizens for the Environment, Environmental Conservation Organization, Public Lands Council, National Wetlands Coalition, and Global Climate Coalition in order to carry out their fight for unlimited mining, logging, grazing, wetlands development, and industrial release of pollutants. Since 1992 a number of major corporations in extractive industry, including some with direct ties to Wise Use/Property Rights, have also adopted the language of greenspeak and have begun flocking to the banner of sustainable development.

"I think that Wise Use is too tied up with protection of its own members' personal interests. If you've got a farmer with one piece of wetland acreage or a developer who wants to build a high-rise on some beachfront, they're not going to draw much sympathy," says Jack Sheehan of the Steelworkers Union. "I think the more important fight in the future will be how we evolve to sustainable development. Whether or not you lay down the framework around market forces, the right to pollute or to continue government regulation to protect the environment is really key from my point of view."

At a Washington, D.C., conference on sustainable development at the swank Madison Hotel, I wander into the wrong reception room and find myself mixing with a group of some thirty sulfur dioxide brokers. Under the 1990 Clean Air Act, industries that produce less than their legal allowable limit of health-threatening, acid-rain-generating sulfur dioxide are permitted to sell their SO_2 pollution "surplus" by the ton on the Chicago Board of Trade. This, the theory goes, creates a "free-market incentive" for pollution reduction, since "cleaner" industries get to sell and dirtier industries have to buy. In the San Francisco Bay Area, SO_2 is selling at around $5,500 per ton, NO_2 (nitrogen oxide) at $7,000 to $20,000 a ton. I recall Farm Bureau economist John Hosemann arguing that this type of pollution-permit trading can win over the public to "free-market environmentalism." But with new EPA and Harvard School of Public Health studies indicating that soot in the air causes fifty to sixty thousand deaths a year, this doesn't seem too likely.[29] Still, the cocktail chatter is alive with the possibility of future trading options in CO_2, or perhaps some hot TRI (toxic release inventory) carcinogens. I end up talking to a pleasant woman in a gray skirt and pearl-colored silk blouse who seems both fascinated and appalled at the idea of an environmental backlash. She'd never consider herself part of this backlash and yet if I offered her enough money she'd gladly sell me a ton or two of dirty air, that being her business.

On my last day in Washington, I leave my hotel early to attend the second quarterly meeting of the President's Council on Sustainable Development. The PCSD was established in June 1993 by Bill Clinton as Al Gore's bully pulpit to demonstrate the connection between environmental protection and economic growth. The council has been mandated to produce a plan of action for sustainable development by June of 1995 and has become the one place in Washington where advocates of the new environmental paradigm, top government leaders, and the corporate powers that be get together on a regular basis.

Just outside my hotel I find two other guests talking to a policeman on the sidewalk. The rear window of their rental car is busted out, glass chips scattered across the curb. Two white-haired ladies who have stopped to observe tell me that their own car had been stolen from a parking lot around the corner. The local media continues to report on the daily shooting deaths and lesser crimes taking place around the district. One of this week's top news stories is the capture of the teenage gunmen who shot and wounded half a dozen kids at a municipal swimming pool during my last visit to the nation's capital. The mayor has requested that the National Guard be mobilized for D.C. crime-fighting duty. I pass through Lafayette Park, with its twenty or so homeless residents, and pass the White House, where an overly cheerful TV correspondent and her camera crew are setting up on the lawn to do an early morning stand-up. I go through the security gate inside the Department of Commerce, where today's meeting of the PCSD is taking place, and open my briefcase for an additional Secret Service handcheck before finding a seat at the front of the stately old auditorium. On the polished wooden stage, a U-shaped table covered in blue bunting and backed by a pair of American flags has been set up for the council's twenty-eight members. Along with Gore, the council membership includes Carol Browner from EPA, Secretary of Interior Bruce Babbitt, Secretary of Commerce Ron Brown, Secretary of Agriculture Mike Espy, Energy Secretary Hazel O'Leary, and Deputy Secretary of Education Madeleine Kunin. The corporate sector is represented by executives and CEOs from Chevron, Enron, Pacific Gas and Electric, Dow Chemical, Ciba-Geigy, Georgia-Pacific, S. C. Johnson & Son, and Browning-Ferris Industries. Labor, civil rights, and environmental groups are represented by the AFL-CIO, NAACP, Columbia River Inter-Tribal Fish Commission, Nature Conservancy, National Wildlife Federation, Environmental Defense Fund, Sierra Club, and Natural Resources Defense Council.

At 8 A.M. former tobacco lobbyist and Secretary of Commerce Ron Brown opens the meeting. "This department is where trade, commerce, and environmental opportunity meet. We reject the notion that economic goals and environmental protection are incompatible. We see this as a false dichotomy," he says before introducing the vice president and disappearing for the remainder of the day.

"I want to underscore the extreme importance placed on the work of this commission by the president, by me, by the entire administration," Al Gore says, appearing more relaxed than normal, wearing a brightly colored tie and flashing an easy smile. "Our world faces a tremendous challenge in reconciling the imperatives of economic progress with the imperatives of protecting the ecological system of the earth and preventing, indeed halting, the rapacious destruction of so many critical elements of that ecological system. The United States must lead the way. And this administration, accepting that challenge, has asked members of this council to play a key role in helping us understand exactly how to reconcile those imperatives and find a path that we must chart into the future. . . . Only with bold new policies to create a partnership of government, business, the environmental community, and the general public can we hope to achieve sustainable

development. It is work that will take decades but that will succeed because of the principles you set forth today."

Following a round of applause, Gore takes off for another
event, promising to return later in the morning. The council's co-
chairs—the tall, lean, mop-haired Jonathan Lash and Dave Buzzelli, a bald, friendly bullfrog of a man from Dow Chemical—get
the morning session under way by asking for preliminary task
force reports. The report on principles, goals, and definitions is
presented by Jay Hair, head of the 4.5-million-member National
Wildlife Federation, and by Bill Ruckelshaus, a former EPA administrator who in 1988 became CEO of Browning-Ferris, the
nation's second largest waste handler. Nineteen eighty-eight was
also the year that hypodermic needles and sludge washed up on
eastern beaches, forcing their closure, and the U.S. solid-waste
industry, under attack for bid rigging, antitrust violations, and
links to organized crime, desperately needed someone like
Ruckelshaus to clean up its image.

Ruckelshaus suggests that the council adopt the definition of
sustainable development as "development that meets the needs
of the present without compromising the needs of the future."
The proposal is readily accepted.

Discussion turns to comparative living standards in the world,
with some agreement that the extreme disparities of today may
be unsustainable by the time world population stabilizes at
around ten billion, fifty years from now. It is suggested that the
council support prudent action now on ozone depletion, global
warming, and loss of biodiversity before these also become critical issues. Dick Clarke, the CEO of Pacific Gas and Electric, asks
if the council should be a contributor and monitor of the president's greenhouse initiative. "What's our responsibility and overlap there?" he wonders without getting a definite response.

The council members wander into a freshman class discussion
of economics and environment. Bill Ruckelshaus rejects "the
zero-sum game that we have to sacrifice economic goals. In fact
environmental protection and economic growth are essential to
each other. Poverty is the greatest threat to the environment," he

claims, offering a pain-free scenario for aligning industry with environmental reform.

"The president's dictate to this group is to emphasize economic vitality without impacting environmental vitality," the NAACP's Ben Chavis believes.

"Are we looking at the environment through an economic lens or the economy through an environmental lens?" wonders Katy McGinty, the twenty-nine-year-old director of the White House Office of Environmental Policy.

"Our principal focus is on the environment in ways that enhance the economy's ability to grow and prosper," replies Dick Clarke.

"Both sides of the equation should get equal weight," claims Fred Krupp, executive director of the Environmental Defense Fund.

"Yes, let's keep it together," agrees Sam Johnson, the Yoda-like chairman of S. C. Johnson & Son, the maker of various cleaning and hygiene products.

"It seems that if the last twenty years have taught us anything it is the inextricable link between the environment and economics," concurs the EPA's Carol Browner. Former Vermont Governor Madeline Kunin offers what may be the first insight of the last twenty minutes. "Until now economic decisions were made first and their environmental impacts studied later," Kunin points out. "We shouldn't always have to play catch-up." Secretary of Interior Bruce Babbitt, seated near the juncture of the U-shaped table, gives a barely perceptible nod of agreement.

Following a task force report on dialogue and education that calls for a national campaign to increase public awareness of sustainable development, the vice president and his security detail return for the sustainable communities task force discussion. Dave Buzzelli asks who'd like to go first. No one volunteers. "Well, I'm not shy," Gore grins and begins talking about how he'd like to link the administration's Reinventing Government initiative with the council through a recently established community-empowerment board. "One of its tasks will be recommending legislation for enterprise zones and beyond that coordinating the work of cabinet departments and agencies to take a more unified approach to lift up the quality of life in devastated communities," he explains. "And in trying to do this we've held a series of workshops and briefings and had a very good session last week on sustainable communities. It was quite interesting, because, like Ben Chavis says, if you talk with people from community groups and at the grassroots level in areas that have not shared in the progress of the country, you will find a greater emphasis on improving the quality of the environment there than a lot of people would expect. So the prospect of trying to alleviate the problems of distressed communities by locating a few smokestack industries or a new business that does not pay attention to its relationship to the environment is seen very differently by people in the community than it is by those who have an emphasis of creating jobs according to the old way of doing things. Reconciling this difference is really at the heart of this council. And the kind of debate unfolding here reflects a very large philosophical shift in our public debate away from single-cause, single-effect analysis that identifies a single problem one day, targets it, and moves on to some other policy the next day.

"We're moving away from that and towards a more systemic approach, identifying communities as living systems that are extremely complex, with many different factors interacting. That's why we must not only examine environmental problems through an economic lens but also look at economic problems through an environmental lens, to bring both perspectives together. We have to find a way to generate economic progress without sacrificing the ability of the next generation and the generation after that to enjoy the same improvements and increases in quality of life."

John Sawhill, president of The Nature Conservancy, talks about the growing sustainable-development movement in communities across the United States. He identifies as key elements intensive planning among politicians, business leaders, and others over land use, transportation, building design, environmental efficiency, and recycling. Gore offers an example from his home state. "In Chattanooga they took protection and enhancement of the local environment as the organizing principle for their efforts to renew and revitalize the city. They have cleaned up the river-bank, built a riverfront park, redesigned the flow of vehicles and people through the downtown area, and will be manufacturing electric buses soon."

Tom Donahue, secretary treasurer of the AFL-CIO, has some suggestions. "We need to integrate concerns of economic development and job growth from toxic cleanup and new energy-efficient buildings, jobs in recycling, and new environmental technologies, and we need to demonstrate this in terms of current economic activity. We also need to talk to people about how they can balance the environment and their jobs, because they don't know what *sustainable development* means." It's uncertain if Donahue is clear on the concept himself. The last time he talked about jobs and the environment was at the Forest Summit in Portland, Oregon, where he was a featured speaker at the anti-enviro Oregon Lands Coalition rally, telling timber industry workers, "We are at your side. We're on the side of preserving jobs of loggers and millworkers, jitney drivers, chain pullers, choke setters, everyone else that depends on this industry for their jobs."[30] At the same time he failed to condemn the timber industry's waste of the resource that was responsible for the loggers' predicament. Jonathan Lash had originally proposed Oil, Chemical and Atomic Workers President Bob Cash to represent labor on the PCSD, but White House staffers, suspicious of Cash's independent politics, opted for the more reliable Donahue instead.

Ken Derr, the CEO of Chevron, presents the energy task force report. "We tried to develop a vision of energy policy with a common understanding of where we are and the significant role fossil fuels play and will continue to play," the round-faced, expensively tailored oil man explains. "We have to look at greater eco-efficiency in the use of our energy sources, given growing world-wide demand." Towards this end he recommends improved utilization of all energy sources, particularly fossil fuels, a suggestion that makes sense in light of Chevron's massive new multibillion-dollar investment in the oil fields of Kazakhstan in the former Soviet Union.

Derr is politely challenged by the Environmental Defense Fund's Fred Krupp, who suggests that if the United States is seen as supporting continued use of fossil fuels, developing countries such as China will take this as a green light to exploit their own coal and oil reserves. He suggests expanding the scope of the energy task force to include meeting the CO_2 reduction goals of Clinton's Climate Change Action Plan. Michele Perrault, president of the Sierra Club, suggests that the task force might also want to put more emphasis on renewable energy sources such as wind and solar power.

Ken Lay, the CEO of Enron, the largest natural gas company in the United States, says that he wants to make sure that whatever policies are adopted on energy, "we get beyond command-and-control regulation. We have to talk about relying on market forces to get things done." Fred Krupp again asks if the energy task force "shouldn't embrace and follow the progress of the CO_2 emissions plan?"

"The issues in energy are much broader than global warming," Derr claims. "I mean, this is an issue with more variance in opinion and data than most. It really depends on your sense of urgency. I think the science is vague."

"I think global warming science is not vague," Fred Krupp counters. "There's wide agreement except for a few fringe people, but let's bring experts in for tutorials if we have to." He goes on to suggest that the energy task force be renamed the energy and global warming task force. "I don't think the president signed onto this international climate treaty because he's some kind of a radical," he says to mild laughter.

However, compared to the oil, gas, and chemical industries even Bill Clinton may appear daringly radical. Just before the PCSD's October meeting, the New Mexico environmental group Forest Guardians called for a national boycott of Chevron because of its many donations to Wise Use outfits, including $92,000 to People for the West. Along with its donations to the Grannells' promining operation, Chevron was blasted for giving money to the National Wilderness Institute, a Wise Use think tank that regularly attacks the environmental groups on the PCSD in a newsletter column titled "Red Alert"; Chevron also funds the Committee for a Constructive Tomorrow (which has compared environmental leaders to Hitler and Stalin) and the Pacific Legal Foundation. "Chevron is hiding behind a green mask," charged the Forest Guardians' Sam Hitt in the group's October 12 press release. "By boycotting Chevron, consumers with an interest in protecting the environment have a way to fight back."

Ken Lay's Enron Corporation, Dave Buzzelli's Dow Chemical, and forty-four other resource industries and associations are also behind the anti-enviro Global Climate Coalition, which was set up in 1989 to convince Congress and the public that global warming is a myth. More sophisticated than other countersci-ence outfits, the Climate Coalition, in its October 1993 newslet-ter, endorsed "the president's reliance on business-government partnerships and voluntary initiatives to reduce greenhouse gas emissions." But it then went on to suggest that the United States was already doing more than its fair share to promote eco-efficiency and that the science on global warming wasn't reliable anyway.[31] More recently, the Climate Coalition attacked Vice President Gore for "politicizing" the global warming issue. The Climate Coalition is the same group that sent reporters copies of the $250,000-video documentary *The Greening of Planet Earth*, claiming that industrial CO_2 buildup in the atmo-sphere is good for plant growth and therefore a potential solution to world hunger.

Before the lunch break, Jonathan Lash notes that the energy task force has been "excellent in provoking discussion."

The Department of Commerce cafeteria is located in the building's basement next to the National Aquarium. Inspired, I order a tunafish sandwich. The food is served on Styrofoam plates with plastic utensils. I share a table with Chuck Ebby, who rep-resents a consortium of agricultural chemical companies. Chuck is spending the day observing the council in order "to tell them if this is anything they have to worry about." He doesn't think it is. We discuss the Clinton administration's interest in voluntary initiatives. Chuck says he also believes in voluntary initiatives— for example, the Responsible Care Program of the Chemical

Manufacturers Association that Dave Buzzelli helped establish. But Chuck admits that no one has ever been thrown out of the association for failing to live up to responsible-care standards. "We're not the government," he shrugs. "I mean, look, if your dad didn't tell you to come home by midnight, would you come home by midnight?"

In the afternoon former Colorado Senator Tim Wirth, who is now a top State Department official, a handsome, large-headed man and old hiking partner of Al Gore's, suggests that a task force be formed to study the issues of population and consumption. "The U.S. must adopt a process to think about its own population and consumption," he explains, using the example of California's 25 percent growth rate between 1980 and 1990. "We don't know what we're sustaining if we don't know our population and consumption levels," he points out. "If we as the sole remaining superpower don't take on this issue for political or other reasons, how will the rest of the world deal with it? Can we lead the world on the population issue without addressing it ourselves?"

"As a Hispanic woman and a Catholic, I know this will be a heated issue," says Judith Espinosa, secretary of New Mexico's Environment Department, who talks about the role of large families in her culture before conceding that the issue deserves serious study and a task force of its own.

Fred Krupp reports for the eco-efficiency task force. He suggests that model eco-industrial parks be established that incorporate green design elements, pollution-prevention technology, and CMA's responsible-care standards. "The government can create a framework and incentives, develop yardsticks for measuring progress, and help facilitate the technology transfers needed," he explains. Jonathan Lash agrees on "the need to improve on market-based incentives, to remove disincentives that exist in the present system."

Adds EPA's Carol Browner, "Over the last twenty years we've had a top-down command-and-control approach to environmental regulation, which has been effective. But in the nineties we have to look for better ways." Later she explains, "If you assume there's a pot of money to be spent on environmental matters, what you want to do is be sure the money is being spent for the best return. And with the laws and regulatory programs we now have that doesn't always happen. It seems to me that philosophically where you'd like to be when you deal with standards is the strongest possible standards necessary to protect the public health but flexibility in how you achieve those standards."

John Adams, the bearded, sun-weathered, executive director of the Natural Resources Defense Council, offers a mild dissent. "We're being asked to give up command and control for flexible management, and I'm not really sure we'll see the results that way."

Ted Strong, a Native American activist in a red shirt and beaded string tie, presents a slide show for the task force on natural-resources management. It includes shots of the Columbia River and regional maps of its tributaries. He explains watersheds as units of resource management. He shows a 1956 picture of Indian fishing platforms on the river's natural falls. "This was the center of our culture," he says. The falls were later submerged by a hydroelectric dam. "The ratio of salmon to people in the 1880s was three times as many salmon as people. Today there's a salmon for every five people," he tells his council mates. "Now there's a $300 million effort to restore the salmon and it may not be working. In the Columbia watershed there's $5 billion of value in farms and dams, $11 billion in commodity shipping, $2 billion in forestry. Fisheries have declined from half a billion to $5 million a year. Some of us would prefer no development and rely on nature to provide us with food and clothing and shelter, as it has since the beginning of time," he concludes.

"Watersheds provide a useful unit of analysis. Our group came quickly to seeing this," says Ted Strong's task force co-chair Richard Barth, CEO of Ciba-Geigy, the Swiss-based multinational that produces drugs, fungicides, and insecticides. At one time Ciba-Geigy was the world's major distributor of DDT. In 1985 the company was fined $1.4 million by the state of New Jersey for illegal dumping at the Toms River plant that OCAW's Bob Cash visited. An accident a year later at the firm's Basel, Switzerland, facility led to a massive release of the herbicide atrazine into the Rhine River. Another council member familiar with watershed issues is Pete Correll, CEO of Georgia-Pacific. In late 1993 GP got the city of Fort Bragg, California (where the Redwood Summer protests took place), to join with the Pacific Legal Foundation in filing an *amicus curia* brief in defense of GP's right to log eight hundred acres of redwood and fir in the local watershed. GP told the city that if a legal challenge filed by area environmentalists prevented them from cutting nine million board feet of lumber, they would have to lay off five hundred millworkers for three months. Fort Bragg City Councilman Lindy Peters, in defending the town's action, said that the lay-offs would have led millworkers to abuse their wives and girlfriends. Environmentalist Judith Vidaver, one of the local women who had filed the suit against GP's logging plan, countered that Georgia-Pacific was using scare tactics. "The industry is overcutting the forest to the point where it cannot sustain business. If it continues in this way, eventually workers will be out of work," she said.[32]

Ciba-Geigy's Dick Barth recommends that the PCSD select four or five watersheds for in-depth study and analysis regarding resource sustainability. Secretary of Interior Bruce Babbitt seems very taken with this approach and suggests that the council could also learn from existing projects, such as the salmon studies now being conducted along the Columbia River basin. Everyone starts bidding their favorite watersheds for study. Carol Browner suggests the Gulf of Mexico off Florida. "Why not the Rio Grande?" Judith Espinosa offers, making a pitch for binationalism. "Being from Minnesota, I'd like to recommend the [mythical NPR] watershed of Lake Wobegon," David Buzzelli grins before he and Jonathan Lash excuse themselves. They have a meeting at the White House with President Clinton to report on the council's accomplishments for the day.

"I think that the president's council is going to become the new target for the Right. The right wing cannot afford to allow the principles of sustainable development to go unchallenged," Ben Chavis tells me after the meeting. He expects this challenge to be very direct, with charges of socialism, shouting protests, and the kinds of vilification of "the preservationist establishment" that are the hallmarks of Wise Use.

The Audubon Society's Brock Evans sees the challenge as taking a more subtle form. "I think there is always going to be 15 to 20 percent of Americans who really believe that all these resources are there for us to use and to hell with future generations or anyone else," he says. "I guess in a way it's a compliment to the environmental movement's power and credibility that we've driven them from outright bragging about their activities like clear-cutting so that now they say what they're doing is sustainable harvesting of timber. Even the Wise Abuse [Wise Use] people say they're the true environmentalists and we're the extremists. Now it's gone beyond that. It's gone to sustainable development. So the same folks who always want to rape and plunder are going to get into sustainable development because it can't be defined, it means different things to different people."

Jonathan Lash believes that, because of the global nature of many of today's environmental problems, the term *sustainable development* has to be defined and put into practice as public policy in the coming years. "I know of no serious scientists who question the chemical change in the atmosphere or the basic model of how the greenhouse effect works," he says. "We're approaching a 90 percent certainty that CO_2 buildup in the atmosphere will increase warming. At some point we'll reach a point on the global-climate issue we've already reached on ozone: that it's a problem and we have to deal with it. What happens when the world gets serious about climate will be much more dramatic than with ozone depletion. It will mean an 80 to 90 percent reduction in fossil fuel use, considerable turbulence in industrialized societies, dislocation and resistance that we have to begin preparing for today."

To date the Wise Use/Property Rights backlash has been a bracing if dangerous reminder to environmentalists that power concedes nothing without a demand and that no social movement, be it ethnic, civil, or environmental, can rest on its past laurels. Of course, only in the cynical argot of Washington where "perception is reality" could a corporate-sponsored environmental backlash successfully sell itself as a populist movement. Despite an intimidating combination of local thugs and national phone/fax guerillas, the anti-enviros lack the broad middle, either ideologically or in terms of real numbers, that is one of the defining elements of authentic social movements. If the anti-enviros' links to the Farm Bureau, Heritage Foundation, NRA, logging companies, resource trade associations, multinational gold-mining companies, Japanese ORV manufacturers, and a Korean billionaire who thinks he's God prove anything, it's that large industrial lobbies and transnational corporations have learned how to play the grassroots game.

If Wise Use's attempt to sponsor a "holy war against the new pagans" of environmental regulation and reform is fully exposed to the public—the right-wing terrorism and vigilante violence, personal profiteering, political sabotage, dirty tricks, and disinformation—the public's reaction will almost certainly force the transnationals into abandoning Wise Use and developing or co-opting a new, more promising "movement."

If Al Gore is right in saying that the environment will become the main organizing principle around which societies restructure in the twenty-first century, then the struggle to define the "sustainable development" movement may become the next generation's green battleground with the "masters and possessors of nature." In the best-case scenario, that effort will take the form of dialogue, education, and inquiry, carried on among American citizens, their government, and a business community newly sensitized to the demands of its customers and employees for a clean, healthy, biologically diverse world. In the worst-case scenario, high-tech industrial combines and international corporate empires will use the rhetoric of sustainable development as a green mask for a new and expanded environmental backlash that seeks to deny the social and biological consequences of their ecologically destructive practices. Between these best- and worst-case scenarios, between the faith that we do have a future and today's backlash despair that says, "Take what you can get while you can get it," lies only the understanding, the heart, and the will of the American people.

Notes

INTRODUCTION: FIRST ENCOUNTERS

1. For additional coverage of the opposing rallies see *San Francisco Examiner,* "Loggers, Activists Square Off" (July 22, 1990): 1; *Santa Rosa Press Democrat* (July 22, 1990): 1.

2. Judi Bari, "The Palco Papers," *Anderson Valley Advertiser* (March 27, 1991): 1. Also a copy of the Pacific Lumber interoffice memo dated April 18, 1990, which reads in part, "Enclosed is a *Press Democrat* article on the environmentalists' internal split over Mississippi Summer. Also enclosed is a flyer with the Earth First! logo, however, as Daryl's name is misspelled, we are not to [sic] sure who put it out."

3. Ron Arnold interview with author, February 5, 1993.

4. A. L. Rawe with Rick Field, "Interview with a 'Wise' Guy," *Common Ground of Puget Sound* (Fall 1992): 1.

5. Chuck Cushman interview with author, March 12, 1993.

6. Keith Schneider, "Environment Gets a Flurry of Final Acts," *New York Times* (January 16, 1993): 1, 9.

7. Ed Knight interview with author and documentary producer Steve Talbot, February 11, 1991. Ed Knight interview with author, July 22, 1993.

8. Pat Costner interview with author, September 8, 1993.

9. From interview broadcast on the syndicated television show "Inside Edition," February 5, 1993.

10. Ibid.

11. As told to private investigator Sheila O'Donnell. Also reported on "60 Minutes," September 20, 1992, and by Alecia Swasy, *Soap Opera: The Inside Story of Procter & Gamble* (New York: Times Books, 1993), p. 222.

12. Sam Hitt interview with author, December 7, 1993.

13. Andy Kerr interview with author, April 20, 1993.

14. Lois Gibbs interview with author, June 25, 1993.

ONE: INSIDE THE BELTWAY

1. *Washington Times* (June 20, 1993).

2. Ben Bolch and Harold Lyons, *Apocalypse Not: Science, Economics, and Environmentalism* (Washington, D.C.: Cato Institute, 1993).

3. Carl Deal, *The Greenpeace Guide to Anti-Environmental Organizations* (Berkeley, Calif.: Odonian Press, 1993), p. 89.

4. A list of the law firms and an explanation of the role Heritage plays in co-ordinating their strategies was provided to the author by Pacific Legal Foundation Attorney James Burling, May 18, 1993.

5. Osha Gray Davidson, *Under Fire: The NRA and the Battle for Gun Control* (New York: Holt, 1993), p. 240.

6. Carole Sugarman, "Pesticide Risk May Be Higher in Children," *Washington Post* (June 28, 1993): A4.

7. "Chavez a 'Worthy Advocate for His Cause,'" *Ag Alert* (April 28, 1993): 1.

8. Although the Farm Bureau's hidden financial structures and transactions are worthy of their own book, the most authoritative work to date, *Dollar Harvest*, by Samuel R. Berger (The Plains, Va.: AAM Publications, 1986), is sadly dated. However, occasional news articles, such as "Bureau Holds Stock in Farm Chemicals," by Dale Rice, *Dallas Times Herald* (April 4, 1989), have continued to spread light on apparent conflicts of interest between the FB's investments and its policies.

9. "Farm Bureau vs. Farmers," lead editorial, *Des Moines Register*, exact 1985 date obscured in photocopy. Also, interviews with former and present FB members.

10. George Rieger, phone interview with author, March 25, 1993.

11. *O'Dwyer's PR Services Report*, January 1991.

12. "The Greening of Planet Earth—The Effects of Carbon Dioxide on the Biosphere," video, copyright Western Fuels Association, 1991.

13. Quoted in Deal, *The Greenpeace Guide*, p. 56.

14. "Clinton Shifts on Grazing Fees," *The Oregonian* (March 31, 1993).

15. *Congressional Record* as quoted in *Land Rights Letter* (Sharpsburg, Md.: June 1993), p. 5.

16. Gordon Smith interview with author, March 11, 1993.

17. Claudia Dreifus, interview with Jim Hightower, *The Progressive* (August 1993): 36.

18. He appeared on CNN's "Crossfire" with Congresswoman Susan Molinary (Republican, New York).

19. Pat Buchanan, speech to the Republican National Convention, August 17, 1992, CNN transcript.

20. *Times Mirror* National Environmental Forum Survey conducted by the Roper organization in June 1992.

21. Richard C. Paddock, "Republicans Form Environmental Group," *Los Angeles Times* (June 15, 1993): 1.

TWO: MASTERS AND POSSESSORS OF NATURE

1. Philip Shabecoff, *A Fierce Green Fire* (New York: Farrar, Straus and Giroux, 1993), p. 9

2. Tom Hayden, *The Love of Possession Is a Disease with Them* (Chicago: Holt, Rinehart and Winston, 1972), pp. 99–100.

3. Ibid., p. 105.

4. Jeremy Rifkin, *Beyond Beef* (New York: Dutton, 1992), p. 78.

5. Quoted by Ed Quillen in "Who Will Coordinate and Inspire the West?" *High Country News* (May 3, 1993): 13.

6. Mike Weiss, "Firetrail—Are Loggers Behind the Rash of Fires in the West?" *Mother Jones* (March/April 1993): 50.

7. Theodore Roosevelt, *Autobiography,* centennial edition, edited and with an introduction by Wayne Andrews (New York: Charles Scribner's Sons, 1958).

8. Jon Krakauer, "Brown Fellas," *Outside* (December 1991): 69.

9. Robert A. Logan with Wendy Gibbons and Stacy Kingsbury, *Environmental Issues for the Nineties: A Handbook for Journalists* (Washington, D.C.: Environmental Reporting Forum, 1992), pp. 179–81.

10. Michael P. Cohen, *The History of the Sierra Club 1892–1970* (San Francisco: Sierra Club Books, 1988), pp. 321–22.

11. David Brower interview with author, March 9, 1993.

12. Shabecoff, *A Fierce Green Fire,* p. 155.

13. David J. Garrow, *Bearing the Cross: Martin Luther King, Jr., and the Southern Christian Leadership Conference* (New York: William Morrow, 1986), p. 553.

14. David Day, *The Environmental Wars* (New York: Ballantine, 1989), pp. 287–90; and other sources.

15. Bernard De Voto, *The Easy Chair* (Boston: Houghton Mifflin, 1955), p. 234.

THREE: REBELS AND REAGANITES

1. "Last Round-Up for the Old West," *The Economist* (March 6, 1993): 16, 23.

2. Bernard Shanks, *This Land Is Your Land* (San Francisco: Sierra Club Books, 1984), p. 266.

3. Ben Santarris, "Landowners Get Sharp Call," *Bellingham Herald* (May 22, 1992): 1.

4. Deane Rhodes interview with author, April 28, 1993.

5. Lou Cannon, *President Reagan: The Role of a Lifetime* (New York: Simon and Schuster, 1991), pp. 86 and 531.

6. Shabecoff, *A Fierce Green Fire,* p. 208.

7. Report by the Comptroller General of the United States, *Deficiencies in the Department of the Interior: OIG Investigation of the Powder River Basin Coal Lease Sale* (Washington, D.C.: U.S. General Accounting Office, June 11, 1984), p. 9.

8. Cannon, *President Reagan: The Role of a Lifetime,* p. 428.

9. Shabecoff, *A Fierce Green Fire,* p. 211.

10. Jonathan Lash, Katherine Gillman, and David Sheridan, *A Season of Spoils* (New York: Pantheon, 1984), p. 67.

11. "The 'Terrible 20' Regulations," *Washington Post* (August 4, 1981).

12. Alan Gottlieb interview with author, March 16, 1993.

13. Trent Clarke, speech to (anti-enviro) Environmental Conservation Organization (ECO) conference, February 20, 1993.

14. Grant Gerber interview with author, May 7, 1993.

15. Ron Arnold interview with author, March 15, 1993.

16. Alan M. Gottlieb, ed., *The Wise Use Agenda* (Bellevue, Wash.: Free Enterprise Press, 1989), pp. 5–18.

17. Quoted by Richard Stapleton in "On the Western Front," *National Parks* (January/February 1993): 34.

18. Chuck Cushman speech to (anti-enviro) Alliance for Environment and Resources conference, January 29, 1993.

19. Based on the official report: Subcommittee on Civil Service of the Committee on Post Office and Civil Service, U.S. House of Representatives, *Interference in Environmental Programs by Political Appointees: The Improper Treatment of a Senior Executive Service Official* (Washington, D.C.: U.S. Government Printing Office, July 1993). Also based on a December 30, 1992, draft report bearing this disclaimer: "This report has not been officially approved by the Committee or Subcommittee and, therefore, may not necessarily reflect the views of all its members."

20. Clark Collins speech to ECO conference, February 19, 1993.

21. Information from a ten-page unpublished article written by Collins titled "Expanded Version of an Article That Appeared in the January 1992 Issue of *Blue Ribbon* (this is the un-edited version)—National Recreational Trails Fund Act Chronology." It reads in part, "Received a grant from the Honda Motor Corporation that coupled with our other funding and membership revenue, enabled the Coalition to hire me as their full time executive director."

22. Ibid., p. 3.

23. Clark Collins interview with author, February 19, 1993.

24. The Captain Mossback character was introduced in *The Mighty Mutanables*, volume 18 of Ninja Turtle Comics, distributed by Creators Syndicate.

25. Joan Smith interview with author, March 10, 1993.

26. "Friday's Forest Summit: What's at Stake—4,600 Owls vs. 32,100 Jobs," *USA Today* (April 1, 1993): 1.

FOUR: THE FOREST FOR THE TREES

1. Deal, *The Greenpeace Guide*, p. 74.

2. Bill Grannell interview with author, February 15, 1993. Also Dave Mazza, "God, Land and Politics, the Wise Use and Christian Right Connection in 1992 Oregon Politics" (Portland, Oreg.: Western States Center and Montana AFL-CIO), pp. 4–6.

3. Typical is the report in the OLC's March 26, 1993, *Network News* that "hundreds of businesses are closing their doors April 2 so employees can be part of history-in-the-making" (an OLC rally at the Portland Timber Summit). The *Albany Democrat-Herald* (Saturday, April 3) reported that Willamette Industries had provided buses to the previous day's rally for two hundred of its Albany, Oregon, employees.

4. This is part of a package of anti-enviro legislation being pushed nationwide by the Washington-based American Legislative Exchange Council (ALEC).

5. Patrick Renshaw, *The Wobblies* (New York: Doubleday, 1967), pp. 163–67, one of several history books that recount the story of Wesley Everest's death.

6. Kathie Durbin and Paul Koberstein, "Forests in Distress," Special Report, *The Oregonian* (October 15, 1990), 28 pages.

7. During the April 1993 Forest Summit, Vice President Al Gore hinted that the export tax incentive might be eliminated for raw logs.

8. Jan TenBruggencate, "Persis Corp. Gift Preserves Forest Lands in Oregon," *Honolulu Advertiser* (December 28, 1992).

9. The original September 1989 broadcast of the Audubon Special, "Ancient Forests: Rage Over Trees" was the target of an OLC/timber industry boycott.

10. Foster Church and Cathy Kiyomura, "Timber Families Stage Rally at Waterfront," *The Sunday Oregonian* (April 4, 1993): A18.

FIVE: GRASSROOTS FOR SALE

1. Bill Grannell interview with author, February 15, 1993.

2. Chuck Cushman interview with author, March 12, 1993.

3. Grant Gerber interview with author, January 26, 1993.

4. Ron Arnold interview with author, March 15, 1993.

5. Jay Hair, *National Wildlife* (October/November 1992): 30.

6. Congressman George Miller interview with author, June 22, 1993.

7. *Land Rights Letter* (June 1992): 1, 5. Also Ron Arnold and Alan Gottlieb, *Trashing the Economy* (Bellevue, Wash.: Free Enterprise Press, 1993), p. 19.

8. Keith Schneider, "When the Bad Guy Is Seen as the One in the Green Hat," *New York Times* (February 16, 1992): E2.

9. Richard Miniter, "Out to Change the Law of the Land," *Insight* (May 2, 1993): 9.

10. Ron Arnold interview with author, March 15, 1993.

11. According to IRS nonprofit returns, in 1991 Blue Ribbon had a total revenue of $138,309.44, CDFE had $55,583.18, WIRF had $144,296, and the Western States Public Lands Coalition (which runs People for the West) had $627,135.

12. Kathy Kvarda interview with author at AER meeting, January 29, 1993.

13. Katherine Bouma, "Forestry Commission Met Illegally," *The Montgomery Advertiser* (November 15, 1992): 1. Also, "State Funds Aided Stewards" (December 1); "Forestry Involved with 2nd Group" (March 28, 1993), and additional reports.

14. Alan Crawford, *Thunder on the Right* (New York: Pantheon, 1980), p. 50.

15. Internal Revenue Service, Form 990, Second Amendment Foundation, 1991.

16. Crawford, *Thunder on the Right*, p. 68.

17. Alan Gottlieb interview with author, March 16, 1993.

18. Court documents copied at Federal Records Center, Seattle, Washington: U.S. Attorney Indictment/Gottlieb; Judgment & Commitment/Gottlieb; and Factual Basis for Plea of Guilty/Gottlieb. Also, Peter Lewis, "Tax Case Against Fundraiser Political, Lawyer Hints," *Seattle Times* (January 14, 1984): A8.

19. As quoted by Josh Sugarmann, *National Rifle Association—Money, Firepower & Fear* (Washington, D.C.: National Press Book, 1992), pp. 132–33.

20. Krakauer, "Brown Fellas," p. 69.

21. Mark W. Wright, "The Color of the Future," *San Francisco Chronicle Sunday Punch* (April 18, 1993): 2.

22. From Ron Arnold, "What's Ahead for Weed Control," Center for the Defense of Free Enterprise speech, delivered to 1981 Washington State Weed Control Association.

23. Ron Arnold, speech to Atlantic Vegetation Management Association, Halifax, Nova Scotia, October 23, 1984.

24. Arnold's advice to Canadian timber giant MacMillan Bloedel, as reported in *Share Groups in British Columbia*, Canadian Library of Parliament report (Ottawa, Canada: December 10, 1991), tracing the establishment of the Wise Use–like Share movement in Canada and the role Arnold played in establishing it.

25. Marked as Exhibit 3 in the deposition of Ron Arnold, April 12, 1988, in U.S. District Court, District of Oregon, *Carol van Strum et al.* v. *John C. Lawn et al.*

26. Quoted in Canadian Library of Parliament report, p. 17.

27. Arnold and Gottlieb, *Trashing the Economy*, p. 179.

28. Canadian Library of Parliament report, executive summary.

29. Richard Cockle, "Cattle-Grazing Advocates Picket Environmentalists' Conference," *The Oregonian* (April 27, 1992).

30. Notices of Default, Sonoma, California, May 21, 1987; May 17, 1989; and other court documents.

31. John McClaughery interview with author, June 9, 1993.

32. Jill Hamburg, "The Lone Ranger," *California Magazine* (November 1990): 90.

33. *The River Reporter* (July 31, 1986): 1, 19.

34. Richard M. Stapleton, "On the Western Front," *National Parks* (January/ February 1993): 32–36.

35. Copy of letter, various articles, including Glen Martin, "The 'Killer Mosquitoes' Deception," *San Francisco Chronicle* (November 11, 1991).

36. Loretta Callahan, "The High Priest of Property Rights," *The Columbian* (May 17, 1992): 1. The *Columbian* has continued to report on Cushman's local activities, even after he led the first ever protest demonstration in front of the newspaper's building.

37. Ibid., A10.

38. Court filings and Daniel Defoe interview with author, August 1, 1993.

39. Loretta Callahan, "Deputies Seize Cushman's Antiques," *The Columbian* (October 17, 1993).

40. Jim Baca interview with author, July 21, 1993.

41. Larry Campbell interview with author, March 11, 1993.

42. Dick Springer interview with author, March 11, 1993.

43. Joan Laatz, "Protection Sought for Trout in Umpqua," *The Oregonian* (April 2, 1993): A25.

44. Memo from Mineral Policy Center, May 2, 1991.

45. IRS Form 990s, Western States Public Lands Coalition, 1991, 1990.

46. The poll was commissioned by the American Mining Congress.

47. Questa's PFW chairperson, Ed Cordova, is identified as MolyCorp's security chief in the *Workbook of the Southwest Research and Information Center* (Spring 1992): 13. In earlier interviews with *Audubon* magazine and CNN, he had identified himself as a miner.

48. John R. Luoma, "Eco-Backlash," *Wildlife Conservation* (November/December, 1992): 34.

SIX: THE GOLDEN ROOSTER

1. "The Story of the Nugget's Gold Rooster," informational brochure, John Ascuaga's Nugget Hotel.

2. General Accounting Office, *Federal Land Management, The Mining Law of 1872 Needs Revision* (Washington, D.C.: U.S. Government Printing Office, March 1989).

3. Michael Satchell, "The New Gold Rush," *U.S. News & World Report* (October 28, 1991): 44–53.

4. Bob Langsencamp interview with author, April 8, 1993.

5. Kit Miniclier, "Mine's Toxic Leaks Render River Lifeless," *Denver Post* (November 11, 1992): 1, 7. Also, *Post* articles from November 20; December 8, 22, 24, and 29; and "The Mine that Killed a River" (January 1993), editorial.

6. Elliot Lord, *Comstock, Mining and Miners* (Berkeley, Calif.: Howell-North, 1959).

7. Dave Barry, *Dave Barry Slept Here* (New York: Random House, 1989), pp. 103–4.

8. Louis Adamic, *Dynamite* (New York: Chelsea House, 1968), pp. 9–21.

9. Richard Hofstaedter and Michael Wallace, *American Violence* (New York: Random House, 1970), pp. 147–51.

10. Adamic, *Dynamite*, p. 140.

11. Ibid., pp. 134–42.

12. Ibid., pp. 157–65. Also Renshwa, *Wobblies*, pp. 21–41.

13. Adamic, *Dynamite*, pp. 152–53.

14. Ibid., pp. 143–56.

15. Hofstaedter and Wallace, *American Violence*, pp. 160–64. Also, Howard Zinn, *A People's History of the United States* (New York: Harper Perennial, 1990), pp. 346–49.

16. Renshwa, *Wobblies*, pp. 144–60.

17. William F. Nolan, *Hammett—A Life at the Edge* (New York: Congdon & Weed, 1983), pp. 13–14.

18. Renshwa, *Wobblies*, pp. 160–63.

19. Harry M. Caudill, *Night Comes to the Cumberlands* (Boston: Little, Brown, 1962), pp. 188–205.

20. Mike Buchner interview with author, September 8, 1993.

21. Michael Satchell, "The New Gold Rush," *U.S. News & World Report* (October 28, 1991): 46.

22. The six-page fundraising letter concludes, "Don't let the 'wise use' enemies of the environment win! Defend your planet by becoming a Sierra Club member today—and receive our special Sierra Club canvas grocery bag FREE with your membership!"

SEVEN: SAVE IT FOR WHAT?

1. Vernon was one of several victims of anti-enviro attacks featured on the syndicated television program "Inside Edition," March 3, 1993.

2. Northern Forest Lands Council, "Northern Forest Lands Overview" (Concord, Mass.: NFLC, 1992), a six-page summary and chronology of the re-

gion's forest issues beginning with the Diamond Match sale. The council was established by Congress with the participation of the governments of Maine, New Hampshire, Vermont, and New York.

3. The most detailed survey of Wise Use/Property Rights activity in New England through 1992 is a twenty-page report put out by the Massachusetts-based Political Research Associates. William Kevin Burke, "The Scent of Opportunity" (Cambridge, Mass.: Political Research Associates, December 12, 1992).

4. Johnson is also secretary of the Alliance for America.

5. The Fly-In was sponsored by the Oregon Lands Coalition in September 1991.

6. Alliance for America, "Signing Away America," *Alliance News* (April 1993): 1–2.

7. As the last state without a Wal-Mart, Vermont's local opposition has received widespread press coverage, including Nancie L. Katz, "Vermont—The Last 'Sprawl-Mart' Holdout," *San Francisco Sunday Examiner/Chronicle* (August 29, 1993): Sunday Punch, p. 4.

8. William Kevin Burke, "The Scent of Opportunity," *Political Research Associates* (December 12, 1992): 6.

9. There are a number of books on Adirondacks history and other related topics, such as Roderick Nash's *Wilderness and the American Mind*, that devote some pages to the subject. For a concise, broad-ranging review, see *Adirondack Park Centennial* magazine (1992, 62 pp.), published by the *Adirondack Daily Enterprise*.

10. The Commission on the Adirondacks in the Twenty-First Century, *The Adirondack Park in the Twenty-First Century* (State of New York, April 1990), 96 pp.

11. Larry Maxwell, "Protestors Confront Council," *Post Star* (April 13, 1990): 1. Descriptions and quotes from protest events between 1990 and 1992 that are not attributed come from forty-two articles printed during that time in four area newspapers: *The Glens Falls Post Star, Plattsburgh Press Republican, Elizabeth Valley News*, and *Adirondack Daily Enterprise* (in Saranac Lake).

12. Eric Siy interview with author, June 1, 1993, and news report.

13. Larry Maxwell, "Adirondack Solidarity Celebrates 1 Year's Fight," *Post Star* (April 24, 1991): 1.

14. Lohr McKinstry, "Liberators Protesting with Arrows, Bulldozers," *Plattsburgh Press Republican* (June 16, 1990): 1.

15. Condemned in a *Plattsburgh Press Republican* editorial, "Bring Your Deer Rifle?" (June 24, 1990): C8. Gerdts's inflammatory leaflets may have marked the beginning of the end of his effectiveness as a political leader in the park.

16. Mathew Russell, "'60 Minutes' Footage of Crane Pond Fight Draws Criticism," *Adirondack Daily Enterprise* (September 22, 1992): 1/6.

17. Harry McIntosh interview with author, April 23, 1993.

18. Jeff Jones, "Getting Wise," *Appalachia Bulletin* (March 1992): 29–31. Also, tape of a local public access television talk show with Birch Society credits.

19. Will Nixon, "Fear & Loathing in the Adirondacks," *E* magazine (Septem-

ber/October 1992): 28–35; also Robert Worth, "Adirondack Battleground: The Struggle over Property Rights in New York State," a report prepared for a college writing course.

20. John Sheehan interview with author, May 5, 1993.

21. From a copy of the two-page "Dear Ron" (Stafford) letter dated August 25, 1992, in which Governor Cuomo outlines the "harassment, intimidation and even life-threatening acts of violence" that culminated in the burning of La-Bastille's barns and spray painting of Gordon Davis's office building. It's signed "Sincerely, Mario Cuomo."

22. The Solidarity Alliance joined the Alliance for America at its founding in St. Louis, November 8–10, 1991.

23. Rose Paul interview with author, August 25, 1993.

24. Carl Reidel interview with author, August 26, 1993.

EIGHT: ROADKILL AN ACTIVIST

1. Laura Parker, "The Island of Dixy Lee Ray," *Seattle Post-Intelligencer* (August 10, 1986): F1.

2. From an ECO brochure.

3. *21st Century Science & Technology* (Winter 1992) and *The New American* (February 8, 1993).

4. Gary Taubes, "The Ozone Backlash," *Science* (June 11, 1993): 1580–83.

5. Florence Williams, "Sagebrush Rebellion 11," *High Country News* (February 24, 1992): 1.

6. Jim Baca interview with author, July 21, 1993.

7. Debra Thunder, "Cowboys Ain't Indians: Buffalo Ain't Cows," *High Country News* (May 31, 1993): 16.

8. TelSpec, Telecommunications Specialists, Inc., of Burnsville, Minnesota, set up the ECO phone system.

9. The reference is to the Sahara Club, a group of southern California dirt bikers who have carried out a campaign of disruption, harassment, and violence directed against environmentalists, elected officials, and the Bureau of Land Management.

10. Other favorite anti-enviro bumper stickers include "Earth Firsters! America's Favorite Speed Bumps," "Hungry and Out of Work?—Eat an Environmentalist," and "Spotted Owl Tastes Just like Fried Chicken!"

11. "The Rest of the Story: The Bill Ellen Horror Story," submitted to U.S. government interagency working group on wetlands by the National Wildlife Federation, two pages; also *Wall Street Journal* (November 18, 1992, and January 15, 1993), editorial pages.

12. *New American* (February 8, 1993): 21–26.

13. Graybiel provided a sampling of thirty articles on Mills and his case that have run in the *Pensacola News Journal* between 1989 and 1993.

14. The source on this case was twenty-two articles and editorials in the *Los Angeles Times* (October 3, 1992–April 21, 1993).

15. Rick Sieman interview with author, May 12, 1993.

16. *Sahara Club Newsletter*, #3 (undated): 2. Other encouragements have included, "Here's a partial list of actions, names and numbers that honest (and

daring) citizens could have some fun with," and "Hit List! Make copies of this list and pass them around to friends. . . . Good hunting!"

17. Susan Sullivan, "Angry Offroaders Say They'll Pack Guns to Defend Rights," *The Press-Enterprise*, Riverside, Calif. (November 17, 1990).

18. Susan Sullivan, "Ten Arrested as Bikers, Rangers Square Off," *The Press-Enterprise* (November 25, 1990). Also, law enforcement sources and BLM agent interview with author.

19. *Sahara Club Newsletter* (February 19, 1993): 5.

20. Candice Boak interview with author and producer Steve Talbot, on December 13, 1990.

21. According to the Arcata Police Department and Steve Talbot.

22. Law enforcement and environmental sources.

23. Ed Knight interviews with author and producer Steve Talbot, February 11 and 12, 1991, and with author, July 22, 1993.

24. Joan Smith interview with author, January 29, 1993.

25. "Land Takeover Threatens NY, VT, NH, and ME!" a flier put out by the John Birch Society. Copy provided by Political Research Associates.

26. Sources on the John Birch Society include Chip Berlet, "Trashing the Birchers: Secrets of the Paranoid Right," *Boston Phoenix* (July 14–20, 1989): 10; Andrea Estes, "Birch Society Claims Gains," *Boston Herald* (May 28, 1991): 1–24; and Robert L. Rose, "Will Communists Take Over in 2002? Ask a John Bircher," *Wall Street Journal* (October 2, 1991): 1.

27. "Greenpeace, Shock Troops for a New Dark Age," *EIR, Executive Intelligence Review* (April 21, 1989): 24–32.

28. Chip Berlet and Joel Bellman, "Lyndon LaRouche—Fascism Wrapped in an American Flag" (Cambridge, Mass.: Political Research Associates, February 7, 1989), 15 pages, pamphlet.

29. "Environmental Hoaxes Kill—Save the Earth with Technology," cover and special reports, *21st Century Science & Technology* (Fall 1992): 11–27.

30. "The Limits of Propaganda: Lyndon LaRouche Goes to Jail," *Special Edition* (May 1989): 1.

31. John Judis, "Rev. Moon's Rising Political Influence," *U.S. News & World Report* (March 27, 1989): 27–31.

32. Daniel Junas, "Rising Moon: The Unification Church's Japan Connection," Working Paper #5 (Seattle, Wash.: Institute for Global Security Studies, 1989).

33. Judis, "Rev. Moon's Rising Political Influence," 27.

34. "The Resurrection of Reverend Moon," a PBS "Frontline" documentary, January 21, 1992.

35. Walter Hatch, "Mainstream Moon," *Seattle Times* (February 13, 1989): 1.

36. Ibid., and the author's own reporting from Honduras.

37. Ross Gelbspan, "The 'New' FBI," *Covert Action* (Winter 1989): 15–16.

38. Edmond Jacoby, "The Mooning of Ralph David Abernathy," *Regardie's* (May 1989): 85–94.

39. Judis, "Rev. Moon's Rising Political Influence."

40. "The Resurrection of Reverend Moon."

41. Ron Arnold interview with author, April 22, 1993.

42. *The Wise Use Agenda* (Bellevue, Wash.: Free Enterprise Press, 1989): p. XV.

43. Merrill Sikorski interview with author, April 23, 1993.

44. This short phone conversation took place on June 17, 1993.

45. Deal, *The Greenpeace Guide to Anti-Environmental Organizations*, pp. 24–25.

46. American Freedom Coalition of Washington filings with the Office of the Secretary of State, Corporations Division, Olympia, Washington, 1988–92.

47. Hatch, "Mainstream Moon."

48. Mark Hume, "Resource-Use Conference Had Links to Moonie Cult," *Vancouver Sun* (July 8, 1989): A6.

49. Copies of these letters were provided to the author by the Montana AFL-CIO.

50. Chuck Malloy, "Wise-Use Promoter Denies Church Ties," *Idaho Falls Post Register* (October 8, 1989): 1–3.

51. Ron Arnold interview with author, March 15, 1993.

52. Junas, "Rising Moon," 25.

53. A second source of information on Moon's holdings in the United States is Alan Green and Larry Zilliox, Jr., "Fishing for Respectability," *Washington City Paper* (June 11, 1993): 1.

54. Frank Greve, "Moon Church Gives Millions to New Right," *San Jose Mercury News* (December 21, 1987): 1A, back page.

NINE: THE MEDIA IS THE MESSAGE

1. "Nightline," ABC, February 4, 1992.

2. Kit Carson interview with author, January 26, 1993.

3. "People Who Call in to Talk Radio More Conservative, Survey Says," *New York Times* (July 16, 1993); Times Mirror survey conducted May 18–24, 1993.

4. "Rather Condemns News Coverage, Colleagues," *New York Times* (October 1, 1993).

5. Mark Hertsgaard, *On Bended Knee* (New York: Farrar, Straus and Giroux, 1988).

6. Herbert J. Gans, *Deciding What's News* (New York: Random House, 1980), p. 186.

7. Ibid., pp. 39–69.

8. Barry Serafin, "TV Reporters Face Extra Ethical Trials," *Society of Environmental Journalists Journal* (Spring/Summer 1993): 7.

9. Randy Lee Loftis, "The Tough Times," *SEJ Journal* (Winter 1992): 1–6, 7.

10. *1993 Writer's Market* (Cincinnati, Ohio: Writer's Digest Books, 1993), pp. 505–14.

11. The American Freedom Coalition in the April 1989 issue of its *Journal*, described *Our Land* magazine as "a unique and powerful voice of moderation in the rising tide of environmental awareness sweeping North America."

12. *Our Land*, vol. 2, no. 2 (Fall 1990).

13. "Big Park Video," produced by Victor E. Williams for Wilderness Impact Research Foundation, Elko, Nevada.

14. Transcripts from New Mexico *Stockman* magazine (November 1992). Also, Pat Wolff, "Cattle Grower's Radio Spots Aren't for Sinking Teeth In," *Santa Fe New Mexican* (March 27, 1993): 88–89, 101.

15. "The Resurrection of Reverend Moon," "Frontline," PBS (January 21, 1992).

16. Chip Berlet, "Taking off the Gloves," *Greenpeace* (September/October 1990): 21.

17. "Radical Environmentalists Fuel Earth Day," *Human Events* (April 28, 1990): 1.

18. Patrick J. Buchanan, "From the Right," *Quarterly* II, vol. 1, no. 6 (1990).

19. David Brooks, "Saving the Earth from Its Friends," *National Review* (April 1, 1990): 28–31.

20. David Horowitz, "Making the Green One Red," *National Review* (March 19, 1990): 39–40.

21. Timothy Egan, "Fund-Raisers Tap Anti-Environmentalism," *New York Times* (December 19, 1991): A18.

22. Rush Limbaugh, *The Way Things Ought to Be* (New York: Simon and Schuster, 1992), p. xiii.

23. Peter J. Boyer, "Bull Rush," *Vanity Fair* (May 1992): 156.

24. James Bowman, "The Leader of the Opposition," *National Review* (September 6, 1993): 44–52.

25. Limbaugh, *The Way Things Ought to Be*, p. 167.

26. Ibid., pp. 161–62.

27. Ibid., pp. 155–56.

28. Ibid., p. 165.

29. Gary Taubes, "The Ozone Backlash," *Science* (June 11, 1993): 1580–83.

30. Limbaugh, *The Way Things Ought to Be*, p. 164.

31. In his history of the environmental movement, *A Fierce Green Fire*, Shabecoff titled a chapter "The Third Wave," referring to a broadening of the environmental movement in the late 1980s. Schneider seemed to be tweaking his predecessor at the *Times* by appropriating the term in the introduction to the five-part antiregulatory series.

32. Keith Schneider, "New View Calls Environmental Policy Misguided," *New York Times* (March 21, 1993): 1, 16.

33. Keith Schneider interview with author, June 18, 1993.

34. Audio cassette, "Covering the Wise Use Movement," Tape 25, Goodkind of Sound, copyright 1992, by the Society of Environmental Journalists, Philadelphia, Pennsylvania.

35. Vicki Monks, "See No Evil," *American Journalism Review* (June 1993): 18–25.

36. Keith Schneider, "In Cattle-Raising West, a County Wants to Help U.S. Manage Federal Lands," *New York Times* (May 6, 1993): A12.

37. Tim Egan interview with author, September 20, 1993.

38. Keith Schneider, "Environment Gets a Flurry of Final Acts," *New York Times* (January 16, 1993): 1.

39. Hertsgaard, *On Bended Knee*, 186–203. Also, author's reporting from Nicaragua and El Salvador.

40. Keith Schneider, "U.S. Backing Away from Saying Dioxin Is a Deadly Peril," *New York Times* (August 15, 1991): 1.

41. Jeff Bailey, "Dueling Studies—How Two Industries Created a Fresh Spin on the Dioxin Debate," *Wall Street Journal* (February 20, 1992): 1.

42. James Ledbetter, "Times White Paper," *Village Voice* (August 27, 1991): 8.

43. Monks, "See No Evil," 18–25.

44. Keith Schneider interview with author, June 18, 1993.

45. Keith Schneider, "Panel of Scientists Finds Dioxin Does Not Pose Widespread Cancer Threat," *New York Times* (September 24, 1992): 9. Also, Rose Gutfeld, "Dioxin's Health Risks May Be Greater than Believed, EPA Memo Indicates," *Wall Street Journal* (October 16, 1992): B3.

46. Associated Press, "More Evidence Found of Dangers of Dioxin" (August 30, 1993).

47. Monks, "See No Evil," 25.

TEN: UP AGAINST THE LAW

1. "Alaska Accuses U.S. of 'Taking' Park Lands," reprinted from the *New York Times* in the *San Francisco Chronicle* (July 24, 1993): A6; also documents provided to the author by Alaska Attorney General Charles Cole.

2. Steven Hayward, "California Should Call the EPA's Smog Bluff," *Orange County Register* (May 5, 1993): op-ed page.

3. Julia Rubin, "Intimidation Lawsuits Chill Public Activism," Associated Press (February 4, 1990); "SLAPPing the Opposition," *Newsweek* (March 5, 1990); Eve Pell, *E* (November/December 1991); and other materials supplied by the Political Litigation Project, University of Denver College of Law.

4. Penelope Canan interview with author, April 29, 1992.

5. Joe Brecher interview with author, April 29, 1992.

6. Quoted in Edward W. McBride, Jr., "The Empire State Strikes Back: New York's Legislative Response to Lawsuits," *Vermont Law Review* (Spring 1993): 931.

7. *Justice for Sale: Shortchanging the Public Interest for Private Gain* (Washington, D.C.: Alliance for Justice, 1993), pp. 10–11.

8. "PLF Argues Against Ballot Box Land Use Planning," *Pacific Legal Foundation* (Fall 1992): 7.

9. List of "Public Interest Law Firms" dated August 4, 1992, provided by Pacific Legal Foundation.

10. IRS Form 990, Mountain States Legal Foundation, 1991.

11. Oliver A. Houck, "With Charity for All," *Yale Law Journal* (July 1984): 1419–563.

12. Ibid., pp. 1465–66.

13. Ibid., p. 1481.

14. Jim Burling interview with author, May 18, 1993.

15. Richard A. Epstein, *Takings: Private Property and the Power of Eminent Domain* (Cambridge, Mass.: Harvard University Press, 1985).

16. W. John Moore, "Just Compensation," *National Journal* (June 13, 1992): 1404–7.

17. Charles Fried, *Order and Law: Arguing the Reagan Revolution—A Firsthand Account* (New York: Simon and Schuster, 1991), p. 183.

18. Nancy Marzulla speech to ECO conference, Reno, Nevada, February 19, 1993.

19. Executive Order #12630; issued by President Reagan on March 15, 1988, and published in the *Federal Register*, vol. 53, no. 53 (March 18, 1988): 8859–62.

20. Presidents Reagan and Bush appointed twelve of the court's judges; President Reagan renominated the other four in 1982.

21. Tom Castleton, "Chief Judge Smith Puts Property Rights Up Front," *Legal Times* (August 17, 1992): 1–16, 17.

22. *Lucas* trial transcript, supra note 44 at 113 as reported by Richard J. Lazarus, "Putting the Correct 'Spin' on Lucas," *Stanford Law Review* (May 1993): 1422.

23. Amicus curiae briefs in support of petitioner and support of respondent as listed in notes 65 and 66 in article by Glenn P. Sugameli, "Takings Issues in Light of *Lucas* v. *South Carolina Coastal Council*," *Virginia Environmental Law Journal* (1993): 439, 453nn.

24. *Stanford Law Review* (May 1993); also *Vermont Law Review* (Spring 1993).

25. John Echeverria interview with author, June 22, 1993.

26. Tom Kenworthy, "Nevada Cowboy Irate Over Discouraging Words on the Range," *Washington Post* (February 16, 1993); also, "Last Round-Up for the Old West," *The Economist* (March 6–12, 1993), and other news reports.

27. Wayne Hage, *Storm over Rangeland* (Bellevue, Wash.: Free Enterprise Press, 1989).

28. Ted Williams, "Taking Back the Range," *Audubon* (January/February 1993): 32.

29. Jon Christensen, "Nevada Sides with Environmentalists Against Rancher," *High Country News* (July 13, 1992): 5.

30. Trent Clarke speech at ECO conference, Reno, Nevada, February 20, 1993.

31. James Wittinghill interview with author, June 23, 1993.

32. Bill Klinefelter interview with author, June 24, 1993.

33. Marianne Lavelle, "The 'Property Rights' Revolt," *National Law Journal* (May 10, 1993): pp. 1, 34.

34. American Farm Bureau Federation, "Farm Bureau Policies for 1993," brochure.

35. Andy Neal interview with author, May 18, 1993.

36. Neil D. Hamilton, "The Next Generation of U.S. Agricultural Conservation Policy," speech delivered at the Soil and Water Conservation conference, March 16, 1993, Kansas City, Missouri.

37. American Legislative Exchange Council, "The Attack of the Killer Watermelons: Flat Earth Science & Zero Risk," *The State Factor* (February 1991). This issue of the council's newsletter consisted of the text of Warren Brookes's speech at the council's 1990 annual meeting. "Watermelon" refers to the anti-

enviro claim that environmentalists are Communists: "green on the outside, red on the inside."

38. Larry D. Hatfield and Dexter Waugh, "Conservative Think Tank Targets States," *San Francisco Examiner* (May 25, 1992): 1, 12.

39. Bill Klinefelter interview with author, June 24, 1993.

40. Hamilton, address to Soil and Water Conservation conference, March 16, 1993.

41. Jonathan Lash interview with author, July 26, 1993.

ELEVEN: THE GREEN P.I.

1. Copies of Investigative Services Companies' "Fire Scene Examination" report and AK Analytical's "Laboratory Report."

2. "CBS Evening News," March 3, 1993.

3. Linda Chase interview with author, April 22, 1993.

4. For more on John Reese, see Chip Berlet, "The Hunt for Red Menace," *Covert Action* (Winter 1989): 3–9; also Ross Gelbspan, "The 'New' FBI," *Covert Action* (Winter 1989): 11–16.

5. Most of the information regarding Judi Bari's case not directly attributed to Sheila O'Donnell comes from interviews with Bari and other subjects, news reports, and other materials collected during a six-month investigation by the author and producer Steve Talbot for "Who Bombed Judi Bari?" a PBS documentary broadcast on KQED, San Francisco, May 24, 1991.

6. From the police department's Affidavit for Search Warrant.

7. From "Who Bombed Judi Bari?"

8. As later recalled by Judi Bari in an interview with author and Steve Talbot, February 12, 1991.

9. From the police affidavit.

10. Nail evidence was also examined in "Who Bombed Judi Bari?"

11. Assistant Special Agent in Charge Edward Appel interview with author and Steve Talbot, May 7, 1991.

12. From the FBI Crime Lab report.

13. "Who Bombed Judi Bari?"

14. Rich McComber interview with author and Steve Talbot, December 10, 1990.

15. From copy of original "Lord's Avenger" letter.

16. Complete lyrics can be found in Susan Zakin, *Coyotes and Town Dogs* (New York: Viking, 1993), pp. 373–74.

17. "Who Bombed Judi Bari?"

18. Pat Costner and Joe Thornton, *Playing with Fire* (Washington, D.C.: Greenpeace, USA, 1991).

19. Chip Berlet, "Taking off the Gloves," *Greenpeace* (September/October 1990): 18–19.

20. Bowman Cox, "Reporter Rejects EPA Protection, Keeps Documents," *SEJ Journal* (Winter 1992): 12.

21. Copies of Incident/Offense reports from Carroll County Sheriff's Department and Eureka Fire Marshal.

22. Kate McConnico, "Raw Deals in Point Comfort," *Texas Observer* (September 18, 1992): 16–17.

23. Ibid., p. 17.

24. Sam Howe Verhovek, "Shrimpers Feel at Bay Over Plant Expansion," *New York Times* (June 20, 1993): 16.

25. Roy Bragg, "Throng of Opposition Envelops Activist," *Houston Chronicle* (March 3, 1991): D1.

26. *Texas Observer* (September 18, 1992): 17.

27. Copy of Calhoun County Sheriff's Department half-page assignment report on the incident.

28. Sheila O'Donnell, "Common Sense Security," brochure for Ace Investigations, November 3, 1992.

29. Charles Spiekerman interview with author, January 15, 1993.

TWELVE: CASUALTIES OF WAR

1. Biddle Duke, "Green Fear Hate Crimes Rising with Tempers," *New Mexican* (December 6, 1992): 1. Also Sam Hitt interview with author, September 23, 1993.

2. Pat Wolff interview with author, April 7, 1993. Also Keith Easthouse, "Activists Inspired by Threat," *New Mexican* (August 22, 1992): 4, 9.

3. Andy Kerr interview with author, April 20, 1993. Also Associated Press, "Worker Threatens Kerr's life" (May 23, 1991).

4. Scott Groene interview with author, September 29, 1993. Also "Opinions from Our Readers," *Moab Times Independent* (March 3, 1993).

5. Charles Pope, "Jury Directs Logger to Pay Environmentalist $31,000," *The State* [South Carolina] (April 22, 1993).

6. Jonathan Franklin, "First They Kill Your Dog," *Muckraker: Journal of the Center for Investigative Reporting* (Fall 1992): 1, 7–11. Also "Inside Edition," syndicated television show, broadcast February 5, 1993.

7. Associated Press, "Newsmen Escape City for Shots in the Desert," *St. George* (Utah) *Spectrum* (October 27, 1991): 5C.

8. Mike Jackson interview with author, September 23, 1993. Also Joan Hamilton, "Streams of Hope," *Sierra* (September/October 1993): 120.

9. Diana Bowen interview with author, October 5, 1993. Also Monty Fowler, "Woman Taping Ashland Oil Says Shots Were Fired," *Herald-Dispatch* (March 4, 1992).

10. Lamar Marshall interview with author, October 7, 1993. Also interview with attorney Ray Vaughn, October 7, 1993.

11. "60 Minutes," "Clean Air, Clean Water, Dirty Fight," CBS, broadcast September 20, 1992.

12. "Inside Edition," February 5, 1993. Also Franklin, "First They Kill Your Dog," story and files.

13. Lyn Mautner, "Ringwood Journal: Development Fight Makes Townspeople Uneasy," *New York Times* (August 15, 1993): 2.

14. Richard C. Sonnichsen; Gail O. Burton; and Thomas Lyons, "A Look Ahead: Views of Tomorrow's FBI," *FBI Law Enforcement Bulletin* (January 1990): 23–27.

15. Jeremy Rifkin, Melinda Mullin, and Liz Einbinder interviews with author, April 27 and 28, 1992.

16. "Alyeska Pipeline Service Company Covert Operation," Report of the Committee on Interior and Insular Affairs of the U.S. House of Representatives, July 1992.

17. "Inside Edition" and Center for Investigative Reporting files.

18. Michael Beebe, "Duped on Dump, Landowners Say," *Buffalo News* (September 8, 1991): 1.

19. Kathy Kellogg interview with author, October 23, 1993.

20. Michael Beebe, "Detective Spies on Landfill Foe," *Buffalo News* (April 5, 1992): 1, 11.

21. "Stop Farmersville Snooping," *Buffalo News*, op-ed page (April 8, 1992).

22. Chani Wiggins, "State: Plant Areas Contaminated," *Albany Herald* (Georgia) (February 28, 1993): 5A.

23. Chani Wiggins, "Merck Sued for Family's Health Problems," *Albany Herald* (Georgia) (February 28, 1993): 1.

24. Tony Winters interview with author, October 24, 1993.

25. Incident reports and supplemental reports from Albany, Georgia, police.

26. Swasy, who spent several weeks in Taylor County, has a chapter in her book called "Fear on the Fenholloway," which documents and recounts the pollution and violence that occurred along the river. Alicia Swasy, *Soap Opera— The Inside Story of Procter & Gamble* (New York: Random House, 1993), pp. 206–34.

27. Ned Mudd interview with author, October 6, 1993.

28. Joy Towles Cummings interview with author, October 9, 1993.

29. As recounted in Swasy, *Soap Opera*, and told to Sheila O'Donnell.

30. "60 Minutes," "Clean Air, Clean Water, Dirty Fight."

31. Jerry Blair interview with author, October 22, 1993.

32. The author was first told the "barroom" version of the sheriff's story during an interview with Putting People First leader Kathleen Marquardt on June 21, 1993.

33. Elizabeth Willson, "Activist's Tale of Attack Is Ruled Untrue," *St. Petersburg Times* (July 14, 1993): 1B.

34. Ibid.

35. Franklin, "First They Kill Your Dog," plus additional research by Franklin.

36. Alaska State Trooper Beldon interview with author, September 27, 1993. *Anchorage News* reporter Tom Kizzia and Charles Dickson interviews with author, September 28. Attorney John Dittman interview with author, September 29.

37. Che Odoum and Ihosvani Rodriguez, "Arson Not Ruled Out in Blaze of Activist's Historic Country Store," *Florida Flambeau* (June 7, 1993): 1.

38. Bob Rackleff interview with author, October 26, 1993. Also "Facts & Common Sense versus Fiction & Distortion #3," a brochure put out by Colonial Pipeline Company.

39. Colin Savage, "Lloyd Activist's Building Was Torched, Fire Investigators Say," *Tallahassee Democrat* (June 10, 1993): 5C. Also press release dated June 8, 1993, from Colonial Pipeline Company.

40. Bill Addington interview with author, October 27, 1993.

41. David Sheppard, "Anti-Sludge Activist: Fire 'Fueled by Hate,'" *El Paso Times* (September 2, 1993): B1.

42. Paul Slopek, "Sludge Company Under Investigation in New York City," *El Paso Times* (March 22, 1992).

43. Lauri Maddy interview with author, October 22, 1993.

44. This technique was explained and confirmed with a slight variation by an instructor at the Skip Barbar Racing School at Sears Point Raceway in northern California and by a California Highway Patrolman. Both agreed it was a maneuver only a professional would attempt.

45. Several reporters' attempts to secure the alleged videotapes from the company have proved nonproductive.

46. Kit Minielier, "Mystery Surrounds Navajo Activist's Death," *Denver Post* (October 25, 1993).

47. Sam Hitt interview with author, December 7, 1993.

48. Brenda Norell interview with author, December 10, 1993.

49. New Mexico State Police Major Frank Taylor interview with author, December 7, 1993.

50. Copy of letter from Representative Bill Richardson to FBI Director Louis Freeh dated October 15, 1993, asking for an investigation of Leroy Jackson's death and a copy of responding letter from Charles E. Mandigo, inspector-deputy chief, FBI Office of Public and Congressional Affairs, dated November 5, 1993, declining to get involved but promising, "If and when there is any evidence developed which would indicate a Federal crime was committed, the FBI will initiate an appropriate investigation."

THIRTEEN: FAILURE TO ENFORCE

1. Federal Bureau of Investigation, U.S. Department of Justice, *National Environmental Actions, April 22, 1970* (Washington, D.C.: June 10, 1970): report and appendix.

2. Senator Edmund Muskie, *Congressional Record* (April 14, 1971): 10313.

3. Ibid. These and other materials were provided by the Edmund S. Muskie Archives at Bates College in Lewiston, Maine.

4. Since the death of J. Edgar Hoover, the FBI has on occasion slipped back into the role of political police force, subverting citizens' constitutional rights. In 1983 FBI agents in Texas initiated a nationwide investigation of CISPES, the Citizens' Committee in Solidarity with the People of El Salvador. CISPES, a protest organization opposed to U.S. policy in Central America, was accused of engaging in terrorist activity. Before its two-year probe was discontinued, the FBI had opened files on 2,375 citizens and had rummaged through people's trash and phone records and spied on their political meetings. At the same time, they ignored more than eighty-five break-ins and thefts of files from homes, offices, and churches involved in Central American refugee and solidarity work. Later the FBI was accused of intimidating a witness to the army massacre of six Jesuit priests, their housekeeper, and her daughter after the witness fled the murder scene in San Salvador to seek protection in the United States. For more

on CISPES, see Ronald Kessler, *The FBI* (New York: Pocket Books, 1993), pp. 148–51.

5. Michael A. Lerner, "The FBI vs. the Monkeywrenchers," *Los Angeles Times Magazine* (April 15, 1990), cover story. Also Susan Zakin, *Coyotes and Town Dogs* (New York: Viking, 1993); U.S. District Court, District of Arizona indictment and additional press reports.

6. Terrorist Research and Analytical Center Counterterrorism Section Intelligence Division, U.S. Department of Justice, Federal Bureau of Investigation, *Terrorism in the United States 1982–1992* (Washington, D.C.), p. 17.

7. Dub and transcript of tape from Tucson news conference.

8. In response to a Freedom of Information request, the FBI wrote on February 5, 1992, "Documents contained in the 'EF!' [Earth First!] files at FBI headquarters amount to approximately 4,000 pages. The corresponding files in our San Francisco office contain approximately 600 pages." In the fall of 1993 the FBI released several thousand pages of files to lawyers for Judi Bari and Daryl Cherney.

9. An official with a third federal law enforcement agency "believed" the FBI to be conducting a terrorist investigation of Earth First! but could not confirm it.

10. Zakin, *Coyotes and Town Dogs*, p. 302.

11. Bari used the incident to illustrate the futility of tree spiking in a two-part series she authored that appeared in the *Earth First! Journal* (Spring 1993) and *Anderson Valley Advertiser* (March 3, 1993). "No matter what you think of L-P's [Louisiana Pacific's] forest practices, this much should be clear. George Alexander is not the enemy," she wrote.

12. Ken Olsen, "Jury Convicts Two of Spiking Trees in Idaho," *High Country News* (May 31, 1993): 2.

13. Both FBI documents were released under the Freedom of Information Act.

14. Biddle Duke, "Environmental Consortium Alleges Harassment," *New Mexican* (June 15, 1993): B-3. Also copy of a DOI memo dated May 24, 1993.

15. Special Agent McElhaney reiterated the FBI's reasons for declining the interview in an official letter dated October 22, 1993, and seal-wrapped in enough brown tape to discourage any postal employee who might think of tampering with the mail.

16. Carla Jones interview with author, July 27, 1993.

17. Christopher Manes, *Green Rage* (Boston: Little, Brown, 1990), pp. 209–12.

18. Grant Gerber interview with author, February 16, 1993.

19. Kurt J. Repanshek, "Environmental War Raging," Associated Press, June 3, 1990.

20. Kathleen Marquardt interview with author, June 21, 1993.

21. Science Reporter Wellington, "Green Campaign Just Cover Says, 'Hit Man,'" *New Zealand Herald* (March 19, 1986).

22. Quoted by columnist Stephanie Salter, "Wake Up, Pro-choicers, and Smell the Acid," *San Francisco Examiner* (October 3, 1993): A17. Also Ana

Puga, "Abortion Clinic Protection Bill OK'd," *Boston Globe* (November 17, 1993).

23. Neil deMause, "If You Can't Beat 'Em Shoot 'Em," *On the Issues* (Fall 1993): 31.

24. Barbara Dudley interview with author, June 29, 1993.

25. Ben Chavis interview with author, October 18, 1993.

26. Chip Berlett interview with author, June 7, 1993.

27. Pete Person interview with author, June 13, 1993.

FOURTEEN: THE MORE THE CHANGE

1. Brock Evans interview with author, October 15, 1993.

2. Michael McCloskey interview with author, October 13, 1993.

3. According to ex-Senator and Counselor of the U.S. Department of State Timothy Wirth speaking at the President's Council for Sustainable Development meeting, October 18, 1993.

4. Associated Press story, "E.P.A. to Study Safety of an Insecticide," reprinted in the *New York Times* (October 24, 1993): 10Y.

5. Glen Martin, "Alarm Over Vanishing Songbirds," *San Francisco Chronicle* (October 26, 1993).

6. Van Blaircom interview with author, March 11, 1993.

7. Editorial, *Wichita Eagle* (October 25, 1993).

8. Tim Egan, "Wingtip 'Cowboys' in Last Stand to Hold on to Low Grazing Fees," *New York Times* (October 29, 1993): 1.

9. Scott Thomsen, "BLM Blast," *Reno Gazette-Journal* (November 1, 1993): 2. Also Tom Gardner, Associated Press, "No Injuries, No Clues in Powerful Blast at BLM," *Nevada Appeal* (November 9, 1993): 1. Also discussions with law enforcement representatives.

10. Jim Baca interview with author, October 14, 1993.

11. Representative Mike Synar interview with author, October 14, 1993.

12. Representative George Miller interview with author during earlier Washington trip, June 22, 1993.

13. Lois Gibbs interview with author, September 28, 1993.

14. Reverend Ben Chavis interview with author, October 18, 1993.

15. The July 13, 1993, letter from Chief Raymond Yowell to the Wise Use Leadership Conference is reprinted in the September 1993 issue of *Western Horizons,* published by the Montana State AFL-CIO and Western States Center. Also Rudolph Ryuser, *Anti-Indian Movement on the Tribal Frontier* (Kenmore, Wash.: Center for World Indigenous Studies, 1993); this research report further details the links between Wise Use activists and the anti-Indian movement.

16. *Congressional Record* (October 26, 1993): H8465.

17. *Congressional Record* (October 6, 1993): H7483.

18. Alston Chase, "Masters of All They Survey?" *Washington Times* (October 18, 1993): A16. The complete numbers on The Nature Conservancy's 1992 sales come from Bruce Selcraig, "The Continuing Saga of New Mexico's Gray Ranch," *High Country News* (February 22, 1993): 1.

19. Dave Roach interview with author, October 15, 1993.

20. Jon R. Luoma, "Eco-Backlash," *Wildlife* (November/December 1992): 36.

21. Timothy Egan, "A Land Deal Leaves Montana Heavily Logged and Hurting," *New York Times* (October 19, 1993): 1, 26.

22. Jack Sheehan interview with author, October 13, 1993.

23. Bob Cash interview with author, October 13, 1993.

24. "A Special Report—Fatal Neglect—Milwaukee's Deadly Water Crisis Shows How Federal Inaction Has Endangered Our Health," *Milwaukee Journal* (September 19–26, 1993), 16 pages.

25. Carol Browner interview with author, October 28, 1993.

26. Richard Rominger interview with author, October 12, 1993.

27. Joel Brinkley, "Cultivating the Grass Roots to Reap Legislative Benefits," *New York Times* (November 1, 1993): 1, A14.

28. Jonathan Lash interview with author, October 13, 1993.

29. Philip J. Hilts, "50,000 Deaths a Year Blamed on Soot in Air," *San Francisco Chronicle* (July 19, 1993): 1, A-15.

30. Foster Church and Cathy Kiyomura, "Timber Families Rally at Waterfront," *The Oregonian* (April 3, 1993): 1, A13.

31. "President Clinton Releases Climate Change Action Plan," *Climate Watch, The Bulletin of the Global Climate Coalition* (October 1993): 2.

32. Ron Sonenshine, "Fort Bragg Joins Suit to Permit Logging," *San Francisco Chronicle* (August 11, 1993).

Bibliography

Adamic, Louis. *Dynamite*. New York: Chelsea House, 1968.

Arnold, Andrea. *Fear of Food*. Bellevue, Wash.: Free Enterprise Press, 1990.

Arnold, Ron. *Ecology Wars*. Bellevue, Wash.: Free Enterprise Press, 1987.

Arnold, Ron, and Alan Gottlieb. *Trashing the Economy*. Bellevue, Wash.: Free Enterprise Press, 1993.

Barry, Dave. *Dave Barry Slept Here*. New York: Random House, 1989.

Berger, Samuel R. *Dollar Harvest*. The Plains, Va.: AAM Publications, 1986.

Birnbaum, Jeffrey A. *The Lobbyists*. New York: Times Books, 1992.

Brown, Lester R., Christopher Flavin, and Hal Kane. *Vital Signs, 1992*. New York: Norton, 1992.

Burnette, Robert, and John Koster. *The Road to Wounded Knee*. New York: Bantam Books, 1974.

Cannon, Lou. *President Reagan: The Role of a Lifetime*. New York: Simon & Schuster, 1991.

Carson, Rachel. *Silent Spring*. Greenwich, Conn.: Fawcett, 1962.

Caudill, Harry M. *Night Comes to the Cumberlands*. Boston: Little, Brown, 1962.

Chase, Alston. *Playing God in Yellowstone*. San Diego: Harcourt Brace Jovanovich, 1987.

Cohen, Michael P. *The History of the Sierra Club 1892–1970*. San Francisco: Sierra Club Books, 1988.

Committee on Interior and Insular Affairs, U.S. House of Representatives. *Alyeska Pipeline Service Company Covert Operation*. Washington, D.C.: U.S. Government Printing Office, 1992.

Crawford, Alan. *Thunder on the Right*. New York: Pantheon, 1980.

Dary, David A. *The Buffalo Book*. Chicago: Swallow Press, 1974.

Davidson, Osha Gray. *Under Fire: The NRA and the Battle for Gun Control*. New York: Holt, 1993.

Day, David. *The Environmental Wars*. New York: Ballantine, 1989.

Deal, Carl. *The Greenpeace Guide to Anti-Environmental Organizations*. Berkeley, Calif.: Odonian Press, 1993.

De Voto, Bernard. *The Easy Chair*. Boston: Houghton Mifflin, 1955.

Editors, Time-Life Books. *This Fabulous Century: 1920–1930*. New York: Time-Life, 1969.

Ellis, Edward. *Lives of the Presidents*. Chicago: Flanagan, 1913.

Environmental and Energy Study Conference. *1993 Briefing Book on Environmental and Energy Legislation*. Washington, D.C.: Environmental and Energy Study Institute, 1993.

Freidel, Frank, and Alan Brinkley. *America in the Twentieth Century*. New York: McGraw-Hill, 1982.

Frohnmayer, John. *Leaving Town Alive: Confessions of an Arts Warrior*. Boston: Houghton Mifflin, 1993.

Gans, Herbert J. *Deciding What's News*. New York: Random House, 1980.

Gore, Albert, Jr. *Earth in the Balance*. New York: Penguin, 1992.

Gottlieb, Alan M. *Gun Rights Fact Book*. Bellevue, Wash.: Merril Press, 1988.

Gottlieb, Alan M., editor. *The Wise Use Agenda*. Bellevue, Wash.: Free Enterprise Press, 1989.

Hage, Wayne. *Storm over Rangelands*. Bellevue, Wash.: Free Enterprise Press, 1989.

Hayden, Tom. *The Love of Possession Is a Disease with Them*. Chicago: Holt, Rinehart and Winston, 1972.

Hertsgaard, Mark. *On Bended Knee*. New York: Farrar, Straus and Giroux, 1988.

Hofstadter, Richard, and Michael Wallace. *American Violence*. New York: Random House, 1970.

Karnow, Stanley. *Vietnam: A History*. New York: Viking, 1983.

Katsiaficas, George. *The Imagination of the New Left*. Boston: South End Press, 1987.

Kerner, Otto, chairman. *Report of the National Advisory Commission on Civil Disorders: The Kerner Report*. New York: Bantam Books, 1968.

Kessler, Ronald. *The FBI*. New York: Simon & Schuster, 1993.

Kohn, Howard. *The Last Farmer: An American Memoir*. New York: Harper & Row, 1988.

LaBastille, Anne. *Women and Wilderness*. San Francisco: Sierra Club Books, 1980.

Lash, Jonathan, Katherine Gillman, and David Sheridan. *A Season of Spoils*. New York: Pantheon, 1984.

Lien, Carsten. *Olympic Battleground*. San Francisco: Sierra Club Books, 1991.

Limbaugh, Rush. *The Way Things Ought to Be*. New York: Simon & Schuster, 1992.

Logan, Robert A., with Wendy Gibbons and Stacy Kingsbury. *Environmental Issues for the Nineties: A Handbook for Journalists*. Washington, D.C.: Environmental Reporting Forum, 1992.

Lord, Eliot. *Comstock: Mining and Miners*. Berkeley, Calif.: Howell-North, 1959.

Makower, Joel. *The E Factor*. New York: Random House, 1993.

Manes, Christopher. *Green Rage*. Boston: Little, Brown, 1990.

McPhee, John. *Encounters with the Archdruid*. New York: Farrar, Straus and Giroux, 1971.

Miller, Nathan. *Stealing from America*. New York: Paragon House, 1992.

————. *Theodore Roosevelt: A Life.* New York: Morrow, 1992.

Millett, Richard. *Guardians of the Dynasty.* Maryknoll, N.Y.: Orbis Books, 1977.

Mitchell, John G., editor, with Constance L. Stallings. *Ecotactics: The Sierra Club Handbook for Environmental Activists*, Pocket Books Edition. New York: Simon & Schuster, 1970.

Nash, Roderick. *Wilderness and the American Mind.* New Haven, Conn.: Yale University Press, 1967.

Oelschlager, Max, editor. *The Wilderness Condition.* San Francisco: Sierra Club Books, 1992.

Ray, Dixy Lee, with Lou Guzzo. *Trashing the Planet.* New York: Harper Perennial, 1990.

Renshaw, Patrick. *The Wobblies.* Garden City, N.Y.: Doubleday, 1968.

Rifkin, Jeremy. *Beyond Beef.* New York: Dutton, 1992.

Roosevelt, Theodore. *The Works of Theodore Roosevelt.* New York: Scribner's, 1926.

Scarce, Rik. *Eco-Warriors.* Chicago: The Noble Press, 1990.

Shabecoff, Phillip. *A Fierce Green Fire.* New York: Farrar, Straus and Giroux, 1993.

Shanks, Bernard. *This Land Is Your Land.* San Francisco: Sierra Club Books, 1984.

Sheehan, Neil. *A Bright Shining Lie.* New York: Random House, 1988.

Shenton, James P. *History of the United States to 1865.* Garden City, N.Y.: Doubleday, 1963.

Slotkin, Richard. *The Final Frontier: The Myth of the Frontier in the Age of Industrialization, 1800–1890.* New York: Atheneum, 1985.

————. *Gunfighter Nation: The Myth of the Frontier in Twentieth-Century America.* New York: Atheneum, 1992.

Soderberg, K. A., and Jackie DuRette. *People of the Tongass.* Bellevue, Wash.: Free Enterprise Press, 1988.

Strategic Analysis & Fifty State Review. *The Wise Use Movement.* Washington, D.C.: The Wilderness Society, 1993.

Subcommittee on Civil Service of the Committee on Post Office and Civil Service, U.S. House of Representatives. *Interference in Environmental Programs by Political Appointees: The Improper Treatment of a Senior Executive Service Official.* Washington, D.C.: U.S. Government Printing Office, 1993.

Sugarmann, John. *National Rifle Association: Money, Firepower and Fear.* Washington, D.C.: National Press, 1992.

Swasy, Alicia. *Soap Opera—The Inside Story of Procter and Gamble.* New York: Random House, 1993.

Tebbel, John. *The Compact History of the Indian Wars.* New York: Tower Books, 1966.

Turner, Frederick. *Rediscovering America: John Muir in His Time and Ours.* San Francisco: Sierra Club Books, 1985.

Turner, William. *Hoover's FBI.* New York: Dell, 1970.

Vanderwerth, W. C., compiler. *Indian Oratory.* New York: Ballantine, 1971.

Van Strum, Carol. *A Bitter Fog: Herbicides and Human Rights.* San Francisco: Sierra Club Books, 1983.

Walls, David. *The Activist's Almanac.* New York: Simon & Schuster, 1993.

Wasserman, Harvey. *Harvey Wasserman's History of the United States.* New York: Harper & Row, 1972.

Wilkinson, Charles F. *Crossing the Next Meridian.* Washington, D.C.: Island Press, 1992.

Woodward, Bob. *Veil: The Secret Wars of the CIA, 1981–1987.* New York: Pocket Books, 1987.

Zakin, Susan. *Coyotes and Town Dogs.* New York: Penguin, 1993.

Zinn, Howard. *A People's History of the United States.* New York: Harper Perennial, 1990.

Index